T5-BQA-675

THE PLAYWRIGHT'S COMPANION 1990

A Submission Guide to Theatres & Contests in the U.S.A.

Compiled and introduced

by

Mollie Ann Meserve

FEEDBACK THEATREBOOKS

Copyright © 1989 by Feedback Theatrebooks

All rights reserved

Except for brief passages quoted in a review, no part of this book may be utilized or reproduced in any form or by any means, mechanical or electronic, including photocopying and recording, or by any information storage and retrieval system, without written permission from the publisher.

Manufactured in the United States of America.

Feedback Theatrebooks
305 Madison Avenue, Suite 1146
New York, NY 10165

Distributed by:

Samuel French Trade
7623 Sunset Blvd.
Hollywood, CA 90046

ISSN 0887-1507
ISBN 0-937657-04-2

Ref
PN
2289
.P57
1990

Contents

321726

Introduction

Using *The Playwright's Companion 1990*

As theatre in America enters the last decade of this century, *The Playwright's Companion*, now in its sixth year of publication, continues to monitor and report the changing interests and needs of those who reward the efforts of America's playwrights. Readers familiar with the book from past years will notice many new features in this, our 1990 edition.

In order to include more listings and to expand each listing, we have reduced our introductory material to this explanation of the book's format, Playscript Format, The Playwright's Checklist and Submission Record. Readers will find changes in many of the listings, as well, in the form of several new headings, among them, "Casting," "Future commitment," "Recent production of unsolicited work" and, in the program section, "Accommodations." These were added to provide and classify additional information which, if our predictions are accurate, will become increasingly important to our readers during the 1990's.

The listings are divided into five major sections: Theatres, Contests, Special Programs, Publishers and Agents. The theatre section includes those theatres, and some producing companies, expressing an interest in new plays for production and/or readings along with a few theatres interested in second productions only. A special list at the end of the theatre section provides information on theatres which have recently issued calls for new scripts. The contest section lists competitions offering cash prizes, productions, staged readings or publication and a few competitions offering commissions. Selected new play festivals are also included in the contest section. The special program section includes membership, service and support organizations and resource information services; play development programs; selected new play festivals; professional appointments; script services; sources of financial suppport; writers' colonies and work spaces. The publisher section includes those publishers expressing a particular interest in plays. Our section on agents includes only contact information. Playwrights wishing to secure the services of an agent should send a query letter with script synopsis, resume and script history. Scripts should be sent only upon the agent's request.

Cross References in the Appendix classify theatres, contests, programs and publishers according to selected special interests and list special programs according to type. For the first time this year, The Playwright's Calendar includes deadlines for special programs as well as for contests.

Again this year we have attempted to arrange our listings in a manner that will be both clear and easy to use. The listings in each section are arranged in alphabetical order, using the first letter of the organization name or contest or program title. Articles are not considered, unless they constitute a vital part of the name or title. When an organization, contest or program bears the name of an individual, the listing is alphabetized under the first letter of the first name,

We believe the material included in the individual listings to be for the most part self-explanatory, but some clarification is necessary.

Information provided in each listing refers to that particular organization's practices and policies regarding original scripts—either unproduced plays or plays that have received one or more previous productions but have not claimed national attention. For example, data listed under the heading entitled "Works" indicate the types of original plays considered, and the heading "Tours" appears in a listing if that organization tours any of the original works it produces.

Each theatre is classified according to type, such as "professional not-for-profit" or "university/college." This classification does not necessarily refer to contractual agreements or tax status; its purpose is to suggest the kind of production a playwright might expect at each theatre.

"Casting" refers to policies and procedures used by producers in selecting performers. (Responses to this heading in our survey, and to our "Special interests" heading as well, indicate a definite trend in 1990 toward "non-traditional" and "multi-ethnic" casting.)

Whether or not they are mentioned under "Submission Policy" or "Procedure" headings, appropriate materials must accompany each submission, entry or application (see The Playwright's Checklist)--

except in the instances of contests and programs which specify other procedures. Several respondents to our 1990 survey indicated that they will not consider any submission (script or query) not accompanied by an adequately stamped, self-addressed return mailer. To our knowledge, no one listed in this book will return scripts not accompanied by such mailers; many will not respond to requests for information that do not include stamped, self-addressed business envelopes. Occasionally, too, respondents indicated that no submitted materials will be returned.

In the theatre and publisher sections the heading "Best time" refers to the months or seasons when each prefers to receive submissions. Unless a listing specifically states otherwise, it may be assumed that submissions are accepted at other times throughout the year, but the stated time is considered optimal. If the heading does not appear in a listing, playwrights may assume that submissions are accepted year round. The "Response" heading refers to the length of time the readers normally require in replying to either a query or a script submission. If both scripts and queries are accepted and only one response time is indicated, that response time applies to both types of submissions.

In the contest and special program sections, "Deadline," unless followed by the word "postmark," indicates the date by which entries or applications must be received. "Notification" refers to the date when contest winners or selected program participants will be notified of their status. For all contests and programs it is advisable to request information well in advance, as policies and deadline dates may change without notice.

Before entering into any kind of agreement or contract, playwrights are advised to understand the exact terms of "Remuneration," i.e., payment resulting from production or publication. The Dramatists Guild, listed in Special Programs, requires that its members accept only the Guild's approved contract and provides them with free contractual advice. "Future commitment" describes options, percentages of future royalties, credits and other commitments required by a producer or publisher.

In the heading "Your chances" the first figure refers to the approximate number of new scripts received by a theatre or publisher each year, plays normally entered in a competition or applications made to a program. In the theatre and publisher sections the second figure indicates the approximate number of new plays given full productions during a normal season or publication during a normal year. In the program section, the second figure indicates the approximate number of participants selected, spaces available or grants or fellowships awarded. In the contest section, the second figure indicates the number of judges normally involved, and the third figure suggests the number of readings each entry is likely to receive. In some listings in the theatre section, "Your chances" is followed by the heading "Recent production of unsolicited work," which indicates the latest year during which material from unsolicited scripts or queries was staged.

In most instances, the "Program" or "Programs" heading in the theatre section provides information on those special programs for playwrights offered in addition to full productions.

Suggestions quoted under the heading "Advice" are intended to assist the playwright in approaching each particular theatre, contest, program or publisher and should not be interpreted as general recommendations on the subject of playwriting or as applicable to any other theatre, contest, program or publisher.

For the past several years, contrary to our title, we have occasionally listed organizations outside the United States, as they came to our attention. This year, more of them than ever before have made themselves known to us, and we believe that it would be a disservice to our readers to refuse to list them simply because of national boundaries. Our subtitle remains *A Submission Guide to Theatres and Contests in the U.S.A.*, although we long ago abandoned the notion of listing only theatres and contests. While we have not yet conducted a large-scale survey abroad, we have by policy included verifiable information from beyond our borders.

The listings in *The Playwright's Companion 1990* are based upon newly received or approved information and include as many quotations from respondents to our annual survey as space allows. In no instance has the intent of a response been altered by editing.

As in past years, we are indebted to the hundreds of artistic directors, literary managers and dramaturgs, board presidents, contest and program coordinators, editors, secretaries and others who help us keep *The Playwright's Companion* up-to-date by responding to our survey. Without their continued and gracious assistance, publication of this book would not be possible.

With each edition of *The Playwright's Companion*, accuracy is our primary goal. Should you find outdated or erroneous information in this book, please let us know. And when you submit your work to a theatre, contest, program or publisher, please mention in your query or cover letter that you are a reader of *The Playwright's Companion*.

M.A.M.

Note: Inclusion of a theatre, contest, program, publisher, agent or publication in *The Playwright's Companion 1990* does not constitute endorsement or recommendation by Feedback Services or Feedback Theatrebooks, nor does exclusion imply a lack of endorsement or recommendation.

Playscript Format

Scripts should be typed on one side only of 8.5"x11" white paper. Pica type is preferred by most playreaders, but a clear elite type is acceptable, provided that the pages do not appear "crowded." If the script is prepared on a word-processor, photocopies of dot-matrix print-outs should be avoided.

The left margin of each page of script is set at 1.5 inches from the left edge of the paper in order to accommodate binding in a folder; the right margin should be at least 1 inch from the right edge.

On the title page, the play's title, in all-caps and underscored, is centered approximately 20 single spaces from the top of the page. Below the underscore line, at 2 single-space intervals, the description (e.g., "A Play in One Act"), the word "by" and the playwright's name (not in all-caps) appear. The Copyright notice—if the play is registered with the United States Copyright Office—is typed in the lower left corner at the margin, and the author's mailing address and phone number are typed in the lower right.

On the page immediately following, entitled "Cast of Characters," the character list is double spaced with character names typed at the left margin, underscored and followed by colons. A description of each character follows on the same line. The tab setting for the descriptions is at the playwright's discretion. If space permits on this page, the descriptions of time and place may be centered below the character list; if not, a separate page should be used for these descriptions.

At the beginning of each scene, set descriptions, following the titles of "SETTING" and "AT RISE," both typed at the left margin and followed by colons, are set 4 inches from the left edge. "SETTING" refers to the appearance of the stage; "AT RISE" refers to the situation and activity on stage as the lights come up or the curtain rises.

Except between speeches by different characters, the text is single spaced. Character titles, which identify the speaker, are typed in all-caps and aligned 4 inches from the left edge.

When a speech continues onto the following page, the character title is retyped in all-caps at the 4-inch setting and followed by the abbreviation "(Cont.)." When two characters speak simultaneously, both speeches occupy the same line, and tab settings for character titles are at the playwright's discretion, depending upon the length of each line of dialogue.

            LINDA   TOM
        Tom, what is it?   Look at that, would you!

Character names appearing in stage directions are typed in all-caps. Stage directions, unless they are one-word descriptions of a character's manner of delivering a line, are typed on a separate line and begin about 2.75 inches from the left edge of the paper; they should not occupy more than 2.5 inches per line.

Stage directions which are one-word descriptions of manner may follow the character title:

                    LINDA (bravely)
        Off with you, then! Give us a kiss!

All stage directions are enclosed in parentheses. Those directions which are complete sentences are punctuated as such.

Stage directions falling within a speech are single spaced within the speech; those which fall between speeches by different characters are set off by double spaces.

Lines of dialogue are the only lines in the body of the script which run from left to right margin.

For emphasis on certain words of dialogue, underscoring, not all-caps, is used.

Page numbers are typed in the upper right corner, 4 or 5 single spaces from the top of the page. In a one-act play, consecutive Arabic numbers are used. If the play is divided into acts, the act number is typed in Roman numerals and precedes the page number. Thus, ACT I, Page 12 would be typed as "I-12." If the acts are broken into scenes, the scene number is typed in Arabic or lower case Roman numerals and is placed between act and page numbers. ACT II, Scene 4, Page 70 would be typed as "II-4-70" or "II-iv-70." In all scripts page numbers run consecutively throughout the script, without regard to act or scene.

Every act and every scene begins on a new page, with act and scene designations centered 8 single spaces from the top of the page. Act designations are typed in all-caps; scene designations are typed in lower case and are located 2 single spaces below the act designations. Both designations begin 4 inches from the left edge of the paper and are underscored:

ACT II

Scene iii

When a scene ends, "(BLACKOUT)" or "(CURTAIN)" is typed 4 inches from the left edge, and in the same style 2 single spaces below this is the designation "(END OF ACT)" or "(END OF SCENE)." On the last page of the script, this final designation reads simply "THE END."

The following three pages provide a sample, reduced in size and not to exact scale, of a title page, character page and first page of text of a play typed in the format described above.

PEGGY'S FAVORITE

A Play in One Act

by

A. D. Woods

Copyright © 1989,
by A. D. Woods

305 Madison Ave.
Suite 1146
New York, NY 10165
(212) 687-4185

Cast of Characters

Linda Harris: A woman in her early 40's.

Tom Eliott: Her brother, 35.

Peggy Harris: Her daughter, 16.

Calvin Soames: Tom's friend, in his late 40's.

Jerry Dobbins: A boy of 11.

Scene

A small bed and breakfast in the Lake District of England.

Time

Spring, 1953.

1

Scene 1

SETTING: We are in the hotel dining
                      room. One door leads to the
                      sitting room, another to the
                      kitchen. There are four small
                      tables, in various stages of
                      preparation for the serving of
                      breakfast.

AT RISE: Morning. Offstage music of
                      the period is heard from a
                      radio in the sitting room.
                      LINDA, carrying table linens
                      and flatware, enters from the
                      kitchen.

LINDA
For pity's sake, Tom! Not at this hour! You **want** a
roomful of angry people?
                      (The radio blares then goes off.)
That'd be your cuppa tea, wouldn't it?
                      (to herself)
But not mine, thank you.

                      (PEGGY, laden with place plates,
                      enters from the kitchen and
                      begins setting a table.)

PEGGY
You always have to yell at him?

LINDA
Don't you start! Haven't I got troubles enough?

PEGGY (cheerfully)
Ask a simple question! What's poor old Uncle Tommy
done this time?

The Playwright's Checklist

A query/synopsis should include the following materials:

☐ A brief, polite and business-like cover letter addressed to an individual, introducing the play, explaining why it may be appropriate for this particular theatre, publisher or program and indicating a willingness to provide the script upon request.

☐ A 1-2 page script synopsis, briefly identifying all characters, indicating the number of acts and scenes, describing locales, set changes and any unusual technical demands—and providing a succinct summary of the play's action.

☐ If requested, a script history, giving details of previous productions, workshops or readings of the play and of any awards the play has won.

☐ If requested, a carefully selected 10-page dialogue sample. (We recommend that, unless so requested, playwrights not send opening scenes as samples.)

☐ The playwright's resume and any available reviews of the play.

☐ A stamped, self-addressed business envelope (#10), or, if requested, a self-addressed postcard, for the reader's response.

A script submission to a theatre, publisher or special program should include the following materials:

☐ A brief and business-like cover letter.

☐ A clear copy (not the original) of the script, typed in proper format (see Playscript Format), and securely bound in a sturdy folder. (Note: Some publishers may prefer that scripts be submitted unbound.)

☐ A cassette tape of original music used in the play, recorded if possible by professional musicians and/or vocalists and marked with the playwright's name, address and phone number and the play's title.

☐ A succinct synopsis and a script history.

☐ The playwright's resume.

☐ A stamped, self-addressed postcard for notification of receipt or for the reader's response.

☐ A stamped, self-addressed mailer for return of the script. (Note: This mailer is essential if the playwright wishes any submitted materials returned. Some readers, in fact, will not consider any script not accompanied by this SASE. Many script readers suggest that the SASE be folded and stapled inside the back cover of the script. The SASE should be large enough to hold the script but should not be so bulky as to complicate the reading and handling process. Playwrights should be aware that Special 4th Class Mail is the most economical means of mailing scripts and should compare the cost of copying and binding a script with the cost of the mailer and return postage. Metered postage is not acceptable for return mailers, and our survey indicates that loose stamps are not appreciated by recipients.)

☐ Any additional materials required or requested by the recipient.

A script entry mailed to a contest should include the following materials:

☐ A brief and business-like cover letter, indicating the playwright's intention to enter the play in the competition.

☐ As many typed, securely bound copies of the script as required by the contest. (Note: Some contests require that all information identifying the playwright be removed from the script prior to submission; in such instances, a second title page with the playwright's name, address and phone number should be attached to the cover letter.)

☐ A cassette tape of any original music used in the play.

☐ All completed application forms, written statements, entry fees and other materials, such as a resume and script history, required by the contest.

☐ A stamped, self-addressed postcard for notification of receipt of submission.

☐   A stamped, self-addressed business envelope for notification of the play's status.

☐   A stamped, self-addressed mailer for return of the script.

A request for information, guidelines and/or application forms should include the following materials:

☐   A polite letter requesting the desired information and materials.

☐   A stamped, self-addressed business envelope.

☐   Any additional materials required or requested by the recipient.

The Playwright's Submission Record

In order to keep track of submissions, playwrights use various record-keeping systems. We suggest use of a submission file containing a record sheet for each play, as shown below:

Play title: _____

Draft: _____

Submitted query:_____, script:_____
              (date)   (date)

Other materials included:_____
_____

To: _____
_____
_____

Response expected: _____, received: _____
                    (date)   (date)

Follow-up: _____

Result: _____

Theatres

Guidelines for submitting materials to the theatres and production companies listed in this section:

Read each listing thoroughly and carefully and follow any advice offered.

Do not expect a theatre or production company to make an exception in the kinds of work it stages, its exclusive interests or its specifications in order to produce your play.

Comply exactly with the submission policy stated in the listing. Be certain that appropriate materials accompany every submission (see The Playwright's Checklist and individual listings).

Do not expect a theatre or production company to return any materials, or respond to any correspondence, not accompanied by self-addressed mailers or envelopes, adequately stamped and large enough to accommodate the materials to be mailed.

ABOUT FACE THEATRE COMPANY
AT THE NAT HORNE THEATRE

442 W. 42nd St., New York, NY 10036 (212) 268-9638
Contact: Sean Burke, Co-Artistic Director **Theatre:** off off Broadway **Works:** full-length plays, one-acts, adaptations, musicals **2nd productions:** no **Exclusive interests:** "New York City area writers interested in long-term residencies and writing for the company. We generate new material monthly. We are a social and political theatre company, interested in plays that explore and reinterpret the American myth and ideology." **Specifications:** "No plays set in New York apartments; no single-set plays." **Tours:** yes **Stages:** proscenium, 99 seats; flexible, 45 seats **Casting:** "Open auditions--Equity and non-Equity actors." **Audience:** "Young--20-40 years of age." **Submission policy:** query/synopsis with resume; agent submission; commission **Best times:** Dec.-Jan. for one-act; Jul.-Aug. for full-length play **Response:** 3 months **Your chances:** full-length plays: 190 submissions/3 productions plus 8 workshops and 15 readings; one-acts: 225 submissions/6 productions plus 16 workshops and 30 readings **Remuneration:** "Varies, depending on funding." **Future commitment:** "Conversion contract." **Programs:** readings, staged readings, workshop productions, development, internships, residencies **Advice:** "We're more interested in the writer's creating material <u>for</u> us, rather than producing scripts from outside the company."

ACACIA THEATRE
Box 11952, Milwaukee, WI 53211 (414) 223-4996
Contact: Dick Gustin, Artistic Director **Theatre:** professional not-for-profit **Works:** full-length plays, one-acts, translations, adaptations, musicals **2nd productions:** yes **Special interest:** "Plays with biblical or spiritual themes. A comedy based on a biblical story would be great." **Maximum cast:** 12 **Tours:** yes **Stage:** arena, 281 seats **Audience:** "Most are Christians from a variety of denominations." **Submission policy:** unsolicited script with SASE; professional recommendation; "word of mouth/perusal copy" **Best time:** fall **Your chances:** 5 submissions/1 production **Advice:** "We are looking for plays written from a Christian World View."

ACADEMY PLAYHOUSE
Box 1843, Orleans, MA 02653 (508) 255-1963
Contact: Maura Hanlon, Theatre Coordinator **Theatre:** professional not-for-profit, community/non-professional **Works:** full-length plays, adaptations, musicals, children's plays **2nd productions:** yes **Tours:** yes **Stage:** thrust, 162 seats **Casting:** open auditions **Audience:** "Tourists and residents, families and senior citizens." **Submission policy:** query/synopsis; commission **Best time:** fall **Response:** 1-2 months script **Your chances:** 3 new plays produced each year **Remuneration:** no **Programs:** workshop productions, development, classes **Advice:** "Write for a general audience."

ACADEMY THEATRE
Box 77070, 173 14th St. NE, Atlanta, GA 30357 (404) 873-2518 Contact: Valetta Anderson, Literary Manager **Theatre:** professional not-for-profit **Works:** full-length plays, one-acts, adaptations, musicals, children's plays **2nd productions:** "If not previously produced in the Southeast." **Special interests:** "Non-traditional plays with elements of poetic language and surrealism; plays that deal with important issues in imaginative ways." **Specifications:** maximum cast: 8; single set preferred **Stages:** modified thrust, 389 seats; flexible, 250 seats; flexible, 80 seats **Audience:** "A cross-sampling of Atlantans interested in alternative theatre-going and good acting." **Submission policy:** query/synopsis with dialogue sample; unsolicited script with SASE from local writer only **Best time:** Aug.-Sept. **Response:** 1 month query; 1-12 months script **Your chances:** 300 submissions/5 productions **Remuneration:** "Varies with type of production." **Future commitment:** for world premiere **Programs:** quarterly readings for students in theatre's playwriting classes; Theatre for

Youth (plays for grades 3-12); Genesis Series: New Play Program for local writers **Advice:** "Writers who have found their own voices and are not imitating current theatrical trends; writers who have a facility with language along with the ability to disturb, amuse and interest an audience in theatrical, dramatic ways."

A CONTEMPORARY THEATER SOUTHWEST
Scottsdale, AZ This theatre is permanently closed.

A CONTEMPORARY THEATRE
100 W. Roy St., Seattle, WA 98119 (206) 285-3220
Contact: Steven Alter, Literary Manager **Theatre:** professional not-for-profit **Works:** full-length plays, translations, adaptations, children's plays **2nd productions:** yes **Special interest:** contemporary issues **Tours:** children's plays **Stage:** thrust, 450 seats **Audience:** "Very mixed." **Submission policy:** query/ synopsis; professional recommendation; agent submission **Response:** 1 month query; 3 months script **Your chances:** 500 submissions/1 production **Remuneration:** "Royalties arranged; often residency for rehearsals." **Program:** Young ACT Company theatre for young audiences (inquire)

THE ACTING COMPANY
Box 898 Times Square Station, New York, NY 10108
(212) 564-3510 Contact: Gerald Gutierrez, Artistic Director **Theatre:** off Broadway, professional not-for-profit **Works:** full-length plays, one-acts, translations, adaptations, musicals **Special interest:** works suitable for an ensemble of 10 men and 4 women, 20-45 years of age **Specifications:** simple, tourable set **Stage:** proscenium, 287 seats **Submission policy:** professional recommendation **Best time:** Nov.-Jan. **Response:** 8-10 weeks

THE ACTING GROUP
Box 1252 Old Chelsea Station, New York, NY 10011
(212) 645-1459 Contact: Celia Barrett, Producing Artistic Director **Theatre:** professional **Works:** full-length plays, one-acts **Special interests:** comedy, drama **Specifications:** maximum cast: 10; no more than 2 sets; "we are an ensemble company of actors, playwrights, directors--major age range 25-45" **Stages:** "Rented per show--in Manhattan only." **Submission policy:** query/synopsis with resume; professional recommendation; agent submission; may accept unsolicited script with SASE **Best time:** spring for following fall-winter **Response:** 10-12 months script **Your chances:** 2000+ submissions/5 productions **Remuneration:** "Usually $50 per one-act." **Programs:** staged

readings, development; "a few playwright members work with us year-round" **Advice:** "Be patient; we're very small but do high quality Equity Showcases."

ACTORS ALLEY REPERTORY THEATRE
4334 Van Nuys Blvd., Sherman Oaks, CA 91403
(818) 986-2278 Contact: John Shaw, Literary Manager **Theatre:** professional not-for-profit **Works:** full-length plays, one-acts, musicals **2nd productions:** yes **Special interests:** comedy, comedy-drama **Maximum cast:** 20 **Submission policy:** unsolicited script with SASE, synopsis and resume **Response:** 2-3 months **Recent production of unsolicited work:** yes **Future commitment:** possibly **Comment:** "Any full-length play submitted is considered for production."

ACTORS' ALLIANCE, INC.
AAI, JAF Box 7370, New York, NY 10116
(718) 768-6110 Contact: Melanie Sutherland, Juanita Walsh, Co-Artistic Directors **Theatre:** off off Broadway, membership company **Works:** full-length plays, one-acts, translations, adaptations **2nd productions:** yes **Tours:** yes **Stage:** proscenium, 99 seats (Nat Horne Theatre) **Casting:** "From a pool, age range 20's-40's." **Audience:** "Subscription list of 4000 in NY, NJ and PA." **Submission policy:** 2 work samples with SASE and resume **Response:** 2 months **Your chances:** 150 submissions/ 1-2 productions **Remuneration:** "Expenses and small stipend." **Programs:** readings, staged readings, workshop productions **Advice:** "Playwrights may submit plays and join the organization, which has a small fee." **Comments:** "Our objective is to produce classical, contemporary and original plays." See Actors' Alliance, Inc. listing in Special Programs.

ACTORS ALLIANCE THEATRE
30800 Evergreen, Southfield, MI 48076
(313) 642-1326 Contact: Jeffrey M. Nahan, Artistic Director/ Literary Manager **Theatre:** professional not-for-profit **Works:** full-length plays, one-acts **2nd productions:** yes **Special interest:** "Contemporary issues." **Maximum cast:** 12 **Stage:** flexible, 99 seats **Audience:** "Black/white--urban, upper middle class." **Submission policy:** query/synopsis **Best time:** Jan.- Apr. **Response:** 6 months query; 6-18 months script **Your chances:** 30-60 submissions/1 production **Remuneration/future commitment:** negotiable **Program:** internships

THE ACTORS' COMPANY OF PENNSYLVANIA

Box 1153, Lancaster, PA 17603 (717) 397-1251
Contact: Jeanne Clemson, Producing Director **Theatre:** professional not-for-profit **Works:** full-length plays, one-acts, translations, adaptations, musicals, children's plays **Specifications:** simple production requirements **Stages:** proscenium, 800 seats; thrust, 200 seats **Submission policy:** query/synopsis **Best time:** summer **Response:** 6 months if interested in query; 3 months script

ACTORS FOR THEMSELVES

Matrix Theatre, 7657 Melrose Ave.,
Los Angeles, CA 90046 (213) 852-1445
Contact: Joseph Stern, Producer **Theatre:** professional not-for-profit **Works:** full-length plays, musicals **2nd productions:** yes **Special interest:** "Naturalistic plays." **Stage:** thrust **Submission policy:** professional recommendation, agent submission preferred; unsolicited script with SASE **Best times:** Jan.-Feb., Aug.-Sept. **Response:** 6 weeks **Recent production of unsolicited work:** no **Future commitment:** yes

ACTORS LAB ARIZONA

7624 E. Indian School Rd., Scottsdale, AZ 85251
(602) 990-1739 **Contact:** Jan Sickler, Artistic Director **Theatre:** professional not-for-profit **Works:** full-length plays, translations, adaptations, children's plays **Special interests:** "Provocative and experimental works." **Specifications:** small cast, simple set **Stage:** thrust, 155 seats **Casting:** "Some local, some from auditions in New York, Chicago." **Submission policy:** query/synopsis **Response:** 2 weeks query; 4-6 months script **Your chances:** 20 submissions/4 productions, usually 2nd productions

ACTORS LABORATORY THEATRE

Kansas City, MO This theatre no longer considers original scripts.

ACTORS OUTLET THEATRE

120 W. 28th St., New York, NY 10019 (212) 807-1590
Contact: Sura Shachnouitz, Literary Manager **Theatre:** off off Broadway **Works:** full-length plays, one-acts, translations, adaptations, musicals **2nd productions:** yes **Specifications:** no more than 2 sets; no "sit-coms" **Stage:** flexible, 99 seats **Audience:** "General." **Submission policy:** unsolicited script with SASE; professional recommendation; agent submission **Response:**

1-2 months **Your chances:** 100 submissions/3 productions **Remuneration:** negotiable **Future commitment:** no **Programs:** readings, staged readings, workshop productions

ACTORS' REPERTORY COMPANY
West Palm Beach, FL Our 1990 questionnaire was returned as "undeliverable," and this theatre's phone has been disconnected.

THE ACTORS SPACE
250 W. 54th St., New York, NY 10019 (212) 925-5020
Contact: Christina Denzingen, Literary Manager **Theatre:** professional not-for-profit **Works:** full-length plays, one-acts, translations, adaptations, musicals **2nd productions:** yes **Special interest:** "High stakes plays in which characters have strong, clear objectives." **Specifications:** simple set preferred; "actors aged 20's-40's preferred but older okay" **Stages:** rented spaces, 50+ seats **Submission policy:** query/synopsis with resume preferred; unsolicited script with SASE and resume **Response:** 3 months **Your chances:** 50-100 submissions/3 productions plus staged readings **Programs:** workshop productions, development **Advice:** "Hard hitting/social issues."

ACTORS THEATRE OF LOUISVILLE
316 W. Main St., Louisville, KY 40402 (502) 584-1265
Contact: Michael Bigelow Dixon, Literary Manager **Theatre:** professional not-for-profit **Works:** full-length plays, one-acts, translations, adaptations **2nd productions:** yes **Special interests:** "Penetrating characterizations, dynamic plot, vivid theatricality." **Maximum cast:** 15 **Tours:** "Occasionally." **Stages:** thrust, 637 seats; thrust, 150 seats **Audience:** "A cross-section of the Louisville community." **Submission policy:** professional recommendation; agent submission; unsolicited script with SASE for one-act contest only **Best time:** Mar.-Oct for shorter response time **Response:** 6-9 months or more script; most scripts returned in fall **Your chances:** 2500 submissions/30 productions **Remuneration:** "Royalties in accordance with Dramatists Guild/LORT contracts." **Future commitment:** minimal and negotiable **Programs:** National One-Act Play Contest, National Ten-Minute Play Contest (see Contests); Humana Festival of New American Plays: 7-14 new works selected each summer and fall for annual presentation the following spring **Advice:** "Submit plays to the National One-Act Play Contest." **Comment:** See Breslin, Jimmy, "TKO in Louisville," *American Theatre* (Jun. 1988), 25-27, 57; DeVries, Hilary, "When Authors Try Their Hand At Writing Plays," *New York Times* (Mar. 26, 1989), 5, 24.

ACTORS THEATRE OF ST. PAUL
28 W. 7th Pl., St. Paul, MN 55102 (612) 297-6868
Contact: Michael Andrew Miner, Artistic Director **Theatre:** professional not-for-profit, LORT regional repertory company **Works:** full-length plays, one-acts, translations, adaptations, musicals **2nd productions:** yes **Special interest:** "High quality scripts." **Specifications:** maximum cast: 15; cast must suit casting needs of resident company **Stage:** proscenium, 330 seats **Audience:** "Varied." **Submission policy:** professional recommendation, agent submission or query/synopsis with dialogue sample preferred; unsolicited script with SASE; submission through Playwrights Center (see Special Programs) **Best time:** Feb.–Jun. **Response:** 2 weeks query; 3 months script **Recent production of unsolicited work:** no **Remuneration:** negotiable royalty **Future commitment:** no **Programs:** staged readings, workshop productions, residencies; Minnesota One-Act Play Festival (inquire) **Advice:** "A carefully prepared query and synopsis can save you postage and time. We solicit many of the scripts described in synopses; discourage ones similar in theme to those we've recently produced and often request an additional script from your resume."

ACTORS' WORKSHOP
Ashland, OR This theatre is not accepting submissions and has requested that we discontinue its listing.

THE ADELPHIAN PLAYERS
8515 Ridge Blvd., Brooklyn, NY 11209 (718) 238-3309
Contact: Russ Bonanno, President **Theatre:** professional not-for-profit **Works:** full-length plays, adaptations **2nd productions:** yes **Special interests:** "Urban problems, senior citizens' issues, contemporary comedies." **Specifications:** "Staff considerations." **Stage:** flexible **Audience:** "Senior citizen and general, Brooklyn-Urban area." **Submission policy:** unsolicited script with SASE and resume; professional recommendation **Best time:** Nov.–Dec. **Response:** 3-4 weeks query; 5-6 weeks script **Remuneration:** no **Comment:** Theatre operates during summer only.

A DIRECTORS' THEATRE
6404 Hollywood Blvd., Hollywood, CA 90028
(213) 465-8431 Contact: Dorothy Lyman, Artistic Director **Theatre:** professional not-for-profit **Works:** full-length plays, translations, adaptations **Special interest:** "Plays by or about women." **Maximum cast:** 10 **Stage:** flexible, 50 seats **Submission policy:** unsolicited script with SASE; query/synopsis

Response: 1 month query; 3-4 months script **Your chances:** readings of approximately 20 new plays each year **Program:** A Directors' Theatre Annual Young Playwrights' Competition (see Contests)

A.D. PLAYERS
2710 W. Alabama, Houston, TX 77098 (713) 526-2721
Contact: Carol Anderson, Literary Manager **Theatre:** professional not-for-profit **Works:** full-length plays, one-acts, translations, adaptations, musicals, children's plays, cabaret/revues **2nd productions:** yes **Exclusive interests:** "All our productions are from a Christian world view: God's reality in Man's everyday world. We are also looking for children's shows." **Specifications:** maximum cast: 12, 10 or fewer preferred; no more than 2 sets; no fly space; low ceiling (11'6"); minimal lighting **Tours:** "Many." **Stage:** proscenium, 212 seats **Audience:** "Majority are conservative, from a wide range economically, ethnically and educationally." **Submission policy:** unsolicited script with SASE; query/synopsis **Response:** 2 weeks query; 2 months script **Your chances:** 100 submissions/1 production **Remuneration:** negotiable royalty

ALABAMA SHAKESPEARE FESTIVAL
Box 20350, Montgomery, AL 36120-0350
(205) 272-1640 Contact: Terry Sneed, Assistant to Artistic Director **Theatre:** professional not-for-profit **Works:** full-length plays, translations, adaptations **2nd productions:** no **Special interests:** "Literary adaptations and plays dealing with Southern black issues." **Specifications:** maximum cast: 18-20; no more than 3-4 sets **Stages:** modified thrust, 750 seats; flexible, 225 seats **Submission policy:** query/synopsis with dialogue sample **Best time:** Apr.-Jul. **Response:** 3 weeks query; 3-4 months script **Your chances:** 50-60 submissions/0 productions **Remuneration:** no

ALASKA REPERTORY THEATRE
Anchorage, AK This theatre did not respond to our 1990 questionnaire, and its phone was not in service when we called.

ALCHEMY THEATRE COMPANY
Box 2408 Times Square Station, New York, NY 10108
(212) 268-7440 Contact: Gita Donovan, Artistic Director **Theatre:** off off Broadway **Works:** full-length plays, one-acts, adaptations **2nd productions:** "If New York premieres." **Stages:** rented spaces **Audience:** "General public, well educated, literate; students; some appeal to ethnic constituency--depends upon the play."

Submission policy: unsolicited script with SASE; query/synopsis; professional recommendation; agent submission; commission **Response:** 1 month **Your chances:** 300-400 submissions/2 productions **Remuneration:** negotiable **Programs:** staged readings, workshop productions, development **Advice:** "We are open to your best work!"

ALHAMBRA DINNER THEATRE
12000 Beach Blvd., Jacksonville, FL 33216
(904) 641-1212 Contact: Tod Booth, Producer **Theatre:** Equity dinner **Works:** full-length plays, musicals **Special interest:** musicals **Specifications:** maximum cast: 8-10; single or unit set **Submission policy:** unsolicited script with SASE **Your chances:** 200 submissions/0 productions **Advice:** "We would love to receive new musicals."

ALICE B. THEATRE
1435 11th Ave. #200, Seattle, WA 98122
(206) 322-5423 Contact: Nikki Appino, Literary Manager **Theatre:** professional not-for-profit **Works:** full-length plays, one-acts, translations, adaptations, musicals, cabaret/revues **2nd productions:** yes **Special interests:** "Gay or lesbian characters or themes; plays which re-examine gender or have a clearly gay, camp or lesbian/feminist perspective." **Tours:** yes **Stages:** proscenium, 295 seats; modified thrust, 148 seats; black box, 99 seats **Casting:** "Wide open: non-traditional, equal opportunity, cross-gender." **Audience:** "1/3 straight, 1/3 gay male, 1/3 lesbian." **Submission policy:** query/synopsis with resume and dialogue sample; professional recommendation; agent submission **Response:** 1 month query; 6 months script **Your chances:** 150 submissions/2 productions **Remuneration:** "$500-$1200 for full length play; $100-$250 for one-act." **Future commitment:** no **Programs:** readings, staged readings, workshop productions, development **Advice:** "We are most excited by original theatre forms and styles, unconventional dialogue and works that take an idiosyncratic or highly skewed perspective on their subjects."

ALLENBERRY PLAYHOUSE
Box 7 Rt. 174, Boiling Springs, PA 17007
(717) 258-3211 Contact: Michael Rothaarr, Director **Theatre:** Equity stock **Works:** full-length plays, musicals **2nd productions:** yes **Special interests:** comedies, farces, musicals, family dramas **Specifications:** cast of 5-7; single set; limited wing and fly space **Stage:** proscenium, 414 seats **Audience:** "Fairly conservative, older." **Submission policy:**

query/synopsis **Best time:** Jan.-Aug. **Your chances:** "We do very few new plays but are always open."

ALLEY THEATRE
615 Texas Ave., Houston, TX 77002 (713) 228-9341
Contact: Gregory Boyd, Artistic Director **Theatre:** professional not-for-profit **Works:** full-length plays, translations, children's plays **2nd productions:** yes **Special interests:** "Revitalized classics, major world dramas, new plays." **Tours:** "May do so in the future." **Stages:** partial thrust, 824 seats; arena, 399 seats **Submission policy:** send SASE for information **Your chances:** 200-400 submissions received each year **Programs:** "All currently in the planning process." **Comment:** When *The Playwright's Companion 1990* went to press, the theatre was in the process of planning its general policies and was not accepting submissions.

ALLIANCE THEATRE
1280 Peachtree St. NE, Atlanta, GA 30309
(404) 898-1132 Contact: Sandra Deer, Literary Manager **Theatre:** professional not-for-profit **Works:** full-length plays, one-acts, children's plays **2nd productions:** yes **Special interests:** works suitable for a large theatre; "strong story lines" **Stages:** proscenium, 864 seats; flexible, 200 seats **Submission policy:** professional recommendation; agent submission **Response:** 1-4 months **Future commitment:** negotiable

AMAS REPERTORY THEATRE
1 E. 104th St., New York, NY 10029 (212) 369-8000
Contact: Rosetta LeNoire, Artistic Director **Theatre:** professional not-for-profit **Works:** musicals, cabaret/revues **2nd productions:** if New York premieres **Special interests:** "Biographical and historical musicals; innovative works." **Specifications:** maximum cast: 12; simple set; "works must be suitable for multi-racial casting and for the whole family" **Tours:** yes **Stage:** modified thrust, 99 seats **Audience:** "Multi-racial, from the New York metro area." **Submission policy:** query/synopsis preferred; unsolicited script with SASE **Best time:** Jul.-Sept. **Response:** 2 months **Your chances:** 150 submissions/ 3 productions **Remuneration:** no **Future commitment:** negotiable **Programs:** workshop productions, internships, residencies **Comments:** "Many of our productions have gone on to receive potentially lucrative commercial productions." See Reed, Claude Jr., "Rosetta LeNoire: Reflections on a Life in the Theatre," *TheaterWeek* (Feb. 29-Mar. 6, 1988), 26-30.

AMERICAN CONSERVATORY THEATRE
450 Geary St., San Francisco, CA 94102
(415) 771-3880 **Contact:** Edward W. Hastings, Artistic Director **Theatre:** professional not-for-profit **Works:** full-length plays, translations, adaptations **2nd productions:** yes **Maximum cast:** 10 **Stage:** black box, 50-60 seats **Audience:** subscription **Submission policy:** query/synopsis with 10-page maximum dialogue sample preferred; unsolicited script with SASE **Response:** 2 months query; 6 months or more script **Your chances:** 100-150 submissions/0 productions **Future commitment:** yes **Program:** Plays-in-Progress staged readings (inquire) **Advice:** "Please inquire before submitting."

AMERICAN ENSEMBLE COMPANY
Box 972 Peck Slip Station, New York, NY 10272
(212) 571-7594 **Contact:** Kelly Masterson, Literary Manager **Theatre:** off off Broadway, professional not-for-profit **Works:** full-length plays, one-acts, musicals **2nd productions:** only if not previously produced off off Broadway **Special interest:** "Socially significant plays written with a concern for language." **Specifications:** unit set; "not interested in avant garde" **Stage:** proscenium, 128 seats **Audience:** "General New York City." **Submission policy:** query/synopsis with dialogue sample **Response:** 2 months **Your chances:** 350 submissions/5 productions plus 8 staged readings; "we hope to do 10 full productions and 15 readings with authors who live in the New York City area" **Programs:** staged readings, workshop productions, residencies

AMERICAN FOLK THEATER, INC.
230 W. 41st St. Suite 1807, New York, NY 10036
(212) 764-1267 **Contact:** David Newman, Literary Manager **Theatre:** professional not-for-profit **Works:** full-length plays **2nd productions:** no **Special interests:** "Cross-cultural social dramas; solid characters, honest dialogue, forward-moving action; scripts for development." **Specifications:** maximum cast: 8; multi-racial cast; "one set if realism or naturalism is required" **Stage:** thrust **Audience:** "College graduates, 20-50, all races, urban." **Submission policy:** unsolicited script with SASE, resume and script history; query/synopsis; professional recommendation; agent submission **Response:** 6 weeks query; 3 months script **Your chances:** 500 submissions/3 productions, "mainly readings and workshops" **Remuneration:** "As per option agreement." **Future commitment:** after full workshop production **Programs:** readings, staged readings, workshop productions, development, classes, internships; Playwrights' Lab (inquire) **Advice:** "Plays that dramatically and musically explore the multi-cultural character of our

changing American society; plays of action, not only of words, especially those with a heightened sense of theatrical realism."

AMERICAN JEWISH THEATRE
307 W. 26th St., New York, NY 10001 (212) 683-7220
Contact: Stanley Brechner, Artistic Director **Theatre:** professional not-for-profit **Works:** full-length plays, translations, adaptations, musicals **2nd productions:** yes **Exclusive interest:** Jewish themes **Maximum cast:** 7 **Stage:** black box, 100 seats **Audience:** "Subscription, mainly middle-class Jewish." **Submission policy:** unsolicited script with SASE; professional recommendation; agent submission **Best time:** Sept.-Jun. **Response:** 2 months **Your chances:** 150 submissions/4-5 productions **Future commitment:** yes **Program:** Jewish Women Playwrights Unit (inquire)

THE AMERICAN LINE
810 W. 183rd St. #5C, New York, NY 10033
(212) 740-9277 Contact: Richard Hoehler, Artistic Director **Theatre:** professional not-for-profit **Works:** full-length plays, one acts **2nd productions:** "Occasionally." **Special interests:** "American plays by American playwrights concerned with a broad vision of American society and ethnic backgrounds; issues relevant to the city and a spectrum of society involving cross-cultural actors and concepts." **Specifications:** maximum cast: 20; no more than 2 sets, "simple is better" **Stages:** rented spaces **Casting:** open auditions once each year **Audience:** "New York; mixed ages, intellectual and ethnic backgrounds." **Submission policy:** query/synopsis **Best times:** Jan., Aug. **Response:** 1 month query; 3 months script **Your chances:** 245 submissions/productions of 2 full-length plays and 4 one-acts plus 5-9 staged readings **Remuneration:** "Contract/royalty."

AMERICAN LIVING HISTORY THEATER
Box 2677, Hollywood, CA 90078 (213) 876-2202
Contact: Dorene Ludwig, Artistic Director **Theatre:** professional not-for-profit **Works:** one-acts **2nd productions:** yes **Exclusive interests:** "American historical and literary characters and events/primary source material; material of interest to multiple age and ethnic groups." **Specifications:** maximum cast: 1-2 preferred; "no set, some props" **Tours:** "Throughout the U.S. on per-performance basis." **Stages:** proscenium, thrust, arena, flexible--"depending upon the client's space" **Audience:** "Ages 4 through over 70, all ethnic groups and white, all educational levels." **Submission policy:** query/synopsis with SAS postcard preferred; unsolicited script with SASE **Response:** 6 months **Your chances:**

12-15 submissions/0 productions; "we rarely produce work outside the company: submissions are not historically accurate/primary source; we have numerous playwrights within the company" **Remuneration:** "Depends upon funding, and how produced—Equity, waiver, reading, etc." **Future commitment:** negotiable **Programs:** "Seminars and consultation available to writers on request. Fees based on services." **Advice:** "Do not send material that has nothing to do with our interests."

AMERICAN MUSIC THEATRE FESTIVAL
One Franklin Plaza, Philadelphia, PA 19103
(215) 988-9050 Contact: Eric Salzman, Artistic Director **Theatre:** professional not-for-profit **Works:** music theatre **2nd productions:** yes **Tours:** "Yes, generally we co-produce." **Submission policy:** unsolicited script with SASE and resume; professional recommendation **Best time:** Jun.-Jul. **Response:** 9 months **Your chances:** 100-150 submissions/4 productions in Mar.-Jun. season **Programs:** staged readings, workshop productions; Spring Festival (inquire)

AMERICAN NOOK & CRANNY THEATRE COMPANY
New York, NY Our 1990 questionnaire was returned as "undeliverable," and this theatre's phone has been disconnected.

THE AMERICAN PLACE THEATRE
111 W. 46th St., New York, NY 10036 (212) 246-3730
Contact: Literary Manager **Theatre:** off Broadway, professional not-for-profit **Works:** full-length plays, one-acts, adaptations, cabaret/revues **2nd productions:** yes **Special interests:** "Innovative works, humorous revues." **Specifications:** American playwrights only **Stages:** flexible, 299 seats; flexible, 100 seats; flexible cabaret, 100 seats **Submission policy:** unsolicited script with SASE from writer who has had professional productions; query/synopsis with up to 25-page dialogue sample from others **Best time:** Sept.-Jun. **Response:** 4 months **Programs:** American Humorist Series (2 programs per season of works by or about American Humorists); Jubilee (annual festival celebrating minority and ethnic American experience) **Comment:** See Shirakawa, Sam H., "American Place: The Original Underground Theatre," *TheaterWeek* (Nov. 7, 1988), 22-29.

AMERICAN PLAYWRIGHTS THEATRE
1742 Church St. NW, Washington, DC 20036
(202) 232-4527 Contact: Debbie Niezgoda, Artistic Associate **Theatre:** professional not-for-profit **Works:** full-length plays, adaptations, musicals **2nd productions:** if D.C. area premieres

Special interest: "A well-crafted conception which fulfills its dramatic mission." **Specifications:** maximum cast: 10; small wing space **Stage:** endstage, 125 seats **Submission policy:** query/synopsis with 10-page dialogue sample, resume and SAS postcard **Best time:** Aug. **Response:** 6 months query; 9-12 months or more script **Your chances:** 300 submissions/4 productions plus 7 staged readings **Remuneration:** yes **Future commitment:** negotiable **Programs:** readings, staged readings, classes, internships; Black Dramatists Festival (see Contests)

AMERICAN RENAISSANCE THEATRE
521 City Island Ave., City Island, NY 10464
(212) 885-1938 Contact: Susan Gert, Literary Manager **Theatre:** off off Broadway, professional not-for-profit **Comment:** This theatre was not accepting submissions when *The Playwright's Companion 1990* went to press; playwrights should inquire before submitting materials.

AMERICAN REPERTORY THEATRE
64 Brattle St., Cambridge, MA 02138 (617) 495-2668
Contact: Arthur Holmberg, Literary Director; R.J. Cutler, Director of New Plays **Theatre:** professional not-for-profit **Works:** full-length plays, one-acts, translations, adaptations, cabaret/revues **2nd productions:** yes **Special interest:** plays with "poetic dimension" rather than "prosaic realism" **Maximum cast:** 15 **Stages:** proscenium, 350 seats; flexible, 556 seats **Submission policy:** agent submission preferred; query/synopsis with 10-page maximum dialogue sample **Best time:** Sept.-Jun. **Response:** 2 weeks query; 4-5 months script **Program:** Monday night readings of works in development

AMERICAN STAGE
Box 1560, St. Petersburg, FL 33731 (813) 823-1600
Contact: Hunt Scarritt, Dramaturg **Theatre:** professional not-for-profit **Works:** full-length plays, adaptations, children's one-acts **Special interest:** works written in the last 10 years by American playwrights **Maximum cast:** 10 **Stage:** flexible, 120 seats **Submission policy:** query/synopsis with 1st act of script preferred; unsolicited script with SASE **Best time:** Jul.-Sept. **Response:** 2 months query; 4 months script **Your chances:** 6-9 readings each year **Comment:** Formerly The American Stage Company.

AMERICAN STAGE COMPANY
Box 336, Teaneck, NJ 07666
Contact: James R. Singer, Producing Director/Literary Manager
Theatre: professional not-for-profit **Works:** full-length plays, musicals **2nd productions:** yes **Special interests:** American playwrights, American themes **Specifications:** maximum cast: 8; single set; low proscenium **Tours:** yes **Stage:** proscenium, 270 seats **Audience:** "New York suburban." **Submission policy:** query/synopsis with resume preferred; unsolicited script with SASE; professional recommendation **Best time:** Jan.-Mar. **Response:** variable time, depending upon interest in play **Your chances:** 200-300 submissions/1 production **Remuneration:** no **Future commitment:** negotiable **Program:** readings

AMERICAN STAGE FESTIVAL
Box 225, Milford, NH 03055 (603) 673-7515, -3143
Contact: Austin Tichenor, Literary Manager **Theatre:** professional not-for-profit **Works:** full-length plays, musicals **2nd productions:** yes **Special interest:** "Innovative works on American society." **Specifications:** maximum cast: 10 for plays, 10 with 5 musicians for musicals; no fly system; no small, intimate pieces; no offensive language **Stage:** proscenium, 497 seats **Submission policy:** professional recommendation; agent submission **Best time:** Sept.-Dec. **Response:** 3 months **Future commitment:** negotiable

AMERICAN STANISLAVSKI THEATRE
485 Park Ave. Apt. 6, New York, NY 10022
(212) 755-5120 Contact: Sonia Moore, Artistic Director
Theatre: off off Broadway **Works:** full-length plays, one-acts, translations, adaptations, musicals **2nd productions:** yes **Special interests:** "Important messages; plays for actors aged 18-45." **Specifications:** maximum cast: 4-6; no offensive language **Tours:** "Some shows." **Stage:** proscenium **Submission policy:** unsolicited script with SASE **Best time:** spring **Response:** Sept.-Oct. **Your chances:** 40 submissions/1 production **Recent production of unsolicited work:** no **Program:** classes year round

AMERICAN THEATRE COMPANY
Box 1265, Tulsa, OK 74101 (918) 747-9494
Contact: Kitty Roberts, Artistic Director **Theatre:** professional not-for-profit **Works:** full-length plays, translations, adaptations, musicals, children's plays **2nd productions:** yes **Special interest:** small-cast comedies **Specifications:** maximum cast: 20, 8 or fewer preferred; single set; low budget **Stage:** proscenium

Submission policy: query/synopsis with letter of introduction and dialogue sample **Best time:** late spring **Response:** 2 months

AMERICAN THEATRE OF ACTORS
314 W. 54th St., New York, NY 10019 (212) 581-3044
Contact: James Jennings, Artistic Director **Theatre:** professional not-for-profit **Works:** full-length plays **2nd productions:** no **Special interest:** dramas **Specifications:** maximum cast: 10; no musicals or avant garde plays **Stages:** proscenium, 140 seats; proscenium, 65 seats **Submission policy:** unsolicited script with SASE **Response:** 2 months **Your chances:** 500 submissions/25 productions **Remuneration:** no **Future commitment:** occasionally **Programs:** readings, staged readings, workshop productions

ANGEL'S TOUCH PRODUCTIONS
7962 Hollywood Way, Sun Valley, CA 91352
Contact: Phil Nemy, Director of Development **Theatre:** off off Broadway, professional not-for-profit **Works:** full-length plays, translations, adaptations, musicals, screenplays **2nd productions:** "Occasionally." **Specifications:** "Best bet is to keep it all to a minimum." **Stages:** flexible, 99 seats; flexible, 65 seats; Equity Agreement houses, 100 or more seats **Submission policy:** unsolicited script with SASE; query/synopsis; professional recommendation; agent submission **Response:** 4 weeks query; 6-7 months script **Your chances:** 80-90 submissions/6-8 productions (stage 1), 6-8 productions (stage 2) **Remuneration:** negotiable **Programs:** readings, staged readings, development **Advice:** "Keep in mind production costs--tailor show to fit low costs."

APPLE CORPS THEATRE
336 W. 20th St., New York, NY 10011 (212) 929-2955
Contact: Bob Del Pazzo, Literary Manager **Theatre:** off Broadway, professional not-for-profit **Works:** full-length plays, one-acts **2nd productions:** occasionally **Special interests:** "American plays for totally integrated, multi-ethnic theatre"; mysteries (contact John Raymond) **Specifications:** maximum cast: 10; some limitations on sets **Stage:** proscenium, 180 seats **Audience:** "Middle-class urban, wide age range, educated." **Submission policy:** query/synopsis; agent submission **Best time:** Sept.-Oct. **Response:** 1-2 weeks query; 4-6 months script **Your chances:** "many submissions/very few productions" **Remuneration:** percentage **Future commitment:** yes **Programs:** readings, staged readings, workshop productions, development

ARENA PLAYERS REPERTORY COMPANY OF LONG ISLAND
296 Rte. 109, E. Farmingdale, NY 11735
(516) 293-0674 Contact: Audrey Perry, Literary Manager
Theatre: professional not-for-profit **Works:** full-length plays
Maximum cast: 12 mainstage, 6 2nd stage **Stages:** arena,
240 seats; 2-sided arena, 100 seats **Submission policy:**
unsolicited script with SASE **Response:** 3 months **Your
chances:** 130 submissions/3-4 productions **Remuneration:**
$600-$1000, a video and reviews from *New York Times* and
Newsday

ARENA STAGE
6th and Maine SW, Washington, DC 20024
(202) 554-9066 Contact: Laurence Maslon, Literary Manager/
Dramaturge **Theatre:** professional not-for-profit **Works:** full-
length plays, one-acts, translations, adaptations, musicals **2nd
productions:** yes **Tours:** "Occasionally." **Stages:** modfied
thrust, 525 seats; arena, 800 seats; cabaret, 180 seats
Submission policy: query/synopsis with dialogue sample and
resume; professional recommendation; agent submission; unsolicited
script with SASE from local playwright only **Best time:**
summer-fall **Response:** 4 weeks query; 2-3 months script **Your
chances:** 600 submissions/2 productions **Remuneration:** "Yes.
Depends." **Future commitment:** negotiable **Programs:**
development; Stage Four new play series (inquire)

ARIZONA THEATRE COMPANY
56 W. Congress, Box 1631, Tucson, AZ 85702
(602) 884-8210 Contact: Gary Gisselman, Artistic Director;
Constantine Arvanitakis, Matthew Wiener, Literary Managers
Theatre: professional not-for-profit **Works:** full-length plays,
one-acts, translations, adaptations **Exclusive interest:** "Plays
that are written by playwrights from the Arizona-Southwest region
or deal with subjects directly connected to this area." **Stages:**
proscenium, 800 seats; proscenium, 526 seats **Submission
policy:** query/synopsis with 10-page dialogue sample and resume
preferred; unsolicited script with SASE may be accepted **Best
time:** spring-summer **Response:** 6 months **Remuneration:** fee,
travel, housing for staged readings **Future commitment:** no

THE ARKANSAS ARTS CENTER CHILDREN'S THEATRE
Box 2137, Little Rock, AR 72203 (501) 372-4000
Contact: Bradley D. Anderson, Artistic Director **Theatre:**
professional not-for-profit **Works:** full-length plays, one-acts,
translations, adaptations, children's plays **Special interests:**

works suitable for family audiences; adaptations of classics **Tours:** yes **Stage:** proscenium, 389 seats **Submission policy:** unsolicited script with SASE **Response:** 6 months

ARKANSAS REPERTORY THEATRE

601 Main St. Box 110, Little Rock, AR 72203-0110
(501) 378-0445 Contact: Brad Mooy, Literary Manager **Theatre:** professional not-for-profit **Works:** full-length plays, one-acts, translations, adaptations, musicals **2nd productions:** yes **Special interest:** "Southern issues." **Maximum cast:** 12; 7 preferred **Tours:** yes **Stage:** flexible **Submission policy:** query/synopsis preferred; unsolicited script with SASE; professional recommendation; agent submission **Response:** 2 weeks query; 3-6 months script **Your chances:** 200 submissions/1 production **Future commitment:** for premiere **Program:** readings

ARROW ROCK LYCEUM THEATRE

Main St., Arrow Rock, MO 65320 (816) 837-3311
Contact: Michael Bollinger, Artistic Producing Director **Theatre:** professional not-for-profit **Works:** full-length plays, translations, adaptations, musicals **2nd productions:** "Not generally; however, a staged reading or non-professional production is okay." **Special interests:** "Plays relating to rural and/or small-town America; the American Dream." **Specifications:** maximum cast: 12; "the fewer sets the better" **Tours:** "At times." **Stage:** proscenium-thrust, 208 seats **Audience:** "Diverse; there tend to be more patrons aged 45+, basically caucasian, rurally based." **Submission policy:** query/synopsis with resume; professional recommendation; agent submission; commission **Best time:** Sept.-Dec. **Response:** 1-2 months **Your chances:** 300 submissions/1 production **Recent production of unsolicited work:** no **Remuneration:** yes **Future commitment:** variable **Program:** Arrow Rock Lyceum Theatre National Playwrights Competition (see Contests)

ARTHUR CANTOR PRODUCTIONS

2112 Broadway, New York, NY 10032 (212) 496-5710
Contact: Arthur Cantor, Owner **Production company:** Broadway and off off Broadway **Works:** full-length plays, musicals, children's plays **2nd productions:** yes **Special interest:** "One-man shows." **Tours:** "Small acts and comedy teams." **Submission policy:** unsolicited script with SASE; agent submission **Best time:** "Anytime, particularly summer." **Response:** 3-4 weeks **Your chances:** 200 submissions/varying number of productions **Remuneration:** contract **Advice:** "Conservative tastes; no gratuitous swearing."

ARTREACH TOURING THEATRE
3074 Madison Rd., Cincinnati, OH 45209
(513) 871-2300 **Contact:** Kathryn Schultz Miller, Artistic Director **Theatre:** professional not-for-profit **Works:** children's plays **2nd productions:** yes **Special interests:** "Cultural, historical and contemporary situations." **Specifications:** cast size: 3; all sets must tour **Stages:** flexible, school spaces **Audience:** children, K-12 **Submission policy:** unsolicited script with SASE and resume; query/synopsis with resume; professional recommendation **Best time:** Jan.-Mar. **Response:** 2-3 weeks query; 1 month script **Your chances:** 20 submissions/0-1 production **Remuneration:** "$10 royalty per performance, approximately 100 performances." **Advice:** "No stereotypes or trite stories."

THE ARTS AT ST. ANN'S
157 Montague St., Brooklyn, NY 11201 (718) 834-8794
Contact: Janine Nichols, Production Manager **Theatre:** professional not-for-profit **Works:** full-length plays **Special interests:** "Inter-cultural relations; American culture and politics." **Specifications:** "Small, informal loft space; limitations on lighting, sets, seating, cast size." **Stages:** church sanctuary, 650 seats; loft, 120 seats **Audience:** "We do such a variety of work that our audience changes all the time. Mostly residents of Brooklyn or lower Manhattan, college-educated, black and white, all ages." **Submission policy:** The theatre is currently presenting concerts and is not open to script submissions in 1990; inquire for future policy.

ARVADA CENTER FOR THE ARTS AND HUMANITIES
Young Adults Drama Camp, 6901 Wadsworth Blvd.,
Arvada, CO 80003 (303) 431-3080
Contact: Jay Levitt, Producing Director **Theatre:** community/non-professional, educational **Works:** one-acts, children's plays **2nd productions:** yes **Maximum cast:** 8-10 **Stage:** thrust **Submission policy:** unsolicited script with SASE **Best time:** winter **Your chances:** 15-20 submissions **Remuneration:** $25 **Advice:** "We desperately need material for teen-aged actors--usually more girls than boys."

ASIAN AMERICAN THEATER COMPANY
403 Aguillo Blvd., San Francisco, CA 94118
(415) 751-2600 **Contact:** Eric Hayashi, Artistic Director **Theatre:** professional not-for-profit **Works:** full-length plays **Special interest:** "Works by and about Asian Americans." **Stage:** flexible **Submission policy:** send SASE for guidelines **Best time:** Jun.-Sept. **Program:** staged readings

ASOLO CENTER FOR THE PERFORMING ARTS
5555 N. Tamiami Tr., Sarasota, FL 34243
(813) 351-9010 **Contact:** John Gulley, Literary Manager
Theatre: professional not-for-profit, LORT **Works:** full-length
plays, musicals, children's plays **2nd productions:** yes
Specifications: small cast preferred; minimal technical
requirements **Tours:** yes **Stages:** proscenium, 499 seats; black
box, 100 seats **Audience:** "Very broad range." **Submission
policy:** query/synopsis **Best time:** Aug.-Dec. **Response:**
immediate query; 6 months script **Your chances:** 500 submissions/
1-2 productions **Remuneration:** negotiable **Future commitment:**
negotiable **Program:** Asolo Touring Theatre Commissions (see
Special Programs) **Comment:** Formerly Asolo State Theater.

ATLANTIC & PACIFIC RENAISSANCE THEATRE
Los Angeles, CA See Mitch Nestor's Playwrights-Actors-
Directors Company listing in this section.

ATLANTIC COMMUNITY COLLEGE THEATRE
Walter Edge Hall, Mays Landing, NJ 08330
(609) 343-5040 **Contact:** John Pekich or Kathie Brown
Theatre: professional not-for-profit, university/college **Works:**
one-acts **2nd productions:** no **Special interest:** "New plays
by Southern New Jersey playwrights residing within a 100-mile
radius of Atlantic City." **Maximum cast:** 8 **Tours:** "Showcased."
Stage: proscenium, 444 seats **Submission policy:** call issued
for unsolicited script with SASE **Best time:** Sept.-Jan. **Response:**
2 weeks query; 6 month script **Your chances:** 20-40
submissions/6 productions **Remuneration:** "All plays are
videotaped; playwright receives a copy." **Programs:** staged
readings, classes; Atlantic Community College Playwrights Weekend
(see Contests) **Advice:** "There are no factors or limitations
considered when selecting plays. The play, on its own merit, is
selected." **Comment:** "1st year, script-in-hand reading; 2nd year,
full production."

AT THE FOOT OF THE MOUNTAIN
2000 S. 5th St., Minneapolis, MN 55454 (612) 375-9487
Contact: Rebecca Rice, Jan Magrane, Co-Artistic Directors
Theatre: professional not-for-profit **Works:** full-length plays,
one-acts, musicals **2nd productions:** yes **Special interests:**
"Plays by and about women, particularly women of color;
experimental works." **Specifications:** small cast, preferably
female; simple set **Stage:** black box, 90 seats **Audience:** "Young
professionals, artists, educators, feminists, blacks, ages 20-50."
Submission policy: query/synopsis; agent submission **Response:**

3-4 weeks query; 4-6 months script **Your chances:** 200 submissions/1 production **Remuneration:** "Royalty based on performances." **Program:** At the Foot of the Mountain Programs (see Special Programs)

ATTIC THEATRE
Box 02457, Detroit, MI 48202   (313) 875-8285
Contact: Lavinia Moyer, Artistic Director **Theatre:** professional not-for-profit **Works:** full-length plays, translations, adaptations, musicals, cabaret/revues **2nd productions:** yes **Special interests:** "Jazz, gospel musicals; cross-cultural themes." **Maximum cast:** 12 **Tours:** "Possibly." **Stage:** proscenium, 299 seats **Casting:** "Mostly ensemble." **Audience:** "Mixed." **Submission policy:** query/synopsis **Best time:** Jan.-May **Response:** 1 month query; 6 months script **Your chances:** 50 submissions/1-3 productions **Recent production of unsolicited work:** 1987 **Remuneration:** "Royalties, occasional grant." **Future commitment:** "Standard." **Programs:** readings, staged readings, workshop productions

ATTIC THEATRE
6562 1/2 Santa Monica Blvd.,
Los Angeles, CA 90038 (213) 462-9720
Contact: James Carey, Artistic Director **Works:** full-length plays, one-acts, translations, adaptations **2nd productions:** yes **Stage:** thrust, 50 seats **Casting:** "From our own in-house company of 30-50 actors." **Audience:** "Mixed, 21-70 age range, wide base of interests." **Submission policy:** unsolicited script with SASE; query/synopsis; professional recommendation; agent submission **Response:** no guaranteed response for query; 4-6 months script **Your chances:** 150-200 submissions/3-4 productions **Recent production of unsolicited work:** 1989 **Remuneration:** one-act: no; full-length play: varies **Future commitment:** "Depends upon the play; usually 1st production rights for full-length play." **Programs:** readings, staged readings, workshop productions, internships, residencies

BACK ALLEY THEATRE
15231 Burbank Blvd., Van Nuys, CA 91411
(818) 780-2240 Contact: Laura Zucker, Allan Miller, Directors **Theatre:** professional not-for-profit **Works:** full-length plays, translations, adaptations, musicals **2nd productions:** yes **Tours:** yes **Stage:** proscenium, 93 seats **Submission policy:** agent submission **Response:** 2-3 months **Your chances:** 400 submissions/6 productions **Remuneration:** "Royalty percentage." **Future commitment:** for world premiere

BAILIWICK REPERTORY
3212 N. Broadway, Chicago, IL 60657 (312) 883-1090
Contact: David Zak, Executive Director **Theatre:** professional not-for-profit **Works:** full-length plays, one-acts, translations, adaptations, musicals, children's plays **2nd productions:** yes **Stage:** thrust **Special interests:** "Plays of political interest or unusual theatricality." **Submission policy:** unsolicited script with SASE; query/synopsis; professional recommendation **Best time:** winter **Response:** 3 months **Your chances:** 1 new play produced each season **Remuneration:** "Royalty fee similar to standard leasing fees." **Programs:** directors' collective (inquire); Bailiwick Repertory Annual Directors' Festival (see Special Programs)

BAINBRIDGE PERFORMING ARTS
Box 10554, Bainbridge Island, WA 98110
(206) 842-8569 Contact: Susan Glass Burdick, Artistic Director **Theatre:** community/semi-professional **Works:** full-length plays, one-acts, translations, adaptations, musicals, children's plays **2nd productions:** "We haven't yet, but it's not out of the question." **Special interests:** "A wide spectrum: children-teen-family-adult." **Specifications:** maximum cast: 50; "budget limits are large scale" **Tours:** international **Stage:** flexible, 200+ seats **Casting:** open auditions **Audience:** "Varies according to project." **Submission policy:** unsolicited script with SASE and resume; query/synopsis with dialogue sample and resume; professional recommendation; agent submission; commission **Best time:** fall-winter **Your chances:** 10-20 submissions/2+ productions **Remuneration:** "Unless the production is a workshop/staged reading, we try to pay a minimum royalty." **Programs:** readings, staged readings, workshop productions, development, internships, classes, contests (inquire)

THE BARBARA BARONDESS THEATRE LAB
281 Ninth Ave., New York, NY 10001
Contact: Leslie (Hoban) Blake, Director **Theatre:** professional not-for-profit **Works:** full-length plays **2nd productions:** no **Special interest:** traditional, well-made plays **Maximum cast:** 6 **Submission policy:** query/synopsis with resume **Response:** 1 month query; 5 months script

BARKSDALE THEATRE
Box 7, Hanover, VA 23069 (804) 537-5333
Contact: Muriel McAuley, David Kilgore, Producers **Theatre:** non-Equity (some Guest Artist Contracts) **Works:** full-length plays, musicals **Specifications:** simple set **Stage:** small thrust **Submission policy:** unsolicited script with SASE **Comment:** "Optional dinner available in separate dining rooms."

BARN PLAYERS

Box 713, Shawnee Mission, KS 66201 (913) 381-4004
Contact: Don Ramsey, President, Board of Directors **Theatre:** community/non-professional **Works:** full-length plays, one-acts, musicals **Specifications:** simple production requirements **Tours:** "Senior Acting Troupe tours church groups and nursing homes and other organizations; about 200 performances a year. The Seniors perform one-acts and a musical review. One-acts are generally light comedies or warm dramas." **Stage:** 1/3 arena, 238 seats **Audience:** "35+, upper mid-income, college educated, professional; audience is expanding to include children and young families." **Submission policy:** unsolicited script with SASE **Best time:** before Sept. 15 **Response:** 4-6 weeks **Your chances:** 30 submissions/1 production **Remuneration:** possible playwriting seminar with stipend during run of show **Comment:** See Senior Acting Program of the Barn Players listing in this section.

BARTER THEATRE

Box 867, Abingdon, VA 24210 (703) 628-2281
Contact: Rex Partington, Producing Director **Theatre:** professional not-for-profit **Works:** full-length plays, translations, adaptations, musicals, children's plays **2nd productions:** yes **Special interests:** social issues, current events **Specifications:** cast size: 4-12; single or unit set **Stage:** proscenium, 394 seats **Submission policy:** unsolicited script with SASE **Best times:** Mar., Sept. **Response:** 6-9 months **Recent production of unsolicited work:** 1978 **Future commitment:** yes

BERKELEY REPERTORY THEATRE

2025 Addison St., Berkeley, CA 94704 (415) 841-6108
Contact: Mame Hunt, Literary Manager **Theatre:** professional not-for-profit **Works:** full-length plays, translations, adaptations **2nd productions:** yes **Special interest:** "Plays whose imaginary worlds are fully realized, but which have resonance for larger society." **Specifications:** maximum cast: 18; no fly space **Tours:** "Educational shows." **Stage:** thrust, 400 seats; "various other capacities and configurations" **Audience:** "Large multicultural urban area with broad education and sophistication." **Submission policy:** professional recommendation; agent submission; unsolicited script with SASE from Bay Area writer **Response:** 3-4 months **Your chances:** 300 submissions/1-2 productions **Remuneration:** varies **Future commitment:** "Sometimes."

BERKELEY SHAKESPEARE FESTIVAL
Box 969, Berkeley, CA 94701 (415) 548-3422
Contact: Michael Addison, Artistic Director **Theatre:** professional not-for-profit **Works:** full-length plays, translations, adaptations **Exclusive interest:** "Shakespeare--in theme, subject, structure." **Stage:** outdoor ampitheatre, 550 seats **Submission policy:** query/synopsis **Response:** 1 month query; 3 months script

BERKSHIRE PUBLIC THEATRE
30 Union St. Box 860, Pittsfield, MA 01202
(413) 445-4631 Contact: Frank Bessell, Artistic Director; Linda Austin, Literary Manager **Theatre:** professional not-for-profit **Works:** full-length plays, one-acts, translations, adaptations, small musicals and operas, children's plays, cabaret/revues **2nd productions:** yes **Special interests:** "Contemporary issues; works dealing with ethics and morality; global concerns." **Tours:** yes **Stage:** proscenium, 300 seats **Casting:** "Non-traditional." **Audience:** "All types. From all over--mostly Northeast." **Submission policy:** unsolicited script with resume; query/synopsis with resume; professional recommendation; agent submission; commission **Response:** 1 month query; 4 months script **Your chances:** 150 submissions/1 production plus 6 staged readings **Remuneration:** "Varies--from nothing to commission." **Future commitment:** no **Programs:** readings, staged readings, workshop production, development, internships, residencies **Advice:** "Hang in!"

BERKSHIRE THEATRE FESTIVAL
Box 797, Stockbridge, MA 01262 (413) 298-5536
Contact: Richard Dunlap, Artistic Director **Theatre:** professional not-for-profit **Works:** full-length plays, musicals **2nd productions:** yes **Special interest:** "Thought-provoking entertainment for vacationers." **Specifications:** maximum cast: 12 for play; minimal requirements, small orchestra for musical; simple set preferred **Stages:** proscenium, 429 seats; thrust, 99 seats **Submission policy:** agent submission **Best time:** Nov.-Dec. **Response:** 6 months **Your chances:** 60 submissions/1-2 productions **Remuneration/future commitment:** yes **Program:** readings

THE BILINGUAL FOUNDATION OF THE ARTS
421 N. Ave. 19, Los Angeles, CA 90031 (213) 225-4044
Contact: Margarita Galban, Artistic Director **Theatre:** professional not-for-profit **Works:** full-length plays, one-acts, translations, adaptations, musicals, children's plays **2nd productions:** no **Exclusive interests:** Hispanic authors, Hispanic subjects **Specifications:** maximum cast: 15; simple set

Stage: thrust, 99 seats **Submission policy:** unsolicited script with SASE **Response:** 6 months

BLOOMINGTON PLAYWRIGHTS PROJECT
409 S. Walnut St. #15, Bloomington, IN 47401
(812) 332-0822 Contact: Rita Kniess, Literary Manager
Theatre: not-for-profit **Works:** full-length plays, one-acts, monologues, "half-acts" **2nd productions:** no **Specifications:** maximum cast: 15; simple sets; small space **Stage:** flexible **Audience:** "Young adults; college students, local community." **Submission policy:** unsolicited script with SASE **Best time:** by Oct. 15, 1990 **Response:** 2 months **Your chances:** 40 submissions/12 productions **Remuneration:** royalty for full-length play **Programs:** readings, staged readings, workshop productions, development; Bloomington Playwrights Project Contest (see Contests)

BLOOMSBURG THEATRE ENSEMBLE
Box 66, Bloomsburg, PA 17815 (717) 784-5530
Contact: Rand Whipple, New Scripts Coordinator; Martin Shell, Dramaturge **Theatre:** professional not-for-profit **Works:** full-length plays, translations, adaptations **2nd productions:** "Not yet. We hope to in future." **Special interests:** "Works suitable for 10-member ensemble in 20-40 age range; new translations of classics." **Specifications:** maximum cast: 6; single or unit set **Stage:** proscenium, 369 seats **Audience:** "We live and create in a rural, small, university town. Our audience is largely professional and on the conservative side." **Submission policy:** query/ synopsis **Best time:** Sept.–Jun. **Response:** 1-6 months **Your chances:** "In 10 years we've done 5 new plays. When we finally get our new stage going, we hope to improve this ratio." **Remuneration:** negotiable contract **Comment:** See McGovern, Michael, "Grassroots Actor-Managers: The Bloomsburg Theater Ensemble," *TheaterWeek* (Oct. 17, 1988), 34-39.

BLUE ISLAND PARK DISTRICT SHOWCASE THEATER
12757 South Western, Blue Island, IL 60406
(312) 388-0482 Contact: Dan Flynn, Producer **Theatre:** community/non-professional **Works:** full-length plays, one-acts, translations, adaptations, musicals **2nd productions:** yes **Maximum cast:** 12 **Tours:** some shows **Stages:** thrust––4 staging areas, 2 side stages **Audience:** "Loyal; 300 season subscribers." **Submission policy:** unsolicited script with SASE **Your chances:** 2-3 submissions/1 production **Remuneration:** no **Programs:** workshop productions, classes

BOARSHEAD: MICHIGAN PUBLIC THEATER
425 S. Grand Ave., Lansing, MI 48933 (517) 484-7800
Contact: John Peakes, Artistic Director **Theatre:** professional not-for-profit **Works:** full-length plays, one-acts, children's plays **2nd productions:** yes **Special interests:** "Social issues; plays that utilize theatrical conventions or create new ones." **Specifications:** maximum cast: 18; little backstage capacity for multiple sets **Stage:** thrust, 249 seats **Audience:** "Average America." **Submission policy:** query with 1-2 page synopsis, 3-5 page dialogue sample and SAS postcard; professional recommendation; agent submission **Response:** 1 month query; 3-9 months script **Your chances:** 300 submissions/7-9 productions plus 7 staged readings **Remuneration:** "It depends upon our budget." **Future commitment:** credit for production in any future publication

BODY POLITIC THEATRE
2261 N. Lincoln Ave., Chicago, IL 60614 (312) 348-7901
Contact: Pauline Brailsford, Artistic Director **Theatre:** professional not-for-profit **Works:** full-length plays, one-acts **Special interest:** works suitable for ensemble company **Specifications:** maximum cast: 10, fewer than 8 preferred; single set **Stage:** 3/4 thrust, 192 seats **Submission policy:** query/ synopsis with resume and dialogue sample **Response:** 6 months query; 1 year script **Program:** Discovery Project: staged readings of new works by authors not known to Chicago-area audiences

BOND STREET THEATRE
2 Bond St., New York, NY 10012 (212) 254-4614
Contact: Joanna M. Sherman, Artistic Director **Theatre:** off off Broadway **Works:** full-length plays, one-acts, adaptations, musicals **2nd productions:** "Not usually." **Special interests:** "Material of political/social significance, satirical but not didactic; surreal, non-linear scripts adaptable to more complex treatment visually and stylistically." **Specifications:** maximum cast: 8-10; experimental musicals only **Tours:** yes **Stages:** various spaces **Casting:** "From ensemble of 7 highly physically trained actors." **Audience:** "Varies considerably; for touring, often non-English speaking." **Submission policy:** query/synopsis with "artistic point of view"; professional recommendation; commission **Response:** 1-3 months **Your chances:** 100 submissions/1 production **Remuneration:** varies **Future commitment:** possibly **Programs:** staged readings, workshop productions; Palenville Interarts Colony (see Special Programs) **Comment:** "Our work is always provocative, stylized to present a heightened reality."

BORDERLANDS THEATER/TEATRO FRONTERIZO
Box 2791, Tucson, Az 85702 (602) 882-8607
Contact: Barkley Goldsmith, Producing Director **Theatre:** non-Equity not-for-profit **Works:** full-length plays, translations, adaptations **2nd productions:** yes **Special interests:** translations and adaptations of Latino American works; plays by U.S. Latino and Native American writers; Southwest border issues **Specifications:** maximum cast: 10-12; small budget **Tours:** yes **Stage:** proscenium, 105 seats **Casting:** open auditions, multi-ethnic **Audience:** mixed **Submission policy:** unsolicited script with SASE; agent submission; commission **Best time:** fall **Response:** 3-4 months **Your chances:** 20 submissions/1 production **Remuneration:** negotiable **Future commitment:** no **Programs:** readings, staged readings, workshop productions, development, internships; Borderlands Theater/Teatro Fronterizo New Play Search (see Contests)

BOSTON POST ROAD STAGE COMPANY
Box 38, Fairfield, CT 06430 (203) 255-4122
Contact: Douglas Moser, Artistic Director **Theatre:** professional not-for-profit **Works:** full-length plays, musicals **2nd productions:** yes **Special interests:** comedies; "dramatic situations in well-constructed plays" **Specifications:** maximum cast: 8; single set; simple technical requirements **Stage:** thrust, 100 seats **Submission policy:** unsolicited script with SASE; query/synopsis **Best time:** spring-summer **Response:** 3 weeks query; 1-3 months script **Your chances:** 1 new script produced in theatre's 3-year life span; 6 readings each season **Future commitment:** limited option following production

BOSTON SHAKESPEARE COMPANY
c/o New Voices, 551 Tremont St., Boston, MA 02116 (617) 267-5600 Contact: Stanley Richardson, Literary Manager **Theatre:** professional not-for-profit **Works:** full-length plays, one-acts, translations, adaptations **2nd productions:** yes **Special interests:** "Politics, history, ideas, the social contract; substantial intellectual content; strong language." **Maximum cast:** 12 **Stages:** thrust, arena, flexible--99-200 and 399-699 seats **Submission policy:** query/synopsis; professional recommendation; agent submission **Best time:** anytime except Jul.-Aug. **Response:** 1 month query; 6 months script **Your chances:** 6 plays "of various sorts" produced each season **Remuneration:** varies **Future commitment:** negotiable **Programs:** staged readings, workshop productions, development, internships **Advice:** "Focus on ideas, language. Forget psychological motivations. Care."

BRASS TACKS THEATRE
401 Third St. N Suite 420, Minneapolis, MN 55401
(612) 341-8208   **Contact:** Patty Lynch, Artistic Director
Theatre: professional not-for-profit   **Works:** full-length plays,
musicals **Special interest:** "Works rich in language." **Maximum
cast:** 10   **Stages:** various spaces   **Submission policy:**
professional recommendation   **Response:** 2-3 months

BRIDGE ARTS THEATRE COMPANY
New York, NY   This theatre is not currently accepting submissions.

BRIGHAM YOUNG THEATRE & FILM DEPARTMENT
BYU, D-581 HFAC, Provo, UT 84602   (801)   378-4574
Contact: Tim Slover, Professor, Theatre/Film   **Theatre:**
university/college **Works:** full-length plays, one-acts, translations,
adaptations, musicals, children's plays   **2nd productions:** yes
Special interest: experimental plays **Specifications:** "Depends
on theatre and space requirements."   **Tours:** yes   **Stages:**
proscenium, 600 seats; flexible arena, 150-200 seats   **Audience:**
"50% students, faculty and staff; 50% townspeople; conservative,
primarily white middle class."   **Submission policy:** unsolicited
script with SASE **Best times:** fall, spring **Response:** "Depends
on time script is received."   **Your chances:** 15 submissions/3
productions   **Remuneration:** "Depends on production, record and
theatre used." **Programs:** development, classes **Advice:** "Plays
should be suitable for family audiences."

BRISTOL RIVERSIDE THEATRE
Box 1250, Bristol, PA 19007   (215) 785-6664
Contact: Ben Janney, Literary Manager   **Theatre:** professional
not-for-profit   **Works:** full-length plays, one-acts comprising full
evening, translations, adaptations, small-scale musicals   **2nd
productions:** yes **Specifications:** maximum cast: 8; "no dead
baby, abortion or excessively sexual themes; no excessive foul
language" **Tours:** yes **Stages:** proscenium, 302 seats; black box,
60 seats   **Audience:** "Broad cross-section from affluent to blue
collar."   **Submission policy:** unsolicited script with SASE
preferred; query/synopsis with dialogue sample and resume;
professional recommendation; agent submission **Best time:** Sept.-
May **Response:** 1 month query; 2 months script **Your chances:**
250 submissions/5 productions on main stage, 4 in black box plus
20-25 staged readings **Remuneration:** "Percentage and
consideration for future production." **Future commitment:** yes
Programs: readings, staged readings, workshop productions,

development, classes, internships **Comment:** "The Bristol Riverside Theatre was founded on the principle of developing new American plays and playwrights, and freshly interpreting often overlooked plays which seem appropriate for our cooperative artistry."

BROADWAY TOMORROW MUSICAL THEATRE
191 Claremont Ave. Suite 53, New York, NY 10027
(212) 864-4736   Contact: Elyse Curtis, Artistic Director **Theatre:** off off Broadway, professional not-for-profit **Works:** full-length and one-act musicals, musical adaptations **2nd productions:** no **Exclusive interest:** "Wholesome material." **Specifications:** maximum cast: 8-10; "writers must be residents of Metropolitan New York area or able to spend time in the city." **Stage:** proscenium, 99 seats **Audience:** general **Submission policy:** professional recommendation **Response:** 6-9 months **Your chances:** 50 submissions/8 productions **Remuneration/future commitment:** "Standard Dramatists Guild Off Broadway contract for first-class production." **Programs:** readings, staged readings, workshop productions, marketing and producing seminars **Advice:** "Submit uplifting material."

BROKEN ARROW COMMUNITY PLAYHOUSE
Box 452, Broken Arrow, OK 74013   (918) 258-0077
Contact: Joyce Polkinghorne, Board of Operations **Theatre:** community non/professional **Works:** full-length plays, musicals, children's plays **2nd productions:** no **Maximum cast:** 35 **Stage:** thrust **Audience:** "White collar, family." **Submission policy:** unsolicited script with SASE **Response:** time varies **Your chances:** "We hope to produce 1 new play each year." **Advice:** "We work with guest directors--we are weak in tech, would hope to have as many ideas on set, costuming and lighting as possible."

BROOKLYN PLAYWORKS
Brooklyn, NY This theatre did not respond to our 1990 questionnaire, and its phone has been disconnected.

BROOKLYN THEATRE ENSEMBLE
c/o Matthew Paris, Director, 850 E. 31st St. Apt. C-6, Brooklyn, NY 11210 (718) 258-5367
Theatre: community/non-professional **Works:** one-acts **2nd productions:** yes **Special interest:** "Brooklyn material." **Specifications:** maximum cast: 5; single set **Stage:** flexible **Audience:** "All kinds." **Submission policy:** unsolicited script with SASE **Response:** 3 months **Your chances:** 10 submissions/2 productions **Remuneration:** no **Advice:** "Make it related to Brooklyn."

BROWN GRAND THEATRE

310 W. 6th St., Concordia, KS 66901 (913) 243-2553
Contact: Susan L. Sutton, President **Theatre:** community/non-professional **Works:** full-length plays, translations, adaptations, musicals, children's plays **2nd productions:** "Possibly." **Special interest:** "Works relevant to the audience and region." **Specifications:** "Cast size and sets within reason." **Tours:** yes **Stage:** proscenium, 650 seats **Audience:** "Midwestern, rural." **Submission policy:** unsolicited script with SASE; query/synopsis **Best time:** fall-winter **Response:** 6 weeks **Remuneration:** "Possibly." **Advice:** "Submit scripts. Just because our in-house performing group has not produced original scripts, that doesn't mean it won't."

BROWNS HEAD REPERTORY THEATRE

Box 312, Monson, ME 04464 (207) 997-9612
Contact: Kathy Huff, Artistic Director; David Greenham, Producing Director **Theatre:** professional not-for-profit **Works:** full-length plays, one-acts, translations, adaptations, musicals, children's plays **2nd productions:** yes **Special interest:** "Plays with rural or ME themes." **Specifications:** "Limited cast and sets are preferred, but we will consider great plays of any size; all plays must tour." **Stages:** various spaces **Casting:** "Mostly by audition in New York or Boston; we will always consider Maine actors." **Audience:** "Varies greatly; mostly working class with a curiosity about the arts rather than lots of arts exposure." **Submission policy:** unsolicited script with SASE and resume; query/synopsis with resume **Response:** 3 months **Your chances:** "We have never solicited new scripts; we have had a company playwright. All of our plays are original scripts." **Remuneration:** "Depends upon production situation and script." **Future commitment:** no **Programs:** "We will consider any work with interested playwrights." **Advice:** "Our audience may not be the right group for your work. If you have questions, call or come see us."

BURBAGE THEATRE ENSEMBLE

2330 Sawtelle Blvd., Los Angeles, CA 90064
(213) 478-0897 Contact: Ivan Spiegel, Artistic Director **Theatre:** professional not-for-profit **Works:** full-length plays, one-acts, musicals **2nd productions:** yes **Special interests:** political-social issues; avant garde, stylized work for ensemble company; Los Angeles premieres **Maximum cast:** 12-15 **Audience:** "People who like well-written plays." **Submission policy:** query/synopsis; professional recommendation; agent submission **Response:** 1 month query; 3-6 months script **Your**

chances: 200 submissions/2 productions **Remuneration:** negotiable **Future commitment:** yes **Program:** readings

THE CABARET THEATRE
Mason Gross School of the Arts, Rutgers University, New Brunswick, NJ 08903 (201) 249-2112
Contact: Michael Bilton, Producer **Theatre:** university/college **Works:** full-length plays, one-acts, adaptations, musicals **2nd productions:** yes **Special interest:** comedies **Specifications:** maximum cast: 15, 8-10 co-ed preferred; relatively simple, single set preferred; "manageable number of props" **Stage:** flexible, 90 seats **Audience:** "Mainly university students, co-ed, some members of surrounding community; basically open minded, like to be entertained." **Submission policy:** query/synopsis with dialogue sample **Best times:** Mar.-Apr., Oct.-Nov. **Response:** 21 days query; 30 days script **Remuneration:** no **Program:** staged readings

CALIFORNIA REPERTORY COMPANY
1250 Bellflower, Long Beach, CA 90840 (213) 985-7891
Contact: Ron Lindblom, Associate Producing Director **Theatre:** professional not-for-profit, university/college **Works:** full-length plays, translations, adaptations **2nd productions:** yes **Special interest:** "We are looking for plays drawn from the international works of playwrights--Europe, Asia, Britain, etc." **Maximum cast:** 15 **Tours:** "Possibly." **Stage:** proscenium-thrust, 90 seats **Casting:** "Open--from company and guest artists." **Submission policy:** unsolicited script with SASE and resume; professional recommendation; agent submission **Response:** 2 weeks query; 2 months script **Your chances:** 50-100 submissions/1-3 productions **Remuneration/future commitment:** "By contracted agreement." **Programs:** readings, staged readings **Advice:** "We are looking for new works with small casts and space in mind." **Comment:** "We are a new company--inaugural season 1989-90."

CALIFORNIA THEATRE CENTER
Box 2007, Sunnyvale, CA 94087 (408) 245-2979
Contact: Will Huddleston, Resident Director **Theatre:** professional not-for-profit **Works:** children's plays **2nd productions:** yes **Specifications:** cast of 3-7 for main stage productions, 10-20 for conservatory productions; single set; works must be no more than 1 hour in length and suitable for touring **Tours:** local, national, international **Stage:** proscenium/small thrust, 200 seats **Casting:** "Professional actors for main season; children in conservatory productions." **Audience:** "Children of all ages." **Submission policy:** unsolicited script with SASE; query/synopsis;

agent submission **Best time:** fall **Response:** 1 month query; 4 months script **Your chances:** 50 submissions/2 productions **Remuneration:** royalty **Future commitment:** no **Advice:** "Plays which can work in a variety of venues are best."

CAL POLY THEATRE & DANCE DEPARTMENT
San Luis Obispo, CA 93407 (805) 756-1465
Contact: Michael Malkin, Dept. Head **Theatre:** university/college **Works:** full-length plays **2nd productions:** no **Specifications:** "No musicals or children's plays." **Stages:** proscenium, 500 seats; flexible, 60 seats **Submission policy:** unsolicited script with SASE and resume; query/synopsis **Response:** 4 months script **Your chances:** 40 submissions/1 production **Recent production of unsolicited work:** 1989 **Remuneration:** $500-$1000 **Future commitment:** no **Advice:** "Deadlines vary; see announcement in Dramatists Guild publications."

CAPITAL REPERTORY COMPANY
Box 399, Albany, NY 12201 (518) 462-4531
Contact: Bruce Bouchard, Peter Clough, Co-Producing Directors **Theatre:** professional not-for-profit **Works:** full-length plays, translations, adaptations **2nd productions:** yes **Special interests:** plays by and about women; works with "broad social conscience" **Specifications:** maximum cast: 10; limited technical requirements; no 3-story sets; no fly space **Stage:** thrust, 258 seats **Audience:** "Intelligent, good theatregoers, willing to listen." **Submission policy:** query/synopsis with 5-10 page dialogue sample **Best time:** summer-fall **Response:** 3-6 months **Your chances:** 400+ submissions/2 productions plus 5-6 readings **Remuneration:** royalty **Future commitment:** for world premiere **Programs:** readings, staged readings, administrative internships, summer workshop residency in Lexington, NY **Advice:** "We are looking for anything we haven't seen."

CARAVAN THEATRE COMPANY, INC.
377 Broome St. Apt. 15, New York, NY 10013
(212) 431-7962 **Contact:** Peter Hodges, Artistic Director **Theatre:** not-for-profit **Works:** full-length plays **2nd productions:** "If New York premieres." **Specifications:** "No sit-coms." **Stages:** rented spaces **Audience:** "Young." **Submission policy:** query/synopsis with resume and reviews of previous productions **Response:** 6 months if interested in query **Your chances:** 15 submissions/2 productions **Remuneration:** no **Program:** development **Advice:** "We want to develop a core of actors, playwrights and directors to work within a similar set of ideas."

CARROLL COLLEGE LITTLE THEATRE
Helena, MT 59625 (406) 442-3450 ext. 308
Contact: Kim DeLong, Director **Theatre:** university/college
Works: one-acts, musicals, children's plays **2nd productions:**
yes **Specifications:** maximum cast: 20; single set **Stage:**
proscenium **Audience:** "College students and townspeople."
Submission policy: query/synopsis with resume; professional
recommendation **Best time:** early spring **Response:** 6 weeks
Your chances: 12-15 submissions/0-1 production **Remuneration:**
"Royalty, maximum $50 per performance."

CASTILLO THEATRE
500 Greenwich St., New York, NY 10013
(212) 941-5800 Contact: Madelyn Chapman, Managing Director
Theatre: off off Broadway **Works:** full-length plays, one-acts,
translations, adaptations, musicals, children's plays **2nd**
productions: yes **Special interest:** social/political works
Tours: yes **Stage:** flexible, 100 seats **Casting:** "Open auditions
and from pool." **Audience:** "Very mixed, multi-racial--across
classes." **Submission policy:** query/synopsis **Response:** 2
weeks query; 2 months script **Your chances:** 10-20 submissions/1
production **Recent production of unsolicited work:** 1989
Remuneration: no **Future commitment:** mention in publication
of program **Program:** "Thursday night readings." **Advice:** "Come
to our theatre and see what we do." **Comment:** "We are a
self-supporting collective (of 50 artists) that canvases support
door-to-door."

THE CAST THEATRE
804 N. El Centro Ave., Hollywood, CA 90038
(213) 462-9872 Contact: Diane Gibson, Literary Manager
Theatre: professional not-for-profit **Works:** full-length plays,
one-acts, musicals, children's plays, cabaret/revues **2nd**
productions: occasionally **Special interest:** "The indomitability
of the human spirit." **Maximum cast:** 12 **Stages:** proscenium,
99 seats; proscenium, 70 seats **Submission policy:** unsolicited
script with SASE **Response:** 6 months or more **Recent**
production of unsolicited work: yes **Future commitment:**
yes **Programs:** readings, staged readings **Advice:** "Be ready to
present a reading."

CELEBRATION THEATRE
1765 N. Highland Ave. #536, Hollywood, CA 90028
(213) 876-4257 Contact: Michael McClellan, Dramaturg
Theatre: professional not-for-profit **Works:** full-length plays,
one-acts, translations, adaptations, musicals **Exclusive interest:**

"Plays which present gay/lesbian life in a positive way." **Specifications:** maximum cast: 6; simple sets; no complex lighting or sound effects **Tours:** yes **Stages:** arena, 45 seats; flexible **Audience:** "All adults are welcome, but our audience consists mostly of gay and lesbian people." **Submission policy:** send SASE for guidelines **Your chances:** 50 submissions/5 productions **Programs:** readings, staged readings, workshop productions, development, internships, classes

CENTER FOR PUPPETRY ARTS
1404 Spring St. NW, Atlanta, GA 30309 (404) 873-3089
Contact: Playreading Committee **Theatre:** professional not-for-profit **Works:** full-length plays, one-acts, translations, adaptations, musicals, children's plays, avant garde, performance art **Specifications:** "Plays must be suitable for puppets or a combination of puppets and live actors." **Tours:** yes **Stages:** proscenium, 350 seats; flexible, 100 seats **Casting:** open auditions **Audience:** "Adult puppetry; adventurous." **Submission policy:** unsolicited script with SASE **Response:** 6-8 weeks **Your chances:** 10-12 submissions/"no productions so far, because they have not been suitable to the meduim" **Remuneration:** royalty **Programs:** workshop productions, internships

CENTER STAGE
700 N. Calvert St., Baltimore, MD 21202
(301) 685-3200 Contact: Rick Davis, Resident Dramaturg **Theatre:** professional not-for-profit **Works:** full-length plays, one-acts, translations, adaptations **2nd productions:** yes **Maximum cast:** 30 **Stage:** modified thrust, 541 seats **Audience:** "Approximately 13,000 subscribers of diverse tastes and interests." **Submission policy:** query/synopsis with dialogue sample, production history and resume; professional recommendation; agent submission **Response:** 4-6 weeks query; 3-6 months script **Your chances:** 300 submissions/varying number of productions **Remuneration:** negotiable **Future commitment:** yes **Programs:** readings, staged readings **Advice:** "Please think carefully before considering Center Stage as a venue for your work; take a moment to review our recent production history and our various statements of artistic policy that are on public record."

CENTER THEATER
1346 W. Devon, Chicago, IL 60660 (312) 508-0200
Contact: Hilary Hammond, Literary Manager **Theatre:** professional not-for-profit **Works:** full-length plays, one-acts, translations, adaptations **Special interests:** comedy; heightened reality; language **Specifications:** maximum cast: 15; equal number of

male/female roles preferred; limited wing space; no fly space **Stages**: modified thrust, 75 seats; black box, 35 seats **Submission policy**: professional recommendation **Best time**: Oct.-Jan. **Response**: 3 months **Program**: Center Theater Youtheatre Program: workshop productions (see Special Programs)

CHAGRIN VALLEY LITTLE THEATRE
40 River St., Chagrin Falls, OH 44022 (216) 247-8955
Contact: Rollin DeVere, Literary Manager **Theatre:** community/ non-professional **Works:** full-length plays, one-acts **2nd productions:** no **Specifications:** maximum cast: 10; single or unit set **Stage:** proscenium, 66 seats **Submission policy:** unsolicited script with SASE; query/synopsis **Response:** 1 month query; 2-3 months script **Your chances:** 20 submissions/1-2 productions **Remuneration:** no **Advice:** "Good character development, sharp dialogue."

THE CHANGING SCENE
1527 1/2 Champa St., Denver, CO 80202
(303) 893-5775 Contact: Alfred Brooks, President
Theatre: professional not-for-profit **Works:** full-length plays, one-acts **2nd productions:** no **Special interest:** unconventional works **Specifications:** small cast, simple set **Stage:** flexible, 76 seats **Submission policy:** unsolicited script with SASE **Response:** 6 weeks-6 months **Your chances:** 100 submissions/ 6 productions in Theatre Workshop **Remuneration:** "We share box office receipts with participants." **Program:** Theatre Workshop: productions of new plays (inquire) **Advice:** "We try to avoid naturalistic plays."

THE CHARLOTTE SHAKESPEARE COMPANY
1236 East Blvd., Charlotte, NC 28203 (704) 377-2354
Contact: Lon Bumgarner, Artistic Director **Theatre:** professional not-for-profit **Works:** full-length plays, one-acts, translations, adaptations, children's plays **Special interests:** new works; translations and adaptations by American writers; ensemble works **Specifications:** small cast; minimal production demands **Stage:** black box, 185 seats **Submission policy:** query/synopsis **Best time:** Sept.-Mar. **Response:** 3 months query; 6 months script

CHECK PLEASE PRODUCTIONS
Los Angeles, CA This theatre did not respond to our 1990 questionnaire, and no phone number is listed.

CHEYENNE LITTLE THEATRE PLAYERS
Box 1086, Cheyenne, WY 82003 **(307) 638-6543**
Contact: Linda McVey, Managing Director **Theatre:** community/
non-professional **Works:** one-acts **2nd productions:** no **Special
interests:** melodramas with 'Old West' flavor; audience inter-active
material." **Specifications:** maximum cast: 15; 1 hour maximum
playing time **Stage:** proscenium, 256 seats **Audience:** "Tourists
out for a good time." **Submission policy:** unsolicited script with
SASE **Best time:** Aug.–Dec. **Your chances:** 3-4 submissions/0-1
production **Remuneration:** negotiable

CHICAGO MEDIEVAL PLAYERS
International House, 1414 E. 59th St., Chicago, IL 60637
(312) 935-0742 **Contact:** Ann Faulkner, General Director
Theatre: professional not-for-profit **Works:** translations,
adaptations, children's plays **2nd productions:** yes **Special
interests:** "Medieval and Renaissance material; new renderings of
old tales." **Tours:** "Occasionally." **Stages:** arena, flexible––
"generally about 100 seats" **Casting:** "EEO-casting without regard
to race, handicap, etc." **Audience:** "Extremely diverse."
Submission policy: query/synopsis with dialogue sample
Response: 30 days **Your chances:** varying number of
submissions/1 production **Recent production of unsolicited
work:** 1988 **Remuneration/future commitment:** negotiable
Advice: "We are especially looking for 3 things: folk-type and
other plays on the early American explorers and colonists to be
produced in 1992; an adaptation of *Beowulf* ; a pre-1650 Eastern
European play, translation or adaptation."

THE CHICAGO THEATRE COMPANY
Parkway Playhouse, 500 E. 67th St., Chicago, IL 60637
(312) 493-1305 Contact: Michael A. Perkins, Artistic Director
Theatre: professional not-for-profit **Works:** full-length plays,
musicals **2nd productions:** yes **Special interests:** African-
American plays; experimental plays **Specifications:** maximum
cast: 10; single set **Tours:** yes **Stage:** thrust, 100 seats
Audience: "Mixed ages and races." **Submission policy:**
unsolicited script with SASE and synopsis **Best time:** summer
Response: 1 month **Your chances:** 20-30 submissions/2
productions; "we have a resident playwright" **Remuneration:** no
Program: staged readings **Advice:** "Get to know our work."

THE CHILDREN'S THEATRE COMPANY
2400 Third Ave. S, Minneapolis, MN 55404
(612) 874-0500 **Contact:** Thomas W. Olson, Literary Editor
Theatre: professional not-for-profit **Works:** full-length plays,

one-acts, translations, adaptations, musicals, children's plays **2nd productions**: yes **Special interest**: "Adaptations of popular classics and contemporary works for young people and families." **Specifications**: maximum cast: 50; "child actors for child roles" **Tours**: "Touring productions are drawn from the mainstage productions." **Stages**: proscenium, 745 seats; studio, 80-100 seats **Audience**: "Public performances: 65% adult; 1987-88 Mainstage total: 240,000." **Submission policy**: query/synopsis preferred; unsolicited script with SASE **Best time**: Oct.-Apr. **Response**: 4-6 months **Your chances**: 125 submissions/0 productions; "scripts are generally read for purposes of referrals and familiarization" **Remuneration**: "Playwrights commissioned receive fee and percentage." **Future commitments**: yes, remount rights in perpetuity; possible video production, rentals to other theatres; negotiable royalty split **Programs**: workshop productions; New Generation Theatre Project (inquire)

CHOCOLATE BAYOU THEATER COMPANY
Houston, TX This theatre is permanently closed.

CINCINNATI PLAYHOUSE IN THE PARK
Box 6537, Cincinnati, OH 45206 (513) 421-5440
Contact: Worth Gardner, Artistic Director; Ara Watson, Playwright-in-Residence **Theatre**: professional not-for-profit **Works**: full-length plays, translations, adaptations, musicals, cabaret/revues **2nd productions**: yes **Special interests**: "Theatricality, excellent writing." **Stages**: thrust, 629 seats; thrust, 220 seats **Audience**: "Every group." **Submission policy**: agent submission preferred; query/synopsis with dialogue sample and available reviews **Best time**: late spring-mid-fall **Response**: 6 months **Your chances**: 600 submissions/2-3 productions **Remuneration**: royalty **Future commitment**: possibly **Program**: Lois and Richard Rosenthal New Play Prize (see Contests) **Advice**: "Absence of the trivial; intelligent, authentic dialogue; characters of substance; compelling situations; language that engages in action."

CIRCA '21 DINNER PLAYHOUSE
Box 784, 1828, Third Ave., Rock Island, IL 61201
(309) 786-2667 Contact: Dennis Hitchcock, Producer **Theatre**: non-Equity dinner **Works**: full-length plays, musicals, children's plays **2nd productions**: yes **Special interests**: comedies, farces, musicals, children's plays **Specifications**: maximum cast: 14; "no star vehicles" **Tours**: yes **Stage**: proscenium/thrust, 336 seats, "dinner theatre seating at 2's, 4's and 6's" **Submission policy**: unsolicited script with SASE **Response**:

3-6 months **Your chances:** 30-50 submissions **Remuneration:** $500, residency with transportation **Programs:** possible readings and staged readings; workshop productions, internships, residences

CIRCLE IN THE SQUARE
1633 Broadway, New York, NY 10019 (212) 307-2700
Contact: Seth Goldman, Literary Advisor **Theatre:** off Broadway, professional not-for-profit **Works:** full-length plays, translations, adaptations **2nd productions:** yes **Stage:** arena, 600 seats **Submission policy:** agent submission preferred; query/synopsis with dialogue sample and resume; professional recommendation **Response:** 1-2 months query; 9 months script **Your chances:** Theatre produces mostly revivals but is open to new plays and receives approximately 300 submissions each year.

CIRCLE REPERTORY
161 Avenue of the Americas, New York, NY 10013
(212) 691-3210 Contact: B. Rodney Marriott, Associate Artistic Director **Theatre:** off Broadway, professional not-for-profit **Works:** full-length plays **2nd productions:** yes **Special interest:** American authors **Stage:** thrust, 177 seats **Submission policy:** unsolicited script with SASE; query/synopsis **Response:** 1 week query; 3 months script **Your chances:** 2000 submissions/4-5 productions plus 30-40 in Friday readings **Programs:** Project in Progress program (inquire); Playwrights Lab (by invitation) **Comment:** See Seff, Richard, "Time of Transition," *TheaterWeek* (Feb. 13, 1989), 16-27.

CITY STAGE THEATRE COMPANY
Box 33155, Washington, DC 20033-0155
(202) 797-7550 Contact: Robert G. Martin, Managing Director **Theatre:** professional not-for-profit **Works:** full-length plays, one-acts **2nd productions:** yes **Special interest:** interracial casting **Specifications:** maximum cast: 8; simple set; "no sitcoms" **Stage:** no permanent space **Audience:** "Urban, racially mixed, well educated." **Submission policy:** submission without SASE will not be considered; unsolicited script with SASE; query/synopsis with dialogue sample **Response:** 2 weeks query; 6 weeks script **Remuneration:** $200 for 3-week production **Your chances:** 300 submissions/2-3 productions **Remuneration:** "50% of gross with $200 advance on royalties." **Future commitment:** "1 year rights in the Washington, DC area." **Special programs:** readings; workshop production program is planned for the future

CITY THEATRE
City College of San Francisco, 50 Phelan Ave., San Francisco, CA 94112 (415) 239-3100
Contact: Don Cate, Chairman, Theatre Arts Dept. **Theatre:** university/college **Works:** full-length plays, translations, adaptations, musicals **2nd productions:** yes **Special interests:** "Large casts; historical, political, social issues." **Specifications:** "Limited budgets." **Stages:** proscenium, 300 seats; flexible, 30± seats **Casting:** "Anyone may audition for a show but must enroll in CCSF if cast. Professional actors sometimes appear in our shows." **Audience:** "College/community; more people per capita attend plays in San Francisco than any other city in the nation." **Submission policy:** query/synopsis **Best time:** "Anytime, but plays are chosen 1-2 years in advance." **Response:** 1 month query; varies script **Your chances:** varying number of submissions/1 production every 2 years; we have produced about 5 new plays in the past 6 years, but all were solicited." **Remuneration:** "For full production $75/$50; musicals negotiable." **Future commitment:** "We would like future productions or publications to indicate CCSF as premiere production, but this is not required." **Programs:** staged readings, workshop productions, possible residencies **Advice:** "Get to know us—personally if possible."

CITY THEATRE COMPANY
B39 CL, University of Pittsburgh, Pittsburgh, PA 15260 (412) 624-1357 Contact: Lynne Conner, Literary Manager **Theatre:** professional not-for-profit **Works:** full-length plays, adaptations, small chamber musicals, children's plays **2nd productions:** yes **Exclusive interest:** "New or recent work by American writers." **Specifications:** maximum cast: 10; no fly space; no multiple realistic sets; "no frivolous comedies or plays that want to be TV pilots" **Tours:** "Only children's plays, which are normally commissioned." **Stage:** thrust, 120 seats **Audience:** "Sophisticated, urban, professional, educated, ages 25-75." **Submission policy:** query/synopsis with dialogue sample and resume; professional recommendation; agent submission **Best time:** Jan-May **Response:** 1 week query; 2-3 months script **Your chances:** 500 submissions/1-2 productions plus 6-8 staged readings **Remuneration:** percentage **Future commitment:** no **Program:** (TNT) Tuesday Night Theatre (inquire)

THE CLARENCE BROWN COMPANY
UT Box 8450, Knoxville, TN 37996 (615) 974-3447
Contact: Thomas P. Cooke, Producing Director **Theatre:** professional not-for-profit **Works:** translations, adaptations **2nd productions:** yes **Special interests:** classical source material;

new Eastern European and Latin American works **Tours:** yes
Stages: proscenium, 600 seats; arena, 500 seats **Audience:**
"From university and community, representing area's
demographics." **Submission policy:** unsolicited script with SASE
and resume; query/synopsis with dialogue sample and resume **Best
time:** fall **Response:** 6-8 weeks **Your chances:** 30 submissions
Remuneration: negotiable

CLAVIS THEATRE
Box 93158, Milwaukee, WI 53203 (414) 272-3043
Contact: Ted Altschuler, Program Director **Theatre:** professional
not-for-profit **Works:** full-length plays, one-acts **Special
interests:** "Provocative, innovative, fun approaches to
contemporary issues"; one-acts for Festival only **Specifications:**
for one-acts: maximum cast: 7; maximum playing time: 1 hour
Stage: flexible, 99 seats **Submission policy:** query/synopsis
Response: 2 months query; 4 months script **Your chances:** 275
submissions/varying number of productions **Remuneration:**
"Negotiated on a per-play basis." **Programs:** Milwaukee Annual
One-Act Festival: unproduced one-acts; readings of full-length plays;
residency for collaborative work with company (inquire)

THE CLEVELAND PLAY HOUSE
Box 1989, Cleveland, OH 44106 (216) 795-7010
Contact: Roger T. Danforth, Literary Manager **Theatre:**
professional not-for-profit **Works:** full-length plays, translations,
adaptations, musicals, children's plays **2nd productions:** yes
Tours: pre-Broadway productions and tours **Stages:** flexible
proscenium, 625 seats; proscenium, 499 seats; proscenium, 160
seats; flexible, 80-100 seats **Submission policy:** agent submission
preferred; query/synopsis with reviews **Response:** 4-6 months
Your chances: 500 submissions/6 productions **Future
commitment:** negotiable **Program:** Playwrights Lab Company
(inquire)

COCONUT GROVE PLAYHOUSE
3500 Main Hwy., Box 616, Miami, FL 33133
(305) 442-2662 Contact: Arnold Mittelman, Producing Artistic
Director **Theatre:** professional not-for-profit **Works:** full-length
plays, musicals **2nd productions:** yes **Special interests:**
"Musicals, comedies, mysteries, entertainment value, commercial
appeal." **Stages:** proscenium, 1100 seats; cabaret, 105 seats
Submission policy: agent submission **Best time:** fall-spring
Response: 2 months **Program:** readings **Comment:** See Chase,
Anthony, "Theater in the Tropics," *TheaterWeek* (Mar. 27, 1989),
52-60.

COLDWATER COMMUNITY THEATER
Coldwater, MI See Robert J. Pickering Award listing in Contests.

COLONY/STUDIO THEATRE
1944 Riverside Dr., Los Angeles, CA 90039
Contact: John Banach, Literary Manager **Theatre:** professional not-for-profit **Works:** full-length plays **2nd productions:** yes **Specifications:** maximum cast: 10; minimal set; plays must be suitable for casting within company **Stage:** thrust, 99 seats **Casting:** "Within resident company of professional actors." **Audience:** "All ages and ethnic backgrounds." **Submission policy:** send SASE for guidelines **Response:** 4 weeks query; 6-9 months script **Your chances:** 300 submissions/2 productions **Remuneration:** royalty **Future commitment:** negotiable **Programs:** staged readings, workshop productions **Advice:** "Scripts should be neat, bound and typed in professional format as detailed in *Guidelines* provided by Samuel French" (see Publishers). **Comment:** Formerly The Colony Theatre Company/Studio Theatre Playhouse.

COMMUNITY CHILDREN'S THEATRE
8021 E. 129th Terrace, Grandview, MO 64030
(816) 761-5775 Contact: E. Blanche Sellens, Chairman, Playwriting Award **Theatre:** elementary schools/non-professional **Works:** children's plays, adaptations and musicals **Specifications:** some limitations on sets **Tours:** yes **Stages:** various spaces **Audience:** "Grades K-6." **Submission policy:** unsolicited script with SASE; query/synopsis **Best time:** Sept.-Dec. **Response:** "Prompt." **Your chances:** 40-60 submissions/1 production **Remuneration:** $500 award **Program:** Margaret Bartle Annual Playwriting Award (see Contests) **Comment:** Theatre may produce some plays other than those submitted to contest.

COMPANY ONE THEATER
30 Arbor St. S, Hartford, CT 06106 (203) 233-4588
Contact: Candace Horter, Managing Director **Theatre:** professional not-for-profit **Works:** one-acts only: plays, translations, adaptations, musicals **2nd productions:** yes **Special interests:** "Non-realistic works, comedies, minority and women playwrights, thought-provoking works, radiodramas." **Specifications:** maximum cast: 6; single set **Stage:** proscenium, 200 seats **Casting:** "Non-traditional." **Audience:** "From the Greater Hartford area, Connecticut, New York and other areas." **Submission Policy:** unsolicited script **Best time:** winter-spring **Response:** 1 month query; 2 months script if rejected, longer if being considered **Your**

chances: 500 submissions/6 productions **Remuneration/future commitment:** negotiable **Programs:** readings, classes **Advice:** "We lean toward non-realistic work, small casts, imaginative sets and design. Audience eats lunch during performance."

COMPANY THEATRE
Box 1324, Cambridge, Ontario, Canada N1R 766
Contact: Katie Wright, Literary Manager **Theatre:** professional not-for-profit **Works:** full-length plays, one-acts, translations, adaptations, musicals **2nd productions:** yes **Exclusive interest:** "Contemporary plays expressing biblical world view." **Specifications:** maximum cast: 12; no large-scale proscenium productions; "we rarely produce Bible stories" **Tours:** yes **Stage:** flexible **Audience:** "Highly educated; college area: Christians and non-Christians." **Submission policy:** query/synopsis with dialogue sample and resume **Best time:** late spring-early summer **Response:** 1 month query **Your chances:** 20 submissions/2 productions **Remuneration:** "Royalties arranged with playwright or representative." **Program:** staged readings

CONEY ISLAND, USA SIDESHOWS BY THE SEASHORE
Boardwalk at W. 12th St., Coney Island, NY 11224
(718) 372-5159 Contact: Dick D. Zigun, Artistic Director **Theatre:** professional not-for-profit **Works:** existing productions of plays and performance-art works **2nd productions:** yes **Special interests:** new and traditional vaudeville; post-modern burlesque; new avant garde works utilizing techniques of American popular entertainments **Maximum cast:** 15 **Stages:** arena, 150 seats; cabaret, 200 seats; open-air spaces (streets, beach, boardwalk) **Submission policy:** query/synopsis with resume and reviews of other works **Best time:** May-Sept. **Response:** 2 months query; 6 months script **Future commitment:** no

CONKLIN PLAYERS DINNER THEATRE
Box 301 Timberline, Goodfield, IL 61742 (309) 965-2545
Contact: Chaunce Conklin, Producer **Theatre:** non-Equity dinner **Works:** full-length plays, musicals, children's plays **2nd productions:** yes **Stage:** thrust, 260 seats **Submission policy:** unsolicited script with SASE

CONTEMPORARY ARTS CENTER
Box 30498, New Orleans, LA 70190 (504) 523-1216
Contact: Julie Hebert, Artistic Director **Theatre:** professional not-for-profit **Works:** full-length plays, one-acts, musicals **Special interests:** political and contemporary issues; experimental or multi-media works; ethnic plays **Submission policy:** query/

synopsis **Best time:** Sept.–Jan. **Response:** 6 weeks query; 6–12 months script **Programs:** readings, staged readings, workshop productions, development; CAC New Play Competition (see Contests); CAC Playwright's Forum (see Special Programs)

CONTEMPORARY THEATRE OF SYRACUSE
1062 Westmoreland Ave., Syracuse, NY 13210
(315) 426-9149 Contact: David Feldman, New Plays Program Director **Theatre:** semi-professional/community **Works:** full-length plays, one-acts **2nd productions:** yes **Special interests:** "Plays by Syracuse area playwrights; plays set in this area." **Tours:** yes **Stage:** flexible, 150 seats **Audience:** "We look to develop a sophisticated audience." **Submission policy:** query/synopsis; professional recommendation; "reference by local theatre people" **Response:** 1 month query; 1–6 months script **Your chances:** 30–40 submissions/9–10 readings; "the only new plays we do are products of our staged reading program" **Remuneration:** $75–$100 **Programs:** readings, staged readings, development (all programs for area writers)

CONTRACT PLAYERS THEATRE
7239 Wales NW, North Canton, OH 44720
(216) 494-8311 Contact: Carla Derr, Executive Producer **Works:** full-length plays **Special interests:** drama, comedy, new plays **Specifications:** small cast; simple set and costume demands; no period plays **Stage:** 45 seats **Submission policy:** unsolicited script with SASE **Best time:** before May 31 for following season **Response:** 2 months

COOPER SQUARE THEATRE
50 E. 7th St., New York, NY 10003 (212) 228-0811
Contact: Jon Michael Johnson, Artistic Director **Theatre:** off off Broadway **Works:** full-length plays, one-acts, translations, adaptations, musicals, children's plays, cabaret/revues **2nd productions:** yes **Special interest:** "New plays." **Specifications:** maximum cast: 10; no more than 2–3 sets **Tours:** yes **Stages:** proscenium-thrust; small proscenium **Casting:** "Open/inclusive." **Audience:** "New York." **Submission policy:** query/synopsis **Best time:** spring **Response:** 1 month query; 6 months script **Your chances:** 100 submissions/1–2 productions **Recent production of unsolicited work:** 1986 **Remuneration:** "Negotiated percentage of box office." **Future commitments:** "For 1st production, negotiated percentage of future production and listing of cast and theatre in published script." **Programs:** readings, staged readings **Advice:** "We love you, but don't expect immediate results."

COOPERSTOWN THEATER FESTIVAL
Box 851, Cooperstown, NY 13326
Contact: Thornton W. Finley, Literary Manager **Theatre:** professional not-for-profit **Works:** full-length plays, adaptations **2nd productions:** yes **Special interests:** "Good stories with good roles; good use of language." **Specifications:** maximum cast: 10-12; "no political or sexual themes" **Stage:** proscenium, 150-200 seats **Audience:** "All types, but mainly of British, French and American descent." **Submission policy:** unsolicited script with SASE; query/synopsis; professional recommendation; agent submission **Best time:** Sept.-May **Response:** 6-12 months **Your chances:** 25 submissions/1 production **Recent production of unsolicited work:** staged reading **Remuneration:** "Small fee, expenses." **Future commitment:** no **Program:** staged readings

CORDEL PRODUCTIONS
Rye, NY This theatre is not accepting submissions in 1990.

THE COTERIE, INC.
2450 Grand, Kansas City, MO 64108 (816) 476-6785
Contact: Pam Sterling, Artistic Director **Theatre:** professional not-for-profit **Works:** children's plays: one-acts, translations, adaptations, musicals **2nd productions:** yes **Special interests:** historical topics, social issues, adaptations of classics, musicals **Specifications:** maximum cast: 14, 6-8 preferred; simple staging requirements; no fairy tales **Tours:** "Limited touring." **Stage:** flexible **Submission policy:** query/synopsis with resume and dialogue sample **Response:** 3-4 months query; 6 months script **Your chances:** 20 submissions/7 productions; "most writing is done in-house" **Remuneration:** negotiable **Advice:** "Quality theatre that educates as well as entertains; honest and serious writing."

COUNTRY DINNER PLAYHOUSE
6875 S. Clinton, Englewood, CO 80112 (303) 790-9311
Contact: Bill McHale, Director **Theatre:** Equity **Works:** full-length plays, musicals **2nd productions:** yes **Special interests:** musicals, comedies, farces **Maximum cast:** 18 **Stage:** arena, 470 seats **Submission policy:** query/synopsis

CO/WORKS
149 Washington St., Mount Holly, NJ 08060
(609) 261-9655 Contact: Daniel Aubrey, President
Theatre: professional not-for-profit **Works:** full-length plays, one-acts, translations, adaptations, children's plays **2nd productions:** yes **Special interests:** "Contemporary social and

personal dilemmas; literary merit." **Tours:** yes **Stages:** various spaces **Submission policy:** unsolicited script with SASE; query/synopsis; commission **Response:** 1 month query; 6 months script **Your chances:** 200 submissions/10 productions **Remuneration:** negotiable **Advice:** "We are interested in discovering and promoting playwrights."

CREATION PRODUCTION COMPANY
127 Greene St., New York, NY 10012 (212) 674-5593
Contact: Anne Hemenway, Managing Director **Theatre:** professional not-for-profit **Works:** experimental pieces **Stage:** no permanent facility **Submission policy:** solicited script with SASE

CREATIVE ARTS TEAM
NYU, 715 Broadway 5th Floor, New York, NY 10003
(212) 598-2360, 998-7380 **Contact:** Miriam Flaherty, Associate Executive Director **Theatre:** professional not-for-profit, university/college **Works:** young people's plays **Special interest:** "Concerns of youth: teen pregnancy, child abuse, substance abuse, employment, literacy." **Specifications:** works must be suitable for touring **Stages:** school auditoriums, fewer than 300 seats **Audience:** teenagers **Submission policy:** query/synopsis of proposed project to be created in collaboration with company **Best time:** spring **Response:** 1 month

CREATIVE PRODUCTIONS
2 Beaver Pl., Aberdeen, NJ 07747 (201) 566-6985
Contact: W. L. Born, Director **Theatre:** community/non-professional **Works:** full-length plays, musicals **2nd productions:** yes **Special interests:** "Players over 55; also folks with disabilities." **Specifications:** maximum cast: 12; no more than 3 sets; "no flying set parts" **Stage:** proscenium, 300 seats **Casting:** "Local and professional (non-union)." **Submission policy:** query/synopsis **Best time:** summer **Response:** 30 days **Your chances:** 6 submissions/0 productions **Remuneration:** negotiable **Advice:** "Only musicals--send professionally produced tape with vocals, orchestra accompaniment."

CREATIVE THEATRE
102 Witherspoon St., Princeton, NJ 08540
(609) 924-3489 **Contact:** Laurie Huntsman, Artistic Director **Theatre:** professional not-for-profit **Works:** children's full-length plays, translations, adaptations and musicals **2nd productions:** yes **Specifications:** maximum cast: 6; simple sets and costumes;

audience participation **Tours:** yes **Stages:** proscenium, arena, flexible—150-200 seats; "we utilize all stages on tour" **Audience:** "Grades K-12." **Submission policy:** unsolicited script with SASE; query/synopsis; commission **Best time:** Dec-Mar. **Response:** 1 week **Your chances:** 20-25 submissions/2-3 productions **Remuneration:** royalty or commission **Programs:** development, classes **Advice:** "Must be children's theatre K-6, 7-9, 9-12; must be suitable for production in open space, with audience participation; must be musical, or suitable for musical adaptation by our composers."

CREEDE REPERTORY THEATRE
Box 269, Creede, CO 81130 (719) 658-2541
Contact: Richard Baxter, Producing/Artistic Director **Theatre:** professional not-for-profit **Works:** full-length plays, translations, adaptations, musicals, children's plays **Special interests:** "The American West and Southwest." **Specifications:** maximum cast: 10; minimal set preferred **Stage:** proscenium, 187 seats **Submission policy:** query/synopsis with resume and dialogue sample **Best time:** Sept.-Nov. **Response:** 1 month query; 9 months script

THE CRICKET THEATRE
9 14th St. W, Minneapolis, MN 55403 (612) 871-3763
Contact: William Partlan, Artistic Director **Theatre:** professional not-for-profit **Works:** full-length plays, long one-acts, musicals, cabaret/revues **2nd productions:** yes **Special interests:** Midwestern subjects and issues **Maximum cast:** 8 **Stage:** modified proscenium, 213 seats **Casting:** open auditions **Audience:** "25-35 years of age." **Submission policy:** query/ synopsis with dialogue sample and resume preferred; professional recommendation **Best time:** Aug.-Sept. **Response:** 1-2 months query **Your chances:** 480 submissions/3 productions **Recent production of unsolicited work:** yes **Remuneration:** royalty **Future commitment:** "A small percentage of future production." **Programs:** readings, staged readings, workshop productions, development

CROSSROADS THEATRE COMPANY
320 Memorial Pkwy., New Brunswick, NJ 08901
(201) 249-5625 Contact: Sydné Mahone, Literary Manager **Theatre:** professional not-for-profit **Works:** full-length plays, one-acts, translations, adaptations, musicals, children's plays, cabaret/revues **2nd productions:** yes **Special interest:** African-American experience "as seen through the eyes of all Americans" **Specifications:** works must be suitable for intimate

stage **Stage**: thrust, 150 seats **Submission policy**: query/
synopsis preferred; unsolicited script with SASE **Response**: 1
month query; 6 months script **Recent production of unsolicited
work**: no **Future commitment**: negotiable

CSC: CLASSIC STAGE COMPANY
136 E. 13th St., New York, NY 10003 (212) 677-4210
Contact: Lenora Champagne, Artistic Associate **Theatre**: off
Broadway, professional not-for-profit **Works**: translations,
adaptations **2nd productions**: yes **Special interests**:
adaptations of major works from other genres; translations and
adaptations of classical European plays **Stage**: flexible, 180 seats
Submission policy: query/synopsis with dialogue sample;
professional recommendation; agent submission; commission
Response: 3 months **Your chances**: 200 submissions/3
productions plus 6 readings **Remuneration**: varies **Future
commitment**: for commissioned work **Programs**: readings,
development **Advice**: "Submit only plays of classic scope or
translations/adaptations of classics."

CUMBERLAND COUNTY PLAYHOUSE
Box 484, Crossville, TN 38555 (615) 484-2300, -4324
Contact: James Crabtree, Producing Director **Theatre**:
professional not-for-profit **Works**: full-length plays, adaptations,
musicals, children's plays **Special interests**: Tennessee history
and culture; Southern or rural settings and themes; plays suitable for
family audiences **Stages**: proscenium, 420-480 seats; thrust, 165
seats; outdoor arena, 200 seats **Submission policy**: query/
synopsis **Best time**: Aug.-Dec. **Response**: 2 weeks if interested
in query; 6-12 months script

DALLAS THEATRE CENTER
3636 Turtle Creek Blvd., Dallas, TX 75219
(214) 526-8210 Contact: Adrian Hall, Artistic Director; Rita
Cumming, Assistant to Artistic Director **Theatre**: professional not-
for-profit **Works**: full-length plays, translations, adaptations **2nd
productions**: yes **Maximum cast**: 20 **Stages**: thrust, 466
seats; flexible, 410 seats; flexible, 150 seats **Casting**: "From
company: 9 men, 6 women, age range 23-60." **Submission policy**:
query/synopsis; professional recommendation; agent submission
Best time: summer **Response**: 3-6 months **Your chances**:
500 submissions/2 productions **Future commitment**: negotiable

DAUGHTER PRODUCTIONS, INC.
37 S. 20th St. Suite 500, Philadelphia, PA 19103
(215) 567-2745 Contact: Lisa Miller, Literary Manager
Theatre: professional not-for-profit **Works:** full-length plays, one-acts **2nd productions:** yes **Special interests:** "Plays by women; non-traditional casting; strong, realistic roles for women." **Specifications:** maximum cast: 6; minimal sets **Tours:** yes **Casting:** "All races, ages, types." **Audience:** "Community centers, colleges/universities, theatregoers." **Submission policy:** query/synopsis with resume **Best time:** spring-summer **Response:** 2 weeks query; 6 months script **Your chances:** 200 submissions/ 2 productions; "we're only 2 years old; all works to date have been found by us" **Programs:** "Future readings, staged readings and workshop productions." **Advice:** "We are a multi-cultural company with a particular focus on plays that lend themselves to post-performance discussion."

DAYTONA PLAYHOUSE
100 Jessamine Blvd., Daytona Beach, FL 32018
(904) 255-2431 Contact: Anne Heflin, President, Board of Directors **Theatre:** community/non-professional **Works:** full-length plays, adaptations, musicals, children's plays **2nd productions:** no **Special interests:** "Scripts of literary merit as well as those farcical bits of froth that are dominant in community theatre circles; we attempt to provide our audiences with a balance of choices." **Specifications:** maximum cast: 8-35; "no excessive profanity" **Stage:** proscenium, 260 seats **Audience:** "Many retired people from northern U.S.; family-oriented; preferences in order: comedy/farce, musicals, mysteries, historical dramas." **Submission policy:** unsolicited script with SASE; query/synopsis; professional recommendation **Best time:** Aug.-Dec. **Response:** 5 months **Your chances:** 5 submissions/0-1 production **Remuneration:** negotiable **Advice:** "Submit scripts that are well composed; write for an intelligent audience--to entertain, not shock."

DEEP ELLUM THEATRE GROUP/UNDERMAIN THEATRE
Box 141166, Dallas, TX 75214 (214) 747-1424
Contact: Lisa Schmidt **Theatre:** professional not-for-profit **Works:** full-length plays, one-acts, musicals **Special interests:** "Language-oriented works; works suitable for ensemble company." **Maximum cast:** 8 **Stage:** flexible thrust, 75 seats **Best time:** Jun.-Aug. **Response:** 3 months query; 6 months script

DELAWARE THEATRE COMPANY
Box 516, Wilmington, DE 19899 (302) 594-1104
Contact: Cleveland Morris, Artistic Director **Theatre:** professional not-for-profit **Works:** full-length plays, translations, adaptations, musicals **2nd productions:** yes **Specifications:** maximum cast: 10-12; single or unit set **Tours:** yes **Stage:** thrust, 300 seats **Audience:** "Educated, professional, middle-aged." **Submission policy:** unsolicited script with SASE and synopsis; query/synopsis with SAS postcard; professional recommendation; agent submission **Best time:** Feb.-May **Response:** 6 weeks query; 4-6 months script **Your chances:** 300 submissions/0-1 production **Recent production of unsolicited work:** yes **Remuneration:** negotiable royalty **Future commitment:** negotiable

DELL'ARTE PLAYERS COMPANY
Box 816, Blue Lake, CA 95525 (707) 668-5411
Contact: Michael Fields, Donald Forrest, Joan Schirle, Artistic Directors **Theatre:** professional not-for-profit **Works:** full-length plays, translations, adaptations, children's plays **2nd productions:** yes **Special interests:** comedy-satire; works for very physical treatment and new vaudeville styles; issue-oriented plays; collaboration with playwright **Specifications:** maximum cast: 5; works must be suitable for touring **Stage:** flexible, 100 seats **Submission policy:** query/synopsis **Best time:** Jan.-Mar. **Response:** 3 weeks query; 1 month script

THE DELRAY BEACH PLAYHOUSE
950 NW 19th St., Box 1056, Delray Beach, FL 33444 (407) 272-1281 **Contact:** Randolph DelLago, Director **Theatre:** community/non-professional **Works:** full-length plays, adaptations, children's plays **2nd productions:** yes **Special interests:** "Mysteries, musicals, comedies, dramas." **Specifications:** simple sets; little capacity for special effects **Stage:** proscenium, 238 seats **Casting:** open auditions **Audience:** "Older, conservative, middle to upper middle class." **Submission policy:** query/synopsis; professional recommendation **Best time:** winter **Your chances:** 20 submissions/1 production **Program:** workshop productions for children **Advice:** "We are always looking for good new mysteries and children's plays that deal intelligently with serious issues; classical farces and melodramas for audiences of children."

DENVER CENTER THEATRE COMPANY
1050 13th St., Denver, CO 80204 (303) 893-4200 ext. 235 **Contact:** Barbara Sellers, Producing Director **Theatre:** professional not-for-profit **Works:** full-length plays **2nd productions:** no **Special interest:** social and political

themes **Maximum cast:** 12 **Stages:** thrust, 642 seats; thrust, 155 seats; arena, 450 seats; proscenium, 196 seats **Submission policy:** unsolicited script with SASE **Best time:** Mar. 1-Dec. 31 **Response:** 1-2 months **Your chances:** 800+ submissions/4 productions; "we accept only 1 script per playwright" **Future commitment:** negotiable **Program:** PrimaFacie/WestFest (see Special Programs)

DERBY DINNER THEATRE
525 Marriott Dr., Clarksville, IN 47130 (812) 288-2632
Contact: Bekki Jo Schneider, Producer **Theatre:** non-Equity **Works:** full-length plays, musicals **Special interests:** comedies, musicals **Maximum cast:** 19 **Stage:** arena **Submission policy:** unsolicited script with SASE **Your chances:** 1 production

DETROIT CENTER FOR THE PERFORMING ARTS
615 Griswold Suite 420, Detroit, MI 48226
(313) 925-7925 Contact: Gary Steward-Jones, Artistic Director **Theatre:** professional not-for-profit **Works:** full-length plays, one-acts, musicals, children's plays, cabaret/revues **2nd productions:** yes **Special interest:** "Ability to cast either black or white." **Specifications:** maximum cast: 8; simple set **Stages:** proscenium, 2000; flexible, 150 seats **Submission policy:** query/synopsis preferred; unsolicited script with SASE **Response:** 3 months query; 6 months script **Your chances:** 60 submissions/2 productions **Remuneration:** negotiable **Future commitment:** no **Program:** Playwrights Development Series: staged readings leading to mainstage production of 1 new play each season (inquire)

DETROIT REPERTORY THEATRE
13103 Woodrow Wilson, Detroit, MI 48238
(313) 868-1347 Contact: Barbara Busby, Literary Manager **Theatre:** professional not-for-profit **Works:** full-length plays, musicals **2nd productions:** yes, but unproduced plays preferred **Special interests:** "Issues. We are an affirmative action theatre and cast without regard to color." **Maximum cast:** 12 **Stage:** proscenium **Audience:** "70% black, lower middle class to professional." **Submission policy:** unsolicited script with SASE; query/synopsis with dialogue sample; professional recommendation; agent submission **Best time:** Sept.-Mar. **Response:** 2 weeks query; 4-6 months script **Your chances:** 100-200 submissions/ 1-3 productions in season of 4 shows **Remuneration:** royalty

DINNER PLAYHOUSE, INC.--NEW PLAYS
Los Angeles, CA This theatre did not respond to our 1990 questionnaire, and no phone number is listed.

THE DIRECTORS COMPANY
311 W. 43rd St. Suite 1404, New York, NY 10036
Contact: Michael J. Norton, Literary Manager **Theatre:** professional not-for-profit **Works:** full-length plays, musicals **2nd productions:** if New York premieres **Maximum cast:** 10 **Submission policy:** query/synopsis with resume and first 10-15 pages of script **Response:** 3 months **Future commitment:** negotiable

DIXIE COLLEGE THEATRE & PIONEER PLAYERS
225 S. 700 E, St. George, UT 84770 (801) 628-3121
Contact: C. Paul Andersen, Director **Theatre:** professional not-for-profit, community/non-professional, university/college **Works:** full-length plays, adaptations, musicals, children's plays **2nd productions:** yes **Special interests:** "19th century Pioneer Movement; 19th century and musical melodrama; scripts which appeal to tourists." **Specifications:** maximum cast: 8; no more than 2 sets **Stages:** proscenium; arena **Audience:** "Community and tourist patrons interested in either a good time or a moving experience." **Submission policy:** query/synopsis with resume **Best time:** Jan.-Mar. **Response:** 1 month **Your chances:** 1-2 new plays produced each season **Remuneration:** "Reasonable royalty." **Advice:** "Family-oriented plays are needed." **Comment:** "Regular theatre season is educational theatre; summer theatre is pre-professional."

DIXON PLACE
37 E. 1st St., New York, NY 10003 (212) 673-6752
Contact: Ellie Covan, Producer **Theatre:** not-for-profit laboratory **Works:** performance pieces **Exclusive interest:** "Works in progress: experimental works, visually oriented works, collaborations." **Specifications:** no more than 4 performers; pieces should be 20-45 minutes in length and suitable for a very small space (10' x 10') **Stage:** living room proscenium, 50 seats **Audience:** "People from the arts community and friends of the performers." **Submission policy:** short proposal with video tape of past work; solicited work **Response:** 2-4 weeks **Remuneration:** "Guaranteed minimum fee of $70 per performance piece." **Advice:** "Take risks." **Comment:** "We are famous for our informal ambiance conducive to creative and social interaction."

DOBAMA THEATRE
1846 Coventry Rd., Cleveland Heights, OH 44118
(216) 932-6838 Contact: Jean Cummins, Literary Manager **Theatre:** community/non-professional **Works:** full-length plays, one-acts, translations, adaptations **2nd productions:** "Previously

unproduced plays are preferred." **Special interest:** "Paired one-acts are preferred over single one-acts." **Specifications:** low ceilings; limited backstage area **Stage:** 3/4 arena **Submission policy:** unsolicited script with SASE and resume **Best time:** May–Sept. **Response:** 6–9 months **Your chances:** 40 submissions/ 3–4 productions **Remuneration:** "Standard fee (about $35 per performance)." **Program:** readings

DORDT COLLEGE THEATRE
Sioux Center, IA 51250   (712) 722-3771
Contact: James Koldenhoven, Theatre Arts Dept.   **Theatre:** university/college **Works:** full-length plays, one-acts, adaptations, musicals **2nd productions:** yes **Special interest:** "Current social or moral questions." **Tours:** yes **Stages:** thrust; arena; flexible **Audience:** "Conservative residents; college crowd." **Submission policy:** unsolicited script with SASE; query/synopsis **Best time:** fall **Your chances:** 10 submissions/1 production **Remuneration:** 1–2 week residency, honorarium **Programs:** readings, staged readings, workshop productions, development, residencies, classes **Advice:** "Write the story. Develop the characters clearly. Don't try to be funny; let the humor as well as the drama evolve from the character and the story."

DORSET THEATRE FESTIVAL
Box 519, Dorset, VT 05251   (802) 867-2223
Contact: Jill Charles, Artistic Director **Theatre:** professional not-for-profit **Works:** full-length plays, adaptations, musicals **2nd productions:** "Yes, but prefer unencumbered plays." **Special interests:** "General audience appeal; depth, whether comedy or drama." **Specifications:** maximum cast: 8; unit set preferred **Stage:** proscenium, 218 seats **Audience:** "Sophisticated; conservative in terms of language." **Submission policy:** professional recommendation; agent submission; workshop in New York City **Best time:** Sept.-Feb. **Response:** 3–4 months **Your chances:** 150 submissions/1 production **Remuneration:** negotiable royalty, transportation, expenses **Program:** Dorset Colony House (see Special Programs) **Advice:** "Have an agent or artistic director of a theatre where the play has been produced send us a query, or inform us of a reading or workshop in New York City."

DOUBLE IMAGE THEATRE
New York, NY   See Double Image Theatre/New Voices at Greene Street Cafe listing in Special Programs and Off-Off Broadway Original Short Play Festival listing in Contests.

DOWLING ENTERTAINMENT CORP.
226 W. 47th St., New York, NY 10036 (212) 719-3090
Contact: Kevin Dowling, Producer **Production company:** off Broadway **Works:** full-length plays **Special interests:** comedies; works suitable for off Broadway productions **Submission policy:** unsolicited script with SASE **Response:** 9 months

DOWNTOWN CABARET THEATRE
263 Golden Hill St., Bridgeport, CT 06604
(203) 576-1634 Contact: Richard C. Hallinan, Executive Producer **Theatre:** professional not-for-profit **Works:** musicals, children's plays, cabaret/revues **Specifications:** cast size: 6-18; simple sets; no fly space **Stage:** proscenium, 294 seats **Submission policy:** solicited script with SASE

DRAMA COMMITTEE REPERTORY THEATRE
118 W. 79th St., New York, NY 10024
Contact: Arthur Reel, Artistic Director **Theatre:** professional not-for-profit **Works:** full-length plays, one-acts, adaptations **2nd productions:** no **Special interest:** adaptations of classics originally written in prose **Specifications:** maximum cast: 10; moveable sets **Submission policy:** query/synopsis with 1st act of script **Response:** 2 months

THE DRAMA GROUP
330 W. 202nd St., Chicago Heights, IL 60411
(312) 755-3444 Contact: Charles Barnett, Business Manager **Theatre:** community/non-professional **Works:** full-length plays, musicals **2nd productions:** "Under consideration." **Maximum cast:** 20 **Stages:** proscenium, thrust, arena, flexible--150-1304 seats **Audience:** "Blue collar; education level tops generally with B.A.; ethnic melting pot; average age 40-60." **Submission policy:** unsolicited script with SASE **Best time:** fall-winter **Remuneration:** "Subject to grant funding." **Program:** contests (inquire) **Comment:** "Production of new plays is currently under consideration by the board."

DREISKE PERFORMANCE COMPANY
1517 W. Fullerton Ave., Chicago, IL 60614
(312) 281-9075 Contact: Nicole Dreiske, Artistic Director **Theatre:** professional not-for-profit **Works:** full-length plays, one-acts **2nd productions:** no **Special interests:** "Non-naturalistic, poetic texts that can be staged with movement by the actors; tech-oriented and visual elements." **Maximum cast:** 15 **Tours:** all shows **Stages:** proscenium; thrust; arena; black box **Audience:** "European festivals, American universities, theatre

and art festivals." **Submission policy:** query/synopsis with dialogue sample; professional recommendation **Response:** 4-6 weeks **Your chances:** 60 submissions/1 production **Remuneration:** "Salary during play development, rehearsals and production." **Programs:** workshop productions, development, internships

DUO THEATRE
Box 1200 Cooper Station, New York, NY 10276
(212) 598-4320 Contact: Michael Alasa, Managing Director **Theatre:** off off Broadway **Works:** musicals **Exclusive interest:** "Hispanic American playwrights writing in English." **Maximum cast:** 10 **Tours:** yes **Casting:** open auditions **Audience:** "We are a theatre for 2nd generation Hispanics. We try to interest all groups of people; we give tickets to people to allow them to experience Hispanic theatre." **Submission policy:** unsolicited script with SASE and resume; query/synopsis with resume; commission **Best time:** early fall **Response:** 3 months script **Your chances:** 50-60 submissions/"8 productions in this season series; this is essentially a showcase theatre, a place for Hispanics to try out their work; in our experience, staged readings are an entree to production" **Remuneration:** "A fee and a piece of the house." **Programs:** readings, staged readings, playwrights' unit for authors who write only in Spanish **Advice:** "A place for playwrights to tell about living in America. Also universal themes, not 'kitchen sink' drama." **Comment:** See Shirakawa, Sam H., "Beyond the Ghetto Mentality," *TheaterWeek* (May 16, 1988), 32-37.

EAST WEST PLAYERS
4424 Santa Monica Blvd., Los Angeles, CA 90029
(213) 660-0366 Contact: Michele Garza, Managing Director **Theatre:** professional not-for-profit **Works:** full-length plays, one-acts, translations, adaptations, musicals, operas, cabaret/revues **Special interests:** "New works dealing with the Asian-American experience in the U.S.; contemporary American works." **Specifications:** works must be suitable for Asian actors **Stage:** 3/4 thrust, 99 seats **Audience:** "Middle-class, college-educated, 60% Asian American, 40% Anglo." **Submission policy:** unsolicited script with SASE **Response:** 3-4 months **Your chances:** 100 submissions/2-3 productions **Remuneration:** negotiable royalty

ECCENTRIC CIRCLES THEATRE
400 W. 43rd St. #4N, New York, NY 10036
(212) 564-3798 Contact: Rosemary Hopkins, Paula Kay Pierce, Janet Bruders, Barbara Bunch, Producing/Artistic Directors **Theatre:** off off Broadway **Works:** full-length plays, one-acts,

musicals **2nd productions:** no **Specifications:** maximum cast: 10; simple set **Stage:** proscenium, 99 seats **Audience:** general **Submission policy:** unsolicited script with SASE; query/synopsis with dialogue sample **Response:** 2 weeks query; 6 weeks script **Your chances:** 150 submissions/1 production **Remuneration:** no

EL TEATRO CAMPESINO
Box 1240, San Juan Bautista, CA 95045 (408) 623-2444
Contact: Phil Esparza, Producer **Theatre:** professional not-for-profit **Works:** full-length plays, one-acts, translations, adaptations, musicals, children's plays, cabaret/revues **Special interests:** social revelance; works reflecting multi-cultural issues; adaptations of classics **Specifications:** maximum cast: 8; simple set **Stage:** flexible, 150 seats **Submission policy:** query/synopsis with resume **Best time:** Jan.-Apr. **Response:** 6 months query; 1 year script

EMMY GIFFORD CHILDREN'S THEATER
3504 Center St., Omaha, NE 68105
(402) 345-4852 **Contact:** James Larson, Artistic Director **Theatre:** professional not-for-profit **Works:** children's plays and adaptations **2nd productions:** yes **Exclusive interest:** "Works suitable for a young audience." **Specifications:** some limitations on sets; no fly space **Stage:** proscenium, thrust--500 seats **Submission policy:** query/synopsis; professional recommendation **Best time:** summer **Your chances:** 48 submissions/2 productions **Remuneration:** negotiable

EMPIRE STATE INSTITUTE FOR THE PERFORMING ARTS
Empire State Plaza, Albany, NY 12223 (518) 443-5222
Contact: James Farrell, Literary Manager **Theatre:** professional not-for-profit **Works:** full-length plays, adaptations, musicals **2nd productions:** yes **Special interests:** unproduced plays for New Works Program; works for family audiences **Tours:** yes **Stages:** flexible thrust, 883 seats; thrust, 450 seats **Audience:** "Adults and families." **Submission policy:** unsolicited script with SASE; query/synopsis; professional recommendation; agent submission **Best time:** Apr.-Aug. **Response:** 3 weeks query; 3-4 months script **Your chances:** 350 submissions/1-2 productions **Remuneration:** varies **Future commitment:** negotiable **Program:** New Works Program (inquire)

THE EMPTY SPACE THEATRE
Box 1748, Seattle, WA 98111-1748 (206) 587-3737
Contact: Kurt Beattie, Artistic Associate **Theatre:** professional not-for-profit **Works:** full-length plays, one-acts, translations,

adaptations, musicals **2nd productions**: yes **Special interests**: "Adventurous themes, contemporary significance, innovative theatrical techniques, imaginative approaches to narrative." **Specifications**: maximum cast: 12; more with doubling; "no excessively derivative or obviously commercial scripts" **Stage**: endstage, 170 seats **Audience**: "Well educated, middle class, intellectually alive." **Submission policy**: query/synopsis with resume and dialogue sample; professional recommendation; agent submission; unsolicited script with SASE from ID, MT, OR, WA, WY only **Best time**: fall **Response**: 2 weeks query; 3-4 months script **Remuneration**: royalty; commission **Future commitment**: negotiable participation in future productions **Recent production of unsolicited work**: no

ENCORE THEATRE
991 North Shore Dr., Lima, OH 45801 (419) 223-8866
Contact: Allyn Barnes, President **Theatre**: community/non-professional **Works**: full-length plays, musicals **2nd productions**: yes **Specifications**: maximum cast: 25; easy set changes; no fly gallery **Stage**: thrust, 309 seats **Audience**: "Upper income, educated, ages 20-70." **Submission policy**: unsolicited script with SASE; query/synopsis **Best time**: fall **Response**: 6-9 months **Your chances**: 2-3 scripts received each year **Advice**: "Complete working script; we would need the playwright present during early rehearsals."

ENSEMBLE STUDIO THEATRE
549 W. 52nd St., New York, NY 10019 (212) 581-9603
Contact: Christopher Smith, Literary Manager **Theatre**: professional not-for-profit **Works**: full-length plays, one-acts **Stages**: flexible mainstage, 98 seats; studio, 45 seats **Submission policy**: unsolicited script with SASE **Best time**: Sept.-Apr. **Response**: 3-4 months **Programs**: readings, staged readings, workshop productions; One-Act Marathon (inquire); Ensemble Studio Theatre Institute (see Special Programs) **Advice**: Do not send query/synopsis. **Comment**: See Myers, Larry, "Curt Dempster: Running a Theatrical Marathon," *TheaterWeek* (Jul. 4, 1988), 52-57.

ENSEMBLE THEATRE OF CINCINNATI
1127 Vine St., Cincinnati, OH 45210 (513) 421-3556
Contact: David A. White III, Artistic Director **Theatre**: Equity Small Professional **Works**: full-length plays, children's plays **2nd productions**: if not previously produced more than once **Special interests**: "Development of new works; ritualistic

devices, stretched boundaries, emotional risks; children's plays."
Specifications: maximum cast: 6; simple set **Tours:** "Possibly."
Stage: thrust, 136 seats **Audience:** "Marketing toward yuppies
whom we want to shake up." **Submission policy:** unsolicited
script with SASE; professional recommendation; agent submission
Best time: before Dec. 1 **Response:** 2 months **Your chances:**
300+ submissions/5 productions **Remuneration:** "Fees are based
on the playwright's background and the number of performances."
Program: staged readings

ENSEMBLE THEATRE OF FLORIDA
Box 1103, Melbourne, FL 32902 (407) 984-0541
Contact: Stuart Smith, Artistic Director **Theatre:** professional
not-for-profit **Works:** full-length plays, translations, adaptations,
musicals, children's plays **2nd productions:** yes **Special
interests:** "Works related to Florida, regional interests." **Stage:**
proscenium-thrust, 100 seats **Casting:** open auditions **Audience:**
"Young, average age 38; educated." **Submission policy:** query/
synopsis with resume **Response:** 6 weeks **Your chances:** 15-20
submissions/2 productions **Remuneration:** negotiable

ENSEMBLE THEATRE OF SANTA BARBARA
Box 2307, Santa Barbara, CA 93120 (805) 965-6252
Contact: Robert Weiss, Artistic Director **Theatre:** professional
not-for-profit **Works:** full-length plays, one-acts, translations,
adaptations **Specifications:** small cast; simple production
requirements **Stage:** proscenium, 140 seats **Submission policy:**
unsolicited script with SASE **Best time:** Sept. 1-Mar. 1 **Response:**
3 months **Program:** 2 Nights Studio Program: staged readings/
discussions

EUCLID LITTLE THEATRE
**c/o Euclid Recreation Department, New City Hall,
585 E. 222 Street, Euclid, OH 44123 (216) 449-8624**
Contact: Jan Petro, Production Manager **Theatre:** community/
non-professional **Works:** full-length plays, one-acts, musicals **2nd
productions:** yes **Special interest:** "Works for audiences who
want to be entertained." **Specifications:** maximum cast: 40; "no
four-letter words" **Stage:** proscenium, 100-200 seats **Casting:**
open auditions **Audience:** "General; mixed." **Your chances:** 100
submissions/1 production **Remuneration:** yes **Program:** staged
readings **Advice:** "Conservative entertainment."

EUREKA THEATRE COMPANY

2730 16th St., San Francisco, CA 94103
(415) 558-9811 Contact: Oskar Eustis, Artistic Director; Ken Grantham, Literary Manager **Theatre:** professional not-for-profit **Works:** full-length plays, one-acts, translations, adaptations **2nd productions:** yes **Special interest:** contemporary social/political issues **Maximum cast:** 15 **Stage:** flexible, 200 seats **Submission policy:** query/synopsis; professional recommendation; agent submission **Best time:** Oct.-Mar. **Response:** 3 months query; 6 months script **Remuneration/future commitment:** negotiable **Program:** readings

EXPERIMENTAL THEATRE
OF THE PUERTORICAN ATHENEUM

Box 1180, San Juan, PR 00902 (809) 722-4839
Contact: Roberto Ramos-Perea, Executive Director **Theatre:** professional not-for-profit **Works:** full-length plays, one-acts, translations, adaptations **2nd productions:** no **Special interests:** "Puertorican subjects; Hispanics' relations with U.S." **Specifications:** maximum cast: 6; single set **Tours:** yes **Stage:** proscenium, 365 seats **Audience:** "Mainly Puertoricans, high and middle education, students, teachers and artists." **Submission policy:** unsolicited script with SASE **Best time:** summer **Response:** 6 months **Your chances:** 15 submissions/3-4 productions, "not necessarily chosen from those submitted" **Remuneration:** royalty **Programs:** readings, staged readings, contests (inquire) **Advice:** "Seriousness in the treatment of political and social issues. Well-written comedies, fresh ideas."

FAIRBANKS DRAMA ASSOCIATION
& FAIRBANKS CHILDREN'S THEATRE, INC.

Box 81327, Fairbanks, AK 99708 (907) 456-PLAY
Contact: Cynthia Steiner, Executive Director **Theatre:** community/non-professional **Works:** full-length plays, one-acts, children's plays **Specifications:** maximum cast: 8; minimal set; "no drops" **Tours:** children's plays **Stage:** flexible, 90 seats **Submission policy:** unsolicited script with SASE; query/synopsis **Best time:** fall **Remuneration:** no

FAIRBANKS LIGHT OPERA THEATRE

Box 2787, Fairbanks, AK 99707 (907) 479-4709
Contact: Diane Egley, President **Theatre:** community/non-professional **Works:** musicals, operas, light operas **2nd productions:** no **Special interest:** "Family-type material." **Specifications:** simple sets **Tours:** yes **Stage:** proscenium, 800 seats **Casting:** "Large chorus; more women than men."

Audience: "Family folks in and around Fairbanks—rural and urban."
Submission policy: query/synopsis **Response:** 2 months
Your chances: theatre would like to produce 1 new musical each
year **Remuneration:** "We're small and non-profit, so we'd have to
talk about it." **Advice:** "Musical theater only; very professional. We
would like to receive new musicals and light operas."

FAIRMOUNT THEATRE OF THE DEAF
8500 Euclid Ave., Cleveland, OH 44106 (216) 229-2838
Contact: Michael Regnier, Associate Artistic Director **Theatre:**
professional not-for-profit **Works:** full-length plays, one-acts,
translations, adaptations, musicals, children's plays **2nd
productions:** yes **Specifications:** maximum cast: 4; sets must
tours **Stages:** various spaces **Audience:** "Deaf and hearing
audiences in a shared-experience setting (preferably). All productions
are staged in sign language and spoken English." **Casting:** "Except in
plays in which race, ethnicity or sex is an issue, casting is decided on
the basis of ability alone." **Submission policy:** unsolicited script
with SASE and resume; query/synopsis with dialogue sample and
resume; professional recommendation; agent submission **Best
time:** Jan-Aug. **Your chances:** 50 submissions/0-1 production
Remuneration: negotiable **Advice:** "Do not assume anything about
deaf theatre."

FERNDALE REPERTORY THEATRE
Box 892, Ferndale, CA 95536 (707) 725-2378
Contact: James Floss, Artistic Director **Theatre:** semi-
professional/community **Works:** full-length plays, musicals **2nd
productions:** "Rarely." **Special interests:** "Contemporary
themes; imagination." **Specifications:** maximum cast: 10; no
domestic comedies, no "bedroom dramas" **Stage:** proscenium, 267
seats **Audience:** "Well educated, 35-65." **Submission policy:**
unsolicited script with SASE; query/synopsis; professional
recommendation **Best time:** spring-summer **Response:** 1 month
query; 6 months script **Your chances:** 125 submissions/1
production **Remuneration:** "$225 royalty for 8 performances."
Program: Ferndale Repertory New Works Competition (see Contests)
Advice: "Simple, small-cast shows, intriguing formats."

FIREHOUSE THEATRE
514 S. 11th St., Omaha, NE 68102 (402) 346-6009
Contact: Richard Mueller, Artistic Director **Theatre:** professional
not-for-profit **Works:** full-length plays, musicals **2nd
productions:** yes **Special interests:** comedies, farces, musicals
Stage: thrust, 289 seats **Submission policy:** unsolicited script
with SASE

THE FIREHOUSE THEATRE, INC.
306 Charles St., Mobile, AL 36604
Contact: Fred Baldwin, Artistic Director **Theatre:** professional not-for-profit **Works:** full-length plays, one-acts, musicals, skits **2nd productions:** no **Special interest:** Southeastern playwrights **Submission policy:** unsolicited script with SASE

FIRELITE DINNER THEATRE
Ventura, CA This theatre is permanently closed.

FLORIDA STUDIO THEATRE
1241 N. Palm Ave., Sarasota, FL 34236 (813) 366-9017
Contact: Jack Fournier, New Play Coordinator **Theatre:** professional not-for-profit **Works:** full-length plays, one-acts, translations, adaptations, musicals, cabaret pieces **2nd productions:** yes **Specifications:** cast size: 4-8; simple unit set preferred **Tours:** yes **Stage:** proscenium, 163 seats **Audience:** "Older community. The theatre tries to educate, enlighten and expand its audience's taste." **Submission policy:** query/synopsis; professional recommendation; agent submission **Best time:** Mar.-Nov. for faster response **Response:** 1-2 months query; 6-9 months script **Your chances:** 750 submissions/2-3 productions **Remuneration/future commitment:** negotiable **Programs:** readings, staged readings, workshop productions; Florida Studio Theatre Mini-Festival/New Play Festival (see Contests); Florida Studio Theatre Artists Colony (see Special Programs)

FMT
Box 92127, Milwaukee, WI 53202 (414) 271-8484
Contact: Mike Moynihan, Co-Founder/Director **Theatre:** professional not-for-profit **Works:** full-length plays, adaptations, musicals, children's plays, cabaret/revues, clown/vaudeville pieces **2nd productions:** "Not usually." **Special interests:** "Writers interested in working with the company to develop a work"; social/political issues, regional themes, mixed-media works; clown/vaudeville pieces; works for young and family audiences **Specifications:** cast size: 1-3; all works must tour **Stages:** flexible; outdoor **Audience:** "General, young to old." **Submission policy:** query/synopsis **Best time:** Sept. only **Response:** 4 months query; 6 months script **Your chances:** 50 submissions/0-1 production **Remuneration:** "Flat fee or royalty." **Program:** ongoing New Works program: script development in collaboration with writer **Advice:** "Know our company's work; work with us on a short-term project."

FOLKSBEINE THEATER
123 E. 55th St., **New York, NY** 10022 (212) 755-2231
Contact: Ben Schechter, Managing Director **Theatre:** off off
Broadway **Works:** full-length plays **2nd productions:** yes
Exclusive interest: Jewish content **Maximum cast:** 10
Stage: proscenium, 445 seats **Audience:** "Jewish, Yiddish-
speaking audiences." **Submission policy:** query/synopsis with
resume **Response:** 3 months **Your chances:** 1 new play
produced each season (Oct.-Dec.). **Advice:** "Plays may be literary
but must also entertain. Interesting subject matter; may have a
message but should not be too philosophical." **Comment:** Plays
written in English will be translated and performed in Yiddish.

FORD'S THEATRE
511 Tenth St. **NW, Washington, DC** 20004
(202) 638-2941 Contact: Frankie Hewitt, Executive Producer
Theatre: professional not-for-profit **Works:** full-length plays,
musicals **2nd productions:** "Possibly." **Special interests:**
small-scale musicals, American authors **Maximum cast:** 15
Stage: proscenium-thrust, 699 seats **Audience:** "Articulate,
intelligent, upwardly mobile." **Submission policy:** query/
synopsis; professional recommendation; agent submission **Best
times:** late spring, late fall **Response:** 3 weeks query; 3 months
script **Your chances:** 200 submissions/1-2 productions
Remuneration: "Standard Dramatists Guild contract." **Programs:**
staged readings, workshop productions

45TH STREET THEATRE
584 **Ninth Ave., New York, NY** 10018 (212) 333-7471
Contact: Seth Gordon, Literary Manager **Theatre:** off off
Broadway **Works:** full-length plays, one-acts **2nd productions:**
if New York premieres **Special interest:** "American plays by
American playwrights." **Specifications:** maximum cast: 10;
single set or minimal stage requirements **Stages:** proscenium, 99
seats; proscenium-thrust, 60 seats **Submission policy:**
unsolicited script with SASE and resume **Best time:** Mar.-Jul.
Response: 2-6 months **Your chances:** 500 submissions/4-5
productions; "we are a development organization and present 3-4
readings each month" **Remuneration:** $200 **Programs:**
readings, staged readings, workshop productions **Advice:** "Off-beat
material, Black Comedy, the kind of thing you do not see on TV."
Comment: "Primary Stages Company (see Special Programs) is the
producing organization."

FOUNTAINHEAD THEATRE COMPANY
New York, NY This theatre is permanently closed.

FOUNTAIN SQUARE PLAYERS
416 E. Main St., Bowling Green, KY 42101
(502) 842-8844 **Contact:** Pat Sprouse
Theatre: community/non-professional **Works:** full-length plays, musicals, children's plays **2nd productions:** yes **Specifications:** "6 free battens to fly set pieces." **Stage:** proscenium, 860 seats **Casting:** open auditions **Audience:** "Middle American; 1/3 university, 1/3 agriculture, 1/3 manufacturing." **Submission policy:** unsolicited script with SASE; query/synopsis **Best time:** spring **Response:** 1 month **Your chances:** 2-3 submissions/"3 productions in 10 years existence" **Remuneration:** negotiable **Advice:** "Crowd pleasers, comedies, mysteries."

FREE STREET THEATER
441 W. North Ave., Chicago, IL 60610 **(312) 642-1234**
Contact: Patrick Henry, Producer/Artistic Director **Theatre:** professional not-for-profit **Works:** full-length plays, musicals **Special interests:** inter-racial or inter-generational issues; documentary projects based on oral histories and experiences of local residents; urban issues **Tours:** all shows **Stage:** mobile outdoor **Submission policy:** solicited script with SASE

FRIENDS & ARTISTS THEATRE ENSEMBLE
1761 N. Vermont Ave., Hollywood, CA 90027
(213) 664-0680 Contact: Play Reading Committee
Theatre: professional not-for-profit **Works:** full-length plays, one-acts, translations, adaptations, musicals **Special interests:** "Political and multi-ethnic themes, experimental works, good roles for women." **Stage:** black box, 60 seats **Casting:** "Open; company members have priority." **Audience:** "Diverse, open-minded." **Submission policy:** unsolicited script with SASE and resume; query/synopsis with resume **Response:** 1 month query; 3 months script **Your chances:** 25 submissions/0-1 production **Recent production of unsolicited work:** 1989 **Remuneration:** negotiable **Future commitment:** no **Programs:** readings, staged readings

THE FULLER YOUNG PEOPLE'S THEATRE
Minneapolis, MN This theatre is inactive.

FULTON OPERA HOUSE
Box 1865, 12 N. Prince St., Lancaster, PA 17603
(717) 394-7133 **Contact:** Kathleen Collins, Artistic Director
Theatre: professional not-for-profit **Works:** full-length plays, children's plays **2nd productions:** yes **Special interests:** "Works on contemporary social issues; non-linear structure; farce."

Specifications: maximum cast: 10-12; single set; simple technical requirements **Tours:** children's shows **Stage:** proscenium, 900 seats **Submission policy:** query/synopsis; agent submission; solicited script with SASE **Response:** 2-3 weeks query; 6 months script **Your chances:** 100-200 submissions/1 production **Remuneration:** negotiable **Future commitment:** yes **Program:** staged readings

THE GALLERY PLAYERS OF PARK SLOPE
Box 150705, Brooklyn, NY 11215 (718) 638-5725
Contact: Jack Kaplan, President **Theatre:** off off Broadway, semi-professional/community **Works:** full-length plays, one-acts, adaptations, musicals, children's plays **2nd productions:** no **Exclusive interest:** Brooklyn playwrights **Specifications:** small cast, simple sets **Stage:** proscenium, 100 seats **Audience:** "All ages; our subscribers tend to be 35-60, but we want to attract younger audiences, too." **Submission policy:** query/synopsis **Best time:** May-Aug. **Response:** 2 weeks query; 6 months script **Your chances:** 10-30 submissions/1-3 productions **Remuneration:** no **Program:** workshop productions

GARY YOUNG MIME THEATRE
23724 Park Madrid, Calabasas, CA 91302
Contact: Gary Young, Artistic Director **Theatre:** professional not-for-profit **Works:** one-act comic monologues and vignettes for adults and children **2nd productions:** yes **Special interests:** "Comedy; physical theatre." **Specifications:** maximum cast: 2; single set must tour; works must be 1-90 minutes in length **Casting:** open auditions **Audience:** "Varies—all types." **Submission policy:** query/synopsis with dialogue sample, resume and SAS postcard **Response:** 1 month query; 2 months script **Your chances:** 50 submissions received each year **Most recent production of unsolicited work:** 1986 **Remuneration:** "Varies according to type of material and use." **Future commitment:** "2-year minimum option." **Program:** development

THE GASLAMP QUARTER THEATRE COMPANY
547 4th Ave., San Diego, CA 92101 (619) 232-9608
Contact: Jean Hauser, Company Manager **Theatre:** professional not-for-profit **Works:** full-length plays, musicals **2nd productions:** yes **Special interest:** literary merit **Specifications:** maximum cast: 10; no more than 2 sets **Stages:** proscenium; thrust **Audience:** "Median age 45, college educated." **Submission policy:** unsolicited script with SASE; query/synopsis with dialogue sample and resume; agent submission **Best time:** Jan.-Mar. **Response:** 12 months **Your chances:** 40 submissions/1

production **Remuneration:** "Depends upon agent." **Future commitment:** negotiable **Program:** California Young Playwrights Project (see Contests)

GENE FRANKEL THEATRE
24 Bond St., New York, NY 10012 (212) 777-1710
Contact: Gene Frankel, Artistic Director **Theatre:** off off Broadway **Works:** full-length plays, one-acts **2nd productions:** yes **Specifications:** some limitations on sets; no fly space, "but creative space" **Tours:** yes **Stage:** flexible, up to 70 seats **Casting:** open auditions and through agents; "depends upon the show" **Audience:** "Varied--from agents and critics to first-time theatregoers." **Submission policy:** unsolicited script with SASE; query/synposis; professional recommendation; agent submission **Best time:** "Now." **Response:** 1-4 months **Your chances:** 100 submissions/varying number of productions **Remuneration:** "By contract." **Future commitment:** varies **Advice:** "Write excellent plays, full of truth. Attend our playwrights and directors workshop."

GEORGE STREET PLAYHOUSE
9 Livingston Ave., New Brunswick, NJ 08901
(201) 846-2895 Contact: Wendy Liscow, Associate Artistic Director **Theatre:** professional not-for-profit **Works:** full-length plays, one-acts, musicals **2nd productions:** yes **Specifications:** maximum cast: 7 preferred, 9 for musicals, 2-3 for one-acts; single set preferred with "multiple locales, flexible staging"; one-acts must be suitable for outreach program **Tours:** "High school outreach program. We tour 3 shows, 3 actors." **Stages:** proscenium-thrust, 367 seats; 3/4 round, 99 seats **Audience:** "Broad-based." **Submission policy:** query/synopis with dialogue sample; professional recommendation **Response:** 1 month query; 4-6 months script **Your chances:** 400 submissions/ production of 2 plays and 1 musical plus 6 staged readings **Future commitment:** varies **Programs:** staged readings; GS Playwrights' Project (see Special Programs) **Advice:** "Plays that have a theatrical approach and universal scope and explore unique situations, world views, characters and relationships."

GERMINAL STAGE DENVER
2450 W. 44th Ave., Denver, CO 80211-1508
(303) 455-7108 Contact: Edward Baierlein, Director/Manager **Theatre:** professional not-for-profit **Works:** full-length plays, translations, adaptations **Specifications:** maximum cast: 8; minimal production requirements **Stage:** 3/4 thrust, 100 seats **Audience:** general **Submission policy:** solicited script with SASE

GEVA THEATRE
75 Woodbury Blvd., Rochester, NY 14607
(716) 232-1366 Contact: Ann Patrice Carrigan, Literary Director **Theatre:** professional not-for-profit **Works:** full-length plays, one-acts, translations, adaptations, musicals **2nd productions:** yes **Special interest:** new plays **Maximum cast:** 10-13 **Stage:** modified thrust, 537 seats **Audience:** "12,500 subscribers, highly educated." **Submission policy:** query synopsis; agent submission **Response:** 1 week query; 4-6 months script **Your chances:** 500 submissions/1 production plus 6 in workshop **Remuneration:** negotiable advance on percentage **Future commitment:** for world premiere **Programs:** development; Plays in Progress: readings (inquire)

GLASS UNICORN PRODUCTIONS
299 Panoramic Way, Berkeley, CA 94707
(415) 644-1780 Contact: Leslie (Hoban) Blake, Artistic Director **Works:** full-length plays **Exclusive interests:** "Plays with multi-generational approaches; good roles for mature men and women (age 45+)." **Submission policy:** query/synopsis with resume **Best time:** Jan.-Mar. **Response:** 1 month query; 6 months script **Programs:** staged readings, development **Comment:** A new company.

THE GLINES
240 W. 44th St., New York, NY 10036 (212) 354-8899
Contact: John Glines, Artistic Director **Theatre:** professional not-for-profit **Works:** full-length plays, one-acts, translations, adaptations, musicals **2nd productions:** if not produced off off Broadway **Exclusive interest:** "The gay experience." **Maximum cast:** 12 **Stages:** various spaces **Submission policy:** unsolicited script with SASE; professional recommendation; agent submission **Response:** 2 months **Your chances:** 100 submissions/ 1-2 productions **Future commitment:** yes **Program:** staged readings **Advice:** "Write something that I won't see on television."

GLOUCESTER STAGE COMPANY
267 E. Main St., Gloucester, MA 01930 (617) 281-4099
Contact: Matthew Hahn, Dramaturg **Theatre:** professional not-for-profit **Works:** full-length plays, one-acts, translations, adaptations, musicals, children's plays **2nd productions:** yes **Special interests:** "New England subjects; contemporary themes." **Specifications:** maximum cast: 12; simple production requirements; no fly space **Stages:** flexible warehouse, 120 seats; 3/4, 40 seats **Audience:** "From Boston theatregoers to local people." **Submission policy:** unsolicited script with SASE and SAS

postcard; agent submission **Best time:** Nov.-Mar. **Response:** 6-9 weeks **Your chances:** 400 submissions/6-8 productions plus 8 staged readings **Remuneration:** "Favored nation payment, $100 per week." **Future commitment:** negotiable, 1-5% **Programs:** staged readings, workshop productions, development, internships

GNU THEATRE
10426 Magnolia Blvd., North Hollywood, CA 91601
(818) 508-5344 Contact: Jeff Seymour, Artistic Director
Theatre: professional not-for-profit **Works:** full-length plays, one-acts, translations, adaptations, musicals **2nd productions:** yes **Special interest:** contemporary themes **Specifications:** maximum cast: 15; "simple sets, but we are interested in sets" **Stage:** proscenium, 50 seats **Casting:** open auditions **Audience:** "Mixed." **Submission policy:** query/synopsis with resume and dialogue sample **Response:** 3 weeks **Your chances:** 100 submissions/4 productions **Remuneration:** royalty **Program:** staged readings **Advice:** "Ideal would be a full-length play of 2 acts, with 5-9 characters and simple but interesting sets."

THE GOLD COAST REPERTORY COMPANY
Pt. Hueneme, CA This theatre is permanently closed.

THE GOODMAN THEATRE
200 S. Columbus Dr., Chicago, IL 60603 (312) 443-3811
Contact: Robert Falls, Artistic Director; Tom Creamer, Literary Manager **Theatre:** professional not-for-profit **Works:** full-length plays, one-acts, translations, musicals **2nd productions:** yes **Special interests:** "Large-scale, highly theatrical works dealing with big ideas; social/political themes." **Stages:** proscenium, 683 seats; proscenium, 135 seats **Submission policy:** professional recommendation, agent submission preferred; query/synopsis with resume **Response:** 1 month query; 6 months script **Your chances:** 400 submissions/"perhaps 1 production every 2 seasons" **Remuneration:** standard royalty **Future commitment:** possibly **Advice:** "Most of the new work we produce is generated in-house, through a commission or a special project originating with one of our directors. Playwrights who have established their careers with productions at other recognized theatres stand the best chance of being produced at the Goodman."

GOODSPEED OPERA HOUSE
East Haddam, CT 06423 (203) 873-8664
Contact: Michael Price, Executive Director **Theatre:** professional not-for-profit **Works:** musicals **2nd productions:** "Not usually." **Specifications:** maximum cast: 20; limited technical requirements

Stages: proscenium, 400 seats; flexible proscenium, 200 seats
Submission policy: send SASE for submission information sheet
Best time: Jan.-Mar. **Response:** 1 month query; 9 months script
Your chances: 300 submissions/3 productions **Remuneration:**
no **Future commitment:** yes **Programs:** readings, staged
readings, workshop productions

THE GREAT-AMERICAN THEATRE COMPANY
Box 92123, Milwaukee, WI 53202 (414) 276-4230
Contact: Annie Jurczyk, Managing Director **Theatre:** professional
not-for-profit **Works:** children's plays, translations and adaptations
2nd productions: no **Special interests:** "New children's plays;
adaptations of classic tales and stories." **Specifications:** maximum
cast: 12; no more than 2 sets; playing time: 45-70 minutes **Tours:**
yes **Stages:** proscenium, 2200 seats; proscenium, 1340 seats
Audience: ages 5-18 **Submission policy:** unsolicited script with
SASE; professional recommendation; showcase **Best time:** Jan.-
Mar. **Response:** 4-6 weeks **Your chances:** 3-5 submissions/
"production of fewer than half of these" **Remuneration:** salary or
negotiable fee

GREAT LAKES THEATER FESTIVAL
1501 Euclid Ave. Suite 250, Cleveland, OH 44115
(216) 241-5490 Contact: Victoria Bussert, Associate Artistic
Director **Theatre:** professional not-for-profit **Works:** full-length
plays **2nd productions:** "Yes and no; depends upon the year."
Specifications: maximum cast 8, minimal sets, simple costumes
Stage: proscenium, 1000 seats **Casting:** "Agent submission,
auditions." **Submission policy:** professional recommendation
Best time: Oct.-Apr. **Response:** 6 months **Your chances:**
"hundreds of submissions/no productions to date"

GREAT NORTH AMERICAN HISTORY THEATRE
30 East 10th St., St. Paul, MN 55101 (612) 292-4323
Contact: Lance Belville, Co-Artisitc Director **Theatre:**
professional not-for-profit **Works:** full-length plays, translations,
adaptations, musicals **2nd productions:** yes **Exclusive
interest:** history **Specifications:** maximum cast: 8-10; few and
simple sets; musicals must be small; no pageants **Tours:** "Yes,
very important." **Stage:** "Thrust that can become arena, 597
seats." **Audience:** "Wide range of ages, economic levels and
educational backgrounds." **Submission policy:** query/synopsis;
professional recommendation; agent submission **Response:** 1 month
query; 3-6 months or more script **Your chances:** 150 submissions;
"we read scripts to find authors we are interested in; then, we
commission scripts from them" **Remuneration:** "Yes, commission."

Programs: readings, staged readings, development, internships
Advice: "Plays must bear some relationship to historical people, places or events--preferably but not exclusively in the U.S."

GREY ENTERTAINMENT & MEDIA
875 Third Ave., New York, NY 10022 (212) 303-2400
Contact: Jeffrey Ash, Producer **Production company:** off Broadway **Works:** full-length plays, musicals **Specifications:** musicals must be small **Submission policy:** unsolicited script with SASE

THE GROUP THEATRE
See The Seattle Group Theatre listing in this section.

GROVE THEATRE COMPANY
12852 Main St., Garden Grove, CA 92640
(714) 636-7213, 638-6747 Contact: Thomas F. Bradac, Producing Artistic Director **Theatre:** professional not-for-profit **Works:** full-length plays, translations, adaptations **Specifications:** maximum cast: 10 preferred; single set **Stages:** proscenium, 172 seats; ampitheatre, 550 seats **Submission policy:** professional recommendation **Best time:** Aug.-Dec. **Response:** 4-6 weeks **Comment:** Formerly Grove Shakespeare Festival.

THE GUTHRIE THEATER
725 Vineland Pl., Minneapolis, MN 55403
(612) 347-1100 Contact: Mark Bly, Literary Manager/ Dramaturg **Theatre:** professional not-for-profit **Works:** full-length plays, translations, adaptations, musicals **2nd productions:** yes **Special interest:** contemporary issues **Stage:** thrust, 1441 seats **Submission policy:** query/synopsis with 10-page dialogue sample; agent submission **Response:** 1-2 weeks query; 1-3 months script **Future commitment:** yes **Comment:** See Stelling, Lucille Johnsen, "The Guthrie Theater: A Dream Turns 25," *TheaterWeek* (Aug. 22, 1988), 44-49.

HANGAR THEATRE
Box 205, Ithaca, NY 14851 (607) 273-8588
Contact: Robert Moss, Artistic Director **Theatre:** professional not-for-profit **Works:** one-acts, children's plays **Stage:** 3/4 thrust, 380 seats **Submission policy:** query/synopsis **Best time:** Oct.-Jan. **Response:** 1 month query; 3 months script **Programs:** 2nd Company performs one-acts before and after mainstage shows; KIDDSTUFF: children's plays performed Saturdays and alternate Thursdays

HARRISBURG COMMUNITY THEATRE
513 Hurlock St., Harrisburg, PA 17110 **(717) 238-7382**
Contact: Thomas G. Hostetter, Artistic Director **Theatre:** community/non-professional **Works:** full-length plays, adaptations, musicals **2nd productions:** no **Specifications:** maximum cast: 25; no fly space **Stage:** proscenium, 450 seats **Casting:** open auditions **Audience:** "Moderate outlook, middle to upper class, largely 40-55 age range, not wildly experimental in taste." **Submission policy:** query/synopsis; professional recommendation **Best time:** Aug.-Oct. **Response:** 6 months **Your chances:** 15-20 submissions/1 production scheduled for 1990-91 season **Remuneration:** negotiable

HARTFORD STAGE COMPANY
50 Church St., Hartford, CT 06103 **(203) 525-5601**
Contact: Literary Associate **Theatre:** professional not-for-profit **Works:** full-length plays, translations, adaptations **2nd productions:** yes **Stage:** thrust, 489 seats **Casting:** "LORT B contract; non-traditional casting." **Audience:** "Subscription—most from this area, some from NY and MA." **Submission policy:** query/synopsis; professional recommendation; agent submission **Response:** 7-10 days query; 3-6 months script **Your chances:** 600 submissions/0-1 production **Recent production of unsolicited work:** 1988 **Remuneration:** standard contract **Future commitment:** only when co-producing

HAVURAT YISRAEL THEATRE GROUP
Havurat Yisrael Synagogue, 106-20 70th Ave.,
Forest Hills, NY 11375 **(718) 997-1899**
Contact: Alan Magill, Artistic Director **Theatre:** community/ non-professional **Works:** full-length plays, one-acts, children's plays, cabaret/revues **2nd productions:** yes **Special interest:** "Works relating to the trials and triumphs of deepening one's Jewish commitment." **Specifications:** maximum cast: 6-8; simple sets **Stage:** open space, 100 seats **Audience:** "Mostly from Forest Hills area—Jewish orientation." **Submission policy:** unsolicited script with SASE **Response:** 2-6 months **Program:** staged readings **Advice:** "Language should be appropriate for presentation at an orthodox synagogue."

HEARTLAND THEATRE COMPANY
c/o McLean County Arts Center, 601 North East St.,
Bloomington, IL 61701 **(309) 829-0011**
Contact: Philip Shaw, Artistic Director **Theatre:** professional not-for-profit **Works:** full-length plays, one-acts, adaptations, children's plays **2nd productions:** yes **Special interest:**

"Plays that treat the theme of living in the Midwest within interesting and challenging stylistic contexts." **Specifications:** maximum cast: 5-8; single set **Tours:** "Some children's shows." **Stage:** flexible, varying number of seats **Casting:** "Some shows are precast from a pool, open auditions are held for other shows." **Audience:** "Very heterogeneous: all ages, social strata." **Submission policy:** unsolicited script with SASE; query/synopsis with dialogue sample **Best time:** Oct.-Apr. **Response:** 2 weeks query; 6 months script **Your chances:** 100--150 submissions/1-2 productions **Remuneration:** $35 per performance, possible transportation **Future commitment:** "If we are interested in further development and production, we prefer a 1-year option." **Programs:** readings, staged readings, workshop productions **Advice:** "Our motto is 'We'll provoke you!' We are looking for gutsy plays that offer the audience the opportunity to be confronted by an aesthetic 'bucket of cold water' in the face! Experimentation with language and theatrical styles are our preferred stock in trade."

HEDGEROW THEATRE
146 W. Rose Valley Rd., Rose Valley, PA 19086
(215) 565-4211 Contact: David zum Brunnen, Managing Director **Theatre:** professional not-for-profit **Works:** full-length plays, children's plays **2nd productions:** yes **Stages:** flexible, 150 seats; studio, 30 seats **Submission policy:** query/synopsis **Best time:** spring **Response:** 1 month query; 2 months script **Remuneration:** negotiable **Comment:** Inquire for detailed information; theatre burned in 1985 and was under construction when *The Playwright's Companion 1990* went to press.

HEIGHTS SHOWCASE
c/o Arts Inter Action, 711 W. 168th St.,
New York, NY 10032 (212) 222-8778
Contact: Eleanor Burke, President **Theatre:** off off Broadway **Works:** full-length plays, one-acts, translations, adaptations, plays for young audiences **2nd productions:** if previous production was not full production **Special interest:** works for inter-racial casting **Submission policy:** unsolicited script with SASE **Stage:** auditorium proscerium, 99 seats **Casting:** "Open audtions with special consideration for Heights Showcase members." **Audience:** "Well mixed: seniors, young people, neighborhood and regular theatregoers." **Program:** readings; Heights Showcase Playwriting Contest (see Contests) **Advice:** "Please send a clean, readable copy." **Comments:** Theatre is located at 54 Nagle Ave., New York City. Small fee for membership. "We are funded by the New York State Council on the Arts and the New York City Cultural Affairs Dept."

HERITAGE ARTISTS, LTD.
Box 586, Cohoes, NY 12047   (518) 235-7969
Contact: Robert W. Tolan, Producing Director   **Theatre:** professional not-for-profit **Works:** full-length and one-act musicals, cabaret/revues, plays with music **2nd productions:** yes **Special interests:** musicals for children; cabarets **Maximum cast:** 12-15, all principals or very small ensemble   **Stage:** thrust, 250-350 seats   **Submission policy:** unsolicited script with SASE; query/synopsis; professional recommendation; agent submission **Response:** 1-2 months **Your chances:** 60-80 submissions/1-2 productions   **Recent production of unsolicited work:** yes **Remuneration:** travel, housing for readings; royalty for production **Future commitment:** negotiable **Program:** readings **Comment:** See Filichia, Peter, "Only 175 Minutes From Broadway," *TheaterWeek* (Jan. 23, 1989), 16-23.

THE HIGHWAY ENSEMBLE
2126 The Highway, Wilmington, DE 19810
(302) 475-9805   Contact: Alicia Ann Chomo, President **Theatre:** community/non-professional **Works:** full-length plays, one-acts, adaptations **2nd productions:** yes **Specifications:** maximum cast: 10; limited lighting **Stage:** flexible outdoor theatre **Audience:** "Small but dedicated, with 100 people attending each performance." **Submission policy:** unsolicited script with SASE; query/synopsis; professional recommendation **Response:** 1-2 months **Remuneration:** no **Programs:** readings, staged readings

HILBERRY THEATRE
Wayne State University, Detroit, MI 48202
(313) 577-2972   Contact: Robert Hazzard, Chairman **Theatre:** college/university, graduate repertory company **Works:** full-length plays, one-acts, translations, adaptations, children's plays   **2nd productions:** yes **Specifications:** maximum cast: 19; no avant garde, no nudity or profanity **Stages:** proscenium; modified thrust, 530 seats **Audience:** "Mixed, city and university." **Submission policy:** unsolicited script with SASE and resume **Best time:** late fall-early winter **Response:** 3 months **Your chances:** 18-20 submissions/1 production   **Remuneration:** negotiable **Advice:** "Open to all styles and approaches."

HIP POCKET THEATRE
1627 Fairmount, Ft. Worth, TX 76104 (817) 927-2833
Contact: Johnny Simons, Artistic Director **Theatre:** professional not-for-profit **Works:** full-length plays, translations, adaptations, musicals **Special interest:** "Plays that have elements of fantasy and do not take place in a New York apartment." **Maximum cast:** 15

(flexible) **Tours:** yes **Stages:** flexible outdoor ampitheatre, 200 seats; flexible, 112 seats **Audience:** "Wide variety of ages and backgrounds from highly educated professionals to working-class folks." **Submission policy:** unsolicited script with SASE **Best time:** summer **Response:** 2-3 weeks **Your chances:** 150 submissions/5 productions **Remuneration:** negotiable **Advice:** "Make your work fresh, exciting, challenging, demanding imagination and creativity to produce."

THE HIPPODROME STATE THEATRE
25 SE 2nd Pl., Gainesville, FL 32601 (904) 373-5968
Contact: Mary Hausch, Producing Director **Theatre:** professional not-for-profit **Works:** full-length plays, one-acts, translations, adaptations, musicals, children's plays, cabaret/revues **2nd productions:** yes **Specifications:** small cast, unit set preferred **Stages:** thrust, 266 seats; flexible, 87 seats **Submission policy:** query/synopsis; agent submission **Response:** 2 weeks query; 4 months script

HOLLYWOOD ACTORS THEATRE, INC.
Santa Rosa, CA This theatre did not respond to our 1990 questionnaire, and its phone has been disconnected.

HOME FOR CONTEMPORARY THEATRE AND ART
44 Walker St., New York, NY 10013 (212) 431-7434
Contact: Douglas Grabowski, Literary Manager **Theatre:** professional not-for-profit **Works:** full-length plays, one-acts, musicals, cabaret/revues **2nd productions:** "If not previously produced in New York." **Maximum cast:** 10 **Stage:** flexible **Casting:** open auditions **Audience:** "Broad range, chiefly from Manhattan and Brooklyn; young (20's-30's); racially mixed." **Submission policy:** unsolicited script with SASE and resume; query/synopsis with resume and dialogue sample; professional recommendation; agent submission **Response:** 2 months **Your chances:** 400 submissions/varying number of productions **Recent production of unsolicited work:** 1989 **Remuneration:** "Fee or percentage." **Future commitment:** "Percentage of future rights for 10 years." **Programs:** readings, workshop productions, internships, residencies **Advice:** "If you approach us with a co-production, we are more likely to work with you."

HONOLULU COMMUNITY THEATRE
529 Makapuu Ave., Honolulu, HI 96816 (808) 734-8763
Contact: Jim Hutchison Artistic Director **Theatre:** community/ non-professional **Works:** full-length plays, one-acts, adaptations, children's plays **2nd productions:** "Sometimes." **Specifications:**

20' x 30' proscenium stage **Audience:** "Middle to upper class, all
races, ages 25-85." **Submission policy:** send SASE for guidelines
Your chances: "few submissions/1 production every other year"
Remuneration: "Equivalent to royalty." **Programs:** readings,
workshop productions, development; "staged reading or production
during a dark night of a regular season production"

HONOLULU THEATRE FOR YOUTH
Box 3257, Honolulu, HI 96801   (808) 521-3487
Contact: John Kauffman, Artistic Director **Theatre:** professional
not-for-profit **Works:** children's full-length plays, one-acts and
adaptations   **2nd productions:** yes   **Special interests:**
"Concerns of contemporary young people; Pacific Rim cultures;
adaptations of fairy tales or classics." **Specifications:** maximum
cast: 10; simple production requirements **Stages:** proscenium, 650
seats; auditorium proscenium, 650 seats; flexible, 300 seats
Audience: "Target audience is youth (K-high school) and their
families." **Submission policy:** unsolicited script with SASE;
query/synopsis **Response:** 1 month query; 6 months script **Your
chances:** 75 submissions/1-2 productions   **Remuneration:**
royalty; commission **Programs:** readings, staged readings

HORIZONS:
THEATRE FROM A WOMAN'S PERSPECTIVE
1041 Wisconsin Ave. NW, Washington, DC 20007
(202) 342-5503 Contact: Carole Myers, Associate Artistic
Director **Theatre:** professional not-for-profit **Works:** full-length
plays, one-acts, translations, adaptations **Exclusive interest:**
women playwrights **Specifications:** single set **Stages:** various
spaces; open endstage, 150 seats (scheduled to open Mar. 1990)
Submission policy: query/synopsis preferred; unsolicited script
with SASE **Response:** 3 months query; 6 months script

HORIZON THEATRE COMPANY
Box 5376, Station E, Atlanta, GA 30307 (404) 584-7450
Contact: Lisa Adler, Jeffrey Adler, Co-Artistic Directors
Theatre: professional not-for-profit **Works:** full-length plays **2nd
productions:** yes **Special interests:** "Atlanta, Southeastern and
world premieres; strong female roles; plays with social or political
implications." **Maximum cast:** 12 **Tours:** yes **Stage:** flexible,
120-200 seats **Casting:** "Ensemble of 2-10 actors aged late
20's-early 30's." **Submission policy:** unsolicited script with
SASE; query/synopsis with resume professional recommendation;
agent submission **Best times:** Nov.-Jan., Jun.-Aug. **Response:** 1
month if interested in query; 2-4 months solicited script; 12 months
script **Your chances:** 300 submissions/1-2 productions

Remuneration: "Percentage of box office plus rehearsal stipend."
Future commitment: negotiable for world premiere **Programs**:
readings, staged readings, workshop productions **Advice**: "We are
particularly interested in satire and comedy of an off-beat nature and
dramas with socio-political significance."

HORSE CAVE THEATRE
Box 215, Horse Cave, KY 42749 (502) 786-1200
Contact: Warren Hammack, Director **Theatre**: professional not-
for-profit **Works**: full-length plays, translations, adaptations **2nd
productions**: yes **Exclusive interests**: Kentucky playwrights;
"unproduced plays about Kentucky life—past, present or future."
Specifications: maximum cast: 10; single or unit set preferred
Tours: yes **Stage**: thrust, 347 seats **Audience**: "All ages,
attitudes, interests, levels of education, ethnic composition."
Submission policy: professional or personal recommendation;
unsolicited script with SASE (reading not guaranteed) **Best time**:
Oct.-Apr. **Response**: several weeks **Your chances**: 30-50
submissions/1-2 productions **Recent production of unsolicited
work**: no **Remuneration**: percentage **Future commitment**:
usually **Programs**: readings, staged readings, internships

HUDSON GUILD THEATRE
441 W. 26th St., New York, NY 10001 (212) 760-9836
Contact: Steven Ramay, Associate Director **Theatre**: off
Broadway **Works**: full-length plays, translations, adaptations,
musicals **2nd productions**: if not produced in New York **Special
interests**: "Social and political significance; entertainment value."
Maximum cast: 7 **Stage**: proscenium, 135 seats **Audience**:
"Various groups; large subscriber base." **Submission policy**:
unsolicited script with SASE **Response**: 4 months **Your chances**:
1200 submissions/5+ submissions **Remuneration**: $1000 **Future
commitment**: yes **Programs**: readings, staged readings,
workshop productions, development, internships **Comment**: See
Raymond, Gerard, "A Neighborhood Theater," *TheaterWeek*, (Jun. 27,
1988), 22-28.

HUNTINGTON THEATRE COMPANY
**Boston University Theatre, 264 Huntington Ave.,
Boston, MA 02115 (617) 353-3320**
Contact: Peter Altman, Producing Director **Theatre**: professional
not-for-profit **Works**: full-length plays, translations, adaptations,
musicals **2nd productions**: yes **Special interests**: New England
authors; new plays with Boston or New England themes **Stage**:
proscenium, 850 seats **Submission policy**: query/synopsis;
professional recommendation **Response**: 2-3 months

IDAHO SHAKESPEARE FESTIVAL
Box 9365, Boise, ID 83707
Contact: Rod Ceballos, Artistic Director **Theatre:** professional not-for-profit **Works:** full-length plays **Special interests:** "Women's issues; regional focus on West and Pacific Northwest." **Stage:** thrust, 650 seats **Casting:** open auditions **Submission policy:** When *The Playwright's Companion 1990* went to press this theatre was not open to query/synopses or unsolicited scripts; playwrights are advised to send SASE for guidelines before submitting any materials.

ILLINOIS THEATRE CENTER
400A Lakewood Blvd., Park Forest, IL 60466
(312) 481-3510 **Contact:** Steve S. Billig, Artistic Director **Theatre:** professional not-for-profit **Works:** full-length plays, musicals **Special interest:** small-cast plays **Maximum cast:** 9 for play, 14 for musical **Stage:** proscenium-thrust, 200 seats **Submission policy:** query/synopsis **Response:** 1 month query; 2 months script

ILLUSION THEATER
528 Hennepin Ave. Suite 704, Minneapolis, MN 55403
(612) 339-4944 **Contact:** Michael Robins, Producing Director **Theatre:** professional not-for-profit **Works:** full-length plays, one-acts, translations, adaptations, musicals **2nd productions:** no **Exclusive interest:** "Collaboration between writer and company to create new works." **Maximum cast:** 12 **Tours:** "Irregular transfer production to touring production." **Stage:** semi-thrust, 250 seats **Audience:** "Educated, adventuresome, thoughtful." **Submission policy:** query/synopsis with resume; professional recommendation **Best times:** May-Jun., Oct.-Nov. **Response:** 8 weeks query; 6 months follow-up **Remuneration/future commitment:** negotiable **Programs:** readings, workshop productions, development, internships **Advice:** "Send resume with cover letter explaining why you are interested in collaborating with the company."

ILLUSTRATED STAGE COMPANY
25 Van Ness Ave., San Francisco, CA 94102
(415) 861-6655 **Contact:** Barbara Malinowski, Artistic Director **Theatre:** professional not-for-profit **Works:** full-length plays, one-acts, adaptations, musicals **2nd productions:** "Yes, but not a priority." **Special interest:** political issues **Stages:** proscenium, 134 seats; thrust, 90 seats; black box, 70 seats **Casting:** "Through open auditions and casting services." **Audience:** "Mixed--wide range." **Submission policy:** introductory letter

followed by unsolicited script with SASE; query/synopsis
Response: 6 months **Your chances:** 400 submissions/2
productions **Programs:** staged readings, development, classes

THE IMMEDIATE THEATRE
1225 W. Belmont, Chicago, IL 60657 (312) 929-1031
Contact: Jeff Ginsberg, Co-Artistic Director **Theatre:**
professional not-for-profit **Works:** full-length plays, one-acts,
translations, adaptations **Special interests:** "Contemporary
American social and political issues; language; unique voices; women
writers." **Specifications:** maximum cast: 8-10, doubling possible;
limited fly space **Stage:** 3/4 thrust, 150 seats **Casting:** "From
resident ensemble: all white, age range 25-40." **Audience:**
"Ethnically diverse; large Hispanic and senior citizen populations."
Submission policy: query/synopsis preferred; unsolicited script
with SASE; professional recommendation; agent submission
Response: 3 weeks query; 3-6 months script **Your chances:** 20
submissions/2 productions in 4 years **Remuneration:** "Something
equitable." **Advice:** "Our spaces are very intimate."

INDEPENDENCE THEATER COMPANY
Box 112, Ft. Lee, NJ 07024 (201) 592-6060
Contact: Michele Ortlip, Producing Artistic Director **Theatre:**
professional not-for-profit **Works:** full-length plays, translations,
musicals, children's plays **2nd productions:** yes **Special
interest:** "Life-affirming works." **Specifications:** maximum
cast: 8; single or simple set; limitations on lighting; musicals must be
simple; "no experimental work" **Tours:** "Yes, plays for children or
young adults with simple or no sets." **Stage:** proscenium-flexible
apron, 450 seats **Audience:** middle to upper class **Submission
policy:** query/synopsis with resume and dialogue sample **Best
time:** Oct.-Mar. **Response:** 2 months **Your chances:** 100
submissions/1 production **Future commitment:** "Credit in all
productions or publications." **Programs:** readings, staged readings,
classes **Remuneration:** no **Advice:** "Simple and honest, humorous
if possible; issues and concepts for a contemporary audience."

THE INDEPENDENT EYE
208 E. King St., Lancaster, PA 17602 (717) 393-9088
Contact: Conrad Bishop, Producing Director **Theatre:** professional
not-for-profit **Works:** full-length plays, related one-acts, musicals
2nd productions: yes **Special interest:** "Well-crafted work."
Specifications: small cast, maximum 4 for musicals; unit set
Stage: open endstage, 100 seats **Casting:** "Local; few minorities
are available." **Submission policy:** query/synopsis with 5-page
dialogue sample **Best time:** Nov.-Dec. **Response:** 1 month query;

3 months script **Your chances:** 100+ submissions/1 production
Remuneration: "Royalty against percentage of receipts."

INDIANA REPERTORY THEATRE
140 W. Washington, Indianapolis, IN 46204
(317) 635-5277 Contact: Janet Allen, Artistic Associate
Theatre: professional not-for-profit **Works:** full-length plays,
translations, adaptations **2nd productions:** yes **Special
interests:** theatricality; rich language; adaptations of classic
material **Specifications:** maximum cast: 10; single or unit set
Stages: modified proscenium, 600 seats; proscenium, 250 seats
Audience: "Average age about 45; mostly white collar
professionals." **Submission policy:** query/synopsis; professional
recommendation; agent submission; commission **Best time:** May-
Aug. **Response:** 2-3 months query; 5-6 months script **Your
chances:** 200 submissions/0 productions **Remuneration:**
"Approximately 6%." **Future commitments:** 120-day production
option after closing in Indianapolis; future billing; 10% of playwright's
compensation for first 5 years after closing, 5% for following 5 years
Program: readings

INTAR HISPANIC AMERICAN THEATRE
Box 788, New York, NY 10109 (212) 695-6134, -6135
Contact: Roger Durling, Literary Manager **Theatre:** professional
not-for-profit **Works:** full-length plays, one-acts, translations,
adaptations, musicals **2nd productions:** if not produced off off
Broadway **Exclusive interests:** Hispanic-American writers
residing in U.S.A. and writing in English; translations and adaptations
of Hispanic works **Specifications:** maximum cast: 10; limited
budget; no wing space **Stages:** proscenium, 99 seats; proscenium,
75 seats **Audience:** "Mixed cultural." **Submission policy:**
unsolicited script with SASE **Best time:** summer **Response:** 3-6
months **Your chances:** 200 submissions/3 productions plus
readings **Remuneration:** varies **Future commitment:** yes
Programs: workshop productions; INTAR Hispanic Playwrights-In-
Residence Laboratory (see Special Programs)

INTERMOUNTAIN ACTORS ENSEMBLE, INC.
1735 S. 1300 E, Salt Lake City, UT 84105
(801) 485-7249 Contact: Ron Burnett, Producing Director
Theatre: professional not-for-profit **Works:** full-length plays,
one-acts, musicals, children's plays **2nd productions:**
"Sometimes." **Special interests:** "American drama; plays of
topical interest; historical plays of this region." **Specifications:**
maximum cast: 8 preferred; no wing space **Stage:** flexible
Audience: "Upwardly mobile who come here to ski in winter and

relax in summer; Mormon residents, generally middle class."
Submission policy: query/synopsis   **Best time:** summer
Response: 3 weeks   **Your chances:** 30 submissions/3 productions
Remuneration: "Depends upon grant situation and audience."
Program: workshop productions   **Advice:** "Present the play in playscript format."

INTIMAN THEATRE COMPANY
Box 19645, Seattle, WA 98109   (206) 626-0775
Contact: Susan Fenichell, Associate Artistic Director **Theatre:** professional not-for-profit **Works:** full-length and one-act translations and adaptations **Special interests:** new adaptations and translations of classics; new plays with classic themes **Maximum cast:** 8 **Stage:** thrust, 410 seats **Submission policy:** query/synopsis **Response:** 6 months **Future commitment:** no **Program:** staged readings **Advice:** "Send query/synopsis only."

INVISIBLE THEATRE
1400 N. First Ave., Tucson, AZ 85719   (602) 882-9721
Contact: Deborah Dickey, Literary Manager **Theatre:** off off Broadway **Works:** full-length plays, one-acts, translations, adaptations, musicals **Special interest:** contemporary issues **2nd productions:** yes **Specifications:** maximum cast: 8; simple sets **Stage:** flexible, 78 seats **Audience:** "Middle to upper middle class, generally liberal." **Submission policy:** query/synopsis **Best time:** Jun.-Jul. **Response:** 1-6 months **Your chances:** 25 submissions/1 production **Remuneration:** percentage **Program:** staged readings

IRONBOUND THEATRE
179 Van Buren St., Newark, NJ 07105   (201) 792-3524, 351-6685 Contact: Henry A. Brown, Playsearch
Theatre: community/non-professional **Works:** full-length plays, one-acts, musicals **2nd productions:** yes **Special interests:** "Contemporary American themes; urban settings; unproduced scripts are given preference." **Specifications:** "Expensive technical effects may prove prohibitive." **Stage:** thrust, 80 seats **Audience:** "Well educated, middle to upper middle class; broad ethnic spectrum and sampling of occupations." **Submission policy:** unsolicited script with SASE and synopsis; query/synopsis **Best time:** fall-winter **Response:** 3-4 weeks query; 3-4 months script **Your chances:** 100+ submissions/1-2 productions plus 7-10 staged readings; "we are committed to producing at least 2 original American plays per season" **Remuneration:** royalty for full production **Program:** staged reading prior to possible mainstage production

Advice: "Send plays that are at least ready for a staged reading. Be willing to participate in reading/development process."

IRONDALE ENSEMBLE PROJECT
782 West End Ave., New York, NY 10025
(212) 633-1292 Contact: Steven Osgood, Dramaturg
Theatre: professional not-for-profit **Works:** full-length plays, one-acts, translations, adaptations, musicals, children's plays **Special interests:** political/social relevance; works to be developed with resident ensemble **Specifications:** maximum cast: 8-9; unit set **Stage:** black box, 50 seats **Submission policy:** query/synopsis preferred; unsolicited script with SASE **Response:** 2-4 weeks query; 6 months script **Comment:** See Kantor, Michael, "Research Theater," *TheaterWeek* (May 1, 1989), 16-21.

IUPUI UNIVERSITY THEATRE
525 N. Blackford St., Indianapolis, IN 46202
(317) 274-0556 Contact: J. Edgar Webb, Director, Theatre Programs **Theatre:** university/college **Works:** full-length plays, one-acts, children's plays **2nd productions:** "Rarely." **Special interests:** "Characters of college age; uplifting subjects; dramatic action is a must." **Specifications:** budget limitations **Stage:** flexible **Audience:** "On site audience is mature. Tour audiences are generally school children, parents and teachers." **Submission policy:** query/synopsis; "our playwriting class" **Best time:** spring for following school year **Response:** 1 week query; time varies script **Your chances:** adult plays: 12-15 submissions/1 production **Remuneration:** standard royalty **Programs:** classes; Indiana University-Purdue University at Indianapolis Playwriting for Youth Competition and Symposium (see Contests)

JACKSONVILLE UNIVERSITY
DIVISION OF ART, THEATRE ARTS AND DANCE
Jacksonville, FL 32211 (904) 744-3950
Contact: Betty H. Swenson, Chair **Theatre:** university/college **Works:** full-length plays, one-acts **2nd productions:** no **Special interest:** "Off-beat, experimental scripts." **Specifications:** maximum cast: 20; "reasonable technical requirements" **Tours:** yes **Stage:** proscenium **Audience:** community and college **Submission policy:** send SASE for guidelines **Best time:** fall

JAM & COMPANY
331 W. 38th St. #5, New York, NY 10018
Contact: John A. Mudd, Artistic Director **Theatre:** off off Broadway **Works:** full-length plays, one-acts, translations, adaptations, cabaret/revues **2nd productions:** yes **Maximum**

cast: 10   Stage: flexible, variable number of seats   **Submission policy:** query/synopsis

JANE HARMON ASSOCIATES
One Lincoln Plaza Suite 28-0, New York, NY 10023
(212) 571-6453, 362-6836   **Contact:** Jane Harmon, Producer
Production company: Broadway   **Works:** full-length plays
Submission policy: query/synopsis; agent submission

JANUS THEATRE COMPANY, INC.
Phoenix, AZ   Our 1990 questionnaire was returned as "undeliverable," and no phone number is listed for this theatre.

JCC CENTER STAGE
1200 Edgewood Ave., Rochester, NY 14618
(716) 461-2000   **Contact:** Herb Katz, Arts Director
Theatre: community/non-professional readers theatre   **Works:** full-length plays, one-acts, translations, adaptations, musicals
Special interest: Jewish subject matter   **Maximum cast:** 10
Stage: thrust **Audience:** "Sophisticated, affluent, all ages."
Submission policy: query/synopsis   **Response:** immediate query; 1 month script   **Your chances:** 25 submissions/variable number of readings   **Comment:** "At this time in our readers theatre we do not do full productions, but we are not closed to the idea."

JEAN COCTEAU REPERTORY
330 Bowery, New York, NY 10012 (212) 677-0060
Contact: Robert Hupp, Artistic Director   **Theatre:** professional not-for-profit **Works:** full-length plays, translations   **Exclusive interest:** "Intellectual, philosophical, poetic content."
Specifications: "No 'thesis plays' or family dramas."   **Stage:** proscenium, 140 seats   **Submission policy:** query/synopsis
Response: 3-4 weeks query; 3-4 months script

JEWISH REPERTORY THEATRE
344 E. 14th St., New York, NY 10003 (212) 674-7200
Contact: Edward M. Cohen, Associate Director   **Theatre:** off Broadway, Equity mini-contract **Works:** full-length plays, one-acts, musicals   **2nd productions:** if not previously produced off off Broadway **Exclusive interest:** Jewish themes   **Maximum cast:** 8 **Stage:** proscenium, 100 seats **Submission policy:** unsolicited script with SASE   **Best time:** Sept.-May   **Response:** 4-6 weeks
Remuneration: "6% of gross."   **Programs:** staged readings, residencies; Writer's Lab: readings with $50 stipend (inquire)
Comment: See Siegel, Fern, "Defining a Jewish Voice," *TheaterWeek* (Jun. 13, 1988), 50-54.

JOMANDI PRODUCTIONS, INC.
1444 Mayson St. NE, Atlanta, GA 30324
(404) 876-6346 Contact: Marsha A. Jackson, Co-Artistic/ Managing Director **Theatre:** professional not-for-profit **Works:** full-length plays, one-acts, adaptations, musicals, children's plays **2nd productions:** yes **Special interests:** "African-American themes or central characters; contemporary themes." **Specifications:** maximum cast: 15; no more than 4 sets; no fly space; minimal orchestra space **Tours:** "National and international." **Stages:** thrust, 378-420 seats; flexible, 150-200 seats **Casting:** "Multi-ethnic." **Audience:** "Multi-ethnic; majority African-American; predominant age: 30-50 and college/university population." **Submission policy:** query/synopsis with resume and dialogue sample **Best time:** spring **Response:** 2 weeks query; 12 weeks script **Your chances:** 15-20 submissions/12 productions **Remuneration:** "Average $750 on unproduced play; percentage of gross on previously produced play." **Future commitments:** "1st presenter royalty and 1st option on commercial production." **Programs:** readings, staged readings, development, classes

THE JULIAN THEATRE
777 Valencia, San Francisco, CA 94110 (415) 626-8986
Contact: Richard Reineccius, Artistic Director **Theatre:** professional not-for-profit **Works:** full-length plays, one-acts, translations **2nd productions:** yes **Special interests:** "Thought, wit, social/political significance; West Coast playwrights; collaboration with playwrights." **Tours:** yes **Stage:** flexible, 150 seats **Audience:** "Multi-cultural." **Submission policy:** query/ synopsis with dialogue sample **Response:** 3 months **Your chances:** 50-250 submissions/2-4 productions **Remuneration:** "5% of gross." **Programs:** classes, internships

JUST US THEATER COMPANY/CLUB ZEBRA
Box 42271, Atlanta, GA 30311-0271 (404) 753-2399
Contact: Pearl Cleage, Artistic Director; Zaron Burnett, Producing Director **Theatre:** professional not-for-profit **Works:** performance art, one-acts, music **2nd productions:** yes **Special interests:** "Black performance artists and writers experimenting with new forms, especially video and movement incorporated into performance." **Specifications:** "No traditional plays." **Stage:** "The Club Zebra performance installation, which is set up to recall the Harlem speakeasies of the 20's." **Audience:** "80%-90% black." **Submission policy:** query/ synopsis **Remuneration:** "Varies with needs or individual artist or performer; competitive artistic fees and all expenses." **Advice:** "It is important to maintain the element of surprise."

KALAMAZOO CIVIC PLAYERS
329 S. Park, Kalamazoo, MI 49007 (616) 343-2280
Contact: David Grapes, Associate Director **Theatre:** community/
non-professional **Works:** full-length plays, musicals, children's
plays **Special interests:** musicals; plays for or about women **2nd
productions:** yes **Stages:** proscenium, 536 seats; arena, 150
seats; flexible **Audience:** "Sophisticated, well educated, somewhat
conservative but open to new work." **Submission policy:**
unsolicited script with SASE; professional recommendation; agent
submission **Best time:** Oct.-Nov. **Response:** 6 months query; 1
year script **Your chances:** 40 submissions/1-3 productions
Remuneration: "Royalty fee, possible transportation." **Programs:**
staged readings, workshop productions **Advice:** "Directors at Civic
also work in other community and non-profit theatres and are always
on the lookout for exciting new works."

KEARNEY STATE COLLEGE THEATRE
905 W. 25th St., Kearney, NE 68849 (308) 234-8409
Contact: Jack Garrison, Festival Coordinator **Theatre:** university/
college **Works:** full-length plays, one-acts, adaptations, musicals
2nd productions: yes **Special interest:** "Scripts should have
subject matter dealing with Great Plains/Midwest region, but we will
accept work from any cultural background." **Specifications:**
maximum cast: 15; single set **Stages:** flexible amphitheatre, 200
seats; black box, 200 seats; proscenium, 334 seats **Casting:** "Open
auditions to students, faculty and community members." **Audience:**
"General population including students and community." **Policy:**
query/synopsis with resume **Best time:** Dec.-Mar. **Your
chances:** 50 submissions/4 productions **Remuneration:** "$500
plus stipend." **Programs:** readings, staged readings, workshop
productions, development, internships, residencies, classes; Great
Platte River Playwrights Festival (see Contests)

KILGORE COLLEGE THEATRE
TEXAS SHAKESPEARE FESTIVAL
Kilgore, TX This theatre is no longer open to submissions.

LACE PRODUCTIONS
23 W. 73rd St., New York, NY 10023
(212) 496-0251 Contact: Francine Mancini, Executive Artistic
Director **Theatre:** off off Broadway, professional not-for-profit
Works: full-length plays, one-acts, children's plays **2nd
productions:** yes **Special interest:** "Women's social issues."
Specifications: maximum cast: 10; single set **Stage:** flexible
Submission policy: unsolicited script with SASE; professional
recommendation **Response:** 6 months **Your chances:** 100's of

submissions/3-5 productions **Remuneration:** no **Programs:** staged readings, readings, workshop productions, development, classes

L.A. DESIGNERS' THEATRE
Box 1883, Studio City, CA 91614
(818) 769-9000, (213) 650-9600 **Contact:** Richard Niederberg, Artistic Director **Theatre:** professional not-for-profit **Works:** full-length plays, thematically related one-acts, translations, adaptations, musicals **2nd productions:** "Yes, especially after extensive re-writes and if no strings are attached from 1st production." **Special interest:** "Controversial material; nudity, street language accepted." **Specifications:** large cast preferred; set must allow for quick changes between acts and shows; one-acts must comprise a full evening; "80-minute shows are ideal" **Tours:** "Not per se, but shows move to larger venues." **Stages:** proscenium, flexible, non-traditional spaces; variable number of seats **Casting:** "Open casting for every show; non-traditional casting encouraged." **Audience:** "Jaded; many television and movie studio personnel." **Submission policy:** unsolictied script; agent submission; commission **Response:** 120 days **Your chances:** 1200+ submissions/25+ productions **Remuneration/future commitment:** "Varies." **Programs:** internships, residencies **Advice:** "Make it unusual, commercial and easy to promote. There is no censorship whatsoever in terms of language, nudity, social themes, religious themes, political themes. Please provide us with information specifically regarding the playwright's involvement with a production beyond what is traditionally considered a playwright's duty." ⁄

LA JOLLA PLAYHOUSE
Box 12039, La Jolla, CA 92037 (619) 534-6760
Contact: Robert Blacker, Associate Director/Dramaturg **Theatre:** professional not-for-profit **Works:** full-length plays, translations, adaptations **2nd productions:** no **Stages:** proscenium, 500 seats; thrust, 300 seats **Submission policy:** professional recommendation **Best time:** Jul.-Nov. **Response:** 4 months

LAKE CHARLES LITTLE THEATRE
813 Enterprise Blvd., Lake Charles, LA 70601
(318) 433-7988 Contact: A. J. Cormier, Board of Directors **Theatre:** community/non-professional **Works:** full-length plays, one-acts, translations, musicals **2nd productions:** yes **Special interest:** "Universal plays that are marketable and not too avant garde." **Specifications:** no complicated technical requirements **Tours:** yes **Stages:** proscenium, 840 seats; proscenium, 134

seats; thrust, 60 seats; flexible, 80 seats **Audience:** "Mixed ages, occupations, ethnic background; generally conservative; some regional interest." **Submission policy:** query/synopsis preferred; unsolicited script with SASE **Best time:** Jan.-Apr. **Response:** 1 month **Your chances:** 8 submissions/1-3 productions **Remuneration:** standard royalty **Advice:** "Scripts need to be relatively complete unless the author is local (within 300-500 miles)."

LAKE GEORGE DINNER THEATRE
Holiday Inn, Box 266, Lake George, NY 12845
(518) 668-5781 **Contact:** David Eastwood, Producer **Theatre:** Equity dinner **Works:** full-length plays, musicals **Exclusive interests:** comedies, farces, musicals **Specifications:** maximum cast: 5; single set **Stage:** arena, 165 seats **Audience:** "Tourists/senior citizens." **Submission policy:** unsolicited script with SASE **Response:** 6 months **Your chances:** 50 submissions/1 production

LAKEWOOD LITTLE THEATRE
Beck Center, 17801 Detroit Ave., Lakewood, OH 44107
(216) 521-2540 **Contact:** LaVerne Lugibihl, Chairman, Selection Committee **Theatre:** community/non-professional **Works:** full-length plays, one-acts, musicals, children's plays, cabaret/revues **2nd productions:** yes **Special interests:** American comedies and mysteries **Specifications:** maximum cast: 20-25, 40 for musical **Stages:** proscenium, 500 seats; flexible, 84 seats **Casting:** open auditions **Audience:** "50% season subscribers." **Submission policy:** unsolicited script with SASE **Best time:** Nov.-Dec. **Response:** 8 weeks **Your chances:** 50 submissions/1 production in studio theatre **Remuneration/future commitment:** no **Programs:** readings, staged readings

LA MAMA EXPERIMENTAL THEATRE
74A E. 4th St., New York, NY 10003 (212) 254-6468
Contact: Ellen Stewart, Founder and Producer **Theatre:** off off Broadway **Works:** full-length plays, one-acts, translations, adaptations, musicals **2nd productions:** no **Special interest:** experimental works **Tours:** yes **Stages:** flexible, 90 seats; flexible, 299 seats **Audience:** "Interested in experimental theatre." **Submission policy:** query/synopsis with resume; commission **Response:** 6 months **Your chances:** 50 submissions/0-1 production **Program:** workshop productions **Advice:** "We must become interested in the playwright's work."

LAMB'S PLAYERS THEATRE
500 Plaza, Box 26, National City, CA 92050
(619) 474-3385 **Contact:** Kerry Cederberg, Literary Manager
Theatre: professional not-for-profit **Works:** full-length plays, translations, adaptations, musicals, children's plays, cabaret/revues **2nd productions:** yes **Special interests:** "Plays which challenge an audience's cultural thinking through a Christian World View; adaptations of classics for junior high and high school audiences." **Specifications:** maximum cast: 11; no nudity or obscenity **Stage:** arena, 180 seats **Submission policy:** query/ synopsis; professional recommendation **Best time:** Sept.-Jun. **Response:** 3-6 months **Future commitment:** yes **Program:** internships

THE LAMB'S THEATRE COMPANY
130 W. 44th St., New York, NY 10036
(212) 575-0300, 221-1031 **Contact:** Carolyn Rossi Copeland, Artistic Director; Sonya Baehr, Literary Manager **Theatre:** off Broadway, professional not-for-profit **Works:** full-length plays, one-acts, translations, adaptations, musicals **2nd productions:** yes **Special interest:** "Theatre that deals with the problems of our time and inspires us to come up with solutions, that makes palpable the brotherhood of man, that can delight and amaze the entire family." **Specifications:** maximum cast: 15, 8 preferred; single set preferred; no nudity or obscenity **Tours:** "We have negotiated both national and international tours." **Stages:** proscenium, 360 seats; flexible, 100 seats **Audience:** "Off Broadway; group sales to high schools and colleges." **Submission policy:** query/synopsis with dialogue sample and SAS postcard; professional recommendation; agent submission **Response:** 6 weeks query; 1-6 months script **Your chances:** 500 submissions/3 productions **Remuneration:** negotiable **Future commitment:** yes **Programs:** readings, staged readings, workshop productions, youth program **Comment:** "We submit scripts to the New Harmony Writer's Project developmental workshops" (see Special Programs).

LAS CRUCES COMMUNITY THEATRE
Box 1281, Las Cruces, NM 88001 (505) 523-1200
Contact: Ken Byers, President **Theatre:** community/ non-professional **Works:** full-length plays, adaptations, children's plays **Specifications:** simple or unit set **Stage:** proscenium **Casting:** open auditions **Audience:** varied **Submission policy:** query/synopsis **Best time:** early spring **Response:** 2 weeks query; 2 months script **Remuneration:** "Equivalent royalty." **Advice:** "Submit family-oriented shows untypical of sit-coms."

LATIN AMERICAN THEATRE ENSEMBLE
Box 1259 Radio City Station, New York, NY 10019
(212) 410-4582   Contact: Margaret Toirac, Administrator
Theatre: off off Broadway, university/ college **Works:** full-length plays, translations, children's plays **Tours:** yes **Stage:** flexible **Audience:** "College students; Spanish- and English-speaking communities; young, old, every kind." **Submission policy:** unsolicited script with SASE and resume; professional recommendation **Your chances:** 6 submissions/3 productions **Programs:** readings, staged readings, workshop productions, classes

LAWRENCE WELK RESORT THEATRE
8975 Lawrence Welk Dr., Escondido, CA 92026
(619) 749-3448   Contact: Frank Wayne, Artistic Director
Theatre: Equity dinner **Works:** full-length plays, musicals **Special interests:** "New musicals with good scores; comedies with merit." **Specifications:** maximum cast: 15; no "off color" language **Audience:** "Senior citizens." **Submission policy:** unsolicited script with SASE

LE PETIT THEATRE DE VIEUX CARRE
616 St. Peter St., New Orleans, LA 70116
(504) 522-9958 Contact: Donald K. Marshall, Executive Director **Theatre:** community/non-professional **Works:** full-length plays, children's plays **2nd productions:** no **Stages:** proscenium, 450 seats; arena, 150 seats **Audience:** 3300 subscribers **Submission policy:** unsolicited script with SASE; professional recommendation **Best time:** summer **Response:** 12 months **Your chances:** 30 submissions/"very few productions" **Remuneration:** no **Program:** Louisiana Playwrights' Project (inquire) **Advice:** "Get other works produced in small spaces; send reviews."

LIFELINE THEATRE
6912 N. Glenwood, Chicago, IL 60626 (312) 761-4477
Contact: Christina Calvit, Literary Services **Theatre:** professional not-for-profit **Works:** full-length plays, one-acts, translations, cabaret/revues **Stage:** proscenium-black box, 89 seats **Submission policy:** query/synopsis with resume **Response:** 2 weeks query; 3 months script

LIGHT OPERA OF MANHATTAN
2112 Broadway, New York, NY 10123
(212) 496-5710 Contact: Steven Levy, Executive Director **Theatre:** off Broadway **Works:** musicals, light operas **2nd productions:** yes **Special interest:** "Light fun." **Specifications:** maximum cast: 22; unit set or no more than 2

sets; no avant garde works **Audience:** family **Submission policy:** query/synopsis with tape; commission **Best time:** before Jan. **Response:** 1 month **Remuneration:** negotiable **Program:** development **Advice:** "Something new and different, relevant to contemporary society; a style that delights." **Comment:** Tapes will not be returned.

LINCOLN CENTER THEATER
150 W. 65th St., New York, NY 10023 (212) 362-7600
Contact: Anne Cattaneo, Dramaturg **Theatre:** professional not-for-profit **Works:** full-length plays, one-acts, translations, adaptations, musicals **Stages:** thrust, 1100 seats; thrust, 300 seats **Submission policy:** agent submission **Response:** 2-4 months

LION THEATRE COMPANY
422 W. 42nd St., New York, NY 10036 (212) 736-7930
Contact: Gene Nye, Artistic Director **Theatre:** off off Broadway **Works:** full-length plays, musicals **2nd productions:** no **Casting:** open auditions **Submission policy:** unsolicited script with SASE **Response:** 2 weeks

LITTLE BROADWAY PRODUCTIONS
Box 15068, North Hollywood, CA 91615 (818) 990-3232
Contact: Jill Shawn Adereth, Producer **Theatre:** professional theatre for young audiences **Works:** children's adaptations and musical adaptations **2nd productions:** yes **Special interest:** "Musical versions of classics." **Specifications:** maximum cast: 8-10; all sets must tour; playing time: 1 hour without intermission **Stages:** various spaces, all proscenium **Audience:** "Family, ages 4-104." **Submission policy:** unsolicited script with SASE **Response:** 2 months **Your chances:** 25 submissions/2productions **Remuneration:** negotiable royalty

LONG ISLAND STAGE
Box 9001, Rockville Center, NY 11571 (516) 546-4608
Contact: Clinton J. Atkinson, Artistic Director **Theatre:** professional not-for-profit **Works:** full-length plays, translations, adaptations **2nd productions:** "Occasionally." **Special interest:** "Translations of unusual classics or little-known works." **Specifications:** maximum cast: 10; single or unit set; simple or contemporary costumes **Stage:** proscenium, 297 seats **Audience:** "Mostly over 50, upper middle class, college educated." **Submission policy:** query/synopsis preferred; unsolicited script with SASE; professional recommendation; agent submission **Best time:** spring-early summer **Response:** 2 weeks query; 3 months script

Your chances: 150 submissions/1-2 productions **Remuneration:** negotiable **Future commitment:** yes

LONG WHARF THEATRE
222 Sargent Dr., New Haven, CT 06511 (203) 787-4284
Contact: John Tillinger, Literary Consultant **Theatre:** professional not-for-profit **Works:** full-length plays, translations, adaptations, musicals **2nd productions:** yes **Special interests:** "Social problems, political awareness, morals, ethics." **Specifications:** small cast preferred; limited space **Tours:** "Occasionally." **Stages:** thrust, 484 seats; flexible, 200 seats **Audience:** "White, majority 40-65, upper middle class." **Submission policy:** agent submission with resume preferred; query/synopsis with resume; professional recommendation **Best time:** summer **Response:** 2 months query; 6 months script **Your chances:** 300 submissions/ "possibly 1 full production, 4 workshops, 4-5 readings" **Remuneration/future commitment:** yes **Programs:** readings, staged readings; Stage II Workshops (see Special Programs)

LOOKING GLASS THEATRE
175 Mathewson St., Providence, RI 02903
(401) 331-9080 Contact: Linda D'Ambra, Producing Director **Theatre:** professional not-for-profit **Works:** children's plays **Special interest:** social issues, with audience participation, for grades K-8 **Specifications:** cast of 3-5; all sets must tour **Stages:** various spaces **Audience:** grades K-8 **Submission policy:** unsolicited script with SASE **Best time:** Mar.-May **Response:** 1 month

LORRAINE HANSBERRY THEATRE
25 Taylor St., San Francisco, CA 94102
(415) 474-8842 Contact: Stanley Williams, Artistic Director **Theatre:** professional not-for-profit **Works:** full-length plays, translations, adaptations, musicals **2nd productions:** yes **Stage:** flexible, 300 seats **Submission policy:** unsolicited script with SASE and resume; query/synopsis with dialogue sample and resume; professional recommendation; agent submission **Response:** 2 months **Your chances:** 20 submissions/1 production **Remuneration:** yes **Programs:** readings, staged readings, workshop productions, development, classes

LOS ALTOS CONSERVATORY THEATRE
Box 151, Los Altos, CA 94022 (415) 941-5228
Contact: Doyne Mraz, Artistic Director **Theatre:** professional not-for-profit **Works:** full-length plays, one-acts, musicals **2nd productions:** yes **Specifications:** maximum cast: 10-12; no

more than 2 sets; simple technical requirements **Submission policy:** query/synopsis with dialogue sample preferred; unsolicited script with SASE **Best time:** Aug.–Sept. **Response:** 1 year

LOS ANGELES THEATRE CENTER
514 S. Spring St., Los Angeles, CA 90013
(213) 627-6500 Contact: Peter Sagal, Stephen Weeks, Literary Co-Managers **Theatre:** professional not-for-profit **Works:** full-length plays, translations, adaptations, musicals **2nd productions:** yes **Special interests:** contemporary social/political issues; women and minority authors; "plays which further the multicultural context of this theatre" **Maximum cast:** 10 **Tours:** "Occasionally." **Stages:** modified thrust, 499 seats; proscenium, 296 seats; thrust, 323 seats; flexible, 99 seats **Submission policy:** query/synopsis with 10-page dialogue sample; professional recommendation; agent submission **Response:** 21 days query; 3–6 months script **Your chances:** 2500 submissions/7-8 productions **Remuneration:** "Royalty varies from 5%." **Future commitment:** yes **Programs:** The Women's Project, Young Playwrights Lab, Latino Theatre Lab, Playwrights' Unit, Asian American Theatre Project, Black Theatre Artists Workshop, Music Theatre Lab (see Los Angeles Theatre Center Programs listing in Special Programs) **Advice:** Request information regarding script submission and critiquing program.

LOS ANGELES THEATRE WORKS
681 Venice Blvd., Venice, CA 90291 (213) 827-0808
Contact: Marianne Powell, Administration Associate **Theatre:** professional not-for-profit **Works:** full-length plays, one-acts, translations, adaptations **2nd productions:** yes **Special interests:** non-realistic new works; adaptations of classic themes **Stages:** various spaces **Submission policy:** query/synopsis with resume and 1st 10 pages of script (opitional); professional recommendation; agent submission **Response:** 2 months query; 6-12 months script **Your chances:** 200+ submissions/1-2 productions **Remuneration:** yes **Program:** staged readings

MABOU MINES
150 First Ave., New York, NY 10009 (212) 473-0559
Contact: Joel Bassin, Company Manager **Theatre:** professional not-for-profit **Works:** full-length plays, one-acts, translations, adaptations **Special interests:** "Contemporary works and issues." **Tours:** yes **Stages:** various spaces **Submission policy:** query/synopsis; professional recommendation **Response:** 4-10 weeks **Your chances:** 200-300 submissions received each year **Advice:** "Send query/synopsis 'Attn: Script Submission.'"

MADISON REPERTORY THEATRE

211 State St., Madison, WI 53703 (608) 256-0029
Contact: Joseph Hanreddy, Artistic Director **Theatre:** professional not-for-profit **Works:** full-length plays, translations, adaptations, musicals **2nd productions:** yes **Special interest:** Midwest themes **Maximum cast:** 15 **Stage:** 3/4 thrust, 335 seats **Submission policy:** query/synopsis preferred; unsolicited script with SASE **Best time:** summer **Response:** 3-4 months **Recent production of unsolicited work:** yes **Future commitment:** no **Programs:** readings, workshop productions

MADISON THEATRE GUILD

2410 Monroe St., Madison, WI 53711 (608) 238-9322
Contact: Board of Directors **Theatre:** community/non-professional **Works:** full-length plays **2nd productions:** no **Specifications:** maximum cast: 20; $1000 set budget **Stage:** proscenium, 205 seats **Audience:** "Older, middle class." **Submission policy:** unsolicited script with SASE **Best time:** summer **Response:** 1 month query; 3 months script **Your chances:** Theatre has not yet produced a new script but will consider doing so. **Remuneration:** no **Programs:** "None yet; hopefully soon." **Advice:** "Send scripts to us, and we'll read them and pass them on to others in town."

MAD RIVER THEATER WORKS

Box 238, West Liberty, OH 43357 (513) 465-6751
Contact: Jeffrey Hooper, Producing Director **Theatre:** professional not-for-profit **Works:** full-length plays, one-acts, adaptations, musicals **2nd productions:** no **Special interests:** "Midwestern and rural issues or themes." **Specifications:** maximum cast: 7-10; simple set and costumes **Tours:** yes **Stage:** flexible, 325 seats **Audience:** "Intended audience: multi-generational, rural, Mid-western." **Submission policy:** query/synopsis; professional recommendation **Response:** 2-3 weeks query; 3-4 months script **Your chances:** 10-12 submissions/0-1 production **Remuneration:** "Royalty; sometimes stipends." **Future commitment:** no

MAGIC THEATRE

Ft. Mason Center, Bldg. D, San Francisco, CA 94123
(415) 441-8001 Contact: Martin Esslin, Dramaturg; Eugenie Chan, Literary Manager **Theatre:** professional not-for-profit **Works:** full-length plays, one-acts **2nd productions:** yes **Specifications:** maximum cast: 6-8; some limitations on sets **Tours:** "Rarely." **Stages:** proscenium, 170 seats; thrust, 156 seats **Audience:** "Well educated and adventurous." **Submission policy:** professional recommendation, agent submission preferred;

query/synopsis with 3-5 page dialogue sample and resume **Response:** 1-3 months query; 3-6 months script **Your chances:** 600 submissions/3 productions **Remuneration:** "Generally 5% of gross with guarantee." **Programs:** workshop productions; Pacific Rim Festival scheduled for summer 1990, Hispanic Playwrights Festival scheduled for summer 1991 (inquire)

MAIN STREET THEATER
2540 Times Blvd., Houston, TX 77005 (713) 524-3622
Contact: Rebecca Green Udden, Artistic Director **Theatre:** non-Equity professional not-for-profit **Works:** full-length plays, one-acts, translations, adaptations, musicals, children's plays **2nd productions:** yes **Special interests:** "We try to present a broad spectrum of points of view. Language is very important. Also good children's plays." **Specifications:** maximum cast: 20; "because our stage is small, some large-scale shows are not appropriate for us" **Tours:** yes **Stage:** arena-thrust, 95 seats **Audience:** "College educated, 30's-40's, generally Anglo, urban, hard-core theatregoers." **Submission policy:** unsolicited script with SASE; query/synopsis; professional recommendation; agent submission **Response:** 2-6 months query; 12-18 months script **Your chances:** 50-100 submissions/4-6 productions and a number of staged readings in New Voices/Different Views program **Remuneration:** "Royalty; sometimes travel and lodging. **Programs:** readings, staged readings, workshop productions

MAIN STREET THEATRE
Box 232, New York, NY 10044 (212) 371-6140
Contact: Worth Howe, Artistic Director **Theatre:** off off Broadway **Works:** full-length plays, translations, adaptations, musicals, children's plays **2nd productions:** no **Specifications:** maximum cast: 12-14; no 2-story sets **Stages:** proscenium; flexible **Audience:** "Upscale middle class; broad ethnic base plus professionals in all aspects of the theatre." **Submission policy:** unsolicited script with SASE; query/synopsis with dialogue sample; professional recommendation; agent submission **Response:** 6 weeks **Your chances:** 150 submissions/3 productions **Future commitment:** possibly **Programs:** readings, staged readings, workshop productions

MANHATTAN CLASS COMPANY AT THE NAT HORNE
Box 279 Times Square Station, New York, NY 10108
(212) 239-9033 Contact: Kent Adams, Literary Manager
Theatre: off off Broadway play development company **Works:** full-length plays, one-acts, musicals **2nd productions:** yes, but unproduced works preferred **Special interests:** contemporary

issues; collaboration with playwright **Maximum cast**: 10 **Stages:** proscenium, 99 seats (at Nat Horne Theatre); black box, 250 seats (on Long Island) **Submission policy:** professional recommendation; agent submission **Best time:** by Oct. 1 for one-acts; anytime for others **Response time:** 3 weeks query; 6 months script **Your chances:** 600 submissions/productions of 4 full-length plays, 6 one-acts; "we rarely produce a play ourselves; usually we workshop a play to the point of option" **Remuneration:** negotiable **Future commitment:** yes **Programs:** workshops, playwrights unit; annual one-act festival (inquire)

MANHATTAN PUNCH LINE THEATRE, INC.
410 W. 42nd St. 3rd Floor, New York, NY 10036
(212) 239-0827 **Contact:** Steve Kaplan, Artistic Director **Theatre:** off off Broadway **Works:** full-length plays, one-acts, adaptations **2nd productions:** New York City premieres **Exclusive interest:** comedies **Stage:** proscenium, 99 seats **Audience:** "All ages; usually the same audience that would go to see a Neil Simon play on Broadway." **Submission policy:** unsolicited script with SASE; professional recommendation; agent submission **Best time:** Jan.-Oct. **Response:** 2 weeks query; 6-10 weeks script **Your chances:** 1400+ submissions/12-15 productions **Remuneration:** "One-act $200, full-length play $400-$600." **Programs:** readings, workshop productions, development, classes, internships; Manhattan Punch Line Festival of One-Act Comedies (see Contests) **Advice:** "Start with the one-act form; we produce 9-15 one-acts each season."

MANHATTAN THEATRE CLUB
453 W. 16th St., New York, NY 10011 (212) 645-5590
Contact: Victoria Abrash, Literary Associate **Theatre:** off Broadway **Works:** full-length plays, one-acts, translations, adaptations, musicals, cabaret/revues **2nd productions:** no **Specifications:** maximum cast: 10-12; single or unit set preferred **Stages:** proscenium-thrust, 300 seats; flexible, 150 seats **Submission policy:** query/synopsis with dialogue sample and resume; professional recommendation; agent submission **Response:** 1 month query; 6 months script **Your chances:** 1200 submissions/ 9 productions **Remuneration:** negotiable fee **Program:** workshop productions

MARIN THEATRE COMPANY
Box 1439, Mill Valley, CA 94942 (415) 388-5200
Contact: Will Marchetti, Artistic Director **Theatre:** professional not-for-profit **Works:** full-length plays, translations, adaptations, children's plays **2nd productions:** yes **Special interests:**

psychological and social issues; new translations of classics **Specifications:** unit set preferred **Stages:** proscenium, 250 seats; black box, 125 seats **Submission policy:** solicited script **Your chances:** 2-3 new plays plus staged readings produced each season **Remuneration:** percentage **Program:** collaboration with West Coast Playwrights Workshop (see Special Programs)

MARKET HOUSE THEATRE
141 Kentucky Ave., Paducah, KY 42001 (502) 444-6828
Contact: April Cochran, Executive Director **Theatre:** community/ non-professional **Works:** full-length plays, one-acts, translations, adaptations, musicals, children's plays **2nd productions:** children's plays **Special interests:** "Full-length, tourable children's plays, 40-50 minutes long; good mysteries for main stage." **Specifications:** small cast; minimal set changes preferred **Tours:** yes **Stage:** proscenium **Audience:** conservative **Submission policy:** send SASE for guidelines **Your chances:** 10 submissions/1 production every 3rd year **Remuneration:** negotiable **Program:** Market House Theatre One Act Playwrighting Competition (see Contests)

THE MARK TAPER FORUM
135 N. Grand Ave., Los Angeles, CA 90012
(213) 972-7251 Contact: Jeremy Lawrence, Literary Administrator **Theatre:** professional not-for-profit **Works:** full-length plays, translations, adaptations, musicals, plays for young audiences, literary cabaret, performance pieces **2nd productions:** yes **Special interests:** social and political issues; innovative forms **Stages:** proscenium, 80-90 seats; thrust, 742 seats; literary cabaret, 200 seats **Submission policy:** query/synopsis; agent submission **Response:** 1-2 weeks query; 8-10 weeks script **Programs:** readings, workshop productions

MARRIOTT LINCOLNSHIRE THEATRE
Lincolnshire, IL 60015 (312) 634-0204
Contact: Dyanne Earley, Artistic Director **Works:** full-length musicals, children's plays **2nd productions:** yes **Special interest:** "Children's shows for 7-12 year olds." **Specifications:** cast of 8-20; no fairy tales **Stage:** arena, 900 seats **Audience:** "Age 30-35, upper middle class, traditionalist." **Submission policy:** unsolicited script with SASE; professional recommendation **Response:** 6-12 months **Your chances:** varying number of submissions/1 production **Recent production of unsolicited work:** no **Remuneration:** no **Future commitment:** yes **Advice:** "Broad-based appeal, musicals only; prefer lighter works; nothing esoteric."

MARY BALDWIN COLLEGE THEATRE
Mary Baldwin College, Staunton, VA 24401
(703) 887-7189 **Contact:** Virginia R. Francisco, Professor of Theatre **Theatre:** university/college **Works:** full-length plays, one-acts, translations, musicals **2nd productions:** yes **Stages:** thrust, 230 seats; flexible, 130 seats **Casting:** "Predominantly women." **Audience:** "Students, staff and community of conservative, college-educated professionals." **Submission policy:** query/synopsis **Best time:** May-Jul. **Response:** 1 month query; 1 year script **Your chances:** 50 submissions/1-2 productions **Remuneration:** "$50/$30 per performance." **Advice:** "Focus on issues of interest to women, either historical or contemporary."

MAXWELL ANDERSON PLAYWRIGHTS SERIES
6 Sagamore Rd., Stamford, CT 06902 (203) 359-9122
Contact: Philip Devine, Executive Producer **Theatre:** community/non-professional **Works:** full-length plays, one-acts **2nd productions:** if play has been revised **Specifications:** maximum cast: 8; no historical dramas **Stage:** black box, 150 seats **Audience:** "Mature, upwardly mobile, sophisticated, college educated." **Submission policy:** unsolicited script; professional recommendation **Response:** 1-2 months **Your chances:** 200-300 submissions/6 staged readings **Remuneration:** stipend, travel **Program:** development through staged readings

McCADDEN THEATRE COMPANY
1157 N. McCadden Pl., Hollywood, CA 90038
(213) 462-9070 **Contact:** Jay Donohue, Joy Rinaldi, Artistic Directors **Theatre:** professional not-for-profit **Works:** full-length plays, one-acts **2nd productions:** no **Maximum cast:** 10 **Stage:** proscenium, 55 seats **Submission policy:** query/synopsis with dialogue sample and resume **Your chances:** 150 submissions/3 productions **Remuneration:** no **Programs:** readings, staged readings, workshop productions

McCARTER THEATRE
91 University Pl., Princeton, NJ 08540 (609) 683-9100
Contact: Robert Lanchester, Associate Artistic Director **Theatre:** professional not-for-profit **Works:** full-length plays, translations, adaptations **2nd productions:** yes **Specifications:** maximum cast: 12 preferred; single or unit set **Stages:** proscenium, 1067 seats; 2nd stage (on stage), 100 seats; black box basement theatre, 100 seats **Submission policy:** unsolicited script with SASE and resume; query/synopsis with resume; professional recommendation; agent submission **Best time:** summer **Response:** 1 week query; 2-3 months script **Your chances:** 600 submissions/1-2 productions

plus 6 staged readings **Remuneration:** "Negotiable fee for mainstage and 2nd stage; $500 plus travel for basement theatre play readings."
Future commitment: negotiable **Programs:** readings, staged readings, workshop productions, development, residencies, classes

MEDICINE SHOW THEATRE ENSEMBLE
353 Broadway, New York, NY 10013 (212) 431-9545
Contact: James Barbosa, Co-Artistic Director **Theatre:** professional not-for-profit **Works:** experimental theatre pieces **Special interests:** social/political issues; comic/satirical works; works developed in collaboration with ensemble **Specifications:** maximum cast: 15; no fly space; no traditional, well-made plays **Stage:** flexible, 60 seats **Submission policy:** query/synopsis **Response:** 2 weeks query; 3 weeks script **Program:** Word/Play: annual Apr. series of readings of poetry, fiction, nonfiction, dramatic works (inquire)

MENDOCINO PERFORMING ARTS COMPANY
Box 800, Mendocino, CA 95460 (707) 937-4477
Contact: Lynne Abels, Artistic Director **Works:** full-length plays **2nd productions:** yes **Maximum cast:** 9 **Stage:** proscenium, 82 seats **Casting:** "Open to anyone in the community." **Audience:** "50% local, 50% tourists." **Submission policy:** query with 1-page synopsis and 5-page dialogue sample **Best time:** Jan.-Apr. **Response:** 2 weeks query; 3 months script **Your chances:** 50 submissions/1 production "in a season for 6 mainstage shows; we don't always achieve that, but it is our goal" **Recent production of unsolicited work:** 1989 **Remuneration:** negotiable royalty **Future commitment:** "Nothing other than future 'Play developed at Mendocino Performing Arts Company.'" **Program:** readings **Advice:** "No unsolicited scripts; provide a postcard for rapid response to your query."

MERRIMACK REPERTORY THEATRE
Box 228, Lowell, MA 01853 (508) 454-6324
Contact: David G. Kent, Literary Manager/Dramaturg **Theatre:** professional not-for-profit **Works:** full-length plays, musicals **2nd productions:** yes **Special interests:** "Plays relating to labor, immigration, cross-cultural experience and the intellectual and historical context of New England." **Specifications:** maximum cast: 12; simple set **Stage:** proscenium-thrust, 280 seats **Audience:** "Blue-collar workers and Asian immigrants." **Submission policy:** query/synopsis; professional recommendation; agent submission **Best time:** Sept.-Jan **Response:** 1 month query; 3-6 months **Future commitments:** credit for premiere production, minimal financial

participation **Program:** Merrimack Repertory Theatre Playwriting Contest (see Contests)

MERRY-GO-ROUND PLAYHOUSE
Box 506, Auburn, NY 13021   (315) 255-1305
Contact: Dennis McCarthy, Literary Manager **Theatre:** professional not-for-profit **Works:** full-length plays, translations, adaptations, musicals, children's plays **Special interest:** audience participation for grades 6-12 **Maximum cast:** 3-4 **Stage:** flexible: 325-seat proscenium or 100-seat thrust **Submission policy:** unsolicited script with SASE **Best time:** Mar.-May **Response:** 1 month

METTAWEE RIVER COMPANY
463 West St. #D405, New York, NY 10014
(212) 929-4777   Contact: Ralph Lee, Artistic Director **Theatre:** professional not-for-profit touring company **Works:** multi-media pieces **Special interests:** "Collaboration between writer and company; works combining dialogue with storytelling, lyrics, masks, puppetry, music, visual elements; works based on myth and legend." **Specifications:** cast size: 6 **Stages:** outdoor (summer) and indoor spaces **Casting:** "From company of 6 performers." **Submission policy:** query/synopsis with dialogue sample **Response:** 4 weeks query; 8 weeks script **Comments:** Theatre's summer (May-Aug.) address is RD 2, Salem, NY 12865 (518) 854-9357. See Hebert, Mary, "Puppets, Masks, and Myths at the Mettawee River Company," *TheaterWeek* (July 31, 1989), 30-33.

MIAMI BEACH COMMUNITY THEATRE
2231 Prairie Ave., Miami Beach, FL 33139
(305) 532-4515   Contact: Jay W. Jensen, Drama Director **Theatre:** community/non-professional **Works:** full-length plays, one-acts, adaptations, musicals, children's plays, cabaret/revues **2nd productions:** yes **Special interest:** "Plays dealing with AIDS-drugs on the teen level." **Specifications:** maximum cast: 25; single set; limited technical requirements **Tours:** yes **Stage:** proscenium, 900 seats **Casting:** open auditions **Audience:** "Students, senior citizens, community people." **Submission policy:** unsolicited script with SASE and resume; query/synopsis with dialogue sample and resume; professional recommendation **Response:** 1 month **Your chances:** 15 submissions/3 productions **Remuneration:** "Open, ususally none, given authors have a chance for their work to be seen and commented upon." **Future commitment:** no **Programs:** readings, classes **Advice:** "Light on sex and violence."

MILL MOUNTAIN THEATRE
Center in the Square, 1 Market Sq., Roanoke, VA 24011
(703) 342-5730 Contact: Jo Weinstein, Literary Manager
Theatre: professional regional **Works:** full-length plays, one-acts, musicals **2nd productions:** yes **Special interests:** "Mixed casts; one-acts (25-35 minutes in length) for Centerpiece series."
Maximum cast: 15, 24 for musical **Stages:** proscenium, 462 seats; flexible, 150 seats **Audience:** "A conservative and provincial community, but becoming more flexible and excited about new, innovative directing and approaches to subject matter."
Submission policy: unsolicited script with SASE and resume; query with resume; agent submission; no synopsis **Best time:** fall-winter **Response:** immediate if interested in query; 4-6 months script **Your chances:** 500 full-length and 300 one-act submissions (including contest entries)/2 productions in Festival, 10 in Centerpieces **Remuneration:** "Each arrangement is individual."
Future commitment: if theatre has a principal role in the script's development **Programs:** staged readings; Mill Mountain Theatre New Play Competition (see Contests); Festival of New Plays; Centerpiece series: lunchtime script-in-hand productions of one-acts

MILLS COLLEGE THEATRE
5000 MacArthur Blvd., Oakland, CA 94613
(415) 430-2169 Contact: James C. Wright, Head, Dept. of Dramatic Arts **Theatre:** university/college **Works:** full-length plays, one-acts, translations, adaptations, musicals, cabaret/revues **2nd productions:** yes **Special interests:** "Minority and women's issues." **Maximum cast:** 15 **Tours:** yes **Stages:** thrust, 187 seats; proscenium, 65 seats **Casting:** "The best person gets the role without regard to race, age, sex, etc." **Audience:** "Mixed." **Submission policy:** query/synopsis **Best time:** "Spring for the following year." **Response:** 1 week query; 3-4 weeks script **Your chances:** 3-4 submissions/"no productions as yet" **Remuneration:** "Standard royalty agreement."

MILWAUKEE CHAMBER THEATRE
Box 92583, Milwaukee, WI 53202 (414) 276-8842
Contact: Montgomery Davis, Artistic Director; Gregory Brennan, General Manager; Lesley Smith, Business Manager **Theatre:** professional not-for-profit **Works:** full-length plays, translations, adaptations **2nd productions:** yes **Special interest:** literary merit **Specifications:** maximum cast: 10-12; single or unit set **Tours:** small productions **Stage:** black box, 216 seats **Audience:** "Usually the older, well-read couple; more and more younger couples." **Submission policy:** query/synopsis with resume; professional recommendation; agent submission **Best time:**

Jul.-Aug. **Response:** 3 months **Your chances:** 200 submissions/ "we consider producing 1 new play each season" **Remuneration:** negotiable **Future commitment:** yes **Advice:** "Have invited staged readings."

MILWAUKEE REPERTORY THEATRE
108 E. Wells, Milwaukee, WI 53202 (414) 224-1761
Contact: Robert Meiksins, Dramaturg **Theatre:** professional not-for-profit **Works:** full-length plays, translations, adaptations, cabaret pieces **2nd productions:** yes **Special interest:** works of substance **Stages:** 3/4 thrust, 700 seats; black box, 200 seats; cabaret, 100 seats **Casting:** "Resident company--non-traditional casting." **Audience:** "Mixed." **Submission policy:** query/ synopsis; professional recommendation; agent submission **Best time:** fall **Response:** 1 month query; 4 months script **Your chances:** 500 submissions/1 production **Remuneration:** "Royalties." **Future commitments:** "Some." **Program:** "Workshops for plays selected for production."

MIMETIC THEATRE
1536 18th St., San Francisco, CA 94107
(415) 621-6002 Contact: Bert Houle, Veera Wibaux, Co-Artistic Directors **Theatre:** professional not-for-profit **Works:** full-length plays, one-acts **2nd productions:** no **Tours:** "We rent theatres for our season in San Francisco, and we tour across the country for college and university audiences." **Submission policy:** unsolicited script with SASE and resume; query/synopsis with resume **Response:** 1 month **Your chances:** 1 play and 5-10 "skits" produced each year **Remuneration:** negotiable **Advice:** "Visual, mystical, spiritual concepts; could be comic. We want to receive original plays."

MIRROR REPERTORY COMPANY
352 E. 50th St., New York, NY 10022
(212) 888-6087 Contact: Robert Lewis, Artistic Director **Theatre:** professional not-for-profit **Works:** full-length plays, one-acts, translations, adaptations **Special interest:** large-cast plays for alternating repertory **Stages:** various spaces **Submission policy:** unsolicited script with SASE **Response:** several months **Programs:** staged readings; summer residency in Unity/Bar Harbor, ME includes readings of approximately 6 plays (inquire)

MISSOURI REPERTORY THEATRE
4949 Cherry St., Kansas City, MO 64110
(816) 363-4541 Contact: Felicia Londré, Dramaturg **Theatre:** professional not-for-profit **Works:** full-length plays, translations,

adaptations **Second productions:** yes **Stages:** proscenium-thrust, 799 seats; black box, 90–100 seats **Submission policy:** query/synopsis; professional recommendation **Best time:** "Academic year." **Response:** time varies **Your chances:** 150 submissions/0–1 production; "we might do an unsolicited translation in 1990–91" **Remuneration:** "Standard LORT contract." **Programs:** readings, staged readings, workshop productions, development, classes; "Second Stage is just getting underway again after a long hiatus" (inquire)

MITCH NESTOR'S PLAYWRIGHTS–ACTORS–DIRECTORS COMPANY
1000 Westgate Ave. Suite 201, Los Angeles, CA 90049
(213) 826–8807   Contact: Mitchell Nestor, Artistic Director **Theatre:** off off Broadway, professional not-for-profit **Works:** full-length plays **2nd productions:** "Plays to be reworked for commerial sales: film, stage, TV." **Special interest:** "1-person or 2-character shows." **Specifications:** maximum cast: 8; single set; open staging **Stages:** proscenium, 99 seats; thrust, 99 seats **Casting:** open auditions **Audience:** "Producers, network executives and general audience." **Submission policy:** unsolicited script with SASE; professional recommendation; agent submission **Response:** 1–3 months **Your chances:** 300 submissions/8 productions **Remuneration:** "If sold as film, TV or Broadway material." **Future commitment:** yes **Programs:** development, classes

MIXED BLOOD THEATRE COMPANY
1501 S. 4th St., Minneapolis, MN 55454   (612) 338–0937
Contact: David Kunz, Script Czar **Theatre:** professional not-for-profit **Works:** full-length plays, one-acts, translations, adaptations, musicals, children's plays, cabaret/revues **Maximum cast:** 10 preferred **Stage:** flexible, 200 seats **Submission policy:** query/synopsis **Response:** 1 month query; 2–6 months script **Program:** Mixed Blood Versus America (see Contests)

MONTANA REPERTORY THEATRE
Performing Arts Center,
University of Montana, Missoula, MT 59812
Contact: Jim Bartruff, Artistic Director **Theatre:** professional not-for-profit **Works:** full-length plays, musicals **2nd productions:** yes **Special interests:** Western characters and themes **Maximum cast:** 20, 6–12 preferred **Submission policy:** unsolicited script with SASE **Best time:** anytime other than Jan.-Mar. **Response:** 6 weeks **Recent production of unsolicited work:** no **Future commitment:** negotiable

MONTFORD PARK PLAYERS

Box 2663, Ashville, NC 28802 **(704) 254-5146**
Contact: Hazel Robinson, Director **Theatre:** community/non-professional **Works:** full-length plays, one-acts, translations, adaptations, children's plays **2nd productions:** yes **Specifications:** maximum cast: 22; 1 or 2 simple sets; budget considerations **Stages:** proscenium; thrust; flexible; outdoor **Audience:** community residents and tourists **Submission policy:** unsolicited script with SASE; query/synopsis **Best time:** fall **Response:** 1 month query; 1 year script **Your chances:** 10 submissions/1 production **Remuneration:** "Usually not; we have commissioned scripts." **Programs:** readings, staged readings, workshop productions **Advice:** "Send request for information with synopsis."

MOUNTAIN VIEW HIGH SCHOOL THEATRE

14609 NE 7th St., Vancouver, WA 98684
(206) 254-7318 **Contact:** Paige Oppenhagen, Theatre Director **Theatre:** high school **Works:** full-length plays, one-acts **2nd productions:** yes **Special interests:** "Good scripts dealing intelligently with issues; large number of female roles." **Specifications:** maximum cast: 50; no more than 2 sets **Stage:** proscenium-thrust, 230-550 seats **Casting:** "Best person for the role." **Submission policy:** unsolicited script with SASE; query with dialogue sample; professional recommendation **Your chances:** 2 submissions received annually **Recent production of unsolicited work:** 1989 **Remuneration:** "Standard royalty." **Advice:** "Don't write 'high school plays'; they are insulting to actors, audiences and directors. We are ready to deal with fine literature."

MUSICAL THEATRE WORKS

440 Lafayette St., New York, NY 10003 **(212) 228-1210**
Contact: Mark S. Herko, Associate Artistic Director **Theatre:** professional not-for-profit **Works:** full-length musicals **2nd productions:** seldom **Special interest:** premieres **Maximum cast:** 12 **Stages:** flexible, 60 seats; flexible, 150 seats **Submission policy:** unsolicited script with SASE; professional recommendation **Response:** 3-4 months **Your chances:** 100 submissions/4 productions plus readings, "20 projects altogether" **Remuneration:** no **Future commitment:** "If project is produced in Premiere Series." **Programs:** readings, staged readings, workshop productions, development **Comment:** See Filichia, Peter, "Musical Theater Works," *TheaterWeek* (Mar. 27, 1989), 38-45.

MUSIC HALL THEATRE
564 Monterey Blvd., San Francisco, CA 94127
This theatre was recently sold, and no phone number is listed. Playwrights are advised to inquire in writing before submitting material.

MUSIC-THEATRE GROUP/LENOX ARTS CENTER
735 Washington St., New York, NY 10014
(212) 924-3108 Contact: John Hart, Project Development **Theatre:** professional not-for-profit **Works:** full-length and one-act musicals, operas, cabaret/revues **2nd productions:** no **Special interest:** "Experimental musicals using music-theatre, dance and visual arts." **Maximum cast:** 15 including musicians **Stages:** flexible, 99 seats; flexible, 75 seats **Audience:** "Well educated, middle class, open-minded, 20's-30's." **Submission policy:** postcard announcement of reading or query/synopsis preferred; unsolicited script with SASE **Best times:** spring, fall **Response:** 1 month query; varying times for script **Recent production of unsolicited work:** no **Future commitment:** negotiable **Advice:** Phone calls are unwelcome. **Comments:** During Jul.-Aug. the theatre's address is Lenox Arts Center, Box 128, Stockbridge, MA 01262 (413) 298-5122. See Carr, Jan, "O Pioneers! A Portrait of Lyn Austin and the Music-Theatre Group/Lenox Arts Center," *TheaterWeek* (Mar. 14-20, 1988), 13-15.

NATIONAL IMPROVISATIONAL THEATER
233 Eighth Ave., New York, NY 10011 (212) 243-7224
Contact: Robert Sherer, Director of Production **Theatre:** off off Broadway **Works:** full-length plays, one-acts, translations, adaptations, musicals, children's plays **2nd productions:** if New York City premieres **Special interests:** "Works which convey positive values; productions which are suitable for all age groups." **Specifications:** maximum cast: 10; single set **Stage:** flexible **Audience:** "Looking for new experiences." **Submission policy:** unsolicited script with SASE and resume **Best times:** summer, early winter **Response:** 2 weeks **Your chances:** 24+ submissions/12 productions including one-acts **Programs:** staged readings, workshop productions, scholarships, playwright's workshop (inquire) **Comment:** Theatre emphasizes full productions.

NATIONAL JEWISH THEATER
5050 W. Church St., Skokie, IL 60077 (312) 675-2200
Contact: Sheldon Patinkin, Artistic Director; Fran Brumlik, Managing Director **Theatre:** professional not-for-profit **Works:** full-length plays, translations, adaptations, musicals **2nd productions:** no **Special interests:** "Contemporary American Jewish experience;

American response to Israel." **Specifications:** maximum cast:
10-12 preferred; unit set preferred; no fly space; contemporary
costumes **Stage:** open, 250 seats **Submission policy:** unsolicited
script with SASE **Response:** 2 months **Recent production of
unsolicited work:** no **Future commitment:** negotiable
Programs: readings, workshop productions, internships; National
Jewish Theater Play Writing Competition (see Contests)

THE NATIONAL THEATRE OF THE DEAF
The Hazel E. Stark Center, Chester, CT 06412
(203) 526-4971   Contact: David Hays, Artistic Director
Theatre: professional not-for-profit **Works:** full-length plays,
one-acts, translations, adaptations, children's plays **Tours:** yes
Stages: various spaces **Submission policy:** send SASE for
guidelines **Response:** 3 months **Comment:** Telecommunications
device for the deaf is available: (203) 526-4974.

NATIVE AMERICANS IN THE ARTS
American Indian Community House, 842 Broadway,
New York, NY 10003   (212) 598-4845
Contact: Muriel Miguel, Theatre Coordinator **Theatre:** off off
Broadway, professional not-for-profit **Works:** full-length plays,
one-acts **2nd productions:** yes **Exclusive interest:** works by
or about native Americans **Maximum cast:** 10 **Tours:** yes
Audience: "Community and New York theatregoers." **Submission
policy:** unsolicited script with SASE; query/synopsis with dialogue
sample and resume; professional recommendation **Best time:** fall
Response: 2 weeks query; 2 months script **Your chances:** 5-10
submissions/1 or more productions **Remuneration:** "Depends upon
grants." **Programs:** readings, staged readings, workshop
productions, classes, internships **Comment:** See American Indian
Community House in Special Programs.

N.C. BLACK REPERTORY COMPANY
610 Coliseum Dr., Box 2793, Winston-Salem, NC 27102
(919) 723-7907   Contact: Larry Leon Hamlin, Director
Theatre: professional not-for-profit **Works:** full-length plays,
one-acts, translations, adaptations, musicals, children's plays **2nd
productions:** yes **Special interests:** "Contemporary dramas
involving African-Americans; historical docudramas; statement
comedies." **Specifications:** maximum cast: 8; multiple sets
discouraged **Tours:** yes **Stages:** proscenium; thrust **Submission
policy:** unsolicited script with SASE and resume; query/synopsis
with resume **Best time:** summer-fall **Response:** 8-12 weeks
query **Your chances:** 25 submissions/4-6 productions
Remuneration: negotiable royalty, option, percentage **Programs:**

staged readings, workshop productions, development, classes
Comment: "NCBRC's Playwright's Division is committed to development of new works by produced and unproduced playwrights."

NEBRASKA REPERTORY THEATRE
Lincoln, NE   This theatre is not currently producing new plays.

NEBRASKA THEATRE CARAVAN
6915 Cass St., Omaha, NE 68132   (402) 553-4890
Contact: Carl Beck, Associate Director   **Theatre:** professional not-for-profit   **Works:** full-length plays, translations, adaptations, musicals, children's plays   **2nd productions:** yes   **Special interest:** translations and adaptations of classics   **Specifications:** maximum cast: 12; single set   **Tours:** yes   **Stages:** various spaces   **Submission policy:** unsolicited script with SASE; agent submission   **Response:** 3 months   **Program:** workshops

NEGRO ENSEMBLE COMPANY
155 W. 46th St. 5th Floor, New York, NY 10036
(212) 575-5860   Contact: Douglas Turner Ward, Artistic Director   **Theatre:** professional not-for-profit   **Works:** full-length plays, one-acts, translations, adaptations   **2nd productions:** no   **Exclusive interest:** "The black experience."   **Tours:** yes   **Stage:** proscenium   **Audience:** "Black middle and upper middle class; white middle class."   **Submission policy:** unsolicited script with SASE; query/synopsis; professional recommendation   **Response:** 6 months-1 year   **Your chances:** 60 submissions/4 productions   **Remuneration:** royalty   **Programs:** staged readings, development, classes, playwriting workshop; McDonald's Literary Achievement Awards (see Contests)

NEIL'S NEW YORKER/BELL PRODUCTIONS
Morristown, NJ   Our 1990 questionnaire was returned as "undeliverable," and no phone number is listed for this theatre.

NEW AMERICAN THEATER
118 N. Main St., Rockford, IL 61101
(815) 963-9454   Contact: J. R. Sullivan, Producing Director   **Theatre:** professional not-for-profit   **Works:** full-length plays, one-acts, translations, adaptations   **Stages:** thrust, 282 seats; black box, 90 seats   **Submission policy:** query/synopsis preferred; unsolicited script with SASE   **Best time:** Sept.-Dec.   **Response:** 3 weeks query; 6 months script

NEWBERRY COLLEGE THEATRE
1935 Nance St., Newberry, SC 29108 (803) 276-5010
Contact: Sidney Pitts, Instructor **Theatre:** university/college
Works: full-length plays, one-acts, translations, adaptations,
musicals **2nd productions:** yes **Maximum cast:** 20 **Stages:**
proscenium, 135 seats; arena, 130 seats **Audience:** middle class,
all ages **Submission policy:** unsolicited script with SASE **Best
time:** May-Aug. **Response:** 3 months **Your chances:** 10
submissions/0-1 productions **Remuneration:** no **Advice:** "Any
subject, any style."

NEW CITY THEATER
1634 Eleventh Ave., Seattle, WA 98122 (206) 323-6801
Contact: John Kazanjian, Artistic Director **Theatre:** professional
not-for-profit **Works:** full-length plays, translations, adaptations,
cabaret/revues **2nd productions:** yes **Special interest:**
non-naturalistic contemporary works **Specifications:** some
limitations on production requirements; 11-foot ceiling **Stage:**
flexible, 100 seats **Casting:** "From a resident company of 5-8."
Submission policy: professional recommendation; agent submission
Response: 5 months **Program:** New City Theater Director's
Festival (see Special Programs)

THE NEW CONSERVATORY
Zephyr Theatre Complex, 25 Van Ness Ave.
Lower Level, San Francisco, CA 94102 (415) 861-4914
Contact: Ed Decker, Artistic Director **Theatre:** professional
not-for-profit **Works:** children's plays and adaptations **2nd
productions:** yes **Special interest:** "Plays featuring youth
dealing with socially relevant issues." **Maximum cast:** 8-12
Tours: yes **Stages:** flexible, 60 seats; flexible, 90 seats;
proscenium, 150 seats **Audience:** families **Submission policy:**
query/synopsis with resume **Response:** 2 weeks query; 10 weeks
script **Your chances:** 75 submissions/2 productions
Remuneration: royalty **Programs:** readings, staged readings

NEW FEDERAL THEATRE
466 Grand St., New York, NY 10002 (212) 598-0400
Contact: Woodie King, Jr., Producer **Theatre:** professional
not-for-profit **Works:** full-length plays **2nd productions:** no
Special interest: "Minority themes (Black, Hispanic, Asian,
Jewish)." **Specifications:** maximum cast: 10; single or simple unit
set **Stages:** proscenium, 340 seats; arena, 146 seats; flexible, 99
seats **Audience:** "Tri-state area (NY, NJ, CT)." **Submission
policy:** unsolicited script with SASE; professional recommendation
Best time: Sept.-May **Response:** 3 months **Your chances:** 300

submissions/6 productions plus readings and staged readings
Remuneration: "$250 for 6 months." **Future commitment:** yes

THE NEW JERSEY PUBLIC THEATRE
1052-A Plainfield Ave.,
Berkeley Heights, NJ 07922 (201) 322-3808
Contact: Robert Vaccaro, Artistic Director **Works:** full-length
plays, one-acts, translations, adaptations, musicals, children's plays
2nd productions: yes **Specifications:** some limitations on sets
Stage: flexible **Audience:** "Various backgrounds." **Submission
policy:** unsolicited script with SASE and resume **Response:** 3
months **Your chances:** 5-10 submissions/1-2 productions
Remuneration: percentage **Program:** staged readings **Advice:**
"Playwrights should be themselves, tell the truth and make sure this
is reflected in their work."

NEW JERSEY SHAKESPEARE FESTIVAL
Route 24, Drew University, Madison, NJ 07940
(201) 377-5330 **Contact:** Paul Barry, Artistic Director
Theatre: professional not-for-profit **Works:** full-length plays,
translations **2nd productions:** yes **Special interests:**
"Positive statements of human potential; rich language; plays which
keep the past alive." **Specifications:** maximum cast: 12 for
contemporary works, larger for classics; minimal sets preferred
Stage: thrust, 238 seats **Audience:** "General." **Submission
policy:** professional recommendation preferred; unsolicited script
with SASE **Best time:** fall **Response:** 3 months **Your chances:**
30 submissions/0-1 production **Future commitment:** varies

NEW MEXICO REPERTORY THEATRE
Box 789, Albuquerque, NM 87103-0789 (505) 243-4577
Contact: David Richard Jones, Literary Manager **Theatre:**
professional not-for-profit **Works:** full-length plays, translations,
adaptations, musicals **2nd productions:** yes **Special interests:**
Hispanic-American and Western American life **Tours:** yes **Stages:**
proscenium, 750 seats; proscenium, 340 seats **Audience:**
"Professional, well educated." **Submission policy:** query/synopsis
with dialogue sample; professional recommendation; agent submission
Response: 1 month query; 4-6 months script **Your chances:** 30
submissions/2 productions **Remuneration:** standard royalty

NEW PHOENIX, INC.
42 Cold Spring Rd., Williamstown, MA 01267
(413) 458-5235 Contact: Ralph Hammann, Director
Theatre: professional/semi-professional not-for-profit **Works:**
full-length plays, translations, adaptations **2nd productions** yes

Special interest: "Thrillers that have some psychological complexity and uniqueness." **Specifications:** maximum cast: 8; small set **Tours:** yes **Stages:** proscenium, 290 seats; flexible, 100 seats **Audience:** "Mixed, mostly college educated." **Submission policy:** query/synopsis with dialogue sample; professional recommendation **Response:** 3 weeks query; 2 months script **Remuneration:** "May offer small royalty." **Programs:** readings, staged readings

NEW PLAY PRODUCTIONS
Box 134, Holmdel, NJ 07733 (201) 583-5420
Contact: Richard Trahan, Executive Director **Theatre:** community/non-professional **Works:** full-length plays, one-acts **2nd productions:** yes **Special interests:** "Political and social satire, psychological themes, farce, black comedy, sensitive subjects. Surreal, absurdist or expressionistic treatments are especially welcome." **Specifications:** maximum cast: 20; "portable set" **Tours:** yes **Stages:** rented spaces **Casting:** "Priority is given to membership, then to local community." **Audience:** "Upscale, scientific/engineering; mixed ethnic backgrounds." **Submission policy:** unsolicited script with SASE **Response:** 1 month query; 3 months script **Remuneration/future commitment:** no **Advice:** "We want plays that can arouse or disturb. If it's suitable for dinner theatre, don't send it."

NEW PLAYWRIGHTS' PROGRAM
Department of Theatre and Dance, University of Alabama, Box 870239, Tuscaloosa, AL 35487-0239
(205) 348-5283 Contact: Paul Castagno, Director **Theatre:** university/college **Works:** full-length plays, one-acts, translations, adaptations, musicals, children's plays **Stages:** mainstage, 338 seats; studio lab, 100 seats **Submission policy:** unsolicited script with SASE **Best time:** Aug.-Apr. **Response:** 60 days if submitted Aug.-Apr. **Your chances:** at least 1 new play produced each season **Programs:** staged readings, development; Plays for a New America (see Contests)

THE NEW ROSE THEATRE
904 SW Main St., Portland, OR 97205 (503) 222-2495
Contact: Michael Griggs, Artistic Director **Theatre:** professional not-for-profit **Works:** full-length plays, translations, adaptations, children's plays **2nd productions:** yes **Special interests:** multi-cultural casting; adaptations and contemporary translations of classics or classical themes **Stages:** 3/4 thrust, 119 seats; flexible, 292-400 seats **Submission policy:** query/synopsis with dialogue sample **Best time:** Aug.-Jan. **Response:** 2-4 weeks

query; 3-6 months script **Remuneration:** negotiable royalty
Program: readings

NEW STAGE THEATRE
1100 Carlisle St., Jackson, MS 39202 (601) 948-3533
Contact: Jane Reid-Petty, Producing Artistic Director **Theatre:**
professional not-for-profit **Works:** full-length plays, one-acts
Specifications: small cast **Stages:** proscenium, 365 seats;
flexible, 100 seats **Submission policy:** query/synopsis **Best
time:** summer-fall **Response:** 2-4 weeks query; 3-5 months script
Your chances: 1 new play is produced in alternate seasons.
Program: Eudora Welty New Plays Series: annual series of
readings (inquire)

THE NEW THEATRE ALLIANCE
AT THE ACTING STUDIO
31 West 21st St., New York, NY 10010 (212) 206-8608
Contact: John Grabowski, Studio Administrator **Theatre:** off off
Broadway **Works:** full-length plays, one-acts, translations,
adaptations, musicals **2nd productions:** yes **Special interest:**
current social issues **Stage:** black box, 60-95 seats **Casting:**
shows are precast from a pool **Audience:** "Mixed New York,
students." **Submission policy:** unsolicited script with SASE;
professional recommendation, agent submission **Best time:**
Jun.-Sept. **Response:** 3 months **Your chances:** 15 submissions/3
productions **Programs:** readings, staged readings, workshop
productions **Advice:** "Original thought."

NEW THEATRE
Box 650696, Miami, FL 33265 (305) 595-4260
Contact: Rafael DeAcha, Artistic Director **Theatre:** non-Equity
not-for-profit **Works:** full-length plays, one-acts, translations,
adaptations, musicals, children's plays **2nd productions:** yes
Special interest: "Non-realistic drama." **Specifications:**
maximum cast: 4-5; "creative sets; no kitchen-sink drama" **Stage:**
black box, 60 seats **Casting:** "Some open auditions, some
precasting from core." **Audience:** "Mixed cultures; young and old."
Submission policy: unsolicited script with SASE; commission
Response: 2 months **Your chances:** 100-200 submissions/3-4
productions; in its 4-season history the theatre has mounted 35
productions, 1/3 of them new plays or 2nd productions
Remuneration: negotiable royalty **Future commitment:** no
Programs: readings, workshop productions, development; children's
program: grant allows school children to attend performances each
Friday **Advice:** "No TV or movie scripts! Use imagination!"

THE NEW THEATRE OF BROOKLYN
465 Dean St., Brooklyn, NY 11217 (718) 230-3366
Contact: Janice Paran, Literary Manager **Theatre:** professional not-for-profit **Works:** full-length plays, translations, adaptations **2nd productions:** if previously produced outside the New York area **Special interests:** women's and minority issues; non-realistic, non-naturalistic comedy and drama; translations **Specifications:** maximum cast: 9; single set; simple requirements; no fly space; low ceiling **Stage:** black box, 99 seats **Casting:** "We use our files and agent submissions." **Audience:** "Wide cross-section." **Submission policy:** query/synopsis with 5-7 page dialogue sample, production history and resume preferred; professional recommendation; agent submission **Response:** 2 months query; 6 months script **Your chances:** varying number of submissions/1 production **Remuneration:** "Small honorarium--varies with production." **Future commitment:** no **Programs:** readings, internships **Advice:** "Please do not send a script without calling."

NEW TUNERS THEATRE
1225 Belmont Ave., Chicago, IL 60657 (312) 929-7367
Contact: George H. Gorham, Associate Producer **Theatre:** professional not-for-profit **Works:** musicals, musical adaptations **2nd productions:** yes **Special interests:** "New and exciting uses of music, as well as more traditional forms. We are less interested in operatic works, but we'll consider. We are particularly interested in scripts using a younger (35 and under) ensemble." **Specifications:** maximum cast: 15; no children's material **Stages:** modified thrust, 148 seats; thrust, 148 seats **Casting:** "Non-Equity, although all performers are paid. We cast absolutely color-blind." **Audience:** "Suburban, traditional theatregoers and younger urban audiences; also out-of-towners." **Submission policy:** unsolicited script with SASE and cassette of score **Response:** "Pretty quick" query; 6 months script **Your chances:** 250 submissions/0-1 production **Most recent production of unsolicited work:** 1985 **Remuneration:** "6%-10% of box office gross, possible stipend." **Future commitments:** "We usually retain the right to remount the show in this territory and 6% of future royalties. We suggest that authors submit now and negotiate later." **Programs:** readings, staged readings, workshop productions, development, internships, classes

NEW VOICES
551 Tremont St., Boston, MA 02116 (617) 357-5667
Contact: Stanley Richardson, Artistic Director **Theatre:** professional not-for-profit **Works:** full-length plays, one-acts, adaptations **2nd productions:** yes **Special interests:**

"Language; socially and politically engaging plays." **Tours:** "Sometimes." **Specifications:** maximum cast: 8; no unit sets **Stages:** various spaces, 99-250 seats **Submission policy:** query/synopsis; professional recommendation; agent submission **Best time:** Sept.-Jun. only **Response:** 1 month query; 4 months script **Your chances:** 100 submissions/10 productions **Remuneration/future commitment:** negotiable **Programs:** staged readings, workshop productions, development, internships; Clauder Competition for Excellence (see Contests) **Advice:** "Focus on ideas, language. Forget psychological motivations. Care."

NEW YORK SHAKESPEARE FESTIVAL
Public Theater, 425 Lafayette St.,
New York, NY 10003 (212) 598-7100, -7129
Contact: Joseph Papp, Producer; Gail Merrifield Papp, Director, New Plays and Musicals Development **Theatre:** off Broadway, professional not-for-profit **Works:** full-length plays, translations, adaptations, musicals, operas **2nd productions:** "Not often." **Special interests:** "Themes of sociological impact; individual and unusual writing talent." **Tours:** "Sometimes." **Stages:** proscenium, 299 seats; proscenium, 200 seats; thrust, 275 seats; flexible, 150 seats; flexible, 100 seats **Audience:** "Totally eclectic." **Submission policy:** unsolicited script with SASE and resume; query/synopsis with dialogue sample and resume; professional recommendation; agent submission **Response:** 2-3 weeks query; 8-10 weeks script **Your chances:** 3000 submissions/15 productions **Remuneration:** negotiable **Programs:** readings, development

NEW YORK STAGE AND FILM COMPANY
450 W. 42nd St. Suite 21, New York, NY 10036
(212) 967-3130 Contact: Jean Wagner, Readings Coordinator **Theatre:** professional not-for-profit **Works:** full-length plays **Special interests:** "New plays; short films; feature films." **Submission policy:** professional recommendation; agent submission **Best time:** fall-winter **Response:** 6 months **Your chances:** 300 submissions/2 productions plus 15 staged readings **Programs:** staged readings, workshop productions, development, internships, residencies, classes

THE NEW YORK THEATRE GROUP
Box 1557, New York, NY 10011 (718) 624-4680
Contact: John Hennessy, Artistic Director **Theatre:** off off Broadway, professional not-for-profit **Works:** full-length plays, one-acts **2nd productions:** yes **Special interests:** "Contemporary social issues; plays that explore the possibilities of

language; theatricality." **Audience:** "Eclectic, young, New York; broad social/cultural base." **Submission policy:** query with 15-20 page dialogue sample   **Your chances:** 200-300 submissions/15 staged readings and workshop productions **Remuneration:** "For full-length play only: percentage of box office on contract." **Programs:** readings, development; New American Plays Series   (see Special Programs) **Advice:** "Send 1 sample at a time--your best!"

NEW YORK THEATRE STUDIO
New York, NY Our 1990 questionnaire was returned as "undeliverable," and no phone number is listed for this theatre.

NEW YORK THEATRE WORKSHOP
220 W. 42nd St. 18th Floor, New York, NY 10036
(212) 302-7737   Contact: Nina Mankin, Literary Manager **Theatre:** professional not-for-profit **Works:** full-length plays, one-acts, translations, adaptations, musicals **2nd productions:** occasionally **Special interests:** "Socially relevant and/or minority issues; innovations in form and language; adaptations of worthy source material." **Specifications:** maximum cast: 8; intimate space; limited budget **Stage:** proscenium, 99 seats **Submission policy:** unsolicited script with SASE; query/synopsis with 10-page sample scene; proposal; solicited work; professional recommendation; agent submission **Response:** 1-3 weeks query; 3-5 months script **Recent production of unsolicited work:** readings **Future commitment:** "Usually." **Programs:** staged readings, development, symposia

THE NEXT THEATRE COMPANY
927 Noyes, Evanston, IL 60201   (312) 475-6763
Contact: Harriet Spizziri, Artistic Director **Theatre:** professional not-for-profit **Works:** full-length plays, adaptations **2nd productions:** yes **Special interests:** well-written plays; current social issues **Specifications:** maximum cast: 15; single or flexible set **Stage:** proscenium, 200 seats **Audience:** "Mixed." **Submission policy:** query/synopsis with dialogue sample, resume and SAS postcard; professional recommendation; agent submission **Response:** 1 month query; 6 months script **Your chances:** 200 submissions/"1 production in 10 years" **Remuneration:** standard royalty **Programs:** staged readings, workshop productions

NIGGLI, WESTERN CAROLINA UNIVERSITY
Cullowhee, NC 28723   (704) 227-7491
Contact: Larry Hill, Chairman **Theatre:** university/college **Works:** full-length plays, one-acts, children's plays **2nd productions:** no **Special interest:** "Plays suitable for college

actors." **Specifications**: small theatre; limited wing space **Tours**: children's plays **Stages**: proscenium, 148 seats; proscenium, 474 seats **Audience**: university and community; senior adults **Submission policy**: unsolicited script with SASE **Best time**: Feb. **Response**: 1 month **Your chances**: 15 submissions/1 production **Remuneration**: no **Programs**: workshop productions; Annual New Playwrights' Festival (see Contests) **Advice**: "Appeal to university theatre students."

NO EMPTY SPACE THEATRE
See No Empty Space Theatre Playwriting Contest listing in Contests.

NORTH CAROLINA SHAKESPEARE FESTIVAL
Box 6066, High Point, NC 27262 (919) 841-6273
Contact: Louis Rackoff, Artistic Director **Theatre**: professional not-for-profit **Works**: full-length plays, translations, adaptations **Special interests**: North Carolina writers; adaptations of classics **Specifications**: mainstage: translations and adaptations of classics, maximum cast: 15, simple set; 2nd stage: new plays, maximum cast: 6, unit set **Stages**: mainstage: proscenium, 620 seats; 2nd stage: arena/thrust, 150-250 seats **Submission policy**: query/synopsis **Best time**: fall **Response**: 3 weeks query; 4 months script

NORTHLIGHT THEATRE
2300 Green Bay Rd., Evanston, IL 60201
(312) 869-7732 Contact: Literary Department
Theatre: professional not-for-profit **Works**: full-length plays, translations, adaptations, musicals **2nd productions**: yes **Special interests**: "Public issues; Chicago and regional subjects; translations and adaptations of 'lost' plays; stylistic exploration and complexity; plays of ideas." **Specifications**: "No domestic realism; no orchestra pit." **Stage**: proscenium-thrust, 298 seats **Audience**: "Upper middle-class, college/post graduates, 35-60." **Submission policy**: query/synopsis with resume; agent submission **Best time**: Sept.-Feb. **Response**: 4-8 weeks query; 2-4 months script **Remuneration**: negotiable **Advice**: "We prefer ambitious plays that acknowledge and utilize the patent theatricality of the medium."

NORTHSIDE THEATRE COMPANY
848 E. William St., San Jose, CA 95116 (408) 288-7820
Contact: Richard T. Orlando, Executive Director **Theatre**: professional not-for-profit young people's theatre **Works**: full-length plays, one-acts and adaptations for young audiences **2nd productions**: yes **Special interest**: "Small-cast plays dealing with concerns of youth: peer pressure, sexual abuse, drug awareness." **Maximum cast**: 8 **Tours**: yes **Stages**: "We have a

modular performance space; touring, we've played them all." **Audience:** "Young and old, rich and poor." **Submission policy:** unsolicited script with SASE; query/synopsis **Best time:** after Jan. **Response:** 4-6 weeks **Your chances:** 20 submissions/3-4 productions **Remuneration:** "Small royalty." **Programs:** readings, staged readings, contests (inquire) **Advice:** "We are looking for touring productions 40-50 minutes in length." **Comment:** "We are not a children's theatre."

OAKLAND ENSEMBLE THEATRE
1428 Alice St. Suite 289, Oakland, CA 94612
(415) 763-7774 Contact: Jeannie Barroga, Literary Manager/Dramaturg **Theatre:** professional **Works:** full-length plays, adaptations, musicals, cabaret/revues **2nd productions:** yes **Special interest:** "Works predominantly about African-American/minority issues." **Specifications:** 0-10 sets **Tours:** yes **Stage:** proscenium, thrust, arena, flexible; 500 seats **Casting:** "Per show; per season; out-ot-town when applicable; racial casts preferred; balance of male/female roles encouraged." **Audience:** "Median income $25,000-$45,000, median age 25-35, college educated, theatregoing, 65% African-American, 35% other." **Submission policy:** unsolicited script with SASE, synopsis, resume, production history and reviews; professional recommendation; agent submission **Response:** 1-2 months, "longer for summer submission" **Your chances:** 50 submissions/0-1 productions **Recent production of unsolicited work:** no **Remuneration/future commitment:** negotiable **Programs:** staged readings, workshop productions, development **Advice:** "Advanced, well-written work; minority sensibilities most applicable; balance of comedy/drama in social issues."

OAK RIDGE COMMUNITY PLAYHOUSE
Box 3223, Oak Ridge, TN 37831 (615) 482-9999
Contact: Stephen F. Krempasky, Managing Director **Theatre:** community/non-professional **Works:** full-length plays, one-acts, translations, adaptations, musicals, children's plays **2nd productions:** yes **Specifications:** maximum cast: 50; small stage; no fly space **Stage:** proscenium, 340 seats **Audience:** "Middle-aged median, 60% female." **Submission policy:** unsolicited script with SASE **Best time:** fall **Response:** 1-2 months **Your chances:** 6 submissions/1 production **Remuneration:** "Very limited." **Advice:** "We are interested in receiving children's plays for Junior Playhouse Program."

ODYSSEY THEATER COMPANY, INC.

2 Bond St., New York, NY 10012 (212) 673-5665
Contact: Andrew Arnault, Co-Artistic Director **Theatre:** off off Broadway **Works:** full-length plays, adaptations **2nd productions:** yes **Special interests:** "Themes of voyagers and their voyages; theatrical image and movement; live musical accompaniment **Maximum cast:** 9 **Stage:** open loft space, flexible seating **Casting:** open auditions **Audience:** "New York cross-section." **Submission policy:** unsolicited script with SASE; query/synopsis with dialogue sample; agent submission; commission **Best time:** summer-fall **Response:** 6 weeks **Your chances:** 10 submissions/0 productions **Remuneration:** "Negotiable-- $200-$400 range." **Future commitment:** no **Program:** readings **Advice:** "We usually produce original adaptations of literary works, stylized investigations of voyagers and their voyages, which include close interaction between actors and musicians."

ODYSSEY THEATRE ENSEMBLE

2055 S. Sepulveda Blvd., Los Angeles, CA 90025
(213) 826-1626 Contact: Jan Lewis, Literary Manager **Theatre:** professional not-for-profit **Works:** full-length plays, translations, adaptations, musicals **2nd productions:** yes **Special interests:** "Provocative subject matter; highly theatrical material." **Tours:** "Sometimes." **Stages:** flexible thrust, 99 seats; L-shaped arena, 99 seats; proscenium, 99 seats **Audience:** "Upper middle-class, urban, primarily over 30." **Submission policy:** query/synopsis with dialogue sample, production history and resume; agent submission **Response:** 2 weeks query; 6 months script **Your chances:** 500 submissions/3-5 productions **Remuneration:** negotiable royalty **Future commitment:** negotiable **Program:** readings **Advice:** "Please check on the kind of work we have done--get to know us before you make submissions."

OFF BROADWAY

1444 NE 26th, Wilton Manor, FL 33305 (305) 566-0554
Contact: Brian C. Smith **Theatre:** professional not-for-profit **Works:** full-length plays, one-acts, translations **2nd productions:** yes **Maximum cast:** 12 **Stage:** proscenium, 300 seats **Audience:** general **Submission policy:** query/synopsis with resume **Best time:** summer **Response:** 4-6 weeks **Your chances:** 40-50 submissions/2+ productions **Remuneration:** negotiable

OFF CENTER THEATRE
1501 Broadway Suite 1310, New York, NY 10036
(212) 768-3277 Contact: Ken Lipman, Literary Manager
Theatre: off off Broadway, professional not-for-profit **Works:**
full-length plays, musicals **2nd productions:** no **Special
interest:** "Issue-oriented comedies." **Stages:** rented spaces
Audience: "New Yorkers." **Submission policy** unsolicited script
with SASE **Response:** 1-5 months **Your chances:** 450
submissions/1 production plus 4 series of readings **Remuneration:**
no **Programs:** staged readings, development

OHIO THEATER
66 Wooster St., New York, NY 10013   (212) 481-0188
Contact: Marcy Drogin, Producer **Theatre:** off off Broadway
Works: full-length plays, one-acts, translations, adaptations,
musicals, children's plays **2nd productions:** yes **Special
interests:** "Social, political and moral issues." **Stage:** black box,
75 seats **Audience:** "Young audiences--18-30." **Submission
policy:** query/synopsis with resume **Best times:** Jan., May
Response: 2-6 weeks **Your chances:** 3 new plays produced each
season **Remuneration:** no **Programs:** staged readings, workshop
productions **Advice:** "Thoughtful plays."

OLDCASTLE THEATRE COMPANY
Box 1555, Bennington, VT 05201   (802) 447-0564
Contact: Eric Peterson, Producing Director **Theatre:** professional
not-for-profit **Works:** full-length plays, musicals **2nd
productions:** yes **Special interest:** "New England subjects."
Specifications: maximum cast: 10; single set **Tours:** yes
Stage: modified proscenium **Audience:** "General New England."
Submission policy: unsolicited script with SASE; query/synopsis;
professional recommendation **Best time:** winter **Response:** 2-3
months **Your chances:** varying number of submissions/1-2
productions **Recent production of unsolicited work:** yes
Remuneration: standard royalty **Program:** readings

OLD CREAMERY THEATRE COMPANY
Box 160, Garrison, IA 52229   (319) 477-3925
Contact: Thomas Peter Johnson,   Artistic and Producing Director
Theatre: professional not-for-profit **Works:** full-length plays,
translations, adaptations, musicals, children's plays **2nd
productions:** yes **Special interests:** touring plays for young
audiences; plays with commercial appeal **Specifications:** maximum
cast: 12 for thrust stage, 2-6 for flexible space; single set preferred;
works must be suitable for touring; limited budget **Stages:** thrust,
265 seats; flexible, 130 seats **Audience:** "Average age 55; avoids

plays with profanity or urban appeal." **Submission policy:** unsolicited script with SASE; query/synopsis **Best time:** Oct.–Jan. **Response:** 4–6 weeks

OLD GLOBE THEATRE
Box 2171, San Diego, CA 92112 (619) 231-1941
Contact: Robert Berlinger, Associate Director **Theatre:** professional not-for-profit **Works:** full-length plays, translations, adaptations, musicals **2nd productions:** yes **Special interests:** "Well-crafted plays; theatricality." **Maximum cast:** 12 preferred **Stages:** thrust, 541 seats; arena, 225 seats; outdoor stage, 620 seats **Audience:** "Wide base." **Submission policy:** query/ synopsis with resume; agent submission **Response:** 1 month query; 3–7 months script **Your chances:** 1000 submissions/1–2 productions plus 4–6 readings **Remuneration/future commitment:** negotiable **Programs:** readings, staged readings, workshop productions, development, internships **Advice:** "Please adhere to guidelines for submission."

OLD LOG THEATER
Box 250, Excelsior, MN 55331 (612) 474-5951
Contact: Don Stolz, Producing Artistic Director **Theatre:** professional year-round stock **Works:** full-length plays, adaptations **2nd productions:** yes **Special interest:** small-cast comedies **Stage:** proscenium, 655 seats **Audience:** "All ages." **Submission policy:** unsolicited script with SASE; query/synopsis **Response:** 1 month query; 6 months script **Your chances:** Theatre receives approximately 200 new scripts each year and intends to produce original scripts in Off Night Series. **Remuneration:** negotiable royalty **Program:** "Occasional readings." **Comments:** Theatre has long run plays. See Stelling, Lucille Johnsen, "The Old Log Theater of Lake Minnetonka, Minnesota," *TheaterWeek* (Jul. 24, 1989), 38–41.

THE OLD SLOCUM HOUSE THEATRE
605 Esther St., Vancouver, WA 98660 (206) 695-5762
Contact: Hermine Duthie Decker, President **Theatre:** community/non-professional **Works:** full-length plays, translations, adaptations, musicals **2nd productions:** yes **Exclusive interest:** "The 19th century or earlier." **Specifications:** maximum cast: 10; simple set **Stage:** proscenium, 61 seats **Submission policy:** query/synopsis **Your chances:** 1 submission/1 production **Remuneration:** no **Advice:** "Our historic site was presented on the premise that we make the plays living history. You do not need a previous production, only the willingness to revise."

OMAHA MAGIC THEATRE
1417 Farnam St., Omaha, NE 68102 (402) 346-1227
Contact: Megan Terry, Literary Manager **Theatre:** professional not-for-profit **Works:** avant garde plays and musicals, experimental youth theatre, performance art **Exclusive interests:** "The most avant of the avant garde; works considered unproducible by other theatres; performance art from musicians, dancers, visual artists." **Tours:** "We tour a total avant garde production or performance event. We do not cut down productions for touring." **Stages:** flexible, 100 seats; non-traditional and outdoor spaces **Audience:** "People from all walks of life." **Submission policy:** unsolicited script with SASE and $30 critique fee **Response:** 3 months **Your chances:** 1300+ submissions/8-10 productions **Remuneration:** standard royatly **Advice:** "Astonish us!"

ONE ACT THEATRE COMPANY
430 Mason St., San Francisco, CA 94102
(415) 421-5355 Contact: Michael Duff, Literary Manager **Theatre:** professional not-for-profit **Works:** one-acts **2nd productions:** yes **Special interests:** "Long one-acts (60-100 minutes); third-world playwrights; political themes; strong female roles." **Specifications:** maximum cast: 8-12; single set or open staging **Stage:** thrust, 140-150 seats **Audience:** "Older, white, educated, politically savvy." **Submission policy:** unsolicited script with SASE; query/synopsis; professional recommendation; agent submission **Response:** 3 months query; 6 months script **Your chances:** 300-400 submissions/1-2 productions **Remuneration:** negotiable **Program:** readings **Advice:** "Innovative, challenging plays that avoid the sit-com format."

ON STAGE PRODUCTIONS: ON STAGE, CHILDREN
50 W. 97th St. #8H, New York, NY 10025
(212) 666-1716 Contact: Frank Lee, Artistic Director **Theatre:** off off Broadway, professional not-for-profit **Works:** full-length plays, one-acts, musicals, children's plays **2nd productions:** yes **Special interest:** "Contemporary social concerns." **Specifications:** maximum cast: 8; interracial cast; minimal sets; small budget **Tours:** yes **Stage:** multi-use space **Audience:** "Families; mixed racially and economically; young audiences." **Submission policy:** query/synopsis **Best time:** Jun. **Your chances:** 4-5 new plays produced each season **Remuneration:** $5 per performance

THE OPEN EYE NEW STAGINGS
270 W. 89th St., New York, NY 10024 (212) 769-4141
Contact: Amie Brockway, Artistic Director **Theatre:** professional not-for-profit **Works:** full-length plays, one-acts, translations, adaptations, musicals, children's plays **2nd productions:** if not previously produced in New York City **Special interests:** "Plays which invite us as artists and audience to take a fresh look at ourselves and the world of which we are a part; plays for a family audience; non-realistic works; plays incorporating music and dance." **Specifications:** maximum cast: 13; no fly space; sets must be easily set up and struck **Tours:** yes **Stage:** modified proscenium, 115 seats **Casting:** "Auditions--announced in *Backstage*." **Audience:** "A typical urban mix." **Submission policy:** unsolicited script with SASE; professional recommendation; agent submission **Best time:** Apr.-Jul. **Response:** 3-6 months **Your chances:** 400 or more submissions/1-5 or more productions **Remuneration:** $500-$1500 **Future commitment:** "Possibly." **Programs:** readings, staged readings, workshop productions; "Eye on Playwrights" festival (inquire) **Advice:** "Please do not send synopsis or dialogue sample."

ORDER BEFORE MIDNIGHT
Philadelphia, PA Our 1990 questionnaire was returned as "undeliverable," and no phone number is listed for this theatre.

OREGON SHAKESPEARE FESTIVAL
Box 158, Ashland, OR 97520 (503) 482-2111
Contact: Cynthia White, Literary Manager **Theatre:** professional not-for-profit **Works:** full-length plays, translations **2nd productions:** yes **Specifications:** small cast preferred for flexible space **Stages:** thrust, 600 seats; outdoor Elizabethan, 1194 seats; black box, 140 seats **Audience:** "90% from 150 miles from Ashland (large cities)." **Submission policy:** query/synopsis with dialogue sample and resume; professional recommendation **Best time:** Jan.-May **Response:** 6 months **Your chances:** 200 submissions/0-1 production plus 4 staged readings **Remuneration:** negotiable royalty **Future commitment:** negotiable **Programs:** new play reading series, development **Advice:** "Don't expect quick responses. Do keep after me, in a nice way, to read your play. And if I say I'm not interested in your play, believe me. "

ORGANIC THEATER COMPANY
3319 N. Clark St., Chicago, IL 60657 (312) 327-5360
Contact: Lawrence Santoro, Literary Manager **Theatre:** professional not-for-profit **Works:** full-length plays, long one-acts, adaptations, small-scale musicals and operas **2nd productions:** no

Special interest: original, unproduced works to be developed in collaboration with the theatre **Specifications:** maximum cast: 10 for lab theatre; playing time for one-acts: 60 minutes or longer **Tours:** yes **Stages:** 3/4 thrust, 400 seats; flexible lab, 80 seats **Audience:** "Young, intelligent." **Submission policy:** query/ synopsis with 10-page dialogue sample strongly preferred; unsolicited script with SASE; agent submission **Response:** immediate query; 3-4 months script **Your chances:** 300 submissions/3-4 productions **Recent production of unsolicited work:** 1989 **Future commitment:** varies **Programs:** staged readings, workshop productions, development, internships; classes planned for future **Advice:** "Please do not call. Send us something that you're passionately interested in, rather than something that you think will sell."

PAN ASIAN REPERTORY THEATRE
47 Great Jones St., New York, NY 10012
(212) 505-5655 **Contact:** Tisa Chang, Artistic/Producing Director **Theatre:** professional not-for-profit **Works:** full-length plays, translations, adaptations, musicals **2nd productions:** yes **Special interest:** "Works suitable for our company of Asian American artists." **Maximum cast:** 8-10 **Tours:** yes **Stage:** proscenium, 151 seats **Casting:** "Resident ensemble." **Audience:** "Half Asian, half non-Asian." **Submission policy:** unsolicited script with SASE and resume **Best time:** summer **Response:** 6-9 months **Your chances:** 60 submissions/3 productions **Recent production of unsolicited work:** no **Remuneration:** "30% of box office." **Future commitment:** yes **Programs:** mainstage readings, staged readings, workshop productions

PAPER MILL PLAYHOUSE
Brookside Dr., Millburn, NJ 07041 (201) 379-3636
Contact: Maryan F. Stephens, Literary Manager **Theatre:** professional not-for-profit **Works:** full-length plays, translations, adaptations, musicals, operas **2nd productions:** yes **Special interests:** new musicals; musical adaptations of previously produced plays; large-scale works **Maximum cast:** 30, 20-25 preferred **Tours:** yes **Stage:** proscenium, 1192 seats **Submission policy:** unsolicited script with SASE and synopsis; query/synopsis **Response:** 2 weeks query; 6-8 weeks script **Future commitment:** option for ongoing production of works developed in workshop or in production **Programs:** readings, staged readings, laboratory productions; Musical Theatre Project: testing of new musicals in a workshop/reading situation (inquire)

PASADENA PLAYHOUSE
39 S. El Molino, Pasadena, CA 9110 (818) 792-8672
Contact: Susan Dietz, Artistic Director **Theatre:** professional not-for-profit **Works:** full-length plays, one-acts, translations, adaptations, musicals, children's plays **2nd productions:** possibly (send reviews) **Specifications:** "Limited mainly by finances." **Stage:** proscenium, 700 seats **Audience:** "They expect and deserve the best." **Submission policy:** query/synopsis with dialogue sample and resume; professional recommendation; agent submission **Response:** 6 months **Remuneration:** negotiable

PAUL BUNYAN PLAYHOUSE
2008 Brewster #301, St. Paul, MN 55108
(218) 751-6238 (Jun.-Aug.) **Contact:** Play Selection Committee **Theatre:** professional not-for-profit, summer stock **Works:** full-length plays, one-acts, translations, adaptations, musicals, children's plays **Special interests:** "Minnesota and Upper Midwest playwrights; works suitable for signing for hearing-impaired." **Specifications:** simple production requirements **Stage:** proscenium, 222 seats **Submission policy:** unsolicited script with SASE **Best time:** fall **Response:** 2-4 months

PAYSON COMMUNITY THEATRE
317 E. 100 S, Payson, UT 85651 (801) 465-3317
Contact: Charles L. Frost, Artistic Director **Theatre:** community/non-professional **Works:** full-length plays, one-acts, children's plays **2nd productions:** no **Tours:** yes **Stages:** proscenium; thrust **Audience:** "Educated, conservative." **Submission policy:** unsolicited script with SASE **Best time:** summer **Response:** 3 months **Your chances:** 7 submissions/1 production **Remuneration:** royalty **Program:** staged readings **Advice:** "Submit--as soon as possible!"

PAYSON PLAYMAKERS
893 S. 880 W, Payson, UT 84651 (801) 465-2752
Contact: Dee Hill, President **Theatre:** community/non-professional **Works:** children's musicals **Special interests:** well-known stories; current issues **Tours:** only in summer **Stages:** high school proscenium; flexible **Casting:** "We have a 4-week summer session for 7-17 year-olds and produce 1 play each summer; all who attend are eligible for acting roles." **Audience:** all ages **Submission policy:** unsolicited script with SASE **Response:** 3 months **Remuneration:** negotiable **Advice:** "We are interested in receiving original works."

PCPA THEATERFEST

Box 1700, Santa Maria, CA 93456 (805) 928-7731
Contact: Cheryl Weiss, Literary Manager **Theatre:** professional not-for-profit; conservatory training program **Works:** full-length plays, one-acts, translations, adaptations, musicals **2nd productions:** yes **Special interests:** unique voices, fresh approaches **Specifications:** large-scale works with broad audience appeal for large theatre; small-cast, minimal-set works on bold and contemporary subjects with appeal to sophisticated audience for intimate staging **Stages:** thrust, 700 seats; thrust, 508 seats; black box-arena, 160 seats; arena, 130 seats **Casting:** "From a pool and state-wide auditions." **Audience:** "Middle to upper class from central coast of California; state-wide and national in summer." **Submission policy:** query with letter of interest; professional recommendation; agent submission **Response:** 5 weeks query; 6 months script **Your chances:** 300-500 query and script submissions/2 productions **Future commitment:** yes **Program:** Outreach projects for children; flexible staging requirements, small cast, minimal set and props (inquire) **Comment:** See Stevens, Rob, "A Tale of Two Cities," *TheaterWeek* (Oct. 3, 1988), 48-53.

PEGASUS PLAYERS

1145 W. Wilson Ave., Chicago, IL 60640 (312) 878-9761
Contact: Arlene Crewdson, Artistic Director **Theatre:** non-Equity not-for-profit **Works:** full-length plays, one-acts, translations, adaptations, musicals, children's plays **2nd productions:** yes **Special interest:** "Topics of social value." **Stage:** proscenium-thrust, 250 seats **Casting:** open auditions **Audience:** "General America—20% of ticket sales are to social service organizations." **Submission policy:** query/synopsis with resume **Best time:** "Beginning of summer." **Response:** 1 month **Your chances:** 10-15 submissions/0-1 production **Recent production of unsolicited work:** 1989 **Remuneration:** negotiable **Future commitment:** "Depends upon situation." **Programs:** development, internships, residencies, classes; Young Playwrights Festival (see Contests) **Advice:** "Plays should have a moral center."

PENGUIN REPERTORY COMPANY

Box 91, Stony Point, NY 10980 (914) 947-3741
Contact: Joe Brancato, Artistic Director **Theatre:** professional not-for-profit **Works:** full-length plays, translations, adaptations, small-scale musicals, revues **2nd productions:** yes **Special interest:** "New works." **Specifications:** maximum cast: 6-8; single set or suggestive settings **Stage:** proscenium-thrust, 108 seats **Submission policy:** unsolicited script with SASE; commission **Best time:** Dec.-Jan. **Response:** 3-6 months **Pecent production**

of unsolicited work: yes **Future commitment:** negotiable
Programs: readings, staged readings

PENNSYLVANIA STAGE COMPANY
837 Linden St., Allentown, PA 18101 (215) 434-8570
Contact: Literary Manager **Theatre:** professional not-for-profit
Works: full-length plays, translations, adaptations, musicals **2nd
productions:** yes **Special interest:** "Works that have a passion
for being presented now, that are entertaining and meaningful to our
community and perpetuate our theatrical and literary heritage."
Specifications: maximum cast: 7 for play, 10 for musical; single
set preferred; "no grossly offensive language" **Stage:** proscenium,
273 seats **Audience:** "Middle class, anglo, fairly conservative,
20-senior citizen." **Submission policy:** query/synopsis with
10-page dialogue sample **Response:** 3 weeks query; 4 months script
Your chances: 300 submissions/productions of 1 play and 1 musical
plus 6 staged readings **Remuneration:** negotiable **Program:** New
Evolving Works: staged readings (inquire) **Advice:** "Plays with
universal and/or mythical scope. Plays that reach beyond discussions
around a kitchen table to touch on larger issues, ask demanding
questions and offer possible solutions. We do not produce one-acts on
mainstage but would be interested in 2-character one-acts."

PENNYRILE PLAYERS THEATRE
410 S. Main, Hopkinsville, KY 42240 (502) 885-2401
Contact: Nita Peacock, Artistic Director **Theatre:** not-for-profit
community/non-professional **Works:** full-length plays, one-acts,
musicals, children's plays **2nd productions:** no **Tours:** yes
Stage: proscenium, 222 seats **Submission policy:** unsolicited
script with SASE **Response:** 1 month **Your chances:** 0-5
submissions/varying number of productions "depending upon quality of
scripts" **Remuneration:** "Each viewed in its own right." **Advice:**
"Low royalties. Family entertainment or children's shows, preferably!
We would like to receive original plays."

THE PENUMBRA THEATRE COMPANY
270 N. Kent St., St. Paul, MN 55102 (612) 224-4601
Contact: Lou Bellamy, Artistic Director **Theatre:** professional
not-for-profit **Works:** full-length plays, one-acts, translations,
adaptations, musicals, children's plays **2nd productions:** yes
Special interest: "The African-American experience." **Tours:**
"Yes, 1-and 2-person shows." **Stage:** proscenium-thrust, 150
seats **Submission policy:** unsolicited script with SASE and
resume **Best time:** Jan.-Mar. **Response:** 6-9 months **Your
chances:** 60 submissions/1 production **Program:** Cornerstone (see
Contests)

PEOPLE'S LIGHT AND THEATRE COMPANY
39 Conestoga Rd., Malvern, PA 19355 (215) 647-1900
Contact: Alda Cortese, Literary Manager **Theatre:** professional
not-for-profit **Works:** full-length plays, one-acts, translations,
adaptations **2nd productions:** yes **Specifications:** maximum
cast: 10-12; single set preferred **Stages:** flexible, 350 seats;
flexible, 200 seats **Submission policy:** query/synopsis with
10-page dialogue sample; agent submission **Response:** 3 weeks
query; 10-12 months script **Your chances:** 350 submissions/1-2
productions **Remuneration:** percentage (5%-7%) **Future
commitment:** for production having at least 12 performances: 5%
of playwright's net receipts above $10,000 per year, for 5 years

THE PERFORMANCE CIRCLE
Gig Harbor, WA 98335 (206) 851-7529
Contact: Patty Benedict **Theatre:** community/non-professional
Works: full-length plays, one-acts, translations, adaptations,
musicals, children's plays **Specifications:** small stage, 9' ceiling
Stage: flexible, 99 seats **Audience:** "Middle aged, conservative,
high education." **Submission policy:** unsolicited script with SASE
Remuneration: "Depends upon quality." **Program:** staged readings

THE PERFORMER'S STUDIO
2906 William Penn Hwy., Easton, PA 18042
(215) 258-5887 Contact: Daniel Kaye, Executive Director
Theatre: "Professional and non-professional repertory company
derived from school of performing arts." **Works:** full-length plays,
one-acts **2nd productions:** "Sometimes." **Specifications:**
minimal cast; no more than 3 sets **Stages:** rented spaces, 75-800
seats **Casting:** "Open auditions combined with students (adults) from
our school." **Submission policy:** unsolicited script with SASE and
resume **Response:** 12-20 weeks **Your chances:** 60
submissions/3-6 productions **Remuneration:** negotiable

PERIWINKLE NATIONAL THEATRE
FOR YOUNG AUDIENCES
19 Clinton Ave., Monticello, NY 12701 (914) 794-1666
Contact: Sunna Rasch, Artistic Director **Theatre:** professional
not-for-profit touring company **Works:** plays for young audiences
Special interests: "Social issues for young audiences, problems of
youth." **Specifications:** playing time: 45-60 minutes; all shows
tour **Stages:** various spaces **Audience:** "Students at various
levels." **Submission policy:** query/synopsis; commission **Best
time:** spring **Response:** 2 weeks query; 6-8 months script
Remuneration: royalty; fee for commission **Advice:** "Contact us
to see what theme interests us."

PERMIAN PLAYHOUSE OF ODESSA, INC.
Box 13374, Odessa, TX 79768-3374 (915) 362-2329
Contact: Coy L. Sharp, Director **Theatre:** community/non-professional **Works:** full-length plays, one-acts, musicals, children's plays **2nd productions:** yes **Tours:** yes **Stage:** proscenium, 402 seats **Casting:** open auditions **Audience:** "Middle-class white, 50% white collar, 35% blue collar; rest ethnic." **Submission policy:** unsolicited script with SASE and resume; query/synopsis with resume; professional recommendation **Best time:** Jun.-Sept. **Response:** 1 week query; 1 month script **Your chances:** 40-45 submissions/0 productions, but would like to produce new plays **Remuneration:** possibly **Programs:** staged readings, workshop productions **Advice:** "Send background information with submission."

PERSEVERANCE THEATRE
914 3rd St., Douglas, AK 99824 (907) 364-2421
Contact: Jack Cannon, Literary Manager **Theatre:** professional not-for-profit **Works:** full-length plays, one-acts **2nd productions:** yes **Special interest:** new plays by Alaska writers **Maximum cast:** 20 **Tours:** "Occasionally." **Stages:** thrust, 150 seats; flexible, 75 seats **Audience:** "Varied: lawyers to fishermen, fairly young, well educated." **Submission policy:** unsolicited script with SASE from Alaskan writer; query/synopsis with resume and list of previous productions from other writer **Response:** 2 weeks query; 6 months script **Your chances:** 25 submissions; plays not sought from outside Alaska **Remuneration:** $500-$1000 **Programs:** readings, staged readings, workshop productions, development, classes

PETERBOROUGH PLAYERS
Box 1, Peterborough, NH 03458 (603) 924-7585
Contact: Ellen M. Dinerstein, Producing Director **Theatre:** professional not-for-profit **Works:** full-length plays, one-acts, adaptations, musicals **2nd productions:** yes **Special interest:** theatrical work that "expands and encourages the imagination" **Maximum cast:** 20 **Stage:** 18th century barn, 207 seats **Submission policy:** unsolicited script with SASE, reviews and recommendations; query/synopsis **Response:** 2 months query; 6 months script **Recent production of unsolicited work:** yes **Future commitment:** usually **Program:** staged readings

PHILADELPHIA DRAMA GUILD
112 S. 16th St. Suite 802, Philadelphia, PA 19102
(215) 563-7530 Contact: Charles Conwell, Director, Playwrights' Project **Theatre:** professional not-for-profit **Works:** full-length plays, related one-acts (pairs or trios), translations,

adaptations **Special interests:** "Plays with moral, political, social or economic as well as personal dimensions; new American plays." **Stages:** proscenium, 120 seats; thrust, 944 seats **Audience:** "Diverse." **Submission policy:** professional recommendation **Best time:** Sept. 1–Dec. 1 **Response:** 1 week query; Jun. 1 script **Your chances:** 88 submissions/3 productions **Remuneration:** $100 for reading; $1000 for production **Programs:** staged readings, workshop productions; Playwrights of Philadelphia Project (POP): staged readings and possible production of 4 plays each year by playwrights living within 25 miles of Philadelphia City Hall (send full-length script with SASE)

PHILADELPHIA FESTIVAL THEATRE
3900 Chestnut St., Philadelphia, PA 19104
(215) 222-5000 **Contact:** Mark Cofta, Literary Associate **Theatre:** professional not-for-profit **Works:** full-length plays, one-acts, translations **2nd productions:** no **Exclusive interest:** unproduced plays (workshop productions and readings do not disqualfy works) **Stage:** black box, 225 seats **Casting:** "Mainly agent submission; send resume to Hilary Missan, Casting Director." **Audience:** "Urban, educated, liberal." **Submission policy:** unsolicited script with SASE; professional recommendation; agent submission **Best times:** by Jan. 15 for fall production; by Jun. 15 for spring production **Response:** 3-4 months **Your chances:** 1500 submissions/6 productions **Remuneration:** yes **Future commitment:** no **Programs:** staged readings, development

THE PHILADELPHIA THEATRE COMPANY
Bourse Bldg. Suite 735, 21 S. 5th St.,
Philadelphia, PA 19106   (215) 592-8333
Contact: Lynn M. Thomson, Artistic Associate/Literary Manager **Theatre:** professional not-for-profit **Works:** full-length plays, small-cast musicals **2nd productions:** on mainstage only **Exclusive interests:** contemporary American drama; contemporary problems; substance **Specifications:** maximum cast: 10; "we shy away from extremely light-weight, so-called 'commercial' pieces" **Stage:** proscenium **Audience:** "Sophisticated, urban, well educated, age cross-section." **Submission policy:** unsolicited script with SASE, synopsis and resume; query/synopsis with dialogue sample and resume; professional recommendation; agent submission **Best time:** Sept.-Dec. **Response:** 1 month query; 3-6 months script **Your chances:** 500 submissions/1 production plus 3 workshops and readings **Recent production of unsolicited work:** yes **Remuneration:** honorarium for workshop; royalty for full

production **Future commitment:** yes **Programs:** staged readings, workshop productions, development; The Philadelphia Theatre Company's Mentor Project (see Special Programs); Stages (see Special Programs)

PHOENIX THEATRE, INC.
749 N. Park Ave., Indianapolis, IN 46202
(317) 635-7529 Contact: Brian Fonseca, Artistic Director **Theatre:** semi-professional **Works:** full-length plays, adaptations **2nd productions:** yes **Special interest:** "New ideas." **Maximum cast:** 15-16 **Stage:** small flexible proscenium, 150 seats **Audience:** "Educated, liberal." **Submission policy:** unsolicited script with SASE; query/synopsis **Best time:** Jan.-Feb. **Response:** 3 months **Your chances:** 400 submissions/3-4 productions **Remuneration:** $500 for full-length play **Programs:** staged readings; FEAT Playwriting Festival (see Contests) **Advice:** "We are a small house with a small budget."

PIER ONE THEATRE
Box 894, Homer, AK 99603 (907) 235-7333
Contact: Lance Peterson, Artistic Director **Theatre:** off off Broadway **Works:** full-length plays, one-acts, translations, adaptations, musicals, children's plays **2nd productions:** yes **Tours:** yes **Stages:** proscenium, thrust, flexible--100 seats summer, 495 seats winter **Submission policy:** unsolicited script with SASE preferred; professional recommendation **Response:** 3 months **Your chances:** 100 submissions/1-3 productions **Remuneration:** percentage **Programs:** readings, staged readings, workshop productions **Advice:** "We gain (or lose) the audience in the 1st 3 minutes of a play; start off your play *in medias res;* save the exposition for an essay."

PING CHONG & COMPANY
New York, NY This theatre no longer accepts submissions.

PIONEER THEATRE COMPANY
University of Utah, Salt Lake City, UT 84112
(801) 581-6356 Contact: Charles Morey, Artistic Director **Theatre:** professional not-for-profit **Works:** full-length plays, translations, adaptations, musicals **Stage:** proscenium, 1000 seats **Submission policy:** query/synopsis **Best time:** fall **Response:** 1 month query; 6 months script

PISGAH PLAYERS
Creative Writing, UNCA, One University Heights, Asheville, NC 28804 (704) 251-6411
Contact: David Hopes, Director **Theatre:** community/non-professional, university/college **Works:** full-length plays, one-acts, translations, adaptations **2nd productions:** yes **Special interests:** "Redemptive, magical works that take language, archetypes and spirituality seriously; class without inflation, ceremony without pomp." **Specifications:** maximum cast: 10; no more than 2-3 sets ("adaptable on this point") **Tours:** yes **Stages:** proscenium, 300 seats; flexible **Casting:** "We look for excellence in acting and commitment to our vision." **Audience:** "College, well educated, students." **Submission policy:** unsolicited script with SASE and resume; query/synopsis with resume **Response:** "Quick." **Your chances:** 100 submissions/"5 productions so far; this is our first year" **Future commitment:** no **Programs:** readings, staged readings, development, classes **Advice:** "Read Shakespeare, Euripides, Yeats, Tennessee Williams. Know something."

PITTSBURGH PUBLIC THEATER
Allegheny Square, Pittsburgh, PA 15212
(412) 323-8200 Contact: William T. Gardner, Producing Director **Theatre:** professional not-for-profit **Works:** full-length plays, translations, adaptations, musicals **2nd productions:** yes **Maximum cast:** 10 **Stage:** arena or thrust, 449 seats **Submission policy:** professional recommendation; agent submission **Best time:** Apr.-Sept. **Response:** 6 months **Future commitment:** "Possibly."

PLAYERS GUILD OF CANTON, INC.
1001 Market Ave., Canton, OH 44718
(216) 453-7619 Contact: Jerry M. Lowe, Artistic Director **Theatre:** community/non-professional **Works:** full-length plays **2nd productions:** yes **Exclusive interest:** "Large-scale productions." **Specifications:** "No 'situation' comedy; no scripts intended for 'bare bones' approaches." **Stages:** proscenium, 496 seats; thrust, 138 seats **Audience:** "Somewhat older, high income, theatrically sophisticated." **Submission policy:** unsolicited script with SASE; query/synopsis with resume; agent submission **Best time:** late spring-summer **Response:** 2 weeks query; 6 months script **Your chances:** 25-30 submissions/2-3 productions; "theatre is committed to the annual production of a new script on the Main Stage" **Remuneration:** negotiable royalty **Program:** workshop productions **Comment:** "Theatre is very large, professionally staffed, with high budget, professional standards; we work closely with Ohio Arts Commission in looking for new plays."

PLAYERS THEATRE OF COLUMBUS
549 Franklin Ave., Columbus, OH 43215 (614) 224-5528
Contact: Steven C. Anderson, Associate Producing Director
Theatre: professional not-for-profit **Works**: full-length plays, translations, adaptations, musicals, children's plays **Special interest**: the Midwestern experience **Stages**: thrust, 750 seats; modified thrust, 250 seats; arena, 100 seats **Submission policy:** query/synopsis **Response**: 3 weeks query; 3-4 months script

PLAYHOUSE IN THE PARK
See Cincinnati Playhouse in the Park listing in this section.

PLAYHOUSE ON THE SQUARE
51 S. Cooper, Memphis, TN 38104 (901) 725-0776
Contact: Jackie Nichols, Executive Director **Theatre:** professional not-for-profit **Works:** full-length plays **2nd productions:** no **Specifications:** maximum cast: 10; single or unit set **Stages:** proscenium, 250 seats; proscenium, 136 seats **Audience:** "25-50 years of age, progressive, open-minded." **Submission policy:** unsolicited script with SASE **Response:** 3 months **Your chances:** 500 submissions/1 production **Remuneration:** $500 **Program:** Midsouth Playwrights Contest (see Contests)

PLAYHOUSE WEST
North Hollywood, CA This is an acting school and no longer produces plays.

PLAYMAKERS
Box 5745, Tampa, FL 33675 (813) 247-7529
Contact: Kathy Tyrell, Associate Director **Theatre:** professional not-for-profit **Works:** full-length plays, one-acts **2nd productions:** yes **Special interests:** traditional and experimental contemporary works **Specifications:** maximum cast: 8; simple set **Stages:** proscenium-thrust, 300 seats; cabaret, 100 seats **Submission policy:** query/synopsis **Best time:** Sept.-Jan. **Response:** 4-6 weeks query; 3-4 months script

PLAYMAKERS REPERTORY COMPANY
Graham Memorial CB #3235
University of North Carolina, Chapel Hill, NC 27599
(919) 962-1122 Contact: Adam Versenyi, Dramaturg
Theatre: professional not-for-profit, university/college **Works:** full-length plays, translations, adaptations, musicals **2nd productions:** yes **Special interests:** "Plays that display theatrical and dramatic action in a manner unique to the stage." **Specifications:** maximum cast: 8; works must be suitable for open

staging **Stage:** thrust, 498 seats **Audience:** "Mixture of university, community and professional people." **Submission policy:** professional recommendation; agent submission **Best time:** Sept.-Dec. for following year's season **Response:** 3-5 months **Remuneration:** negotiable **Programs:** residencies, classes

THE PLAY WORKS COMPANY
Box 25152, Philadelphia, PA 19147 (215) 236-8488
Contact: Christopher J. Rushton, Artistic Director **Theatre:** art service, new play development organization **Works:** full-length plays, one-acts, adaptations, musicals **2nd productions:** no **Exclusive interest:** "Current material." **Specifications:** maximum cast: 15; some set limitations **Tours:** yes **Stage:** flexible **Submission policy:** query/synopsis with resume and references preferred; unsolicited script with SASE and resume **Best time:** spring **Response:** 2 months query; 3 months script **Your chances:** 200 submissions/14 staged readings **Remuneration/ future commitment:** no **Dues:** $45 per year **Programs:** private readings, public staged readings, playwright "labs," marketing service, workshops for new musicals, interdisciplinary workshop project including radio and video (inquire); New Independents Project, Playwright Exchange (see Special Programs)

PLAYWRIGHT'S ALLIANCE
8 Tompkins Ave., Babylon, NY 11702 (516) 587-8945
Contact: Robert Mantione, Artistic Director **Theatre:** professional not-for-profit **Works:** full-length plays, one-acts, translations, adaptations, performance art **2nd productions:** no **Special interests:** "Social, political, psychological, ideological works; avant garde." **Specifications:** maximum cast: 4; simple sets or no set **Stages:** thrust; arena; flexible **Audience:** "All ages, educated, literate, informed, culturally active." **Submission policy:** unsolicited script with SASE; query/synopsis with dialogue sample; professional recommendation **Response:** immediate query; 8-10 weeks script **Your chances:** 40-50 submissions/5 productions **Remuneration:** no **Programs:** readings, staged readings, workshop productions **Advice:** "Be prepared to be present at auditions and as many rehearsals as possible."

PLAYWRIGHTS HORIZONS
416 W. 42nd St., New York, NY 10036 (212) 564-1235
Contact: Tim Sanford, Literary Manager; Ira Weitzman, Musical Theatre Program Director **Theatre:** off Broadway, professional not-for-profit **Works:** full-length plays, musicals **2nd productions:** "Yes, but not often." **Specifications:** "Original

works only." **Stages:** proscenium, 160 seats; black box, 74 seats **Casting:** "Equity regulations; open casting." **Audience:** "Intelligent, urban, well-versed, older." **Submission policy:** unsolicited script with SASE and resume; query/synopsis with resume; agent submission; commission **Response:** 1-4 weeks query; 1-4 months script **Your chances:** 2000 submissions/7 productions **Remuneration/future commitment:** negotiable **Programs:** readings, internships, residencies, professional theatre training program (inquire) **Advice:** "Personal, relevant, articulate, theatrical."

PLAYWRIGHTS WORKSHOP
Stamford, CT Our 1990 questionnaire was returned as "undeliverable," and this theatre's phone was not in service when we called.

PLYMOUTH PLAYHOUSE
Plymouth Place Hotel, 2705 Annapolis Ln., Plymouth, MN 55411 (612) 333-3302
Contact: Curt Wollan, Producer/Director **Theatre:** professional **Works:** full-length plays, musicals **2nd productions:** yes **Exclusive interest:** "Light fun." **Specifications:** maximum cast: 6; unit set; "no serious drama" **Tours:** yes **Stage:** thrust, 211 seats **Audience:** "Aged 25-55, white, business white collar, college or technical school education." **Submission policy:** query/synopsis with dialogue sample **Best time:** spring **Response:** 6 months query; 1 year script **Your chances:** 400 submissions/0-1 production **Remuneration:** royalty **Future commitment:** for premiere **Advice:** "Send video tape of previous production."

PONCA PLAYHOUSE
Box 1414, Ponca City, OK 74602 (405) 765-7786
Contact: John A. Robinson, Managing/Artistic Director **Theatre:** community/non-professional **Works:** full-length plays, adaptations, musicals **2nd productions:** yes **Special interest:** "A good, clear dramatic plot and point of view." **Specifications:** maximum cast: 12; single set **Stage:** proscenium, 412 seats **Audience:** "Average age 45, upper middle class, college educated; no interest in excessive vulgarity or nudity; prefer comedies over heavy drama." **Submission policy:** unsolicited script with SASE; query/synopsis, professional recommendation; "I go out and look for them" **Best time:** Sept.-Mar. **Response:** 1-2 weeks **Your chances:** 20-30 submissions/2-3 productions **Remuneration:** "Up to $500 plus a 2-week residency." **Programs:** readings, staged readings, workshop productions, development, residencies **Advice:** "Must be theatrically exciting. No vague self-discovery epics, please!"

PORTHOUSE THEATRE COMPANY
See Theatre Kent & Porthouse Theatre Company listing in this section.

PORTLAND REPERTORY THEATER
25 SW Salmon St., Portland, OR 97204 (503) 244-4491
Contact: Brenda Hubbard, Artistic Director **Theatre**: professional not-for-profit **Works**: full-length plays, translations, children's plays **Special interests**: adaptations of classics for holiday presentation for young and family audiences; Northwest writers; comedies **Specifications**: maximum cast: 8; simple set **Stage**: proscenium, 230 seats **Submission policy**: query/synopsis with resume and dialogue sample **Best time**: summer **Response**: 2 months query; 6-12 months script **Program**: readings

PORTLAND STAGE COMPANY
Box 1458, Portland, ME 04104 (207) 774-1043
Contact: Richard Hamburger, Artistic Director **Theatre**: professional not-for-profit **Works**: full-length plays, one-acts, translations, adaptations, small musicals **2nd productions**: yes **Special interest**: "Works which engage, educate, challenge and entertain our audience." **Specifications**: maximum cast: 10; maximum of 4 instruments for musical **Stages**: proscenium, 290 seats; flexible, 90 seats (used for readings only) **Casting**: one-acts must be suitable for young actors **Audience**: "Primarily professionals from early 30's to mid-60's." **Submission policy**: query/synopsis with dialogue sample; professional recommendation; agent submission **Response**: 1 month query; 2-6 months script **Your chances**: 130 submissions/1 production **Remuneration**: royalty **Advice**: "Small cast, neatly typed script." **Programs**: readings, staged readings, workshop productions

POST THEATRE COMPANY
Greenvale, NY 11548 (516) 299-2353
Contact: Bonnie J. Eckard, Chairman **Theatre**: university/college **Works**: full-length plays, translations, one-acts **2nd productions**: yes **Special interest**: "Just good, serious theatre." **Stages**: black box; small studio **Audience**: "College plus Long Island community." **Submission policy**: query/synopsis with dialogue sample; professional recommendation **Best time**: Jan. **Response**: 1 year **Remuneration**: "Yes, limited." **Programs**: development; Festival of the Americas (translations from Spanish, contact David Scanlan for information)

POTOMAC THEATRE PROJECT
269 W. 72nd St., New York, NY 10023
Contact: Susan Sharkey, Literary Manager **Theatre:** professional not-for-profit **Works:** full-length plays, one-acts, translations, adaptations **2nd productions:** yes **Exclusive interests:** "Current social and political interests; we use Robert Brustein's phrase: 'to illuminate the nightmares and hoaxes by which we live' as a guideline for an operating aesthetic. Hopefully there is a balance between development of issue and character." **Specifications:** maximum cast: 12; single set **Stage:** arena, 125 seats **Casting:** "For the most part, referrals and submission of photo and resume. Baltimore/DC actors are given strong consideration. Middlebury College students make up our '2nd company.'" **Audience:** "We attempt to reach audiences in all areas of the community, not only politically oriented but those who need a public voice: the homeless, battered women, people in prison." **Submission policy:** query/ synopsis with resume; professional recommendation; agent submission **Best time:** autumn **Response:** 6-9 weeks query; 7-10 months script **Your chances:** 10-15 submissions/0-2 productions **Recent production of unsolicited work:** 1982 **Remuneration:** negotiable **Future commitment:** "Exclusive U.S. production rights up to 1 year." **Programs:** readings, staged readings, workshop productions, development **Advice:** "Please send only a treatment or synopsis. Do not send a script." **Comment:** "Plays are produced in Washington, DC."

PRAIRIE PLAYERS, INC.
Box 291, Kingman, KS 67068 (316) 532-3321
Theatre: community/non-professional **Works:** full-length plays, one-acts, translations, adaptations, children's plays **2nd productions:** "Occasionally." **Special interest:** "Comedy-farce." **Specifications:** maximum cast: 8-11; some set limitations **Tours:** "We haven't toured outside of 50 miles." **Stage:** proscenium, 120 seats **Audience:** "Primarily 30-65 age range." **Submission policy:** unsolicited script with SASE **Response:** 30 days **Your chances:** Theatre has not yet produced new plays but is willing to do so. **Remuneration:** "Small royalty possible." **Programs:** "By contract and prior arrangement." **Advice:** "Royalty is a problem; we are a very small volunteer group."

PRAIRIE PLAYERS YOUTH THEATRE
45 S. Kellogg St., Galesburg, IL 61401 (309) 343-9097
Contact: Jeffrey R. Kellogg, Youth Theatre Managing Director **Theatre:** community/non-professional **Works:** full-length plays, one-acts, adaptations, children's plays **2nd productions:** yes **Special interests:** "Social/political one-acts; teens in crisis;

children's holiday scripts; single-actor shows." **Specifications:** maximum cast: 70; limited wing space **Tours:** "Occasionally." **Stages:** proscenium/thrust, 970 seats; proscenium, 120 seats; arena, 50-300 seats **Casting:** "Adults: open auditions; children: open auditions with preference given to those who have taken creative drama at Prairie Players." **Audience:** "Adult productions: 50% middle class blue collar and agrarian, 25% professional and academic, 25% senior citizens; youth productions: 40% children, 30% senior citizens." **Submission policy:** unsolicited script with SASE and resume; query/synopsis with resume **Best time:** winter for following season **Response:** 7-10 days query; 2-6 weeks script **Your chances:** 15 submissions/1-5 productions **Recent production of unsolicited work:** 1987 **Remuneration/ future commitment:** no **Advice:** "Obscenities and nudity are unacceptable. Remember that our audience is mainly rural, Midwestern, conservative."

PRATHER PRODUCTIONS
Lancaster, PA This theatre is not currently producing new works and has asked that we discontinue its listing.

PRINCETON REP COMPANY
13 Witherspoon St., Princeton, NJ 08542
(609) 921-3682 Contact: Victoria Liberatori, Artistic Director **Theatre:** professional, Small Professional Theatre Contract **Works:** full-length plays **2nd productions:** yes **Special interests:** "Realistic and non-realistic dramas and comedies; daring and exciting subject matter." **Specifications:** maximum cast: 5-7; single or non-realistic set **Tours:** yes **Stage:** flexible **Audience:** "Eclectic: well educated and affluent to working class; average age 40." **Submission policy:** query/synopsis with dialogue sample; professional recommendation; agent submission **Best times:** spring, fall **Response:** 2 months query; 6 months script **Your chances:** 300 submissions/2 productions **Remuneration:** negotiable **Programs:** readings, staged readings, workshop productions **Advice:** "We are not interested in soap opera or standard domestic drama. We like work that takes risks and emphasizes character."

PROCESS STUDIO THEATRE
257 Church St., New York, NY 10019
(212) 226-1124 Contact: Bonnie Loren, Artistic Director **Theatre:** off Broadway, not-for-profit **Works:** full-length plays, one-acts, musicals **2nd productions:** yes **Tours:** yes **Stages:** proscenium; thrust; flexible **Audience:** "Varied, sophisticated." **Submission policy:** query/synopsis with dialogue sample; professional recommendation; agent submission **Remuneration:**

"Only if the production makes a substantial profit." **Programs:** readings, staged readings, workshop productions, development, internships

PRODUCERS CLUB
358 W. 44th St., New York, NY 10036 (212) 246-9069
Contact: Vincent Gugleotti, Artistic Director **Theatre:** off Broadway **Works:** full-length plays, one-acts **2nd productions:** yes **Specifications:** maximum cast: 6; no more than 2 sets **Stage:** proscenium **Submission policy:** unsolicited script with SASE; professional recommendation; agent submission **Response:** 2-6 weeks **Your chances:** 300 submissions/3 productions **Remuneration:** option; royalty **Programs:** readings, staged readings, workshop productions, development

PROVO COMMUNITY THEATRE
760 W. 1340 S, Provo, UT 84601 (801) 373-8509
Contact: Judy Porray **Theatre:** community/non-professional **Works:** full-length plays, one-acts, musicals **2nd productions:** yes **Special interests:** "New dramas and comedies; small musicals." **Tours:** "Periodically." **Stages:** proscenium; arena/thrust; combined **Casting:** open auditions **Audience:** "Contemporary, educated, multi-aged; children/family." **Submission policy:** unsolicited script with SASE; query/dialogue sample **Best time:** summer **Response:** 2 months **Your chances:** 10-15 submissions/1 production **Remuneration:** royalty **Future commitment:** no **Programs:** readings, staged readings; future contest (inquire)

PS PRODUCTIONS
PS, Inc., 9 W. 57th St. 34th Floor, New York, NY 10019
Contact: Terry Burstein **Theatre:** off off Broadway **Works:** full-length plays, one-acts **2nd productions:** yes **Specifications:** maximum cast: 10; simple sets **Stage:** proscenium, 100 seats **Audience:** "Cosmopolitan upward." **Submission policy:** unsolicited script with SASE; query/synposis; agent submission **Response time:** 2 weeks query; 3 months script **Your chances:** 150 submissions/3 productions **Remuneration:** no **Program:** development **Advice:** "Material should be comedic, cosmopolitan in nature."

PUERTO RICAN TRAVELING THEATRE
141 W. 94th St., New York, NY 10025 (212) 354-1293
Contact: Miriam Colon Valle, Artistic Director **Theatre:** professional not-for-profit **Works:** full-length plays, translations, adaptations, musicals **Special interests:** social issues relevant to

contemporary Hispanic experience; short musicals (60 minutes) **Specifications:** maximum cast: 8 preferred; single or unit set; no fly or wing space **Stage:** proscenium, 196 seats **Submission policy:** unsolicited script with SASE **Response:** 6 months **Your chances:** 15 submissions/0 productions **Future commitment:** "Contract negotiable." **Programs:** Puerto Rican Traveling Theatre Playwrights' Workshop, Puerto Rican Traveling Theatre Training Unit for Youngsters (see Special Programs) **Comment:** "We are a bilingual organization; all works are produced in English and in Spanish."

PULSE ENSEMBLE THEATRE
870 Sixth Ave., New York, NY 10001 (212) 213-0231
Contact: Alexa Kelly, Artistic Director **Theatre:** off off Broadway, Equity showcase **Works:** full-length plays, translations, adaptations, musicals, children's plays, cabaret/revues **2nd productions:** yes **Special interests:** "Politically and socially relevant works; works with appeal to a broad audience and with depth and relevance, whether comedic or not; children's Christmas plays." **Specifications:** "We are not interested in fluff." **Tours:** possibly **Stage:** flexible, 50 seats **Casting:** from company of 30 people **Submission policy:** unsolicited script with SASE **Response:** 6 months **Your chances:** 2 new plays and 1 musical produced each year **Programs:** monthly readings, workshops **Advice:** "No first drafts. We prefer works with previous readings."

PUSHCART PLAYERS
197 Bloomfield Ave., Verona, NJ 07004 (201) 857-1115
Contact: Ruth Fost, Executive Producer **Theatre:** professional not-for-profit **Works:** children's plays **2nd productions:** yes **Special interest:** "Curriculum or current event orientation." **Specifications:** maximum cast: 4; all shows must tour **Stages:** schools **Audience:** grades K-12 **Submission policy:** send SASE for guidelines **Programs:** staged readings, workshop productions

QUAIGH THEATRE
205 W. 89th St., New York, NY 10024 (212) 595-6185
Contact: Dennis Rickabee, Literary Manager **Theatre:** professional not-for-profit **Works:** full-length plays, one-acts **Stage:** thrust, 100 seats **Submission policy:** unsolicited script with SASE and synopsis **Response:** 3-6 months one-act; 6-9 months full-length play **Program:** Lunchtime Series: semi-monthly workshop productions of one-acts presented Oct.-May (inquire)

THE QUARTZ THEATRE
Box 465, Ashland, OR 97520 (503) 482-8119
Contact: Robert Spira, Artistic Director   **Theatre:** community/
non-professional   **Works:** full-length plays, one-acts, musicals,
children's plays   **2nd productions:** "If there is rewriting to be
done."   **Stage:** flexible, 80 seats   **Audience:** "General."
Submission policy: query/synopsis with dialogue sample
Response: 1 week query; 2 months script   **Your chances:** 30
submissions/3 productions   **Remuneration:** "Tape; if box office
exceeds expenses, the playwright gets a share."   **Advice:** "Literate
writing."

RAFT THEATRE
432 W. 42nd St., New York, NY 10036 (212) 947-8389
Contact: Martin Zurla, Artistic Director   **Theatre:** professional
not-for-profit **Works:** full-length plays, one-acts **Specifications:**
maximum cast: 7; no more than 2 sets or unit set **Stage:** 2-sided L
Audience: middle class; professionals   **Submission policy:** send
SASE for guidelines   **Best time:** spring   **Response:** 4 months
Your chances: 500 submissions/4 productions **Remuneration:**
option **Advice:** Request statement of artistic purposes; do not type
scripts in European format. **Comment:** Theatre is dedicated to new
plays by American playwrights.

RAINBOW COMPANY CHILDREN'S THEATRE
821 Las Vegas Blvd., Las Vegas, NV 89101
(702) 386-6553   Contact: Brian Strom, Artistic Director
Theatre: community/non-professional   **Works:** full-length plays,
one-acts, adaptations, children's plays   **2nd productions:** yes
Stages: proscenium; thrust; arena; black box **Audience:** "Varied:
from children to adults."   **Submission policy:** query/synopsis;
commission **Best time:** Feb.-Jun. **Response:** 1 year **Your
chances:** 25 submissions/1 production   **Remuneration:** royalty
Programs: workshop productions, internships for playwrights

RAIN COUNTRY PLAYERS
**c/o Ralph Eaton, Treasurer, 17319 32nd Ave. W,
Lynnwood, WA 98037 (206) 743-4240**
Theatre: community/non-professional   **Works:** full-length plays
Special interest: "Family-oriented plays." **Specifications:** cast
of 2-10, various ages; single set **Stage:** proscenium, 92 seats
Audience: "Approximately 40% over 60, 50% adult, 10% children
12 and under." **Submission policy:** unsolicited script with SASE
Best time: fall-spring **Response:** 6 months **Your chances:**
Theatre has not produced new plays for several years but is willing to
do so. **Remuneration:** "Reasonable royalty."

R.A.P.P. RESIDENT THEATRE COMPANY
220 E. 4th St., New York, NY 10009   (212) 529-5921
Contact: Philip Langer, Managing Director   **Theatre:** professional not-for-profit   **Works:** full-length plays, translations, adaptations **2nd productions:** yes **Exclusive interests:** "Works of epic size and historical scope; translations and adaptations of classics; spectacles." **Maximum cast:** 12-15 **Stages:** proscenium/flexible, 299 seats; flexible, 85-99 seats; flexible, 50 seats **Submission policy:** unsolicited script with SASE and synopsis; query/synopsis **Best time:** Jun.-Sept.   **Response:** 4-6 weeks query; 2-4 months script   **Your chances:** 100-200 submissions/2-5 productions **Remuneration:** "For production."   **Future commitment:** negotiable   **Programs:** staged readings, workshop productions, internships   **Advice:** "We are looking for new voices on relevant, universal issues."   **Comment:**   See Anderson, Wayne, "Artist's Oasis: The R.A.P.P. Arts Center," *TheaterWeek* (Mar. 7-13, 1988), 12-15.

RED BARN THEATRE
Box 707, Key West, FL 33040   (305) 296-9911
Contact: Richard A. Magesis, Artistic Director   **Theatre:** professional not-for-profit   **Works:** full-length plays, one-acts, translations, adaptations, musicals, children's plays, cabaret/revues **Maximum cast:** 8 for mainstage, 6 for cabaret **Tours:** children's plays **Stage:** proscenium, 94 seats **Submission policy:** unsolicited script with SASE; query/synopsis with dialogue sample and resume **Best time:** Apr.-Jun. **Response:** 1 month

REMAINS THEATRE
1300 W. Belmont, Chicago, IL 60657 (312) 549-7725
Contact: Amy Morton, William L. Petersen, Co-Artistic Directors **Theatre:** professional not-for-profit   **Works:** full-length plays, adaptations, musicals   **Special interests:** political works, local issues, adaptations **Specifications:** maximum cast: 15; large stage area   **Stages:** various spaces   **Casting:** from resident ensemble: 7 men, 4 women, age range 20-38   **Submission policy:** query/synopsis   **Response:** 3 weeks query; 3 months script

RENDEZVOUS PRODUCTIONS
New York, NY   This theatre is no longer producing plays.

RENEGADE THEATER COMPANY
Box M109, Hoboken, NJ 07030 (201) 659-1480
Contact: David Gilman, Eileen Lynch, Literary Managers **Theatre:**   professional not-for-profit   **Works:** full-length plays, one-acts **Special interest:** works suitable for ensemble company

Maximum cast: 10-12 **Stage:** flexible, 99 seats **Submission policy:** query/synopsis **Response:** 2-4 weeks query; 2-4 months script

REPERTORIO ESPAÑOL
138 E. 27th St., New York, NY 10016 (212) 889-2850
Contact: Rene Buch, Artistic Director **Theatre:** professional not-for-profit **Works:** full-length plays, adaptations, children's plays, operas **Exclusive interests:** Hispanic themes; plays in Spanish or plays in English suitable for translation into Spanish **Specifications:** maximum cast: 10; single set **Stage:** proscenium, 140 seats **Audience:** "Predominantly Hispanic audience; some English-speaking audience for musical and dance events." **Submission policy:** unsolicited script with SASE **Best time:** May **Response:** 2 months **Comment:** See Bensussen, Melia, "Something to Celebrate," *TheaterWeek* (Apr. 24, 1989), 31-33.

THE REPERTORY THEATRE OF ST. LOUIS
130 Edgar Rd., St. Louis, MO 63119 (314) 968-7340
Contact: Steven Woolf, Artistic Director **Theatre:** professional not-for-profit **Works:** full-length plays, musicals **2nd productions:** yes **Specifications:** maximum cast: 8, fewer preferred, 16 for musical; single set; no naturalistic works **Stages:** thrust, 735 seats; flexible, 125 seats; storefront, 40 seats **Audience:** "30 and up, literate, cultured, middle and upper class, educated, professionals, conservative." **Submission policy:** query/synopsis to Susan Gregg, Associate Artistic Director; professional recommendation; agent submission **Best time:** late winter-early spring **Response:** 1 month query; 12 months script **Your chances:** 100+ submissions/"number of productions depends upon need and quality of work" **Future commitment:** for a premiere **Program:** workshop productions **Advice:** "Good story, strong emotions."

RICHMOND SHEPARD THEATRES
6476 Santa Monica Blvd., Hollywood, CA 90038
(213) 462-9399 Contact: Richmond Shepard, Artistic Director **Theatre:** Equity-waiver **Works:** full-length plays **2nd productions:** yes **Specifications:** maximum cast: 10, fewer preferred; no large spectacles **Stage:** proscenium **Audience:** varied **Submission policy:** unsolicited script with SASE **Response:** 2-7 weeks **Your chances:** 200 submissions/2 productions **Remuneration:** "In initial production, royalty after recoupment of investment; subsequently, straight royalty." **Advice:** "Write a hit: great story, brilliant dialogue, depth, pith."

RITES & REASON
Box 1148, Brown University, Providence, RI 02912
(401) 863-3558 Contact: Rhett S. Jones, Research Director
Theatre: professional not-for-profit, university/college **Works:** full-length plays, one-acts, musicals **2nd productions:** yes **Special interest:** "Developing new plays and ideas by and about Afro-Americans using our research to performance method." **Maximum cast:** 10-12 **Tours:** "National tours." **Stage:** black box, 150 seats **Submission policy:** query/synopsis with resume and references **Response:** 6 months if interested in query **Your chances:** 2-4 new plays produced each season **Remuneration:** "Varies." **Future commitment:** yes **Programs:** readings, staged readings, workshop productions, development

RIVER ARTS REPERTORY
Byrdcliffe Theatre, Box 1166,
Woodstock, NY 12498 (914) 679-2100, -2493
Contact: Lawrence Sacharow, Artistic Director; Marguerite Feitlowitz, Literary Manager **Theatre:** off off Broadway **Works:** full-length plays, translations **2nd productions:** yes **Special interests:** "Translations of classics; social issues; works with poetic dimension." **Maximum cast:** 8 **Stages:** 3/4 arena, 250 seats; flexible, 125 seats; flexible, 100 seats (used for readings only) **Audience:** "Broad spectrum." **Submission policy:** professional recommendation **Best time:** fall **Response:** several months **Your chances:** "infinite number" of submissions/3 productions plus 4 staged readings **Remuneration:** "Generally a fee against percentage." **Programs:** staged readings, development; The Playwrights in Residence New Works Program (see Special Programs)

RIVERWEST THEATER
155 Bank St., New York, NY 10014 (212) 243-0259
Contact: Nat Habib, Artistic Director **Theatre:** off off Broadway **Works:** full-length plays, musicals **2nd productions:** "Only occasionally." **Stage:** proscenium, 28'x18' **Audience:** "Eclectic. People who go to the theatre once a month and find nothing pleasing on Broadway." **Submission policy:** unsolicited script with SASE; professional recommendation; commission **Best time:** fall **Response:** "Depends upon the play and our interest in it--the number of people who want to read it." **Your chances:** 250 submissions/ 5-6 productions (4 plays, 2 musicals or 5 plays, 1 musical) **Remuneration:** negotiable royalty **Advice:** "The play should be ready for an audience to see it."

THE ROAD COMPANY
Box 5278-EKS, Johnson City, TN 37603 (615) 926-7726
Contact: Christine Murdock **Theatre:** professional not-for-profit, community-based **Works:** full-length plays **2nd productions:** yes **Special interests:** "Social value; plays that can teach us something and make us think." **Maximum cast:** 8 **Stage:** proscenium, 150 seats **Audience:** "Young to middle age, liberal, college educated, rural." **Submission policy:** query/synopsis; professional recommendation **Response:** 3 months query; 1 year script **Your chances:** 20 submissions/1-2 productions **Remuneration:** negotiable royalty **Advice:** "Non-traditional form, social significance, Southern or rural in location."

ROADSIDE THEATER
Box 743, 306 Madison St., Whitesburg, KY 41858
(606) 633-0108 Contact: Dudley Cocke, Director **Theatre:** professional not-for-profit **Works:** full-length plays **2nd productions:** no **Exclusive interest:** Appalachian subject matter **Specifications:** maximum cast: small cast; simple sets suitable for touring **Stage:** thrust, 150 seats **Audience:** "All ages, educated and uneducated, largely 'working class.'" **Submission policy:** unsolicited script with SASE; query/synopsis with dialogue sample **Response:** 2 weeks query; 1 month script **Programs:** readings, workshop productions, residencies

ROCHESTER CIVIC THEATRE
Mayo Park, Rochester, MN 55901 (507) 282-7633
Contact: Christopher Schario, Artistic Director **Theatre:** community/non-professional **Works:** full-length plays, one-acts, musicals, children's plays **Special interests:** "Local, regional, upper Midwest concerns." **Stage:** proscenium, 299 seats **Audience:** "Bi-polar: half are highly educated professionals." **Submission policy:** query/synopsis **Best time:** summer-early fall **Response:** 4 weeks **Your chances:** 2-4 submissions/0 productions

ROCK VALLEY COLLEGE STUDIO/STARLIGHT THEATRE
3301 N. Mulford Rd., Rockford, IL 61111 (815) 654-4296
Contact: Mike Webb, Managing Director **Theatre:** community/non-professional, university/college **Works:** full-length plays, one-acts, translations, adaptations, musicals **2nd productions:** "Occasionally." **Special interest:** "We seek reputable playwrights to write commissioned works that they have always wanted to write but have never gotten around to writing." **Stages:** proscenium, 599 seats; endstage, 223 seats; thrust, 166 seats **Casting:** "Open to all residents of community of 175,000; we are not required to cast

students; we cast age for age." **Audience:** "Urban cross section."
Submission policy: unsolicited script with SASE; query/synopsis;
commission **Response:** 3 months **Your chances:** 1200
submissions/3-4 productions **Remuneration:** "Commission fee plus
royalties." **Future commitment:** negotiable **Advice:** "Submitted
scripts are read by a panel. If dialogue is interesting, we will contact
playwright about the possibility of commissioning an original work.
The Playwright must have an idea for an unwritten work."
Comment: "We guarantee production of commissioned works."

ROUNDABOUT THEATRE COMPANY
100 E. 17th St., New York, NY 10003 (212) 420-1360
Contact: Mark Michaels, Literary Manager **Theatre:** off
Broadway, professional not-for-profit **Works:** full-length plays,
translations, adaptations **2nd productions:** yes **Stages:**
proscenium; thrust **Audience:** "Diverse, sophisticated New York
audience." **Submission policy:** query/synopsis; professional
recommendation; agent submission **Response:** 2 months query; 1
year script **Your chances:** 200 submissions/0-1 production plus
1-3 readings on mainstage **Programs:** readings, classes;
Roundabout Theatre's Creative Connection (see Special Programs)

ROUND HOUSE THEATRE
12210 Bushey Dr., Silver Spring, MD 20902
(301) 468-4233 Contact: Jerry Widdon, Artistic Director
Theatre: professional not-for-profit **Works:** full-length plays,
translations, adaptations, children's plays **Special interests:**
social/political issues; experimental pieces; new translations of
lesser-known classics **Specifications:** maximum cast: 7-8; single
set preferred **Stage:** modified thrust, 216 seats **Submission
policy:** professional recommendation **Response:** 1 year or more

ROYAL COURT REPERTORY
300 W. 55th St., New York, NY 10019 (212) 956-3500
Contact: Phyllis Craig, Artistic Director **Theatre:** professional
Works: full-length plays, musicals **Special interests:** murder
mysteries; "we are particularly interested in promoting musicals"
Casting: open auditions **Submission policy:** unsolicited script
with SASE **Response:** 2 weeks **Your chances:** 70-80
submissions/12- 14 productions

THE RYAN REPERTORY COMPANY, INC.
2442 Bath Ave., Brooklyn, NY 11214 (718) 265-7011
Contact: Script Review Committee **Theatre:** professional
not-for-profit **Works:** full-length plays, musicals, children's plays,
cabaret/revues **2nd productions:** no **Specifications:** cast of

1-10; no more than 2 sets; "no nudity" **Stage:** flexible **Casting:** open auditions **Audience:** "Mixed." **Submission policy:** unsolicited script with SASE **Your chances:** 4 new plays produced each season **Remuneration:** "Very little." **Future commitment:** no **Programs:** readings, staged readings, workshop productions, development **Advice:** "Call us."

SACRAMENTO THEATRE COMPANY
1419 H St., Sacramento, CA 95814 (916) 446-7501
Contact: Mark Cuddy, Producing Director **Theatre:** professional not-for-profit **Works:** full-length plays, one-acts, translations, adaptations, cabaret/revues **Maximum cast:** 7 for black box **Stages:** proscenium, 297 seats; black box, 80 seats **Submission policy:** query/synopsis; solicited script **Best time:** Nov.-Jan. **Response:** 8-12 months

ST. BART'S PLAYHOUSE
New York, NY   This theatre is not accepting submissions in 1990.

THE SALT LAKE ACTING COMPANY
168 W. 500 N, Salt Lake City, UT 84103
(801) 363-0526   **Contact:** Shaun Elam, Literary Manager **Theatre:** professional not-for-profit **Works:** full-length plays, one-acts, translations, musicals **Special interests:** contemporary western social issues; experimental, non-traditional works **Stage:** proscenium-thrust, 140-200 seats **Submission policy:** query/synopsis with SAS postcard **Response:** 2-3 weeks if interested in query; 6 months script **Program:** readings

SALTWORKS THEATRE COMPANY
The Design Center, 5001 Baum Blvd.,
Pittsburgh, PA 15213 (412) 687-8883
Contact: Lynn George, Managing Director **Theatre:** professional not-for-profit touring company **Works:** full-length plays, one-acts, translations, adaptations, musicals, children's plays **Special interests:** "Values of contemporary society; social issues affecting health and well-being; 1- and 2-person shows on Christian themes." **Maximum cast:** 10 **Submission policy:** unsolicited script with SASE **Response:** 3-4 months

SAN DIEGO REPERTORY THEATRE
79 Horton Plaza, San Diego, CA 92101 (619) 231-3586
Contact: Walter Schoen, Associate Producer **Theatre:** professional not-for-profit **Works:** full-length plays, translations, adaptations, musicals, literary cabaret, multi-media works **2nd productions:** yes **Special interests:** "U.S. and West Coast

premieres; innovations in form and perspective; works by and about women and minorities; multi-media works." **Specifications:** maximum cast: 16; no fly space **Stages:** proscenium, 212 seats; modified thrust, 535 seats; flexible, 225 seats **Audience:** "Middle to upper middle class, white, 35-50." **Submission policy:** unsolicited script with SASE **Response:** 6-12 months **Your chances:** 500 submissions **Recent production of unsolicited work:** no **Remuneration/future commitment:** negotiable **Programs:** readings, workshop productions, residencies

SEASIDE MUSIC THEATER
Box 1310, Daytona Beach, FL 32015 (904) 252-3394
Contact: Lester Malizia, General Manager **Theatre:** professional not-for-profit **Works:** musicals, children's musicals, cabaret/revues **Specifications:** maximum cast: 8 for Winter Dinner Theater; 30 for Summer Repertory Theater, 10 for Theater for Children; fly space in summer theatre only **Stages:** Winter Dinner Theater: thrust, 159 seats; Summer Repertory Theater: proscenium, 550 seats; Theater for Children: modified thrust, 150 seats **Submissior policy:** query/synopsis with cassette **Best time:** Sept.-Nov. **Response:** 1 month query; 3 months script

SEATTLE CHILDREN'S THEATRE
Seattle Center, 305 Harrison, Seattle, WA 98109
(206) 443-0807 Contact: Linda Hartzell, Artistic Director **Theatre:** professional not-for-profit **Works:** children's full-length plays, one-acts, adaptations and musicals **Exclusive interest:** "Sophisticated works on contemporary issues for young audiences." **Stage:** proscenium, 280 seats **Submission policy:** professional recommendation **Best time:** Feb.-Dec. **Response:** 6 months

THE SEATTLE GROUP THEATRE
3940 Brooklyn Ave. NE, Seattle, WA 98105
(206) 545-4969 Contact: Tim Bond, Literary Manager **Theatre:** professional not-for-profit **Works:** full-length plays, one-acts, translations, adaptations, musicals **2nd productions:** yes **Special interests:** "Plays suitable for multi-ethnic casting; serious plays on social/cultural issues; satires or comedies with bite." **Specifications:** maximum cast: 10; unit or simple set preferred **Tours:** yes **Stage:** modified thrust, 200 seats **Audience:** "Median age 35, liberal, socially conscious; college graduates; variety of occupations; various ethnic backgrounds; middle income." **Submission policy:** query/synopsis with dialogue sample and resume **Best time:** before Nov. 1, 1990 for 1991-92 season **Response:** 6 weeks query; 3-6 months script **Your chances:** 400 submissions/"6-8 productions as part of Playwrights' Festival;

regular season varies" **Remuneration:** "Royalty, fee negotiable."
Future commitment: negotiable for world premiere **Programs:** readings, staged readings, workshop productions, development; Multicultural Playwrights' Festival (see Contests)

SEATTLE REPERTORY THEATRE
155 Mercer St., Seattle, WA 98109 (206) 443-2210
Contact: Douglas Hughes, Associate Artistic Director **Theatre:** professional not-for-profit **Works:** full-length plays, translations, adaptations **Tours:** "Each season at least 1 play tours WA, CA and HI." **Stages:** proscenium, 856 seats; arena, 142 seats **Submission policy:** professional recommendation **Response:** 2-3 months **Your chances:** 1000 submissions/2 or more productions plus 4 or more in workshop **Remuneration:** travel, per diem for workshop production **Programs:** internships, residencies; New Plays in Process workshop productions (inquire) **Advice:** "No conventional domestic melo-dramas or 'sit-com'-like material. We seek playwrights with unique voices to whom language and authentic theatricality are most important." **Comment:** See Egan, Timothy, "He'll Take Seattle (The Rain's Good for Business)," *New York Times* (July 15, 1989), 5, 12.

THE SECOND STAGE
Box 1807 Ansonia Station, New York, NY 10023
(212) 787-8302 **Contact:** Jim Lewis, Literary Manager
Theatre: professional not-for-profit **Works:** full-length plays, adaptations, musicals **2nd productions:** exclusively: revivals of works that have had major productions in past 20 years **Special interests:** social/political issues; "heightened realism" **Stage:** endstage, 110 seats **Submission policy:** unsolicited script with SASE, synopsis and production history **Response:** 3 months **Your chances:** readings of 6-8 new and previously produced plays each year **Future commitment:** no **Comment:** See Reiter, Susan, "Second Stage's Second Decade," *TheaterWeek* (Dec. 5, 1988), 8-15.

SENIOR ACTING PROGRAM OF THE BARN PLAYERS
Box 713, Shawnee Mission, KS 66201 (913) 381-4004
Contact: Don Ramsey, President **Theatre:** community service touring theatre **Works:** one-acts **2nd productions:** no **Exclusive interest:** "Works suitable for performers over 55 years of age." **Specifications:** no scenery for touring; minimum props; maximum playing time: 30 minutes **Stages:** "Various spaces--from platforms to living rooms." **Audience:** retired persons; elementary, high school and college students **Submission policy:** unsolicited script with SASE **Your chances:** 125 submissions/6 productions **Remuneration:** $10 per performance **Comment:** See The Barn Players listing in this section.

SEVEN STAGES
c/o George R. Wren,
New Play Development Coordinator,
956 Seville Dr., Clarkston, GA 30021 (404) 522-0911
Theatre: professional not-for-profit **Works:** full-length plays, related or compatible one-acts, translations, adaptations, musicals, performance-art pieces **2nd productions:** yes **Special interests:** socio/political works; non-traditional, experimental works on contemporary issues; comedies; works by young black writers and women **Specifications:** maximum cast: 10, fewer preferred; small space **Stages:** flexible modified thrust, 250 seats; flexible L-shape, 100 seats **Audience:** "Racially and culturally mixed; inner-city, professional and working class." **Submission policy:** unsolicited script with SASE; query/synopsis with resume; solicited script **Best time:** summer-fall **Response:** 1 month query; 3 months solicited script; 8 months script **Your chances:** 150 submissions/3 productions **Remuneration:** commission; royalty; per diem; residency **Future commitment:** film and video rights **Programs:** readings, staged readings, workshop productions, development, internships **Advice:** "No domestic melodramas. Avoid realism. Be a poet--include music." **Comment:** Theatre is located at 1105 Euclid Ave., Atlanta, GA 30307.

SEVENTH SIGN THEATRE COMPANY
Box 8314 FDR Station, New York, NY 10150-1919
Contact: Donna Niemann, President **Theatre:** off off Broadway **Works:** full-length plays, one-acts, translations, adaptations, children's plays **2nd productions:** "We might consider them." **Specifications:** moderate cast size; simple sets **Stage:** open arena, 60-80 seats **Audience:** "Varying, with quite a number of senior citizens." **Submission policy:** unsolicited script with SASE and resume; professional recommendation; agent submission; in-house commission **Best time:** summer **Response:** 1 month **Remuneration:** no **Program:** Writer's Roundtable: monthly readings (request application)

SHAKESPEARE & COMPANY
The Mount, Lenox, MA 01240 (413) 637-1197
Contact: Tina Packer, Artistic Director; Stanley Richardson, Literary Manager **Theatre:** professional not-for-profit **Works:** two-act plays, one-acts, adaptations, children's plays (1 hour in length) **2nd productions:** no **Special interests:** adaptations of works by Edith Wharton, Henry James and their contemporaries; works dealing with social change, c. 1900-1910 **Specifications:** maximum cast: 6; single set **Stages:** outside amphitheatre, 500

seats; outside amphitheatre, 150 seats; flexible, 100 seats
Audience: "Mixed: city, rural, area people and people from across
U.S.A." **Submission policy:** query/synopsis preferred; unsolicited
script with SASE **Best time:** Feb. **Response:** 4 weeks **Your
chances:** 100 submissions/0 productions **Future commitment:**
negotiable **Programs:** staged readings, workshop productions
Advice: "Irish plays; Protestant/Catholic problem; Irish
playwrights." **Comment:** The Mount, Edith Wharton's former home,
may be used as a set.

THE SHAKESPEARE THEATRE AT THE FOLGER
Washington, DC This theatre no longer produces new plays.

THE SHALIKO COMPANY
151 Second Ave. Suite 1E, New York, NY 10003
(212) 475-6313 Contact: Mary Ellen Kernaghan, Administrative
Director **Theatre:** professional not-for-profit **Works:** full-length
plays, one-acts, translations, adaptations, musicals, children's plays,
cabaret/revues **Maximum cast:** 10 **Submission policy:**
query/synopsis **Best time:** spring **Response:** 1 month

THE SHAZZAM PRODUCTION COMPANY
418 Pier Ave. Suite 104, Santa Monica, CA 90405
(213) 396-0984 Contact: Edward Blackoff, Producer
Theatre: off off Broadway **Works:** full-length plays **2nd
productions:** occasionally **Special interests:** emotional works,
social comment **Specifications:** maximum cast: 15; 1 or 2 sets
Stages: proscenium; thrust; arena **Submission policy:**
unsolicited script with SASE; query/synopsis; professional
recommendation; agent submission **Best time:** Mar.-Sept.
Response: 6 weeks **Your chances:** 100 submissions/2
productions **Remuneration:** $15 per performance **Future
commitment:** no

SHEBOYGAN COMMUNITY PLAYERS
607 S. Water St., Sheboygan, WI 53081 (414) 459-3779
Contact: Ralph Maffongelli, Director of Theatre **Theatre:**
community/non-professional **Works:** full-length plays, children's
plays **2nd productions:** "We would consider it." **Specifications:**
maximum cast: 6-8; simple sets **Stage:** thrust **Audience:**
"Conservative!" **Submission policy:** query/synopsis **Response:**
2 weeks query; 2 months script **Your chances:** 3-4 submissions/"1
production every few years" **Remuneration:** "Small stipend."
Program: readings **Advice:** "We will consider new plays for
mainstage, but must be very careful as our box office must support a
substantial part of our budget. We also produce children's shows and,

from time to time, special projects, for all of which we would consider new plays."

SIDEWALKS BY THE SEASHORE
See Coney Island, USA listing in this section.

SIDEWALKS THEATER
40 W. 27th St., New York, NY 10001 (212) 481-3077
Contact: Gary Beck, Artistic Director **Theatre:** off off Broadway, professional not-for-profit **Works:** full-length plays, one-acts, translations, adaptations **2nd productions:** "Possibly." **Special interests:** "We want serious playwrights, not amateurs with first plays. Serious, meaningful, sophisticated plays." **Specifications:** maximum cast: 12; single set; "nothing set in bars or cafes" **Stage:** black box, 74 seats **Audience:** "Depends on play; New York." **Submission policy:** query/synopsis with resume **Response:** 6-12 months **Your chances:** 150 submissions/1-2 productions **Remuneration:** negotiable **Programs:** readings, staged readings, workshop productions, internships, residencies **Advice:** "Work through our workshop development procedure. All plays are done in this manner: reading, workshop, production."

THE SNOWMASS REPERTORY THEATRE
Box 6275, Snowmass Village, CO 81615 (303) 923-2618
Contact: Gordon Reinhart, Artistic Director **Theatre:** professional not-for-profit **Works:** full-length plays, translations, adaptations, musicals, children's plays **2nd productions:** yes **Special interests:** non-realistic comedies, musicals and nightclub and period pieces for repertory production **Specifications:** maximum cast: 13; single set preferred **Tours:** yes **Stages:** proscenium, 488 seats; proscenium-thrust, 253 seats **Audience:** "Tourists interested in healthy fun." **Submission policy:** query/synopsis **Best times:** Apr., Oct. **Response:** 6 weeks query; 6 months script **Your chances:** 300 submissions/2 productions **Remuneration:** percentage **Future commitment:** yes **Program:** workshop productions

SOCIETY HILL PLAYHOUSE
507 S. 8th St., Philadelphia, PA 19147 (215) 923-0210
Contact: Walter Vail, Literary Manager **Theatre:** professional not-for-profit **Works:** full-length plays, translations, adaptations, musicals, children's plays **2nd productions:** if not previously produced in Philadelphia **Specifications:** maximum cast: 6; simple set preferred; plays must be suitable for production in repertory **Stages:** proscenium, 223 seats; flexible, 90 seats **Audience:** "General theatregoers from the Delaware Valley." **Submission**

policy: query/synopsis preferred; unsolicited script with SASE; professional recommendation; agent submission **Response**: 1 month query; 6 months script **Your chances**: 300+ submissions/2-6 productions **Remuneration**: negotiable **Future commitment**: no **Programs**: staged readings, workshop productions

SOHO REPERTORY THEATRE
80 Varick St., New York, NY 10013 (212) 925-2588
Contact: Rob Barron, Director of Play Development **Theatre**: off off Broadway **Works**: full-length plays, one-acts, translations, adaptations, musicals **2nd productions**: "If not off off Broadway shows." **Special interests**: "Plays that are intellectually stimulating, use 3-dimentional space imaginatively, have plenty of action and are unlikely to be done by other theatres; mixed-media and experimental works; offbeat new musicals and operas." **Specifications**: maximum cast: 12; high ceilings; no realistic sets **Stage**: apron proscenium, 100 seats **Audience**: "Educated, sophisticated, median age about 50." **Submission policy**: query/synopsis with dialogue sample and SAS postcard **Response**: 1 month query; 3 months script **Your chances**: 100 submissions/1-2 productions **Remuneration**: "About $400 for 30 performances." **Future commitment**: yes **Programs**: staged readings, One Night Stand Series: "performance pieces, music"; New Voices for the Musical Theatre: excerpts from unproduced musicals (inquire) **Advice**: "Request guidelines; if you have a director interested in staging your play, his/her input might be useful."

SOURCE THEATRE COMPANY
1809 14th St. NW, Washington, DC 20009
(202) 462-1073 Contact: Pat Murphy Sheehy, Artistic Director **Theatre**: professional not-for-profit **Works**: full-length plays, one-acts, translations, adaptations, musicals **2nd productions**: yes **Special interest**: contracted mysteries for one-night gala fund-raisers (contact Garland Scott) **Specifications**: small stage; suggestive settings **Stage**: 3/4 thrust, 107 seats **Submission policy**: unsolicited script with SASE, synopsis and resume; query/synopsis with resume **Best time**: Sept. 15-Mar. 15 **Response**: 6 months **Programs**: readings; SourceWorks and The Washington Theatre Festival (see Special Programs); Source Theatre National Playwriting Competition (see Contests)

SOUTH COAST REPERTORY
Box 2197, Costa Mesa, CA 92628 (714) 957-2602
Contact: Jerry Patch, Dramaturg; John Glore, Literary Manager **Theatre**: professional not-for-profit **Works**: full-length plays, one-acts, musicals **2nd productions**: yes **Maximum cast**:

15-20 **Tours:** yes **Stages:** proscenium, 507 seats; thrust, 161 seats **Audience:** "Cosmopolitan." **Submission policy:** query/synopsis; professional recommendation; agent submission **Response:** 2 weeks query; 3-6 months script **Your chances:** 600-700 submissions/5-6 productions **Remuneration:** "Negotiable, usually about 5%." **Future commitment:** participation in subsidiary rights **Programs:** readings, staged readings, workshop productions, development; Hispanic Playwrights Project (see Contests); California Playwrights Festival (inquire)

SOUTHERN APPALACHIAN REPERTORY THEATRE
SART, Box 53, Mars Hill, NC 28754
(704) 689-1384, -1203 Contact: James W. Thomas, Managing Director **Theatre:** professional not-for-profit **Works:** full-length plays, musicals **2nd productions:** "Sometimes." **Special interest:** "Southern Appalachian themes, but not exclusively." **Stage:** proscenium, 152 seats **Audience:** "Well educated; upper-middle income; generally about 45-50 years of age; many retired and summer residents." **Submission policy:** unsolicited script with SASE and resume; query/synopsis with resume; professional recommendation **Best time:** fall **Response:** 1 month query; 6 months script **Your chances:** 65-70 submissions/1-2 or more productions **Remuneration:** "$500 plus expenses while attending rehearsals and/or performances." **Future commitment:** no **Programs:** readings, staged readings, development; Southern Appalachian Playwrights Conference held each Jan. (inquire) **Advice:** "Submit finished draft in proper form."

SOUTHERN REP
1437 South Carrollton Ave.,
New Orleans, LA 70118 (504) 861-8163
Contact: R. H. O'Neill, Artistic Director **Theatre:** professional not-for-profit **Works:** full-length plays, translations, adaptations, musicals, children's plays, cabaret/revues **Special interest:** Southern works **Stage:** proscenium, 200 seats **Submission policy:** unsolicited script with SASE **Best time:** late summer **Response:** 6-12 months

SOUTH JERSEY REGIONAL THEATRE
Bay Ave, Somers Point, NJ 08244 (609) 653-0553
Contact: Joanna Papada, Producing Director **Theatre:** professional not-for-profit **Works:** full-length plays, adaptations, musicals, revues **Specifications:** maximum cast: 8; minimal or unit set; no fly space **Stage:** proscenium, 299 seats **Submission policy:** query/synopsis **Response:** 3 weeks query; 3-6 months script

SPOKANE INTERPLAYERS ENSEMBLE
Box 1961, Spokane, WA 99210 (509) 455-7529
Contact: Robert A. Welch, Managing Director **Theatre:** professional not-for-profit **Works:** full-length plays, related one-acts, translations, adaptations, cabaret/revues **Specifications:** maximum cast: 8 preferred; single set **Stage:** thrust, 255 seats **Submission policy:** query/synopsis with dialogue sample, production history and reviews **Best time:** Jun.-Aug. **Response:** 3 weeks if interested in query; 6 months script

SPRINGBOARD THEATRE
386A Sackett St., Brooklyn, NY 11231 (718) 875-2405
Contact: Sasha Nanus, Artistic Director **Theatre:** off off Broadway **Works:** full-length plays, one-acts **2nd productions:** yes **Specifications:** some limitations on sets **Stages:** proscenium; thrust; flexible **Casting:** "Age range 20-40; more female roles." **Audience:** "Educated New York audience." **Submission policy:** unsolicited script with SASE; query/synopsis; agent submission **Response:** 1 week query; 1 month script **Your chances:** 75-100 submissions/5-10 productions **Remuneration:** "Depends upon each individual project." **Programs:** readings, staged readings, workshop productions **Advice:** "Contemporary, realistic works."

STAGE ONE: LOUISVILLE CHILDREN'S THEATRE
425 W. Market St., Louisville, KY 40202
(502) 589-5946   Contact: Moses Goldberg, Producing Director **Theatre:** professional not-for-profit **Works:** children's full-length plays, one-acts, translations, adaptations and musicals **2nd productions:** yes **Special interests:** "Stageworthy, respectful dramatizations of the classic tales of childhood, both ancient and modern; plays relevant to the lives of young people and their families; plays directly related to school curriculum." **Maximum cast:** 12-14 Equity actors; no limit on students in cast **Tours:** yes **Stages:** thrust, 626 seats; arena, 350 seats **Audience:** "Young people, ages 5-18, and family audiences." **Submission policy:** unsolicited script with SASE and resume; professional recommendation; agent submission **Best time:** Aug.-Dec. **Response:** 4-6 months **Your chances:** 100-200 submissions/1-2 productions **Remuneration/ future commitment:** possible **Program:** readings **Advice:** "Please do not send plot summaries or reviews."

STAGES REPERTORY THEATRE
3201 Allen Pkwy. Suite 101, Houston, TX 77019
(713) 527-0220 Contact: Joe Cantu, Associate Artistic Director **Theatre:** professional not-for-profit **Works:** full-length plays, one-acts, children's plays, cabaret/revues **Special interest:** new

plays by Texas authors **Specifications:** small cast, simple set
preferred **Tours:** children's plays tour schools **Stages:** thrust,
195 seats; arena, 248 seats **Submission policy:** unsolicited
script with SASE and synopsis **Best time:** fall **Response time:**
10 months **Your chances:** 200 submissions/2 productions
Remuneration: for full production **Programs:** readings,
workshops, residencies; Women Playwrights Repertory, Texas
Playwrights Festival (inquire)

STAGES TRILINGUAL THEATRE
1540 N. McCadden Pl., Hollywood, CA 90028
(213) 463-5356 Contact: Stephen Sachs, Executive Director
Theatre: professional not-for-profit **Works:** full-length plays,
one-acts, translations, adaptations **Special interests:** works by
foreign writers in either original languages or translation; plays in
Spanish, French and English; experimental works **Maximum cast:** 5
preferred **Stages:** outdoor flexible, 99 seats; proscenium, 49 seats;
classroom Lab, 25 seats **Submission policy:** query/synopsis
Response: 1 month query; 2 months script

STAGE WEST
One Columbus Center, Springfield, MA 01103
(413) 781-4470 Contact: Eric Hill, Artistic Director
Theatre: professional not-for-profit **Works:** full-length plays,
translations, adaptations **2nd productions:** yes **Special
interests:** adaptations of material from non-dramatic genres; new
translations and adaptations of neglected classic and 20th-century
European plays **Maximum cast:** 8 **Stages:** thrust, 480 seats;
flexible, 99 seats **Submission policy:** query/synopsis **Response:**
3-6 months **Future commitment:** yes **Program:** staged readings

STAGE WEST
Box 2587, Ft. Worth, TX 76113 (817) 332-6265
Contact: Jerry Russell, Artistic Director **Theatre:** professional
not-for-profit **Works:** full-length plays, translations, adaptations,
musicals, cabaret/revues **2nd productions:** yes **Special
interest:** contemporary issues **Maximum cast:** 9 preferred
Stage: flexible, 175 seats **Submission policy:** query/synopsis
Best time: Jan.-Mar. **Response:** 1 month query; 3 months script
Remuneration: "Varies."

STAGEWRIGHTS, INC.
165 W. 47th St., New York, NY 10036 (718) 946-5891
Contact: Gary Apple, Literary Manager **Theatre:** off off Broadway
Works: full-length plays, one-acts **2nd productions:** if free of
commitments **Special interests:** works that take risks; strongly

motivated characters; conflict **Stages:** various spaces
Submission policy: query/synopsis with 1st scene **Response:** 3
months **Future commitment:** no **Programs:** Manhattan Monday
Night Playwrights Workshop, Annual One-act Festival (inquire)
Advice: "Participate in our weekly playwright's workshop and
become a member. All are welcome to pay a visit and see how we
operate."

STAMFORD THEATRE WORKS
95 Atlantic St., Stamford, CT 06901 (203) 359-4414
Contact: Steve Karp, Artistic Director **Theatre:** professional not-
for-profit resident company **Works:** full-length plays **2nd
productions:** yes **Special interest:** "Quality work on any
subject matter that speaks to our audience." **Stage:** pit stage with
raked audience, 150 seats **Casting:** "Mostly Equity; some
non-Equity." **Audience:** "Stamford area, affluent and sophisticated."
Submission policy: unsolicited script with SASE **Response:** 3-6
months **Remuneration:** royalty **Program:** staged readings
Advice: "We are interested in new plays."

STANLEY HOTEL THEATRE
333 Wonderview Rd., Estes Park, CO 80517
(303) 586-3371 (hotel) **Contact:** Melody Page, Producer
Theatre: non-Equity **Works:** full-length plays, musicals **Special
interests:** mysteries, melodramas, dramas, comedies, farces,
musicals **Specifications:** maximum cast: 10; simple, moveable
sets; no sit-coms **Submission policy:** query/synopsis

STEPPENWOLF THEATRE COMPANY
2851 N. Halsted St., Chicago, IL 60657 (312) 472-4515
Contact: Randall Arney, Jeff Perry, Artistic Directors **Theatre:**
professional not-for-profit **Works:** full-length plays, adaptations
Specifications: maximum cast: 8; single set **Stage:** modified
thrust, 211 seats **Submission policy:** query/synopsis **Best
time:** Oct.-Dec. **Response:** 1 month query; 6 months script

STOP-GAP COMPANY
523 N. Grand Ave., Santa Ana, CA 92701
(714) 648-0135 **Contact:** Don Laffoon, Executive Director
Theatre: professional not-for-profit **Works:** full-length plays
Special interests: "Social issues and disabilities: alcoholism,
families in crisis, senior topics, forms of abuse, etc."
Specifications: maximum cast: 6; some limitations on sets
Stage: proscenium, 200 seats **Audience:** "General audience and
those interested in specific social themes presented." **Submission
policy:** unsolicited script with SASE; query/synopsis **Response:**

4 months **Your chances:** 20 submissions/2 productions
Remuneration/future commitment: no **Advice:** "In an issue-oriented play, beware of the issue 'taking over' the play."

STOREFRONT THEATRE
615 NW Couch, Portland, OR 97209 (503) 224-9598
Contact: Shirley Suttles, Literary Manager **Theatre:** professional not-for-profit **Works:** full-length plays, adaptations, musicals **2nd productions:** yes **Specifications:** "We are Portland's 'alternative' theatre--not interested in mainstream, Broadway-type material; small-scale or non-traditional musicals only." **Stages:** flexible (usually proscenium), 300 seats; proscenium, 150 seats **Submission policy:** query/synopsis with dialogue sample and SAS postcard; professional recommendation **Response:** 1 month query; 6 months script **Your chances:** 50-100 submissions/1-2 productions **Remuneration:** standard royalty

STRAND STREET THEATRE
2317 Mechanic St., Galveston, TX 77550
(409) 763-4591 Contact: Susan Permenter, Managing Director **Theatre:** professional not-for-profit **Works:** full-length plays, one-acts, adaptations **Specifications:** small cast; single-story set, unit preferred **Submission policy:** send SASE for guidelines **Programs:** readings, workshop productions

STREET PLAYERS THEATRE
Box 2687, Norman, OK 73070 (405) 364-0207
Contact: Robert Woods, Artistic Director **Works:** full-length plays, children's plays **Special interests:** comedy, drama **Specifications:** cast size: 4-7; single set or open staging; playing time for children's plays: 55 minutes **Tours:** children's plays **Stage:** flexible, 70-99 seats **Casting:** open auditions for season company **Audience:** largely university faculty and students and senior citizens **Submission policy:** query/synopsis preferred; unsolicited script with SASE **Response:** 3 months **Your chances:** 25-30 submissions received each year **Remuneration:** negotiable **Program:** Fall Festival Playwrights Contest (see Contests) **Advice:** "Small theatre."

THE STREET THEATER
228 Fisher Ave. Room 226, White Plains, NY 10606
(914) 761-3307 Contact: Gray Smith, Executive Director **Theatre:** professional not-for-profit touring theatre **Works:** one-acts, plays for young audiences **Special interests:** ensemble pieces; plays for young audiences (not children's plays) **Specifications:** minimal production requirements **Stages:**

summer; outdoor mobile stages; winter; school stages **Submission policy:** query/synopsis; commission **Best time:** Nov.-Feb. **Response:** 2-4 weeks **Comment:** Playwrights interested in commissions should write for information.

STUDIO ARENA THEATRE
710 Main St., Buffalo, NY 14202 (716) 856-8025
Contact: Ross Wasserman, Associate Director/Dramaturg **Theatre:** professional not-for-profit **Works:** full-length plays, translations, adaptations, children's plays **2nd productions:** yes **Special interests:** "Issues of power in America; the roles of women and minorities in our society; work that celebrates theatricality and the act of performance itself." **Specifications:** maximum cast: 12; limited wing space; no fly system **Stage:** thrust, 637 seats **Audience:** "Broad spectrum." **Submission policy:** query/ synopsis with dialogue sample; agent submission **Response:** 2 weeks query; 3 months script **Your chances:** 300 submissions/1-2 productions **Remuneration:** "Fee." **Program:** PlayWorks: staged readings, 1-week residency (inquire)

THE STUDIO THEATRE
1333 P St. NW, Washington, DC 20005 (202) 232-7267
Contact: Maynard Marshall, Literary Manager **Theatre:** professional not-for-profit **Works:** full-length plays, translations, adaptations, musicals **Special interests:** American "lyric realism"; translations of new Asian and European plays **Stage:** modified thrust, 200 seats **Submission policy:** professional recommendation **Best times:** Dec.-Jan., Aug.-Sept. **Response:** 2 months

STUDIO X
The Ashland Performing Arts Center,
208 Oak St., Ashland, OR 97520
(503) 488-2011 Contact: Scott Avery, Artistic Director **Theatre:** professional not-for-profit **Works:** full-length plays, one-acts **2nd productions:** yes **Maximum cast:** 8 **Stage:** flexible **Audience:** "All types." **Submission policy:** unsolicited script with SASE **Best time:** Mar. **Your chances:** 150 submissions/13 productions **Programs:** staged readings, classes

SUNSET PLAYHOUSE, INC.
800 Elm Grove Rd., Elm Grove, WI 53122
(414) 782-4430 Contact: Alan Furlan, Managing Director **Theatre:** community not-for-profit **Works:** full-length plays **Special interest:** comedies with appeal to an older audience **Stage:** proscenium **Audience:** "Mature--30-70." **Submission**

policy: unsolicited script with SASE **Your chances:** 50 submissions/"perhaps no productions" **Remuneration:** royalty **Comment:** "Season normally consists of Broadway plays."

SYNTHAXIS THEATRE COMPANY
North Hollywood, CA (213) 877-4726 Our 1990 questionnaire was returned as "undeliverable," and, although the above number appears to be correct, we received no response to our messages.

SYRACUSE STAGE
820 E. Genessee St., Syracuse, NY 13210
(315) 443-4008 **Contact:** Howard A. Kerner, Literary Manager **Theatre:** professional not-for-profit **Works:** full-length plays, translations, musicals **2nd productions:** yes **Special interests:** plays by and about women; anti-nuclear plays; experimental works **Maximum cast:** 12 **Stages:** proscenium, 199 seats; flexible, 499 seats **Audience:** "Cultural cross-section; high school to senior citizen." **Submission policy:** professional recommendation, agent submission preferred; unsolicited script with SASE; query/synopsis with dialogue sample **Best times:** Apr.-Oct. for query/synopsis; May-Jun. only for script **Response:** 1 month if interested in query; 3-5 months script **Future commitment:** varies **Your chances:** 150 submissions/1-2 productions **Remuneration:** "Standard royalty." **Program:** staged readings

TACOMA ACTORS GUILD
1323 S. Yakima Ave., Tacoma, WA 98405
(206) 272-3107 **Contact:** Bruce K. Sevy, Artistic Director **Theatre:** professional not-for-profit **Works:** full-length plays, translations, adaptations, musicals **2nd productions:** yes **Special interest:** strong characterization **Specifications:** maximum cast: 10; unit set preferred; intimate setting; "no strong language or nudity" **Stage:** modified thrust, 298 seats **Audience:** "Older, middle-of-the-road, not adventurous." **Submission policy:** query/synopsis with SAS postcard **Best time:** spring-summer **Response:** 1-2 months query; 6 months script **Your chances:** 30 submissions/0 productions **Remuneration:** "Negotiable." **Future commitment:** 5% of royalties **Program:** staged readings

TAKOMA THEATRE, INC.
Box 56512, Washington, DC 20011 (202) 291-8060
Contact: Andrea Hines, Artistic Director **Works:** full-length plays, musicals **Special interests:** realistic plays; comedy and drama; multi-ethnic casting **Submission policy:** unsolicited script with SASE **Response:** 3 months **Remuneration:** negotiable

TALE SPINNERS THEATER
Attn: Studio Eremos, 401 Alabama St. #127, San Francisco, CA 94110 (415) 861-7950 **Contact:** Kate Mendeloff, Artistic Director **Theatre:** professional not-for-profit **Works:** full-length plays **2nd productions:** yes **Exclusive interest:** "The development of new plays from Bay Area oral history." **Tours:** yes **Stage:** black box, 99 seats **Audience:** "Varied." **Submission policy:** unsolicited script with SASE and resume **Best time:** spring **Response:** 6 weeks **Your chances:** 4 new plays produced each year **Remuneration:** negotiable **Programs:** readings, staged readings, workshop productions, development

THE TAMPA PLAYERS
601 S. Florida Ave., Tampa, FL 33602 (813) 229-1505 **Contact:** Bill Lelbach, Artistic/Managing Director **Theatre:** professional not-for-profit **Works:** full-length plays **2nd productions:** yes **Stage:** flexible, 220 seats **Submission policy:** professional recommendation **Response:** "No response guaranteed." **Future commitment:** possibly **Programs:** staged readings, development

TEATRO DALLAS
222 S. Montclair, Dallas, TX 75208 (214) 943-4429 **Contact:** Cora Cardona, Artistic Director **Theatre:** professional not-for-profit **Works:** full-length plays, one-acts, translations, adaptations, children's plays **2nd productions:** yes **Special interests:** "Hispanic and ethnic/minority interests; plays on historical, educational and social issues." **Specifications:** maximum cast: 8-10; simple sets **Tours:** yes **Stages:** "Small rented spaces; flexible." **Casting:** open auditions **Audience:** "Cultural mix--from senior citizens to children." **Submission policy:** unsolicited script with SASE **Best time:** summer **Response:** 1 month **Your chances:** 6 submissions/1 production **Remuneration:** "Everyone is paid; negotiable." **Future commitment:** no **Programs:** readings, staged readings, workshop productions **Advice:** "Write or call Cora Cardona."

TENNESSEE REPERTORY THEATRE
427 Chestnut St., Nashville, TN 37203 (615) 244-4878 **Contact:** Mac Pirkle, Artistic Director; Jennifer Orth, Production Manager **Theatre:** professional not-for-profit **Works:** full-length plays, adaptations, musicals **2nd productions:** yes **Special interests:** new American musicals; Southern plays **Maximum cast:** 8 **Stage:** workshop setting, 90 seats **Submission policy:** unsolicited script with SASE; query/synopsis with dialogue and

music/lyrics samples **Best time**: spring-summer **Response**: 6-12 months **Your chances:** 6-12 submissions/0 productions to date; "no new works on mainstage; we might consider them for 2nd stage only" **Future commitment:** yes **Comment:** "Theatre has a playreading committee of actors, designers and directors who evaluate submitted scripts. Because of limited resources and a very conservative audience base, the number of new works actually produced is extremely small."

TEXAS A & I UNIVERSITY THEATRE
Box 178, Texas A & I University, Kingsville, TX 78363 (512) 595-2614
Contact: Randall J. Buchanan, Director of Theatre **Theatre:** university/college **Works:** full-length plays, one-acts, translations, children's plays **2nd productions:** yes **Specifications:** cast size: 8-10; single set or space **Tours:** yes **Casting:** "At least as many female as male roles." **Stages:** proscenium, 1000 seats; proscenium, 240 seats; flexible, 100 seats **Audience:** "Fairly conservative; mixture of university and community; Hispanic and Anglo; small Black population." **Submission policy:** unsolicited script with SASE; query/synopsis **Best time:** spring **Response:** 1 month query; 3-4 months script **Your chances:** 3-4 submissions/0-1 production **Remuneration:** standard royalty **Advice:** "We hope to produce at least 1 new play each year."

THALIA SPANISH THEATRE
Box 4368, Sunnyside, NY 11104 (718) 729-3880
Contact: Silvia Brito, Artistic/Executive Director **Theatre:** professional not-for-profit **Works:** full-length plays, translations, adaptations **Exclusive interest:** plays in Spanish **Specifications:** maximum cast: 6; single set **Stage:** proscenium, 74 seats **Submission policy:** unsolicited script with SASE **Best time:** Dec.-Jan. **Response:** 3 months

THEATER ARTISTS OF MARIN
Box 473, San Raphael, CA 94915 (415) 454-2380
Contact: Charles Brousse, Artistic Director **Theatre:** professional not-for-profit **Works:** full-length plays, one-acts, musicals **2nd productions:** yes **Special interest:** "Plays which illuminate contemporary American life in a broader sense, not merely personal relationships." **Audience:** "Varied in age, well educated, affluent, liberal." **Submission policy:** unsolicited script with SASE; query/synopsis **Response:** 2 months query; 6 months script **Your chances:** 80-100 submissions/1 production plus 3 staged readings **Remuneration:** "$400 for full production." **Programs:** staged readings, workshop productions, development

THE THEATER AT MONMOUTH
Box 385, Monmouth, ME 04259 (207) 933-2952
Contact: Ted Davis, Artistic Director; Margaret M. Sterling, Business Manager **Works:** full-length plays, children's plays **Special interest:** traditional plays for young audiences **Specifications:** simple set **Stage:** raked thrust, 275 seats **Submission policy:** query/synopsis **Best time:** Nov. **Response:** 4-6 weeks query; 4-6 months script

THEATER EMORY
Annex B, Emory University, Atlanta, GA 30322
(404) 727-0523 Contact: Geoffrey Reeves, Artistic Director **Theatre:** professional not-for-profit **Works:** full-length plays, one-acts, translations, adaptations **Special interests:** translations and adaptations of classics **Stages:** flexible, 100-150 seats; flexible, 40-60 seats **Casting:** "Casts combine Equity members and students." **Submission policy:** query/synopsis with resume **Best time:** Oct.-Nov. **Response:** 1 month query; 3 months script

THEATER FOR THE NEW CITY
155 First Ave., New York, NY 10003
(212) 254-1109 Contact: Crystal Field, George Bartenieff, Artistic Directors **Theatre:** off off Broadway, professional not-for-profit **Works:** full-length plays, one-acts, musicals, operas, cabaret/revues, dance, performance art **2nd productions:** no **Special interests:** social issues; experimental American works; plays integrating music, dance and poetry **Tours:** "Annual Street Theatre production tours New York City." **Stages:** proscenium, 140 seats; arena, 80-90 seats; black box, 45 seats; cabaret, 45 seats **Submission policy:** unsolicited script with SASE; professional recommendation; commission **Best time:** spring **Response:** 9-18 months **Your chances:** 780 submissions/40 productions **Remuneration:** "For a play that we commission and when the playwright attends every performance." **Programs:** readings, staged readings, classes, internships **Comment:** TNC is committed to "the creation and performance of new American theatre and to new artists, lesser known writers and young performers."

THEATER LUDICRUM, INC.
64 Charlesgate E #83, Boston, MA 02215
(617) 424-6831 Contact: George Bistransin, President **Theatre:** professional not-for-profit **Works:** full-length plays, one-acts **2nd productions:** yes **Special interest:** "Works which rely upon the written word and acting." **Specifications:** "We are unable to present works that require expensive or difficult

sets and effects." **Stages:** various spaces **Submission policy:** unsolicited script with SASE **Response:** 1 month **Your chances:** 50 submissions/1 production **Remuneration:** $15-$30 per performance **Programs:** readings, staged readings

THEATER OF UNIVERSAL IMAGES
360 Central Ave., Newark, NJ 07104 (201) 645-6927
Contact: Clarence C. Lilley, Executive Producer **Theatre:** professional not-for-profit **Works:** full-length plays one-acts, musicals, cabaret/revues **Special interest:** "New works that project a positive image." **Specifications:** maximum cast: 8-10; single set **Tours:** yes **Stages:** proscenium, 400 seats; thrust, 100 seats **Casting:** open auditions **Audience:** "Multi-ethnical." **Submission policy:** query/synopsis; professional recommendation

THE THEATER STUDIO
New York, NY This theatre did not respond to our 1990 questionnaire, and its phone has been disconnected.

THEATRE AMERICANA
Box 245, Altadena, CA 91001-1235 (818) 397-1740
Contact: Elaine Hamilton, Chairman, Playreading Committee **Theatre:** community/non-professional **Works:** full-length plays **2nd productions:** yes **Specifications:** cast of 4-10 preferred; simple sets; minimum set changes; no elaborate, expensive costumes; no musicals **Stage:** "Simple raised stage with curtains, 100-150 seats." **Audience:** "Mostly conservative; middle-aged and senior citizens." **Submission policy:** unsolicited script with SASE **Best time:** before Apr. 1 **Response:** 2-3 months query; several months script **Your chances:** 175-200 submissions/4 productions **Remuneration:** "No; however, there is an annual $500 award to the best of the 4 plays produced each year." **Future commitment:** no **Program:** David James Ellis Memorial Award (see Contests)

THEATRE ARTS GROUP
1612 Metropolitan, Las Vegas, NV 89102
(702) 877-6463 Contact: Lori Noble, Trustee
Theatre: community not-for-profit **Works:** full-length plays **Specifications:** maximum cast: 20; small stage **Stage:** proscenium, 90 seats **Audience:** "Mainly middle-class white." **Submission policy:** unsolicited script with SASE **Response:** 6 weeks **Your chances:** 1 submission/"1 production in 3 and a half years" **Remuneration:** "Would depend." **Programs:** workshop productions, classes **Advice:** "Appeal to a general audience."

THEATRE DE LA JEUNE LUNE
Box 25170, Minneapolis, MN 55458-6170
(612) 332-3968 Contact: Emily Stevens, Business Director **Theatre:** professional not-for-profit **Works:** full-length plays, translations, adaptations, musicals **2nd productions:** yes **Special interests:** "Large casts; universal themes." **Specifications:** "No small-cast, psychological dramas." **Tours:** yes **Stages:** prosenium, 200 seats; thrust, 325 seats **Audience:** "All ages and backgrounds; majority 25-65, college educated." **Submission policy:** query/synopsis with resume **Response:** 2 months **Your chances:** 40 submissions/0 productions **Remuneration:** "Negotiated fee or royalty."

THEATREFEST
c/o Phillip Oesterman, Producer-Artistic Director,
529 W. 42nd St. #9T, New York, NY 10036
(212) 307-7856
Theatre: professional try-out center; university/college **Works:** full-length plays, musicals **2nd productions:** if not previously produced in New York **Stages:** mainstage, 1009 seats; studio, 199 seats **Submission policy:** unsolicited script with SASE and synopsis; query/synopsis **Best time:** no submissions before fall 1990 **Program:** developmental workshops **Comment:** Theatre is located at Montclair State College, Montclair, NJ.

THEATRE IV
114 W . Broad St., Richmond, VA 23220 (804) 783-1688
Contact: Russell Wilson, Production Associate **Theatre:** professional not-for-profit **Works:** full-length plays, translations, adaptations, musicals, children's plays **2nd productions:** yes **Special interest:** children's plays **Specifications:** maximum cast: 6 for children's plays; moderate production budget **Stages:** proscenium, 222-650 seats; flexible, 100 seats **Audience:** "Broad base." **Submission policy:** query/synopsis with resume; professional recommendation; commission **Response:** 2 weeks query; 2-6 months script **Your chances:** 50 submissions/3-7 productions; new plays, other than new children's plays, are rarely produced **Remuneration:** "Negotiated royalty." **Programs:** readings, staged readings

THEATRE IN THE PARK
Box 12151, Raleigh, NC 27605 (919) 755-6936
Contact: Ira D. Wood, Executive Director **Theatre:** community/ non-professional **Works:** full-length plays, one-acts, translations, adaptations, musicals, children's plays **2nd productions:** yes **Maximum cast:** 60 **Tours:** yes **Stages:** flexible, 200 seats;

proscenium, 40 seats **Audience:** college community; young professionals **Submission policy:** unsolicited script with SASE **Response:** 2 months **Your chances:** 50 submissions/1 production **Remuneration:** "Negotiated royalty." **Programs:** staged readings, workshop productions, classes, contest (inquire)

THEATRE-IN-THE-WORKS, INC.
Box 532016, Orlando, FL 32853 (407) 365-7235
Contact: Literary Manager **Theatre:** professional not-for-profit, Equity small professional **Works:** full-length plays, one-acts, translations, adaptations, musicals, children's plays, operas **2nd productions:** yes **Exclusive interest:** Florida playwrights **Stage:** flexible, 150 seats **Audience:** "Varies from show to show; we use each production as an opportunity to reach new audiences." **Submission policy:** send SASE for guidelines **Best time:** fall **Response:** 6-12 months **Your chances:** 40-50 submissions/2 productions; "all works are carefully read and conscientiously critiqued; no cursory treatment" **Remuneration:** $100 **Programs:** staged readings, workshop productions, development **Advice:** "Patience. We have a small staff of readers who are often involved in other area productions. We also seek out at least one individual with in-depth knowledge on the subject of the play."

THEATRE KENT & PORTHOUSE THEATRE COMPANY
B141 Music & Speech Bldg., Kent State University, Kent, OH 44242 (216) 672-2082, 929-4416
Contact: Michael Nash, Artistic Director **Theatre:** professional not-for-profit, university/college **Works:** full-length plays, one-acts, translations, musicals **2nd productions:** yes **Specifications:** "Balance of male/female roles; no fly system." **Tours:** "Rarely." **Stages:** thrust, 500 seats; flexible, 150-200 seats **Submission policy:** query/synopsis preferred; unsolicited script with SASE; professional recommendation; agent submission **Response:** 2 months query; 3 months script **Your chances:** "We produce 1 new play every 2 years or so. Unsolicited submission is <u>very</u> difficult, given the lack of any literary staff." **Remuneration:** "We would try!"

THEATRE NOUVEAU
Boston, MA This theatre did not respond to our 1990 questionnaire, and its phone was not in service when we called.

THEATRE OFF PARK
224 Waverly Pl., New York, NY 10014
(212) 627-2556   Contact: Albert Harris, Artistic Director
Theatre: professional not-for-profit   **Works:** full-length plays, one-acts, musicals   **2nd productions:** "Occasionally." **Special interest:** small-cast contemporary plays **Specifications:** maximum cast: 8; single set   **Stage:** 99 seats   **Submission policy:** agent submission   **Best time:** summer   **Response:** 2-3 months   **Remuneration:** yes **Programs:** readings, staged readings, internships, classes

THE THEATRE OF NEWBURYPORT
Box 6027, Newburyport, MA 01950
(508) 462-3332   Contact: Hanna Trautman, Director, Formative Stage   **Theatre:** professional not-for-profit   **Works:** full-length plays, one-acts, translations, adaptations, cabaret/revues   **Special interests:** translations, adaptations; Northeastern writers   **Maximum cast:** 5-7   **Stage:** flexible, 70 seats   **Submission policy:** unsolicited script with SASE **Best time:** Sept.-Mar.   **Response:** 2 months   **Program:** Formative Stage: staged readings possibly leading to full productions (inquire)

THEATRE OF YOUTH COMPANY
681 Main St., Buffalo, NY 14205
(716) 856-4410   Contact: Meg Pantera, Artistic Director **Theatre:** professional not-for-profit   **Works:** full-length plays, translations, adaptations, children's plays   **2nd productions:** yes   **Special interest:** contemporary issues for young audiences   **Specifications:** maximum cast: 6; small sets for touring shows   **Stages:** proscenium; 908 seats; arena, 200 seats; school auditoriums   **Audience:** "Children pre-K and grades K-12, adults."   **Submission policy:** unsolicited script with SASE;   query/synopsis with dialogue sample;   commission **Best time:** Sept.   **Response:** 2 weeks   **Your chances:** 12-15 submissions/2 productions   **Remuneration:** fee plus royalty **Programs:** development, internships

THEATRE ON THE SQUARE
450 Post St., San Francisco, CA 94102 (415) 433-6461
Contact: Jonathan Reinis, Owner **Theatre:** professional **Works:** full-length plays, musicals **2nd productions:** yes **Special interests:** musicals, comedies **Specifications:** maximum cast: 12; no more than 6 sets **Tours:** yes **Stage:** proscenium, 700 seats **Submission policy:** professional recommendation; agent submission **Best time:** spring **Response:** immediate query; 3 months script **Your chances:** 40-50 submissions/1-2 productions **Remuneration:** percentage

THEATRE PROJECT COMPANY
634 N. Grand St. Suite 10H, St. Louis, MO 63103
(314) 531-1315 **Contact:** William Freimuth, Artistic Director **Theatre:** professional not-for-profit **Works:** full-length plays, translations, children's plays **Exclusive interests:** "We produce compelling, alternative theatre: hard-edged comedy, drama and farce. Emphasis on the absurd, fantastical and controversial." **Maximum cast:** 15; no more than 2 sets **Stage:** thrust, 200 seats **Submission policy:** query/synopsis with dialogue sample **Best time:** Apr.-Jun. **Response:** 2 weeks query; 2 months script **Your chances:** "We are committed to producing 1 new play per season."

THEATRE RAPPORT
8128 Gould Ave., Hollywood, CA 90046 (213) 660-0433
Contact: Crane Jackson, Artistic Director **Theatre:** professional not-for-profit **Works:** full-length plays **2nd productions:** "Yes, a special interest." **Special interests:** "Unique, issue-oriented dramas; fast-moving farce-comedies; contemporary work." **Specifications:** maximum cast: 8; single set **Stage:** proscenium, 50 seats **Audience:** "From young people to adults." **Submission policy:** send script with SASE and reviews **Response:** 1 month if interested **Your chances:** 50 submissions/4 productions **Remuneration:** 20% of box office **Programs:** workshop productions, internships

THEATRE RHINOCEROS
2926 16th St., San Francisco, CA 94103
(415) 522-4100 **Contact:** Kenneth R. Dixon, Artistic Director **Theatre:** community/non-professional **Works:** full length plays, one-acts, musicals **2nd productions:** yes **Special interest:** "Gay/lesbian issues." **Specificiations:** maximum cast: 8; simple set **Tours:** yes **Stages:** 2 flexible spaces **Audience:** "60% male, 40% female, 15% people of color." **Submission policy:** unsolicited script with SASE; query/synopsis; professional recommendation **Response:** 1 month query; 3-4 months script

Your chances: 200 submissions/6+ productions **Remuneration:** royalty **Future commitment:** negotiable for a premiere **Programs:** readings, staged readings, workshop productions, development **Advice:** "Contemporary subject matter with lesbian/gay characters, people of color, other minorities functioning together."

THEATRE SOUTHWEST
Houston, TX This theatre is not currently accepting submissions.

THEATRE TESSERACT
820 E. Knapp St., Milwaukee, WI 53202 (414) 273-7529
Contact: Sharon McQueen, Producer/Artistic Director **Theatre:** professional not-for-profit **Works:** full-length plays, translations, adaptations, musicals, cabaret/revues **Special interests:** "Slightly controversial, cutting-edge works; Broadway and off Broadway-type material." **Specifications:** maximum cast: 6; simple production requirements **Stages:** proscenium, 180 seats; proscenium-thrust, 130 seats; proscenium, 120 seats **Submission policy:** professional recommendation **Best time:** Jun.-Aug. **Response:** time varies

THEATRE THREE PRODUCTIONS
Box 512, Pt. Jefferson, NY 11777 (516) 928-9202
Contact: Jerry Friedman, Associate Artistic Director **Theatre:** professional not-for-profit **Works:** full-length plays, children's plays, cabaret/revues **Specifications:** single set or suggested settings **Stages:** thrust, 475 seats; 3/4 thrust, 75 seats **Submission policy:** unsolicited script with SASE **Response:** 6 months **Program:** staged readings

THEATREVIRGINIA
2800 Grove Ave., Richmond, VA 23221-2466
(804) 367-0840 Contact: Bo Wilson, Literary Manager **Theatre:** professional not-for-profit **Works:** full-length plays, adaptations, musicals **2nd productions:** yes **Maximum cast:** 20 **Tours:** "Possibly." **Stage:** proscenium, 500 seats **Submission policy:** query/synopsis with 15-20 page dialogue sample **Best time:** late spring **Response:** 2-4 weeks query; 2-5 months script **Remuneration/future commitment:** negotiable

THEATRE WEST
3333 Cahuenga Blvd. W, Los Angeles, CA 90068
(213) 851-4839 Contact: Jan Harris, Writer's Workshop Moderator **Theatre:** professional not-for-profit membership workshop **Works:** full-length plays, one-acts, translations,

adaptations, musicals, children's plays **2nd productions:** yes **Specifications:** very limited wing and fly space **Tours:** "Occasionally." **Stage:** proscenium, 200 seats **Audience:** "Fairly sophisticated theatrically; wide financial spectrum; many from entertainment industry." **Submission policy:** sponsorship by 1 or more of approximately 200 members; unsolicited script with SASE from playwright desiring membership; no unsolicited script for production **Response:** 2 months **Your chances:** 30-40 submissions/1-3 productions **Remuneration:** negotiable **Program:** Theatre West Writer's Unit: a membership workshop offering developmental programs and full productions; $66 initiation fee, $34 monthly dues **Advice:** "L.A. area writers can greatly increase their chances for production by applying to join our Writer's Unit."

THEATRE WEST VIRGINIA
Box 1205, Beckley, WV 25802 (304) 253-8317
Contact: Megan Greenlee, Production Manager **Theatre:** professional not-for-profit touring company **Works:** full-length plays, one-acts, translations, adaptations, musicals, children's plays **Special interests:** adaptations of well-known works; historical subjects **Specifications:** maximum cast: 5; single set suitable for touring **Audience:** family-oriented **Submission policy:** unsolicited script with SASE **Best time:** Sept. **Response:** 2 months

THEATREWORKS
1305 Middlefield Rd., Palo Alto, CA 94301
(415) 328-0606 Contact: Robert Kelley, Artistic Director **Theatre:** professional not-for-profit **Works:** full-length plays, translations, adaptations, musicals **2nd productions:** yes **Special interests:** new musicals; non-traditional casting; entertainment value; works that celebrate the human spirit **Stages:** proscenium, 425 seats; proscenium, 275 seats; flexible, 70 seats **Audience:** "Wealthy and educated; heavily subscribed; very active." **Submission policy:** unsolicited script with SASE, synopsis, production history and resume; professional recommendation; agent submission **Best time:** Oct.-Dec. **Response:** 1-2 months; longer for summer submissions **Your chances:** 200 submissions/0-1 production **Recent production of unsolicited work:** yes **Remuneration:** royalty **Future commitment:** negotiable **Programs:** staged readings, workshop productions (request flyer) **Advice:** "Extremely well-written work; interesting subject matter; send reviews if previously produced."

THEATREWORKS/USA
890 Broadway, New York, NY 10003 (212) 688-0745
Contact: Barbara Pasternack, Artistic Associate **Theatre:** professional not-for-profit touring **Works:** children's musicals **2nd productions:** yes **Special interests:** "Historical plays, fairy tales, issues, classics, contemporary literature." **Specifications:** maximum cast: 5-6; single, touring set **Stages:** proscenium; flexible **Audience:** "6-14 year olds." **Submission policy:** query/synopsis preferred; unsolicited script with SASE **Best time:** summer **Response:** 3 months query; 6 months-1 year script **Your chances:** 100 submissions/3 productions **Remuneration:** "$1500 available for commission (advance against royalty); 6% total divided among collaborators." **Programs:** readings, workshop productions; Theatreworks/USA Commissioning Program (see Contests)

THEATRE X
Box 92206, Milwaukee, WI 53202 (414) 278-0555
Contact: John Schneider, Co-Artistic Director **Theatre:** professional not-for-profit **Works:** full-length plays **2nd productions:** yes **Special interests:** plays written with or for the company; performance art; avant garde works **Specifications:** small cast **Stage:** flexible, 99 seats **Audience:** "Mixed, educated." **Submission policy:** professional recommendation **Response:** 6 months **Your chances:** 20 submissions/0-1 production **Remuneration:** standard royalty **Program:** readings **Advice:** "Get to know us and our work; get us to see your work somewhere."

THIRD STEP THEATRE COMPANY
1179 Broadway 3rd Floor, New York, NY 10001
(212) 545-1372 Contact: Margit Ahlin, Literary Manager **Theatre:** off off Broadway, professional not-for-profit **Works:** full-length plays, one-acts, translations, adaptations **2nd productions:** no **Special interests:** "Women and minority playwrights are strongly encouraged; social relevance." **Specifications:** "No 1-person 'plays' or kitchen drama." **Stage:** rented space, 99 seats **Casting:** "Interracial, often non-traditional." **Audience:** "General New York audience." **Submission policy:** query/synopsis with character analysis and 15-page dialogue sample **Best time:** Sept. 1-Jan. 15 only **Response:** 3 months **Your chances:** 100 submissions/2-3 productions plus 10-12 in staged reading festival **Remuneration:** "Royalty based on agreement." **Future commitment:** "Conversion and subsidiary rights." **Programs:** readings, staged readings, workshop productions; Third Step Theatre Company Spring Festival of Staged

Readings (see Contests)   **Advice:** "All submissions should be highly dramatic, lean toward the avant garde, the daring."

THE THIRTEENTH STREET CHILDREN'S THEATRE ENSEMBLE
**The Thirteenth Street Repertory Theatre,
50 W. 13th St., New York, NY 10011 (212) 675-6677**
Contact: Greg Ward, Director   **Theatre:** off off Broadway, professional not-for-profit   **Works:** children's musicals, adaptations of classic fairy tales, original non-musicals for children   **2nd productions:** yes   **Specifications:** works must be 45-60 minutes in length and suitable for adult ensemble company; small cast; sets suitable for small spaces   **Tours:** "All shows."   **Stage:** proscenium, 70 seats   **Audience:** "Parents and children ages 3-8."
Submission policy: unsolicited script with SASE and resume   **Response:** 2 weeks   **Your chances:** 10-15 submissions/5 productions   **Remuneration:** no   **Advice:** "Send a cassette tape of songs, sample lead sheets and/or piano arrangements."

THE THIRTEENTH STREET REPERTORY COMPANY
50 W. 13th St., New York, NY 10011 (212) 675-6677
Contact: Gordon Farrell, Literary Manager   **Theatre:** off off Broadway   **Works:** short full-length plays, one-acts, musicals, children's plays   **2nd productions:** New York premieres   **Specifications:** maximum cast: 10; uncomplicated sets--"simple and fun!"   **Tours:** "Not yet--may."   **Audience:** "City dwellers from New York, Brooklyn, New Jersey--mixed."   **Submission policy:** unsolicited script with SASE   **Best time:** summer   **Response:** 6 months   **Your chances:** 200 submissions/10 productions   **Remuneration:** no   **Programs:** readings, development, playwright's unit   **Advice:** Inform literary manager of readings; "come to our theatre; see our productions."   **Comments:** Theatre is interested in working with playwrights to develop new plays. See McGovern, Michael, "The Line-up on 13th Street," *TheaterWeek* (Apr. 10, 1989), 37-39.

THREE BROTHERS THEATRE
216 Falmouth Rd., Scarsdale, NY 10583 (914) 723-8169
Contact: Wendell Batts, Artistic Director   **Theatre:** professional not-for-profit   **Works:** full-length plays, one-acts, translations, adaptations, musicals, children's plays   **2nd productions:** yes   **Special interest:** "The contemporary Black experience, particularly from 1964 to present--post Civil Rights."   **Specifications:** simple   **Tours:** yes   **Stage:** proscenium, 388 seats   **Audience:** "Black and white, middle class."   **Submission policy:** query/synopsis with resume   **Best time:** Sept.-Mar.

Response: 3 months **Your chances:** 30-35 submissions/1 production **Remuneration:** no **Programs:** readings, staged readings, workshop productions **Advice:** "Emphasis on the Black experience; good writing."

3-DOLLAR BILL THEATRE
Box 1105 Madison Square Station,
New York, NY 10159 (212) 989-3750
Contact: Kate Moira Ryan, Literary Manager **Theatre:** professional not-for-profit **Works:** full-length plays, one-acts **2nd productions:** "If previously produced outside New York." **Special interest:** "Lesbian or gay themes." **Stage:** proscenium, 175 seats **Casting:** open auditions **Audience:** "Mix of gay and straight." **Submission policy:** unsolicited script with SASE **Response:** 2-3 months **Your chances:** 200 submissions/2 productions **Remuneration:** "Option payment and royalties." **Future commitment:** negotiable **Program:** staged readings

THREE RIVERS SHAKESPEARE FESTIVAL
B-39 CL, University of Pittsburgh,
Pittsburgh, PA 15260 (412) 624-6805
Contact: Attilio Favorini, Producing Director **Theatre:** professional not-for-profit, university/college **Works:** full-length plays, translations, adaptations **Special interests:** new translations and adaptations of classics **Stage:** modified thrust, 600 seats **Submission policy:** query/synopsis with resume **Best time:** fall **Response:** 3 months

THE THUNDERBIRD THEATER COMPANY
Box 468, Venice, CA 90204-0468 (213) 396-5228
Contact: Martin Isenberg, Literary Manager **Theatre:** professional not-for-profit **Works:** full-length plays, one-acts **2nd productions:** yes **Special interest:** "Mature writing concerned with characters under the age of 30." **Stages:** rented spaces **Submission policy:** unsolicited script with SASE; professional recommendation; agent submission **Response:** 2 months **Your chances:** 200 submissions/2-3 productions **Remuneration:** "Varies: as much as possible, sometimes very little." **Program:** Agit Pop: The Boardwalk Project: "We are looking for 10-15 site-specific, environmentally integrated short pieces to be performed on the Venice Boardwalk (send SASE for guidelines)." **Advice:** "Please send us strong and serious work. TTC yearns for comedic scripts, but please do not submit scripts that resemble sitcoms. It is never our intention to serve as a Hollywood showcase. Please write with a big heart and a sharp mind, and create plays that are emotionally vital, intellectually rigorous and theatrically inventive."

TOLEDO REPERTORY THEATRE
16 Tenth St., Toledo, OH 43624 (419) 243-9277
Contact: Paul Causman, Resident Director **Theatre:** community/ non-professional **Works:** full-length plays, one-acts, children's plays **Tours:** yes **Stage:** proscenium **Submission policy:** unsolicited script with SASE; query/synopsis with dialogue sample **Remuneration:** yes

TOUCHSTONE THEATRE
321 E. 4th St., Bethlehem, PA 18105 (215) 867-1689
Contact: William George, Producing Director **Theatre:** professional not-for-profit **Works/exclusive interest:** ensemble pieces to be created in collaboration with theatre **Specifications:** maximum cast: 4; small performance space (18'x20') **Stage:** black box, 74 seats **Submission policy:** query with proposal for project

THE TOWER PLAYERS OF HILLSDALE COLLEGE
Hillsdale, MI 49242 (517) 437-7341
Contact: R. J. Pentzell, Professor of Theatre Arts **Theatre:** university/college **Works:** full-length plays, one-acts, translations, adaptations **2nd productions:** yes **Specifications:** maximum cast: 20 (cast of 8-16 preferred); single set, "including multi-scene 'space staging' shows; no run-of-the-mill Leftist cliches or standard targets of satire" **Stage:** thrust, 180 seats **Casting:** "We always have more female than male performers available." **Audience:** "Students and townspeople; tendency toward intelligent political and religious conservatism." **Submission policy:** unsolicited script with SASE; professional recommendation **Best time:** Sept.-Jan. **Response:** 2 weeks script; 1 month or more script **Your chances:** 5-10 submissions/0-1 production **Remuneration:** royalty, possible residency **Program:** workshop productions **Advice:** "Our directors, overall, prefer 'theatricalist' or 'Brechtian' styles."

TRIAD ENSEMBLE
c/o Keith McGregor, Literary Manager,
Box 280, Monroe, WA 98272 (206) 322-1398
Contact: Victor Janusz, Artistic Director **Theatre:** professional not-for-profit **Works:** full-length plays, one-acts; translations and adaptations may be considered **2nd productions:** yes **Special interests:** "New works from the Pacific Northwest (AK, ID, MT, OR, WA, BC)." **Specifications:** maximum cast: 10; single or unit set; "limited facilities and resources"; no fly space **Stage:** flexible, 80-120 seats **Casting:** "Open auditions each fall with additional auditions as needed for each show." **Audience:** "Eclectic; willing to

take chances with us." **Submission policy:** query/synopsis with resume and dialogue sample preferred; unsolicited script with SASE **Best time:** Aug.-Feb. **Response:** 4 weeks query; 3-4 months script **Your chances:** "50 submissions and growing"/2 productions **Remuneration:** "A percentage royalty." **Future commitment:** "Not at this time." **Advice:** "Send us a readable copy of an exciting, challenging play with no impossible production requirements. Also, for new works, the playwright should plan to be available for at least part of the rehearsal process."

TRIANGLE THEATRE COMPANY
316 E. 88th St., New York, NY 10128 (212) 860-7245
Contact: Molly O'Neil, Managing Director **Theatre:** off off Broadway **Works:** full-length plays, musicals **2nd productions:** New York premieres **Special interests:** "Small chamber productions; non-naturalistic, theatrical plays and musicals." **Specificiations:** maximum cast: 8; simple unit set or skeleton **Stages:** proscenium; arena; 3/4 flexible **Audience:** "Yorkville area of Upper East Side New York. Many young professionals." **Submission policy:** unsolicited script with SASE and resume; professional recommendation; agent submission **Best time:** Apr.-Jul. **Response:** 1 month **Your chances:** 200-300 submissions/4 productions **Remuneration:** "Depends—$500-$1000." **Programs:** readings, staged readings

TRINITY REPERTORY COMPANY
201 Washington St., Providence, RI 02903
(401) 521-1100 Contact: Anne Bogart, Artistic Director **Theatre:** professional not-for-profit **Works:** full-length plays, translations, adaptations, musicals **Stages:** thrust, 500 seats; thrust, 297 seats **Submission policy:** query/synopsis **Best time:** Aug.-Oct. **Response:** 1 month query; 12 months script

TRINITY SQUARE ENSEMBLE
927 Noyes, Evanston, IL 60201 (312) 328-0330
Contact: Karen L. Erickson, Artistic Director **Theatre:** professional not-for-profit **Works:** full-length plays, translations, adaptations, children's plays **2nd productions:** yes **Maximum cast:** 10 **Stages:** various spaces, 70-190 seats **Audience:** "Upper middle class, white and some minorities; college educated, white-collar workers and professionals, 30-60 years of age." **Submission policy:** query/synopsis with reviews and resume; professional recommendation **Best time:** Apr.-Jun. **Response:** 2-18 months **Your chances:** 10 submissions/1 production **Remuneration:** "Sometimes. Varies." **Program:** staged readings **Advice:** "Get to know our ensemble and what our seasonal theme is—in advance!"

UBU REPERTORY THEATER
15 W. 28th St., New York, NY 10001 (212) 679-7540
Contact: François Kourilsky, Artistic Director; Catherine Temerson, Literary Manager **Theatre:** professional not-for-profit theatre center **Works:** full-length and one-act translations from French **2nd productions:** yes **Exclusive interests:** English translations of contemporary plays originally written in French; American plays dealing with French themes **Maximum cast:** 10 **Tours:** "Perhaps in the future." **Stage:** flexible **Audience:** "New York off Broadway." **Submission policy:** unsolicited script with SASE; query/synopsis; professional recommendation; agent submission; commission **Best time:** summer **Response:** 3 months **Your chances:** 100 submissions/2 productions plus readings; "most of our submissions come from France or other French-speaking countries" **Remuneration:** royalty **Future commitment:** yes **Programs:** readings, staged readings, workshop productions, script evaluations, translation referrals, international theatre panels and workshops, French-English reference library, publication of series of English translations of contemporary French plays (inquire)

UKIAH PLAYERS THEATRE
1041 Low Gap Rd., Ukiah, CA 95482 (707) 462-1210
Contact: Catherine Babcock Magruder, Artistic Director **Theatre:** semi-professional not-for-profit **Works:** full-length plays, one-acts, musicals, children's plays, cabaret/revues **2nd productions:** yes **Special interest:** "Unpublished, unproduced full-length comedies." **Specifications:** small cast, simple sets preferred **Tours:** yes **Stage:** proscenium, 133 seats **Casting:** "We cast the best actors from the available local pool." **Audience:** "A mixed audience in age and background in this rural, northern California community 150 miles north of San Francisco." **Submission policy:** query/synopsis **Best time:** before Feb. 1, 1990 **Response:** 2 weeks query; May 1, 1990 script **Your chances:** 200 submissions/2 productions **Programs:** staged readings, workshop productions, children's training; New American Comedy Festival (see Contests)

UNDERGROUND RAILWAY THEATER
21 Notre Dame Ave., Cambridge, MA 02140
(617) 497-6136 Contact: Wes Sanders, Artistic Director **Theatre:** professional not-for-profit **Works:** full-length plays, one-acts, translations, adaptations, musicals, children's plays, multi-media pieces **2nd productions:** "We could." **Special interests:** "Social/political themes; highly visual works combining actors, puppets and music; works created in collaboration with company." **Maximum cast:** 6 **Tours:** "Preferred." **Stages:**

various spaces: proscenium, thrust, arena, flexible **Audience:** "Diverse." **Submission policy:** professional recommendation preferred; query/synopsis with resume; commission **Response:** 2 weeks query; 4-6 weeks script **Your chances:** 5 submissions/"no productions so far; so far we have worked with playwrights we know, but we are always open" **Remuneration:** "We raise grants to pay collaborating artists." **Programs:** staged readings, workshop productions

UNICORN THEATRE
3820 Main St., Kansas City, MO 64111 (816) 531-7529
Contact: Cynthia Levin, Artistic Director **Theatre:** professional not-for-profit **Works:** full-length plays **2nd productions:** if not previously produced by Equity theatre **Special interest:** social issues **Specifications:** maximum cast: 10; contemporary settings and themes **Stage:** thrust, 150 seats **Submission policy:** query/synopsis **Response:** 1 month query; 6 months script **Recent production of unsolicited work:** yes **Future commitments:** 5% of subsidiary rights; credit for premiere production **Program:** Unicorn Theatre National Playwright Competition (see Contests)

UNIVERSITY OF ARIZONA DEPARTMENT OF DRAMA
Tucson, AZ 85721 (602) 621-7008
Contact: Robert C. Burroughs, Acting Department Head **Theatre:** university/college **Works:** full-length plays, one-acts, adaptations, musicals **2nd productions:** yes **Special interest:** "Hispanic and Native American themes." **Specifications:** unit set preferred **Tours:** yes **Stages:** proscenium, 330 seats; proscenium, 120 seats; flexible, 100 seats **Audience:** "Varies; majority are university-affiliated." **Submission policy:** unsolicited script with SASE and resume; professional recommendation; university's playwriting program **Best time:** fall **Response:** 2-6 weeks **Your chances:** 75 submissions/3-4 productions **Remuneration:** "Non-student playwright receives royalty." **Programs:** readings, staged readings, workshop productions, development, classes

UPSTAIRS DINNER THEATRE
221 S. 19th St., Omaha, NE 68102 (402) 344-3858
Contact: Anne Ausdemore, Producer **Theatre:** non-Equity dinner **Works:** full-length plays, musicals, children's plays **Exclusive interests:** comedies, musicals **Maximum cast:** 14 **Submission policy:** unsolicited script with SASE

VERMONT THEATRE COMPANY
31 Green St., Brattleboro, VT 05301 (802) 257-0607
Contact: Ray Jenness, Artistic Director **Theatre:** community/ non-professional **Works:** full-length plays, one-acts, musicals, children's plays **2nd productions:** yes **Special interests:** "Vermont and other New England writers." **Tours:** yes **Stage:** flexible **Audience:** "Cross section." **Submission policy:** unsolicited script with SASE; query/synopsis with resume; agent submission **Best time:** late spring **Response:** 2 weeks query; 6 months script **Remuneration:** "$500-$1000." **Programs:** readings, staged readings, workshop productions, development

VETCO
1457 Broadway Suite 1203, New York, NY 10036
(212) 869-6090 **Contact:** Thomas Bird, Artistic Director **Theatre:** professional not-for-profit **Works:** full-length plays **Special interest:** "Political statements." **Specifications:** maximum cast: 8; single, flexible set **Tours:** yes **Stages:** rented spaces **Audience:** general **Submission policy:** unsolicited script with SASE; query/synopsis; professional recommendation **Best time:** summer **Response:** 6 weeks **Your chances:** 200 submissions/3 productions **Remuneration:** "Option; royalty; 6%-7% of box office." **Programs:** staged readings, development **Advice:** "Present plays in a professionally typed format with a synopsis. A polite follow-up will indicate the author's seriousness." **Comment:** See Paller Michael, "Dispatches from The Front," *TheaterWeek* (Nov. 21, 1988), 28-33.

VICTORIAN THEATRE
4201 Hooker St., Denver, CO 80211 (303) 433-5050
Contact: S. Jenkins, Artistic Director **Theatre:** community/ semi-professional **Works:** full-length plays **2nd productions:** "Occasionally." **Specifications:** maximum cast: 8; single set; no fly space; small wings; modest light and sound facilities **Tours:** "Possibly, not normally." **Stage:** proscenium, 90 seats **Casting:** "Open, affirmative action." **Audience:** "Mixed urban and suburban, wide age range." **Submission policy:** send SASE for information **Remuneration:** standard royalty **Comment:** When *The Playwright's Companion 1990* went to press, new play production had been temporarily suspended.

VICTORY GARDENS THEATER
2271 N. Lincoln Ave., Chicago, IL 60614 (312) 549-5778
Contact: Charles Smith, Literary Manager **Theatre:** professional not-for-profit **Works:** full-length plays, one-acts, small-cast musicals **2nd productions:** yes **Special interests:** "Plays

which address contemporary social issues; plays by Chicago and Midwest playwrights; plays by or about minorities." **Specifications:** maximum cast: 8; small stage; no wing space **Tours:** yes **Stages:** thrust, 200 seats; thrust, 60 seats **Submission policy:** query/synopsis; professional recommendation; agent submission **Response:** 1 month query; 6 months script **Your chances:** 800 submissions/3-4+ productions **Remuneration:** standard royalty **Programs:** readings, staged readings, workshop productions, development, internships, classes; contests (inquire)

VICTORY THEATRE
3326 W. Victory Blvd., Burbank, CA 91505
(818) 843-9253 **Contact:** Tom Ormeny, Maria Gobette, Artistic Directors **Theatre:** professional not-for-profit **Works:** full-length plays, small-scale musicals **2nd productions:** yes **Special interest:** "Relationships." **Specifications:** maximum cast: 12; single set; low ceiling precludes 2-story set **Stages:** proscenium, 91 seats; proscenium, 48 seats **Casting:** open auditions **Audience:** "Traditional." **Submission policy:** unsolicited script with SASE; professional recommendation **Response:** 4 months **Your chances:** 500 submissions/4 productions **Remuneration:** "Option fee and some travel expense." **Future commitment:** "Some subsidiary rights." **Programs:** readings, development, residencies; contests (inquire)

VINEYARD THEATRE
108 E. 15th St., New York, NY 10003;
309 E. 26th St., New York, NY 10010 (212) 353-3366
Contact: Douglas Aibel, Artistic Director **Theatre:** professional not-for-profit **Works:** full-length plays, grouped one-acts, musicals **2nd productions:** yes **Special interests:** works with strong poetic quality; plays with unique structural incorporation of music; original book musicals with strong narrative **Maximum casts:** 10 for play; 15 for musical **Stages:** thrust, 70 seats; black box, 175 seats **Submission policy:** query/synopsis with 10-page dialogue sample and resume preferred; unsolicted script **Response:** 2 months query; 4-6 months script **Future commitment:** yes **Programs:** New Works at the Vineyard: readings; Concert Readings of New American Musicals: developmental workshop for new musicals or produced musicals needing revision (inquire)

VIRGINIA STAGE COMPANY
Box 3770, Norfolk, VA 23514 (804) 627-6988
Contact: Charles Towers, Producing Director **Theatre:** professional not-for-profit **Works:** full-length plays, translations, adaptations, musicals **2nd productions:** yes, particularly when

playwright wants to revise work **Special interests:** "Talented writers who understand the stage's unique requirements for theatricality, vital language and metaphor, as distinct from television and movie media; developing writers who are giving voice to the current American experience." **Tours:** "Perhaps in the future." **Stages:** proscenium, thrust, arena, flexible--125-600 seats **Audience:** "All ages from students to senior citizens; ethnically diverse; the majority of adults are college educated." **Submission policy:** professional recommendation; agent submission **Response:** 6 months **Your chances:** 100 submissions/1 production **Remuneration/future commitment:** negotiable **Programs:** readings, staged readings, workshop productions

THE WALDO ASTORIA THEATRE
1116 W. 25th St., Kansas City, MO 64108
(816) 523-1704 Contact: Karla Evans, Artistic Director; Donn G. Miller, Literary Manager **Theatre:** dinner **Works:** full-length comedies **2nd productions:** yes **Special interest:** reality-based humor **Specifications:** maximum cast: 10, smaller preferred; no more than 2 sets; no sex-based comedies **Stage:** 3/4 round, 300+ seats **Audience:** "Very, very conservative, middle-to-upper middle class, from Kansas City and surrounding area." **Submission policy:** unsolicited script with SASE; query/synopsis with dialogue sample; professional recommendation; agent submission **Response:** 3 days query; 10 weeks script **Your chances:** 150 submissions/2 productions **Remuneration:** negotiable **Future commitment:** yes

WALNUT STREET THEATRE
9th and Walnut Sts., Philadelphia, PA 19107
(215) 574-3550 Contact: Bernard Havard, Executive Director **Theatre:** professional not-for-profit **Works:** full-length plays, translations, adaptations, musicals **2nd productions:** yes **Special interests:** historical plays; experimental works for studio; broad popular appeal for main stage **Specifications:** maximum cast: 14, fewer preferred for main stage; 5 for studio; 35 for musical; simple technical requirements **Stages:** proscenium, 1052 seats; proscenium, 99 seats; flexible, 77 seats **Audience:** "Conservative; prefer modern plays. We are open, however, to 'wild' material that is well written." **Submission policy:** query/synopsis with dialogue sample and resume; agent submission **Response:** 1 month query; 6 months script **Your chances:** 450 submissions/3-4 productions **Remuneration/future commitment:** negotiable **Program:** classes

WASHINGTON UNIVERSITY
PERFORMING ARTS DEPARTMENT
Campus Box 1108, St. Louis, MO 63130 (314) 889-5858
Contact: Henry Schvey, Chair **Theatre:** university/college
Works: full-length plays, one-acts, translations, adaptations,
children's plays **Tours:** yes **Stages:** proscenium; arena
Submission policy: unsolicited script with SASE; agent submission
Response: 1 week query; 4 weeks script **Your chances:** 50
submissions/1 production **Remuneration:** "Sometimes; $500 or
transportation and lodging." **Programs:** staged readings,
development, classes **Comment:** Theatre also receives submissions
from the St. Louis Playwrights Festival (inquire).

WATERLOO COMMUNITY PLAYHOUSE/
BLACK HAWK CHILDREN'S THEATRE
Box 433, Waterloo, IA 50704 (319) 235-0367
Contact: Charles Stilwill, Managing Director **Works:** full-length
plays, one-acts, adaptations, musicals, children's plays **2nd
productions:** yes **Specifications:** no fly space **Tours:**
elementary schools **Stage:** proscenium **Audience:** "All ages, 3%
black." **Submission policy:** unsolicited script with SASE;
query/synopsis with dialogue sample; agent submission **Best time:**
winter-spring **Response:** 3 months query; 1-4 years script **Your
chances:** 400 submissions/1 or more productions **Remuneration:**
"Royalty plus travel if money is available."

THE WAYSIDE THEATRE
Box 260, Middletown, VA 22645 (703) 869-1782
Contact: Christopher Owens, Artistic Director **Theatre:**
professional not-for-profit **Works:** full-length plays, musicals,
children's plays **2nd productions:** yes **Special interest:**
contemporary comedy **Specifications:** maximum cast: 10-12;
simple technical demands; no wing or fly space; no more than 2 sets;
contemporary works only **Tours:** "Small-cast children's shows;
simple 1-set mainstage shows." **Stage:** proscenium, 195 seats
Submission policy: query/synopsis with reviews preferred;
unsolicited script with SASE **Best time:** winter **Response:** 2-3
months **Your chances:** 20 submissions/1 production **Future
commitment:** for main stage premiere **Advice:** "Send synopsis;
if we are interested we will request full script."

WEST BANK DOWNSTAIRS THEATRE BAR
311 W. 42nd St., New York, NY 10036 (212) 695-6909
Contact: Rand Foerster, Artistic Director **Theatre:** off off
Broadway **Works:** one-acts, musicals **2nd productions:**
"Occasionally, but primarily we present premiere productions."

Special interests: "One-act plays and short musicals."
Specifications: "Minimal sets. Our focus is what's on the page as opposed to what's on the stage, set wise; 1 hour maximum running time." **Stage:** thrust/flexible, 130 seats **Casting:** "Playwright casts with his or her directorial choice, or we will cast out of our files." **Audience:** "Majority are theatre professionals and entertainment industry people." **Submission policy:** unsolicited script with SASE **Response:** 3-6 months **Your chances:** 300-400 submissions/100-120 productions **Remuneration:** "The door is split 50/50 between the theatre bar and the production." **Future commitment:** "We ask for billing as 'Originally presented and/or developed at the West Bank Downstairs Theatre Bar, Theatre Row, New York, New York.'" **Advice:** "The majority of plays we do are by established writers such as Jack Heifner, John Ford Noonan, Jim McClure. Please send only final drafts of your very best work. Comedy, drama, musicals are all treated equally; avoid 1-person monologues."

WESTBETH THEATRE CENTER
151 Bank St., New York, NY 10014 (212) 691-2272
Contact: Ted Snowdon, Literary Manager **Theatre:** off off Broadway, professional not-for-profit **Works:** full-length plays **2nd productions:** if not produced in New York City **Specifications:** maximum cast: 10; no more than 1-2 simple sets **Stage:** proscenium, 60-99 seats **Audience:** "Downtown New York City, industry and Greenwich Village." **Submission policy:** query/synopsis with 10-20 page dialogue sample; professional recommendation; agent submission **Best time:** late summer **Response:** 2-6 months **Your chances:** 150 submissions/5 productions **Future commitments:** credit for production, percentage **Programs:** readings, development; American Playwright Program (see Special Programs)

WEST COAST ENSEMBLE
Box 38728, Los Angeles, CA 90038 (213) 871-8673
Contact: Les Hanson, Artistic Director **Theatre:** professional not-for-profit **Works:** full-length plays, one-acts, musicals **2nd productions:** "Yes; we encourage submissions for 2nd productions of scripts that have been reworked." **Specifications:** maximum cast: 12; single set **Stages:** proscenium, 60 seats; flexible arena, up to 99 seats **Casting:** "Mainly from the company; there is also a policy of non-tradtional casting." **Audience:** "Wide variety of Southern Californians including Hispanic, Black and Asian." **Submission policy:** unsolicited script with SASE; query/synopsis **Best times:** Jan.-Jun. for full-length plays, Sept.-Dec. for one-acts **Response:** 2 weeks query; 6 months script **Your chances:** one-

acts: 700 submissions/6-9 productions; full-length plays: 600 submissions/2 productions **Remuneration:** $500 for Celebration of One Acts; negotiable royalty for full-length play **Future commitment:** credit for first production **Programs:** readings, staged readings, workshop productions, development, classes; Celebration of One-Acts and West Coast Ensemble Full-Length Play Competition (see Contests)

WEST END DINNER THEATRE
4615 Duke St., Alexandria, VA 22304 (703) 823-9061
Contact: James J. Matthews, Producer **Works:** full-length plays, musicals **Special interests:** family-oriented comedies, farces and musicals **Specifications:** maximum cast: 20-25; no fly space **Submission policy:** unsolicited script with SASE

THE WESTERN STAGE OF HARTNELL COLLEGE
Salinas, CA See The Steinbeck Playwriting Competition listing in Contests.

W.H.A.T.
WELLFLEET HARBOR ACTORS' THEATRE
Box 1118, Wellfleet, MA 02667 (508) 349-6835
Contact: Gip Hoppi, Artistic Director **Theatre:** professional/ semi-professional not-for-profit **Works:** full-length plays, translations, adaptations **2nd productions:** yes **Special interests:** "Contemporary American topics; social/political issues." **Specifications:** maximum cast: 10; no farce **Tours:** yes **Stage:** proscenium, 70 seats **Casting:** open auditions and precasting from pool **Audience:** "Sophisticated, adventurous." **Submission policy:** query/synopsis with resume; professional recommendation; agent submission **Best time:** Nov.-Jan. **Response:** 1 month query **Your chances:** 30-40 submissions/0-3 productions **Recent production of unsolicited work:** yes **Remuneration/future commitment:** negotiable **Program:** staged readings **Advice:** "Be imaginative; avoid theatrical clichés."

THE WHOLE THEATER
544 Bloomfield Ave., Montclair, NJ 07042
(201) 744-2996 Contact: Daniel DeRaey, Associate Artistic Director **Theatre:** professional not-for-profit **Works:** full-length plays **2nd productions:** yes **Specifications:** maximum cast: 7; single or unit set **Stage:** endstage, 200 seats **Submission policy:** agent submission preferred; query/synopsis **Best time:** Oct.-Apr. **Response:** 3 weeks query; 3-4 months script **Future commitment:** yes **Programs:** readings, staged readings; New Play Development Unit (selection by professional recomendation;

inquire); The Gathering (see Special Programs)   **Comment:** See Ledford, Larry S. with Bonnie Kramen, "On Becoming The Whole Theater," *TheaterWeek* (Feb. 8-14, 1988), 28-29.

THE WILL GEER THEATRICUM BOTANICUM
Box 1222, Topanga, CA 90290 (213) 455-2322
Contact: Ellen Geer, Artistic Director   **Theatre:** professional not-for-profit **Works:** full-length plays, one-acts, translations, adaptations, musicals, cabaret/revues   **2nd productions:** yes **Special interests:** social issues; new translations of classics **Specifications:** maximum cast: 5-10; works must be suitable for large outdoor stage   **Stage:** rustic outdoor arena, 350 seats **Submission policy:** query/synopsis with dialogue sample preferred; unsolicited script with SASE   **Best time:** Sept. **Response:** 3-4 weeks query; 6 months script   **Your chances:** 100-150 submissions/1 production   **Recent production of unsolicited work:** yes   **Remuneration:** negotiable royalty **Future commitment:** no   **Programs:** Sunday workshops; series of one-acts (inquire)

WILLIAMSTOWN THEATRE FESTIVAL
Box 517, Williamstown, MA 01267 (413) 597-3377
Contact: Peter Hunt, Austin Pendleton, Artistic Directors **Theatre:** professional not-for-profit **Works:** full-length plays, translations, adaptations   **2nd productions:** no   **Exclusive interest:** ensemble pieces **Specifications:** maximum cast: 14; simple set   **Stages:** proscenium, 500 seats; flexible, 96 seats; outdoor theatre   **Audience:** "Wide range."   **Submission policy:** query/synopsis with dialogue sample and resume; professional recommendation; agent submission   **Best time:** Oct.-Mar. 15 **Response:** 1 month query; 2 months script   **Your chances:** 300-400 submissions/4-7 productions   **Remuneration:** "A modest fee."   **Future commitment:** yes   **Program:** staged readings **Advice:** "Small cast, simple production values, important subject matter."   **Comment:** See Chansky, Dorothy, "Williamstown After Nikos," *TheaterWeek* (Jun. 19, 1989), 20-25.

WILLOW CABIN THEATRE COMPANY
c/o Max Daniels, Box 171, New York, NY 10024
Contact: Ed Berkeley, Artistic Director   **Theatre:** professional **Works:** full-length plays, adaptations, musicals   **Special interests:** large casts; "plays that communicate something meaningful; physical action"   **Submission policy:** unsolicited script with SASE   **Programs:** readings, development   **Comment:** See Paller, Michael, "Making A Willow Cabin In New York," *TheaterWeek* (Oct. 16, 1989), 28-32.

THE WILMA THEATRE

2030 Sansom St., Philadelphia, PA 19103
(215) 963-0249 **Contact:** Jiri Zizka, Blanka Zizka, Artistic Directors **Theatre:** professional not-for-profit **Works:** full-length plays, one-acts, translations, adaptations, musicals **2nd productions:** yes **Special interests:** translations and adaptations of international works; social issues; poetic dimensions; innovative staging; multi-media works and ensemble works **Specifications:** maximum cast: 10-12; "simple but inventive sets" for 30'x22' stage; limited set changes **Tours:** yes **Stages:** proscenium, 100 seats; flexible **Submission policy:** query/ synopsis with dialogue sample; professional recommendation; agent submission **Best time:** Mar.-Sept. **Response:** 4-6 months **Your chances:** 1-2 new plays produced each season **Remuneration:** fee and royalty **Future commitment:** yes

WINGS THEATRE COMPANY

521 City Island Ave., City Island, NY 10464
(212) 885-1938 **Contact:** Jeffery Corrick, Artistic Director **Theatre:** off off Broadway **Works:** full-length plays, musicals, children's plays **2nd productions:** seldom **Exclusive interest:** "American playwrights; also interested in unproduced plays and 'strong themes.'" **Specifications:** maximum cast: 12; small stage **Stage:** flexible, 75 seats **Audience:** "Very mixed, New York City." **Submission policy:** unsolicited script with SASE; professional recommendation; agent submission **Best time:** Sept.-Dec. **Response:** 9 months **Your chances:** 500 submissions/ 8-10 productions **Remuneration:** "$100 advance against 3% of box office gross." **Programs:** readings, staged readings, workshop productions, internships; Wings Theatre Company 1990 New Plays Contest (see Contests)

WISDOM BRIDGE THEATRE

1559 W. Howard St., Chicago, IL 60626 (312) 743-0486
Contact: Jeffrey Ortmann, Producing Director; Joshua F. Pollack, Literary Manager **Theatre:** professional not-for-profit **Works:** full-length plays, one-acts, translations, adaptations, musicals **2nd productions:** yes **Special interests:** "New plays that deal with contemporary social/political issues; plays by women and minority writers; adventurous treatments of classic texts." **Specifications:** maximum cast: 8-12; works must be suitable for a small stage **Stage:** proscenium, 196 seats **Audience:** "Ethnically diverse; Chicago dwellers as well as people from the suburbs; largely in the 30-40 age range." **Submission policy:** query/synopsis; professional recommendation; agent submission **Response:** 4

months query; 6 months script **Your chances:** 800 submissions/4 productions **Remuneration/future commitment:** negotiable **Program:** in-house readings

WOMEN IN THEATRE NETWORK
New York, NY This theatre is permanently closed.

WOMEN'S INTERART CENTER
549 W. 52nd St., New York, NY 10019 (212) 246-1050
Contact: Margo Lewitin, Artistic Director **Theatre:** off off Broadway **Works:** full-length plays **2nd productions:** "Yes, co-producing." **Special interest:** "Women's plays and themes." **Specifications:** small cast; simple set **Stage:** flexible **Submission policy:** query/synopsis with dialogue sample **Response:** "We do our best but are very backlogged and have a very small staff." **Program:** staged readings **Advice:** "Invite us to your workshop production, if possible."

THE WOMEN'S PROJECT AND PRODUCTIONS
220 W. 42nd St. 18th Floor, New York, NY 10036
(212) 382-2750 Contact: Suzanne Bennett, Literary Manager **Theatre:** professional not-for-profit membership/service organization **Works:** full-length plays **Exclusive interest:** "Plays by women; also interested in works of social or political significance." **Stage:** proscenium, 180 seats **Submission policy:** query/synopsis **Response:** 1-2 months **Your chances:** 500 applications/3-4 new members accepted **Advice:** "The theatre produces plays only by women but is interested in subjects of wide-ranging import to men and women." **Stage:** proscenium, 180 seats **Programs:** staged readings, workshop productions, development, directors' forum, discount tickets, dramaturgical counsel to members; members receive *Dialogues* newsletter **Comment:** Works are staged at the Apple Corps Theatre (see listing in this section).

WOODSTOCK PLAYHOUSE ASSOCIATION
Woodstock, NY This theatre burned recently and has no plans to rebuild.

WOOLLY MAMMOTH THEATRE COMPANY
1401 Church St. NW, Washington, DC 20005
(202) 393-3939 Contact: Martin Blank, Literary Manager **Theatre:** professional not-for-profit **Works:** full-length plays, translations, adaptations, musicals **2nd productions:** yes **Exclusive interest:** "Plays that are highly unusual, either in form or content." **Maximum cast:** 10 **Stage:** flexible, 130 seats

Audience: "Yuppies and older." **Submission policy:** unsolicited script with SASE **Response:** 8 weeks **Your chances:** 120 submissions/1-2 productions

WORCESTER FOOTHILLS THEATRE COMPANY
074 Worcester Center, Worcester, MA 01608
(508) 754-3314 Contact: Greg DeJarnett, Literary Manager **Theatre:** professional not-for-profit **Works:** full-length plays, one-acts, translations, adaptations, musicals **2nd productions:** yes **Special interest:** plays of interest to a multi-generational audience **Specifications:** maximum cast: 8-10; single or simple set; musicals must be small scale; "no strong language or gratuitous violence" **Stage:** proscenium, 349 seats **Audience:** "Multi-generational." **Submission policy:** query/synopsis **Response:** 3-4 weeks query; 3 months script **Future commitment:** negotiable

THE WORKLIGHT PERFORMING SPACE
17714 Saticoy St., Reseda, CA 91335 (818) 996-8688
Contact: Anne Dunkin, Producing Director **Theatre:** Los Angeles Equity 99 seat plan **Works:** full-length plays, musicals, children's plays **2nd productions:** "We would consider them." **Special interests:** "Contemporary settings appropriate for family audiences." **Specifications:** maximum cast: 6; single, simple set **Stage:** proscenium, 46 seats **Casting:** open auditions **Audience:** "Middle-class families and metropolitan-area professionals." **Submission policy:** unsolicited script with SASE **Response:** 2-4 weeks query; 2-4 months script **Remuneration:** no **Future commitment:** "Mention in credits." **Program:** staged readings **Comment:** "This is a new theatre; our first season is this year."

WORKS BY WOMEN
11 Fifth Ave. #14P, New York, NY 10003
(212) 674-7381 Contact: Laura Padula, Script Consultant **Theatre:** off off Broadway, professional not-for-profit **Works:** full-length plays, one-acts, translations **2nd productions:** "If not previously produced in New York City, or if it is a completely new draft." **Exclusive interest:** plays by women from any country **Specifications:** some limitations on sets; minimal lighting; no works-in-progress **Stage:** flexible, 150 seats **Audience:** "Theatre professionals and others interested in good theatre." **Submission policy:** unsolicited script with SASE; professional recommendation; agent submission **Response:** 3 weeks query; 3-5 months script **Your chances:** varying number of submissions/6-8 staged readings **Remuneration:** "Small honorarium for staged reading." **Comment:** Theatre was founded to give exposure to women playwrights; all productions and staged readings are directed by women.

WPA THEATRE
519 W. 23rd St., New York, NY 10011
(212) 691-2274 Contact: Donna Lieberman, Managing Director
Theatre: professional not-for-profit **Works:** full-length plays,
musicals **2nd productions:** no **Special interest:** "Contemporary
American realism dealing with important social issues."
Specifications: maximum cast: 10; single set preferred **Tours:**
"No, but several have had commercial transfers." **Stage:**
proscenium, 124 seats **Submission policy:** query/synopsis with
dialogue sample; agent submission **Best time:** summer **Response:**
3 weeks query; 6 months script **Your chances:** 250 submissions/1
production **Remuneration:** $1500 **Programs:** readings, staged
readings

THE WRITERS THEATRE
145 W. 46th St., New York, NY 10036 (212) 869-9770
Contact: Byam Stevens, Literary Manager **Theatre:** professional
not-for-profit developmental theatre **Works:** full-length plays,
one-acts, translations, adaptations, poetry pieces **2nd
productions:** "Only if the playwright wants to do substantial
rewriting." **Exclusive interest:** "Scripts for development."
Specifications: "No finished works." **Stage:** flexible, 74 seats
Submission policy: unsolicited script with SASE and resume;
professional recommendation; agent submission **Best time:**
development season runs Sept. 1-Jun. 30 **Response:** 6 months
Your chances: 350 submissions/2-3 productions **Remuneration:**
$150 for workshop production; "Favored nations on Actors Equity
Association Tier Code basis." **Program:** 10-step development
process including in-house and informal readings, staged readings,
workshop and full productions **Advice:** "If the playwright feels that
a work is finished and is looking for immediate production, he or she
would be better served submitting to another company."

YALE REPERTORY THEATRE
222 York St., New Haven, CT 06520 (203) 432-1560
Contact: Lloyd Richards, Artistic Director **Theatre:** professional
not-for-profit, university/college **Works:** full-length plays,
translations, adaptations, musicals **2nd productions:** yes **Special
interests:** new plays; new translations of classics and contemporary
foreign plays **Stage:** modified thrust, 487 seats **Submission
policy:** query/synopsis; agent submission **Response:** 6 weeks
query; 2-3 months script **Remuneration/future commitment:**
yes **Program:** Winterfest: production of 3-4 new plays each
Jan.-Feb.

YORK COMMUNITY SCHOOL
355 St. Charles Rd., Elmhurst, IL 60126 (312) 617-2400
Contact: Les Zunkel, Director of Drama and Speech **Theatre:** high school **Works:** musicals, children's plays, reader's theatre **Stages:** thrust; arena; flexible **Audience:** community and school **Submission policy:** query/synopsis; commission **Best time:** spring **Response:** 4 months **Remuneration:** stipend based upon work

THE YORK THEATRE COMPANY
2 E. 90th St., New York, NY 10128 (212) 534-5366
Contact: R. David Westfall, Literary Manager **Theatre:** off off Broadway **Works:** full-length plays, musicals **2nd productions:** no **Specifications:** maximum cast: 10; "some limitations on sets, subject matter and extremes in language (the theatre has been located for the past 20 years in an Episcopal church)" **Stage:** flexible **Audience:** "Adults with New York demands for good theatre." **Submission policy:** unsolicited script with SASE; professional recommendation **Response:** 6 months **Your chances:** 80-90 submissions/1 production **Remuneration:** no **Programs:** readings, staged readings

YOUNG PEOPLE'S THEATRE COMPANY
OF DELAWARE VALLEY
121 South Dr., Newtown, PA 18940 (215) 860-6888
Contact: Karin Kasdin, Executive Director **Theatre:** professional not-for-profit **Works:** full-length plays, adaptations, musicals, children's plays **2nd productions:** yes **Exclusive interests:** "Family-oriented theatre: dramatic, comic or musical; subjects relevant to the lives of young people in the 80's; historical subjects." **Specifications:** maximum cast: 35, always including adults, teens and children; simple unit set; no works for children under 8 years of age **Audience:** "Affluent, well-educated suburban families." **Submission policy:** unsolicited script with SASE; query/synopsis with dialogue sample; professional recommendation; agent submission **Best time:** Jun.-Aug. **Response:** 8-12 weeks **Your chances:** 200 submissions/2 productions **Remuneration:** negotiable

YOUNG PERFORMERS THEATRE
Ft. Mason Center Bldg. C Room 300,
San Francisco, CA 94123 (415) 346-5550
Contact: Matilda Kunin, Executive Director **Theatre:** professional not-for-profit **Works:** children's plays **2nd productions:** yes **Special interest:** "Family entertainment." **Specifications:** maximum cast: 12; no more than 3 set changes; limited lighting; maximum length 60-70 minutes **Tours:** yes **Stages:** thrust;

flexible **Casting:** mixed cast of adults and children **Audience:** "Urban, 3-12 years of age, ethnic mixture, poor to wealthy." **Submission policy:** unsolicited script with SASE and resume; professional recommendation **Response:** 2-6 weeks **Your chances:** 15-20 submissions/1 production **Remuneration:** negotiable **Programs:** readings, staged readings **Advice:** "Don't write 'down' to children; don't try to write 'hip' scripts; make submitted material neat and easy to read."

YOUNG PERFORMERS THEATRE ADULT WING
Ft. Mason Center Bldg. C Room 300,
San Francisco, CA 94123 (415) 346-5550
Contact: Matilda Kunin, Executive Director **Theatre:** professional not-for-profit **Works:** full-length plays, one-acts, translations, adaptations, musicals **2nd productions:** yes **Special interests:** "Thought-provoking plays; politics, religion." **Maximum cast:** 12-16 **Stage:** flexible **Submission policy:** unsolicited script with SASE and resume; professional recommendation **Response:** 2-6 weeks **Your chances:** 150 submissions/2 productions **Remuneration:** "7% of gate." **Advice:** "A good, solid play with a story line."

ZACHARY SCOTT THEATER CENTER
Box 244, Austin, TX 78744 (512) 476-0597
Contact: Candace Thompson, Office Manager **Theatre:** professional performing arts school, community/semi-professional, professional children's theatre **Works:** full-length plays, children's plays **2nd productions:** yes **Specifications:** "maximum cast: 8 for children's plays, 30 for adult plays; unit set **Tours:** "INTER ACT--professional children's theatre." **Stage:** thrust, 200 seats **Audience:** "Yuppies, professionals, retirees." **Submission policy:** unsolicited script with SASE; professional recommendation **Best time:** summer-early fall **Response:** 6 months **Your chances:** 50 submissions/0-1 production **Remuneration:** travel; 2-week residency **Advice:** "Take a course in playwriting. Learn your craft. Only 1 out of every 100 scripts we read has possibilities."

ZEPHYR THEATRE
25 Van Ness Ave. Suite 50,
San Francisco, CA 94102 (415) 861-6655
Contact: Michael Lojkovic, Operations Manager **Theatre:** 3 not-for-profit theatres **Works:** full-length plays, translations, adaptations, musicals **2nd productions:** "Yes, but not a priority." **Special interests:** musicals, political works **Maximum cast:** 16 **Tours:** yes **Stages:** proscenium, 50 seats; thrust, 99 seats;

flexible, 140 seats **Audience:** "All ethnic groups, highly educated, ages 25-60." **Submission policy:** query/synopsis with dialogue sample; agent submission **Response:** 1 month query; 8-10 months script **Your chances:** 120 submissions/2 productions **Remuneration:** 4%-6% of box office **Future commitment:** yes **Programs:** staged readings, workshop productions, development

ZOILUS II PRODUCTIONS
281 Ninth Ave., New York, NY 10011 (212) 255-2334
Contact: Leslie (Hoban) Blake, Co-Artistic Director **Theatre:** off off Broadway, professional not-for-profit **Works:** translations, adaptations **2nd productions:** "Possibly." **Special interests:** "Broad interests, including TV scripts." **Stages:** proscenium; thrust; arena **Audience:** "Sharp and knowledgeable, New York off off Broadway." **Submission policy:** unsolicited script with SASE; query/synopsis with dialogue sample and resume; professional recommendation **Best time:** Sept.-Jun. **Response:** 5 months **Programs:** staged readings, development **Advice:** "Be willing to start with a reading and to work on development." **Comment:** "We are attached to, but separate from, the New Theatre."

During the past few months, the following theatres and producers have issued calls for scripts. As they either did not respond to our 1990 questionnaire or came to our attention too late to be included in our survey, we advise that playwrights inquire before submitting materials.

THE ALTERNATIVE TRAVELING THEATER (ATT)
8 Jones St. Suite 2A, New York, NY 10014
(212) 633-1021 Contact: Michelle Lundquist, Artistic Director

ANGEL ENTERPRISES
c/o Kathryn Kelly
One Essex St. Apt. 3B, New York, NY 10002

THE ARTIST THEATRE GROUP
c/o Anthony Alexandre, 4415 1/2 Tujunga Ave.,
North Hollywood, CA 91602

ASIAN AMERICAN OUTREACH THROUGH THE ARTS
Henry Street Settlement, 466 Grand St.,
New York, NY 10002 (212) 598-0400 Contact: Fay Chiang

AVALON PRODUCTIONS
2064 Watsonia Terrace, Los Angeles, CA 90068
Contact: Jeames Higgins, Isobel Grandin, Artistic Directors

CAREB PRODUCTIONS
c/o Actors Institute, 48 W. 21st St.,
New York, NY 10010

ENSEMBLE THEATRE OF THE HAMPTONS
c/o Box 1259, Quogue, NY 11959

FIRST STREET PLAYHOUSE
423 First St., Ithaca, NY 14850
Contact: Richard Brandt, Artistic Director

FRIENDS THEATRE COMPANY
1245 Park Ave. #19C, New York, NY 10128
(212) 534-6005 Contact: Barbara Pitcher, Artistic Director

GALLERY PLAYERS OF OREGON
Box 245, McMinville, OR 97128 Contact: Carol Burnett

GAY PERFORMERS THEATRE
Box 1617 Old Chelsea Station, New York, NY 10011
(212) 595-1445 Contact: Don Barrington

KAARIN RAUP, MAGGIE WYSOCKI
Box 55 Times Square Station, New York, NY 10108

LAURA LEWIS-HARTOS
The Pyramid Group, 159 W. 53rd St. #21F,
New York, NY 10019

MOYOGI PRODUCTIONS
380 Union St., Brooklyn, NY 11231

NEVERTHELESS, RADIO INC.
655 W. Roscoe, Chicago, IL 60657
(312) 472-2315 Contact: Sandy Kenyon, Literary Manager

OBERON THEATRE ENSEMBLE
10 Oxford St., Islip, NY 11751

OPEN CIRCLE THEATRE FOR TELEVISION
Open Circle Productions, Box 1155,
Northampton, MA 01061

P & M PRODUCTIONS
7985 Santa Monica Blvd. Suite 109, Box 430,
Los Angeles, CA 90046

RADIO THEATRE OF GLENDALE
American Radio Theatre, 1616 W. Victory Blvd. #104,
Glendale, CA 91201

SOUPSTONE PROJECT
309 E. 5th St. #19, New York, NY 10003
Contact: Literary Manager

STILLWATERS THEATRE COMPANY
c/o Brent Fadem, 10 Manhattan Ave. Apt. 1E,
New York, NY 10025

T. HARTNETT
2 Chestnut St., Boston, MA 02108

THEATREINC-NEW VOICES SERIES
328 Flatbush Ave. Suite 282, Brooklyn, NY 11238
Contact: Charles Pekunka, Associate Artistic Director

WHITBELL PRODUCTIONS, INC.
Box 2459 Times Square Station, New York, NY 10108

Contests

Suggestions for submitting works to the competitions and festivals listed in this section:

Read each entry carefully and observe all regulations.

Request guidelines for all competitions; any contest or festival may chance its regulations and/or deadlines during the year. Always enclose a stamped, self-addressed business envelope when requesting application forms, guidelines or other information.

Submit well in advance of deadlines.

Include all appropriate materials, as described in The Playwright's Checklist and individual listings, with each submission. Enclose a self-addressed, stamped postcard for acknowledgement of receipt of your entry materials.

After a script has been submitted, do not send revisions or other materials unless the competition sponsor requests that you do so.

Do not expect a competition or festival to return any material not accompanied by a stamped, self-addressed mailer of adequate size to accommodate the material.

ACTORS ALLEY REPERTORY THEATRE'S ANNUAL NEW PLAY COMPETITION
Sherman Oaks, CA   This contest has been discontinued.

ACTORS' GUILD OF LEXINGTON'S NEW THEATRE FESTIVAL
161 North Mall, Lexington, KY 40507
(606) 233-7330, -0663 Contact: Vic Chaney, Artistic Manager
Frequency: annual   **Awards:** $300 stipends, production for 3 winners **Works:** full-length plays, one-acts **Special interest:** "Works that address the social, political and personal dilemmas of our time." **Regulations:** entries must be unpublished and unproduced **Specifications:** small cast, single set **Casting:** open auditions **Audience:** local **Procedure:** send script with cover letter and SASE **Deadline:** inquire (Oct. 31 in 1989); no submissions before Sept. 30, 1990 **Your chances:** 100 entries/6 judges/3 readings per entry **Future commitment:** credit in future programs

ACTORS THEATRE OF HOUSTON
& MASTERSCRIPTOR'S LITERARY SERVICE
NATIONAL PLAYWRIGHT COMPETITION
Box 711067, Houston, TX 77271-1067
Frequency: annual **Awards:** 1st prize production; 2nd prize
staged reading; travel and housing **Works:** full-length plays
Regulations: entries must be unproduced **Procedure:** send SASE
for guidelines **Deadline:** Jan. 21, 1990

A DIRECTORS' THEATRE
ANNUAL YOUNG PLAYWRIGHTS' COMPETITION
6404 Hollywood Blvd. Suite 329,
Hollywood, CA 90028 (213) 465-8431
Contact: Dorothy Lyman, Artistic Director **Awards:** $1000
savings bond, production, travel for each of 3 winners; $500 to
teachers of winning writers **Works:** one-acts **Exclusive
interest:** comedies **Regulations:** authors must be under age 19
and enrolled in local area schools; entries must be unproduced
Playing time: 30-40 minutes **Procedure:** request guidelines; 3
copies of script required upon entry **Deadline:** spring 1990 (inquire)
Comment: Formerly Carol Burnett Young Playwrights' Competition.

AGGIE PLAYERS PLAYWRITING COMPETITION
Texas A & M University, College Station, TX 77843
(409) 854-2526 **Contact:** Roger Shultz, Director of Theatre
Frequency: annual **Award:** $1000 or more, production, $1000
expenses to attend rehearsals **Works:** full-length plays
Regulations: authors must be American playwrights; entries must
be unpublished, unproduced and must deal with "the American
experience"; winning author must be in residence in fall 1990
Specifications: cast size: 5-12; entries must be suitable for
cross-cultural casting **Procedure:** send script with SASE and
1-page synopsis **Deadline:** Feb. 15, 1990 **Notification:** Apr.
1990 **Comment:** Although the 1989 contest announced 10 finalists,
no alternate was named when the winning script was withdrawn.

ALLEN CLARK MEMORIAL AWARD
See La Pensee Dicovery! Theatre Awards listing in this section.

AMERICAN COLLEGE THEATRE FESTIVAL AWARDS
ACTF XXIII
Michael Kanin Playwriting Awards Program,
John F. Kennedy Center, Washington, DC 20566
(202) 416-8850 Contact: David Young, Producing Director
Frequency: annual **Regulations:** authors must be students in
accredited institutions of higher learning; entries must be original,

copyrighted works produced by ACTF participating schools; no translations; adaptors must secure permission; adaptations "must involve substantial changes in form and/or expression" **Procedure:** request guidelines; application form to be completed by producing school; $150 fee and tape of any music required upon entry **Notification:** spring 1991 **Comment:** The judges reserve the right to withhold any award if in their opinion no entry merits it.

ACTF COLLEGE MUSICAL THEATER AWARD
Awards: $1000 each for lyrics, music and book; $1000 to producing school **Works:** full-length musicals, related one-act musicals, musical adaptations **Regulations:** authors must be full-time students **Deadline:** Dec. 1, 1990 postmark **Your chances:** 10 applications/2 judges/2 readings per application

COLUMBIA PICTURES TELEVISION AWARD
FOR COMEDY PLAYWRITING
Award: assignment to write a completed teleplay for one of Columbia Pictures Television's series, expenses for story conference in Los Angeles, Writers Guild Scale for completed teleplay, fellowship to Shenandoah Playwrights Retreat (see Special Programs) **Works:** full-length plays, related one-acts, adaptations, musicals **Exclusive interest:** comedies **Regulations:** authors must be full-time students **Deadline:** Dec. 1, 1990 **Your chances:** 35 applications received each year **Advice:** "Scripts should be sent as soon as possible after the last performance on campus."

DAVID LIBRARY
OF THE AMERICAN REVOLUTION
AWARD FOR PLAYWRITING ON FREEDOM
OR AMERICANA
Awards: $3000 divided among winners; 1 fellowship to Shenandoah Playwrights Retreat (see Special Programs); 2nd prize $1000 **Works:** full-length plays, adaptations, musicals **Exclusive interest:** entries must "examine or reflect some aspect of Americana and reveal, either in primary statement or underlying theme, the nature of freedom in its broadest sense" **Regulations:** authors must be full-time students **Procedure:** application form must be filed with both ACTF national office and Ezra Stone, National

Chairman, Box 748, Washington Crossing, PA 18977
(215) 493-6776 **Deadline:** Oct. 15, 1990, or 12
weeks prior to initial ACTF production, whichever is
earlier

LORRAINE HANSBERRY PLAYWRITING AWARD

Awards: 1st prize $2500, fellowship to Shenandoah
Playwrights Retreat (see Special Programs); 2nd
prize $1000; grants ($750 and $500) to schools
producing 1st and 2nd place winners **Works:**
full-length plays, adaptations, musicals **Exclusive
interest:** entries must deal with the black experience
Regulations: authors may be part-time students
Deadline: Dec. 1, 1990 **Your chances:** 15
applications/2 judges/2 readings per application
Advice: Playwrights may submit scripts to ACTF
regional playwriting chairs for assistance in securing
productions.

NATIONAL STUDENT PLAYWRITING AWARD

Awards: $2500, production at Kennedy Center,
offer of contract with William Morris Agency (see
Agents), active membership in The Dramatists Guild
(see Special Programs), publication by Samuel French
(see Publishers), cash award to producing school
Works: full-length plays, adaptations, musicals
Regulations: authors must be full-time students;
entries must be selected for and presented at ACTF
regional festivals; entries are not eligible for other
ACTF playwriting awards, but performers are eligible
for ACTF's Irene Ryan Acting Scholarship **Deadline:**
Dec. 1, 1990 **Your chances:** 30 applications/3
judges/2-4 readings per application **Comment:** The
producing department of each regional winner of the
National Student Playwriting Award is eligible for the
ANGELS NEW PLAY PRODUCTION AWARD of
$500 to be used for production costs of the next
production entered in the Michael Kanin Playwriting
Awards Program within 3 years; a request for the
award should accompany the entry form for the 2nd
original play.

THE SHORT PLAY AWARDS PROGRAM

Awards: $1000, publication by Samuel French (see
Publishers), membership in The Dramatists Guild (see
Special Programs), offer of contract with William

Morris Agency (see Agents), possible production at Kennedy Center; awards to each of 2-3 winners **Works:** one-acts **Regulations:** authors must be full-time students; entries must be selected for and presented at ACTF regional festivals; entries are not eligible for other ACTF playwriting awards, but performers are eligible for ACTF's Irene Ryan Acting Scholarship **Playing time:** 20-40 minutes **Deadline:** Dec. 1, 1990

AMERICAN COLLEGE THEATRE FESTIVAL NEW PLAY PREVIEW PROGRAM
See listing in Special Programs.

AMERICAN MUSICAL THEATER FESTIVAL
Box S-3565, Carmel, CA 93921 (408) 625-5828
Contact: Moss Hall, Dramaturg **Frequency:** annual **Awards:** $2000, possible production and/or staged reading; possible readings for runners-up; finalists receive critiques **Works:** full-length musicals and musical adaptations **Special interest:** "Commercial rather than experimental works." **Regulations:** entries must have completed scores and must be unpublished and unproduced and may not have won major awards; adaptors must secure permission **Stage:** flexible, 160 seats **Audience:** general **Procedure:** send SASE for guidelines and application form; $20 fee upon entry **Deadline:** inquire (Dec. 31 in 1989)

ANNA ZORNIO MEMORIAL CHILDREN'S THEATRE PLAYWRITING AWARD
Theater Department, Paul Arts Center M211, University of New Hampshire, Durham, NH 03824
(603) 862-2291 Contact: Carol Lucha-Burns, Director of Youth Drama **Frequency:** annual **Award:** $250, production **Works:** children's plays **Regulations:** authors must be U.S. or Canadian residents; entries must be unpublished and not professionally produced; no more than 3 entries per author **Specifications:** maximum cast: 22; no more than 2 sets; playing time: 45-60 minutes **Casting:** college students **Audience:** "Age range 6-10." **Procedure:** request guidelines **Deadline:** May 1, 1990 **Your chances:** 20 entries usually received **Future commitment:** "Original program included in publication."

ANNUAL AT THE UPRISING PLAYWRIGHT'S AWARD
Long Beach, CA Our 1990 questionnaire was returned as "undeliverable," and no phone number is listed for this organization.

ANNUAL NEW PLAYWRIGHTS' FESTIVAL
Speech and Theatre Arts, Western Carolina University, Cullowhee, NC 28723 (704) 227-7491
Contact: D. L. Loeffler **Awards:** 1st prize $1000, production, 2-week residency; 2nd prize $250, staged reading **Works:** full-length plays **Regulations:** entries must be unproduced **Stages:** proscenium, 148 seats; proscenium, 474 seats **Audience:** university and community **Procedure:** request guidelines **Deadline:** inquire (Oct. in 1989)

THE ANN WHITE THEATRE
7TH ANNUAL NEW PLAYWRIGHTS CONTEST
5266 Gate Lake Rd., Ft. Lauderdale, FL 33319
(305) 722-4371 Contact: Ann White, Founder/Executive Director **Frequency:** annual **Award:** $500, production **Works:** full-length plays **Special interest:** "Relevant, contemporary, issue-oriented works." **Regulations:** entries must be unpublished, unproduced and free of royalty and copyright restrictions **Specifications:** maximum cast: 12, single set **Stage:** proscenium, 300 seats **Casting:** open auditions **Audience:** adults **Procedure:** send script with SASE and tape of any music **Deadline:** Nov. 15, 1990 postmark; no submissions before Aug. 1 **Notification:** Apr. 15, 1991 **Your chances:** 500 entries/6 judges/8 readings per entry **Future commitment:** "Current Equity-Dramatists Guild contract for future productions." **Comment:** The screening committee reserves the right to select no winner or more than one winner.

ARNOLD AND DOROTHY BURGER
PLAYWRITING COMPETITION
Euclid Recreation Dept., New City Hall, 585 E. 222nd St., Euclid, OH 44123 (216) 449-8624
Contact: Jan Petro, Representative **Frequency:** annual **Award:** "Cash award varies depending upon funding; production." **Works:** full-length plays, one-acts, adaptations, musicals **Regulations:** authors must be residents of Ohio; entries must be unpublished and unproduced except in a staged reading **Stage:** proscenium, 100-200 seats **Audience:** "General; mixed." **Procedure:** send SASE for guidelines **Deadline:** Aug. 1, 1990 postmark **Notification:** Oct. 15, 1990 **Your chances:** 40-50 entries/5 judges/1 or more readings per entry **Comment:** Winning play is produced at Euclid Little Theatre (see Theatres).

ARNOLD WEISSBERGER AWARD
New Dramatists, 424 W. 44th St.,
New York, NY 10036 (212) 757-6960
Contact: Beth Nathanson, Artistic Associate **Frequency:** annual
Award: $5000 **Works:** full-length plays **Regulations:** entries
must not be published or professionally produced; no more than 1
entry per author **Procedure:** send SASE for guidelines **Deadline:**
Feb. 1, 1990; no submission before Sept. 15 for 1991 competition
Notification: Sept. 1990 **Your chances:** 700 entries/3 final
round judges/1-3 readings per script

ARROW ROCK LYCEUM THEATRE
NATIONAL PLAYWRIGHTS COMPETITION
Main St., Arrow Rock, MO 65320 (816) 837-3311
Contact: Michael Bollinger, Artistic Producing Director
Frequency: biennial even years **Award:** $1000, possible
production, transportation **Works:** full-length plays **Regulations:**
entries must be unpublished and unproduced and must deal with rural
or small-town America **Specifications:** maximum cast: 12; unit
set preferred **Procedure:** send SASE for guidelines **Deadline:**
Dec. 1990 (inquire) **Your chances:** 300 entries **Comment:**
Formerly On Themes of Rural America.

ASF TRANSLATION PRIZE
The American-Scandinavian Foundation,
127 E. 73rd St., New York, NY 10021 (212) 879-9779
Contact: Publishing Office **Frequency:** annual **Works:**
translations from a Scandinavian language into English **Award:**
$1000, publication of excerpt in *Scandinavian Review* **Regulations:**
entries must be unpublished; original work must be written by a
Scandinavian born after 1880 **Length:** 75 pages minimum for prose,
35 pages minimum for poetry **Procedure:** send SASE for guidelines
Deadline: Jun. 1, 1990 **Notification:** Nov. 1, 1990

ATA AWARD
FOR LITERARY TRANSLATION FROM GERMAN
American Translators Association,
109 Croton Ave., Ossining, NY 10562 (216) 234-6345
Contact: Betty Becker-Theye, Chair, Honors and Awards Committee,
Kearny State College, Kearny, NE 68849 (308) 234-8521
Frequency: biennial odd years **Award:** $1000, certificate
Regulations: entries must have been published in U.S. after Jan. 1,
1988, and must conform to PEN guidelines **Procedure:** "Any party
directly associated with publication of the book may request
application form and guidelines; ATA members may nominate books."
Deadline: Mar. 1991 (inquire)

ATLANTIC COMMUNITY COLLEGE
PLAYWRIGHTS' WEEKEND
Humanities Division, ACC, Mays Landing, NJ 08330
(609) 343-5040, -4959 Contact: John Pekich, Kathie Brown
Frequency: annual **Award:** reading, possible production **Works:**
one-acts **Regulations:** entries must be unpublished and not under
consideration or option elsewhere; no more than 1 entry per author;
no musicals, adaptations, film or TV scripts **Specifications:**
minimum cast: 4-6; limited sets; limited scene changes **Audience:**
"General, mixed." **Procedure:** send script with SASE **Deadline:**
Jan. 31, 1990 **Notification:** Feb. 20, 1990 **Your chances:** 100
entries/5 judges/several readings per entry **Comment:** "The
reviewers reserve the right to accept or reject any and all
manuscripts."

BARN PLAYERS PLAYWRIGHTING CONTEST
Shawnee Mission, KS   This contest in inactive in 1990.

BEVERLY HILLS THEATRE GUILD–
JULIE HARRIS PLAYWRIGHT AWARD COMPETITION
2815 N. Beachwood Dr., Los Angeles, CA 90068
(213) 465-2703 Contact: Marcella Meharg, Competition
Coordinator **Frequency:** annual **Awards:** 1st prize $5000 plus
$2000 to a theatre company to help finance a showcase production in
the Los Angeles area within 1 year after receipt of award; 2nd prize
$1000; 3rd prize $500 **Works:** full-length plays **Regulations:**
authors must be U.S. citizens; entries must be unpublished, unproduced
and unoptioned; no more than 1 entry per author; previous entries and
plays that have won other contests are ineligible **Procedure:**
request guidelines and application form **Deadline:** Nov. 1, 1990
postmark; no submissions before Aug. 1 **Notification:** Jun. 1991
Your chances: 500+ entries/5 judges/2+ readings per entry
Advice: "Don't send 1st draft--competition is tough; play should be
as well-developed as possible without a production."

BIENNIAL PROMISING PLAYWRIGHT AWARD
Colonial Players, Inc., c/o Doris Cummins,
104 Stewart Dr., Edgewater, MD 21307 (301) 956-3397
Frequency: biennial, even years **Award:** $750, possible production
Works: full-length plays, adaptations **Regulations:** authors must
reside in U.S. or U.S. possession; entries may not have been formally
produced and must be free of restrictions; no more than 2 entires per
author; adaptors must secure permission **Specifications:** maximum
cast: 20, 12 or fewer preferred; entries must be suitable for arena
staging **Stage:** arena, 170 seats **Procedure:** send SASE for
guidelines; $5 fee upon entry **Deadline:** Dec. 31, 1990 **Your**

chances: 75 entries/24 judges/3 readings per entry **Comment:** "The judges reserve the right to withhold the award if no play is deemed suitable for production in Colonial Players' theatre."

BLACK DRAMATISTS FESTIVAL
American Playwrights Theatre, 1742 Church St. NW, Washington, DC 20036 (202) 232-4527
Contact: Debbie Niezgoda, Artistic Associate **Awards:** 1st prize cash remuneration, production in spring 1991; staged readings of a total of 4 plays in fall 1990 **Works:** full-length plays **Regulations:** authors must be black playwrights **Procedure:** send SASE for guidelines **Deadline:** Jun. 1990 (inquire) **Notification:** late summer

BLOOMINGTON PLAYWRIGHTS PROJECT CONTEST
409 S. Walnut St., Bloomington, IN 47401
(812) 334-1188 **Contact:** Rita Kniess, Literary Manager **Frequency:** annual **Award:** $250, production **Works:** full-length plays **Regulations:** entries must be unpublished and unproduced **Specifications:** simple set; entries must be suitable for small theatre **Stage:** flexible, 50 seats **Audience:** young adults, college students **Procedure:** send script with SASE, cover letter and $5 fee **Deadline:** Oct. 15, 1990 **Notification:** Jan. 1991 **Your chances:** 15 entries/3 judges/3 or more readings per entry **Advice:** "We consider the playwright's ability to take part in the rehearsal process."

BMI UNIVERSITY MUSICAL SHOW COMPETITION
320 W. 57th St., New York, NY 10019
(212) 586-2000 ext. 258 **Contact:** Jean Banks, Senior Director; Norma Grossman, Director, Musical Theater **Frequency:** periodic **Awards:** $2500 to each composer of best music, writer of best lyrics, organization or class sponsoring winning show; $1000 to librettist **Regulations:** authors must be students in accredited institutions of higher learning and must have been under 26 years of age as of Dec. 31, 1989; entries must be certified by a dean of students and must have been sponsored during the 1988-89 academic year as a recognized student activity; no more than 1 entry per author **Procedure:** send SASE for guidelines **Deadline:** Jun. 1990 (inquire) **Comment:** "If, in the opinion of the judges, the quality of the entries does not warrant the awarding of any prizes, the amount not awarded shall be added to the awards for the following year's competition."

BOB CLARK NEW PLAYWRIGHT CONTEST
University of Miami, Dept. of Theatre Arts,
Box 248273, Coral Gables, FL 33124 (305) 284-6439
Contact: Robert Ankrom, Chairman **Frequency:** annual **Award:** $1500, production, student showcase in New York **Works:** full-length plays, musicals **Specifications:** small cast; entries must be suitable for college conservatory members **Procedure:** send script with SASE **Deadline:** Mar. 31, 1990 **Notification:** Aug. 1990

BORDERLANDS THEATER/TEATRO FRONTERIZO NEW PLAY SEARCH
Box 2791, Tucson, AZ 85702 (602) 882-8607
Contact: Barkley Goldsmith, Producing Director **Frequency:** annual **Award:** $100 honorarium, staged reading (Jun. 1990), air fare, housing and meals for residency **Works:** full-length plays, translations, adaptations **Special interests:** Native American, Latino American and Southwest writers; Southwest border area issues; translations and adaptations of Latino American works **Regulations:** entries must be unpublished; previously produced entries must be re-worked; entries may be in English or Spanish; no more than 2 entries per author; winning writers must be available for residency **Stage:** proscenium, 105 seats **Casting:** open auditions; multi-ethnic **Procedure:** send script with SASE and brief resume **Deadline:** Mar. 1, 1990 postmark **Notification:** Apr. 1 **Future commitment:** negotiable **Comment:** The judges reserve the right to withhold the award if in their opinion no entry merits it.

BREAKTHROUGH SERIES
University of Missouri Press, 200 Lewis Hall,
Columbia, MO 65211 (314) 882-7641
Contact: Janice Smiley, Administrative Assistant **Frequency:** biennial odd years **Award:** publication **Works:** full-length plays, one-acts **Regulations:** authors "must have published in other media than book form, although established writers using a new creative form are eligible"; entries must be unpublished; no simultaneous submissions **Length:** 130 pages maximum **Procedure:** send SASE for application form, guidelines; $10 fee upon entry **Deadline:** Mar. 31, 1991 postmark; no submission before Feb. 1, 1991 **Your chances:** 50 entries/3 judges/2 readings per script

CAC NEW PLAY COMPETITION
Contemporary Arts Center, Box 30498,
New Orleans, LA 70190 (504) 523-1216
Contact: Elena Ronquillo, Performing Arts Director **Frequency:** annual **Awards:** 1st prize $500, staged reading; 2 runners-up receive staged readings **Works:** full-length plays, musicals **Special**

interest: "The Southern region." **Regulations:** authors must reside in AL, GA, LA or MS; entries must be unpublished and unproduced; no more than 2 entries per author; previous entries ineligible **Procedure:** send SASE for guidelines **Deadline:** Nov. 1, 1990 **Notification:** Feb. 1991

CALIFORNIA PLAYWRIGHTS FESTIVAL
South Coast Repertory, Box 2197,
Costa Mesa, CA 92628 (714) 957-2602
Contact: John Glore, Literary Manager **Frequency:** undetermined (inquire) **Awards:** 1st prize $5000, 2nd prize $3000, 3rd prize $2000, production; 5 staged readings of works by California writers **Works:** full-length plays **Regulations:** entries must not have been professionally produced and must be unoptioned; authors must have principal residence in California; no more than 2 entries per author **Procedure:** send SASE guidelines **Your chances:** 300-500 entries/variable number of judges and readings per entry **Deadline:** inquire (Nov. 15 in 1989)

CALIFORNIA YOUNG PLAYWRIGHTS PROJECT
The Gaslamp Quarter Theatre Company,
547 4th Ave., San Diego, CA 92101-6904
(619) 232-9608 Contact: Deborah Salzer, Director
Frequency: annual **Award:** variable cash award, production, script development, variable travel **Works:** full-length plays, single and related one-acts, musicals, children's plays **Regulations:** authors must be residents of California under 19 years of age at date of submission; entries must not be published or professionally produced **Stage:** 3/4 round, 95 seats **Audience:** "Many young people (usually over age 12), families and theatre patrons. We don't cater to any element in the audience." **Procedure:** send script and cover letter giving date of birth and biographical information **Deadline:** May 1, 1990 postmark **Notification:** late fall 1990 **Your chances:** 170 entries/6 or more judges/2 or more readings per entry **Advice:** "We consider the quality of script as follows: sense of truth, imagination, skillful use of language, grasp of dramatic format. Writers are encouraged to write about ideas of importance to them, using whatever subject matter, form or language they choose." **Comment:** Scripts are not returned.

CAROL BURNETT YOUNG PLAYWRIGHTS' COMPETITION
See A Director's Theatre Annual Young Playwrights' Competition listing in this section.

CELEBRATION OF ONE-ACTS
West Coast Ensemble, Box 38728,
Los Angeles, CA 90038 (213) 871-8673
Contact: Les Hanson, Artistic Director **Frequency:** annual **Award:** production, staged reading **Works:** full-length plays, one-acts **Regulations:** no more than 3 entries per author; previous entries ineligible **Specifications:** maximum cast: 12 for full-length play, 6 for one-act; no more than 2 sets **Stages:** proscenium, 65 seats; flexible, 70 seats **Casting:** "From the company; policy of non-traditional casting." **Audience:** "Wide range of Southern California." **Procedure:** send script with SASE **Deadline:** Oct. 15, 1990 postmark **Notification:** Feb. 1991 **Your chances:** 700 entries/15 judges/5 readings per entry **Future commitment:** "Credit, if published." **Comment:** The judges reserve the right to withhold the award if in their opinion no entry merits it."

CHARLOTTE FESTIVAL/NEW PLAYS IN AMERICA
Charlotte Repertory Theatre, Spirit Square,
110 E. 7th St., Charlotte, NC 28202 (704) 375-4796
Contact: Claudia Carter Covington, Literary Manager **Frequency:** annual **Awards:** production with royalty, travel, housing for 5 winners **Works:** full-length plays **Regulations:** entries must not be professionally produced; no musicals or children's plays; winning authors must participate in Festival process **Procedure:** send script with SASE and resume **Deadline:** ongoing program **Notification:** 3-4 months **Your chances:** 600 entries/3 judges **Advice:** "Just your best work."

CHARLOTTE REPERTORY THEATRE
PLAY COMMISSION
Charlotte, NC This commission has been discontinued.

CHICANO LITERARY CONTEST
Dept. of Spanish and Portuguese,
University of California at Irvine, Irvine, CA 92717
(714) 856-5702 Contact: Julie Foraker, Coordinator
Frequency: annual **Awards:** cash awards subject to funding: 1st prize $400, publication; 2nd prize $250 possible publication; 3rd prize $150, possible publication **Works:** short plays and one-acts **Regulations:** authors must be U.S. residents, either Chicano playwrights or playwrights with strong identification with Chicano community; entries must be unpublished and may be written in Spanish, English or both; "awards with honorable mention do not disqualify the artist from re-entry" **Procedure:** "Manuscripts must be typed and submitted in triplicate with SASE. The Title page must bear the title 'Sixteenth Chicano Literary Contest' and the author's full

name, address, telephone number and social security number. The author's name should not appear anywhere else on the script." **Deadline:** Jan. 8, 1990 **Notification:** May 1990 **Advice:** "Since entries are judged anonymously, their thematic content and relation to Chicanismo is of primary importance."

CHRISTINA CRAWFORD AWARDS
ATHE Playwrights Workshop, Theatre Arts Dept., Humboldt State University, Arcata, CA 95521
(707) 826-3566 Contact: Louise Williams, Vice-President for Workshop **Frequency:** annual **Awards:** 1st prize $1000, 2nd prize $500, 2 Honorable Mention Awards: $150 each; staged readings at annual conference **Works:** full-length plays, one-acts **Special interest:** one-acts **Regulations:** for 1st and 2nd prizes, authors must have been enrolled in college on or since Jun. 1, 1990; no more than 1 entry per author; winning authors must attend conference **Procedure:** send SASE for guidelines; 2 copies of script required upon entry **Deadline:** Feb. 1, 1990 postmark **Notification:** May 1990 **Advice:** "Short plays have an advantage because of convention session length."

CLAUDER COMPETITION FOR EXCELLENCE
New Voices, 551 Tremont St., Boston, MA 02116
(617) 357-5667 Contact: Stanley Richardson, Artistic Director **Frequency:** biennial even years **Awards:** $3000, production; runners-up may receive $500 and staged reading **Works:** full-length plays **Regulations:** authors must be residents of New England (CT, MA, ME, NH, RI, VT); entries must not be published or professionally produced; no translations, adaptations, musicals or children's plays **Specifications:** maximum cast: 8; no more than 1 unit set; playing time: 1-3 hours **Procedure:** send SASE for guidelines **Deadline:** Jun. 29, 1990; no submissions before Jan. 3 **Notification:** fall 1990 **Your chances:** 200 entries/6 judges/2 or more readings per entry **Advice:** "Focus on ideas, language. Forget psychological motivation. Care."

CLEVELAND PUBLIC THEATRE
FESTIVAL OF NEW PLAYS
6415 Detroit Ave., Cleveland, OH 44102
(216) 631-2727 Contact: Linda Eisenstein, Festival Director **Awards:** staged readings (May-Jun., 1990) of as many as 12 plays, housing **Works:** full-length plays, one-acts **Special interests:** northeast Ohio writers **Regulations:** entries must be unproduced or significantly revised **Stage:** flexible arena-proscenium, 150-175 seats **Procedure:** send script with SASE, $10 entry fee **Deadline:** Feb. 1, 1990 **Notification:** late Apr. 1990

COLUMBIA ENTERTAINMENT COMPANY'S CHILDREN'S THEATRE PLAYWRITING CONTEST

See Regional Children's Theatre Competition 1990 listing in this section.

COLUMBIA THEATRE PLAYERS ANNUAL NEW PLAY CONTEST

103 Greenleaf Dr., Hammond, LA 70401 (504) 567-2411
Contact: Carroll Bass **Award:** $300, staged reading, possible production **Works:** full-length plays **Regulations:** entries must be unpublished; no musicals **Stage:** black box, 100 seats **Audience:** "Community theatre; cross section, all kinds." **Procedure:** send script with SASE **Deadline:** Feb. 1, 1990 **Notification:** Mar. 1, 1990 **Your chances:** 50-100 entries/ "usually 3 judges/1 reading per script in 1st round, usually 3 readings for finalists" **Advice:** "Use standard script form. Binding makes our life easier and makes your script look better." **Advice:** "We want the best quality. We promise a staged reading. A full production is possible if we think we can do it justice. The award will be given to the best play, regardless."

CORNERSTONE: PENUMBRA THEATRE COMPANY NATIONAL PLAYWRIGHT COMPETITION

270 N. Kent St., St. Paul, MN 55102 (612) 224-4601
Contact: Lou Bellamy, Artistic Director **Frequency:** annual **Award:** $1000, travel for workshop, possible production **Works:** full-length plays **Exclusive interest:** "The African American experience" **Regulations:** entries must not be professionally produced **Stage:** thrust/ proscenium, 150 seats **Procedure:** send script with SASE and resume **Deadline:** Feb. 15, 1990 **Notification:** Sept. 1, 1990 **Your chances:** 75 entries/4 judges/3 readings per entry

DALTON LITTLE THEATRE NEW PLAY PROJECT

Box 841, Dalton, GA 30722-0841 (404) 226-6618
Contact: Coordinator **Frequency:** annual **Award:** $400, production (Sept.), travel and expenses **Works:** full-length plays, musicals **Regulations:** entries must be unproduced; no more than 2 submissions per author; no one-acts **Specifications:** entries must be suitable for a small playing area **Procedure:** send SASE for guidelines **Deadline:** May 1, 1990; no submissions before Mar. 1 **Your chances:** 200 entries/6 judges/6 readings per entry

DAVID JAMES ELLIS MEMORIAL AWARD
**Theatre Americana, Box 245,
Altadena, CA 91001-1235 (818) 397-1740
Contact:** Elaine Hamilton, Chairman, Playreading Committee
Frequency: annual **Award:** $500, production **Works:** full-length
plays **Special interest:** "Preference is given to American
authors." **Regulations:** entries must be unpublished and must deal
with "the American scene"; no musicals, TV or movie scripts
Specifications: maximum cast: 20, 4-10 preferred; simple sets;
minimal set changes; no elaborate, expensive costumes; playing time:
90 minutes-2 hours; "no pornography" **Procedure:** send script with
SASE **Deadline:** Apr. 1, 1990 postmark **Notification:** time varies
Your chances: 200-250 entries/3 judges/2-7 readings per entry
Advice: "Originality is important. Oscenity for shock value is
unacceptable." **Comment:** Season runs from Jul. 1-Jun. 30 with 1
award each season for the best of 4 plays produced.

DAYTON PLAYHOUSE PLAYWRITING COMPETITION
**1301 E. Siebenthaler Ave., Dayton, OH 45414
(513) 277-0144 Contact:** Jim Payne, Managing Director
Frequency: annual **Award:** $1000, possible production **Works:**
full-length plays, translations, adaptations **Special interests:**
"Plays for and about, but not limited to, women and minorities."
Regulations: entries must be unpublished and unproduced except in
staged readings and/or workshops **Stage:** flexible, 180 seats
Audience: "Open." **Procedure:** send SASE for guidelines
Deadline: Nov. 30, 1990 postmark; no submissions before Sept. 1
Notification: May 30, 1991 **Your chances:** 200 entries/5-8
judges/at least 3 readings per entry **Comment:** The judges reserve
the right to withhold the award if in their opinion no entry merits it.

DC ART/WORKS PLAYWRIGHTS COMPETITION
**410 8th S. NW Suite 400, Washington, DC 20004
(202) 724-3412 Contact:** Selim Garner, Acting Executive
Director **Frequency:** annual **Award:** $1000, production, travel
Works: one-acts **Exclusive interest:** concerns and problems of
inner-city youth: substance abuse, pregnancy, crime, health, peer
pressure, etc. **Specifications:** maximum cast: 11; works must be
suitable for touring; playing time: 45 minutes **Regulations:**
authors must be over 18 years of age; entries must be unpublished and
unproduced **Procedure:** request guidelines; 6 copies of script
required upon entry **Deadline:** inquire (Oct. 1 in 1989)

THE DOGWOOD NATIONAL ONE-ACT PLAY COMPETITION

The Little Green Theatre Company
2040 Old Salem Rd., Watkinsville, GA 30677
(404) 769-6576 **Contact:** David Muschell, Contest Coordinator
Frequency: annual **Award:** $100, possible production
Regulations: entries must be unpublished **Stages:** 300 seats;
150 seats **Procedure:** send script with SASE and $5 fee
Deadline: Jul. 15, 1990 **Notification:** Sept. 15, 1990 **Your chances:** 50+ entries/7 judges/2+ readings per entry

DRAMA LEAGUE OF NEW YORK PLAYS-IN-PROGRESS COMPETITION

165 W. 46th St. Suite 601, New York, NY 10036
(212) 302-2100 **Contact:** Playwrights Awards Committee
Frequency: annual **Awards:** $1000 or workshop production;
professional readings, script development for as many as 6 finalists;
winner to be chosen after rewriting **Works:** full-length plays-in-progress **Special interests:** "We like to see human beings represented at their best; we prefer plays that resonate to the community rather than plays about narrow psychological perceptions; we invariably choose plays of literary as well as theatrical merit."
Regulations: authors must be U.S. citizens or permanent residents; entries must be "undeveloped," unpublished and unproduced at time of submission **Procedure:** send SASE for guidelines and application form **Deadline:** inquire (Nov. 1 in 1989) **Your chances:** 300 entries/15 judges/2-15 readings per entry

DRAMARAMA90

Playwright's Center of San Francisco,
1001 Pine St. #803, San Francisco, CA 94109
(415) 928-4451 **Contact:** Lois Myers **Frequency:** annual
Awards: concert readings of 6 plays; 3 $100 post-performance awards **Works:** full-length plays, one-acts **Regulations:** entries must not have been produced in Bay Area; no musicals, children's plays, pageants, screenplays or TV scripts; no more than 1 entry per author **Specifications:** small stage; "no pornographic works" **Stage:** 50 seats **Audience:** general **Procedure:** send script with SASE, synopsis (50-100 word plot summary, character descriptions), production history and bio **Deadline:** inquire (Dec. 1 in 1989) **Your chances:** 140 entries/9 judges/3 readings per entry **Advice:** "Send the best script you have available for a small stage; script-in-hand staged reading."

DRURY COLLEGE 1-ACT PLAYWRITING CONTEST
900 N. Benton Ave., Springfield, MO 65802
(417) 865-8731   Contact: Sandy Asher, Writer-in-Residence
Frequency: biennial even years   **Awards:** 1 prize of $300, 2
prizes of $150 each; possible production   **Regulations:** entries must
not be committed, published or professionally produced; no more than
1 entry per author   **Specifications:** "Some preference is given to
small cast, one-set plays running between 20 and 45 minutes."
Stage: proscenium, 200 seats   **Audience:** "College students,
faculty, staff, general public."   **Procedure:** send SASE for guidelines
Deadline: Dec. 1, 1990 postmark   **Notification:** Mar. 1, 1991
Your chances: 200 entries/14 judges/1-3 readings per entry

DUBUQUE FINE ARTS PLAYERS
13TH ANNUAL ONE-ACT PLAYWRITING CONTEST
569 S. Grandview, Dubuque, IA 52001   (319) 582-5558
Contact: Sally T. Ryan, Contest Director   **Awards:** 1st prize $200,
2nd prize $150, 3rd prize $100; production   **Regulations:** entries
must be unpublished and unproduced; no musicals or children's plays;
no more than 1 entry per author   **Specifications:** maximum cast:
6-8; playing time: 45 minutes maximum   **Procedure:** send SASE
for guidelines and application form; $5 fee upon entry   **Deadline:**
Jan. 31, 1990 postmark; no submission for 1991 contest before Nov.
1, 1990   **Notification:** Jun. 1990   **Your chances:** 180 entries/2
judges/2-5 readings per entry   **Advice:** "Small cast, minimum scene
changes, minimal costume requirements."

EMERGING PLAYWRIGHT AWARD
Playwrights Preview Productions,
1160 Fifth Ave. #304, New York, NY 10029
(212) 996-7287   Contact: Thais Fitzsimmons, Literary Manager
Frequency: annual   **Award:** $500, production, travel   **Works:**
full-length plays, one-acts   **Special interests:** "Minority
playwrights, among all other writers"; full-length plays and related
one-acts preferred   **Regulations:** entries must not have been
produced in New York   **Maximum cast:** 8   **Procedure:** send script
with SASE   **Deadline:** ongoing program   **Notification:** spring
Comment: The judges reserve the right to withhold the award if no
play of merit is found.

EUCLID LITTLE THEATRE
PLAYWRITING COMPETITION
See Arnold and Dorothy Burger Playwriting Competition listing in this
section.

EXPOSURE/STAGES '90
S.T.A.G.E., 4633 Insurance, Dallas, TX 75221
(214) 559-3917 Contact: Julie Holman, Executive Director
Frequency: annual **Awards:** stipend, staged reading for each of 4 winners **Works:** one-acts **Regulations:** entries must be unproduced **Specifications:** "Keep it simple." **Stage:** "Usually arena." **Casting:** "Open auditions; actors must be members of S.T.A.G.E." **Audience:** "Wide range: professional, community." **Procedure:** send script with SASE **Deadline:** Apr. 15, 1990 **Your chances:** 40 entries/3 or more judges/3 or more readings per entry **Advice:** "Playwright should be at rehearsals--1 week." **Comment:** The judges reserve the right to withhold the award if in their opinion no entry merits it.

FALL FESTIVAL PLAYWRIGHTS CONTEST
Street Players Theatre, Box 2687,
Norman, OK 73070 (405) 364-0207
Contact: Robert Woods, Artistic Director **Frequency:** annual **Award:** $250, possible production **Works:** full-length plays **Regulations:** entries must be unpublished and may not have been professionally produced **Specifications:** small cast; simple production requirements **Stage:** flexible, 70-99 seats **Casting:** open auditions for season company **Audience:** largely university faculty and students and senior citizens **Procedure:** send SASE for guidelines and application form **Deadline:** Jun. 1, 1990 postmark **Notification:** by Aug. 7 **Your chances:** 25-30 entries/3-6 judges/5 readings per entry **Future commitment:** no **Comment:** The judges reserve the right to withhold the award if in their opinion no entry merits it.

FEAT PLAYWRITING FESTIVAL
Phoenix Theatre, 749 N. Park,
Indianapolis, IN 46204 (317) 635-7529
Contact: Brian Fonseca, Artistic Director **Frequency:** annual **Awards:** $500 for full-length play, $250 for one-act; production (summer 1990), housing **Works:** full-length plays, single and related one-acts, translations, adaptations **Regulations:** entries must be unpublished; professionally produced plays accepted; no more than 1 entry per author **Specifications:** entries must be suitable for 150-seat theatre **Audience:** "University educated, liberal, interested in social issues." **Procedure:** send script with SASE, biography "of self and play," $5 entry fee **Deadline:** Apr. 30, 1990 **Notification:** Jun. 1990 **Your chances:** 300 entries/14-15 judges/1-3 readings per entry

FERNDALE REPERTORY NEW WORKS COMPETITION
Box 892, Ferndale, CA 95536 (707) 725-2378
Contact: James Floss, Artistic Director **Frequency:** annual
Award: production with royalty **Works:** full-length plays
Regulations: entries must be unproduced **Stage:** proscenium-thrust, 267 seats **Procedure:** send SASE for guidelines **Deadline:** Oct. 1, 1990 **Notification:** Dec. 1, 1990 **Your chances:** 250 entries/7 judges/2-4 readings per entry **Advice:** "Highly entertaining, theatrical works."

FESTIVAL OF FIRSTS PLAYWRITING COMPETITION
Sunset Center, Box 5066, Carmel, CA 93921
(408) 624-3996 Contact: Richard Tyler, Director **Frequency:** annual **Award:** $1000, possible production **Works:** full-length plays, related one-acts, adaptations **Regulations:** entries must be unpublished and unproduced; no musicals or children's plays **Specifications:** related one-acts must constitute a full evening's entertainment **Procedure:** send SASE for guidelines and application form; $5 fee upon entry **Deadline:** Aug. 30, 1990 **Your chances:** 200 entries/3 judges/1-3 readings per entry

FESTIVAL OF NEW WORKS
See University of Cincinnati Playwriting Contest/Festival of New Works listing in this section.

FESTIVAL OF SOUTHERN THEATRE
Dept. of Theatre, University of Mississippi,
University, MS 38677 (601) 232-5816
Contact: Scott McCoy, Producing Director **Frequency:** annual
Awards: 3 awards of $1000, expenses **Works:** full-length plays
Regulations: authors must be Southerners, or plays must have "markedly Southern themes"; entries must not be published or professionally produced; winning authors must be in residence in mid-July, 1990 **Stage:** proscenium **Audience:** "General; we must avoid extreme and unwarranted vulgarity." **Procedure:** send SASE for guidelines **Deadline:** inquire (Dec. 1 in 1989) **Your chances:** 150 entries **Advice:** "Theatricality and resolution--we're tired of dialogue pieces." **Comment:** "National critics are on hand for critique of winners; there are usually printed reviews."

FESTIVAL THEATRE OF BIOGRAPHY
AND HISTORY COMMISSIONS
Division of the Wooden O, Inc., 600 W. 58th St.
Suite 9194, New York, NY 10019 (212) 874-6147
Contact: Gayther Myers, Artistic Director **Award:** at least $500 commission, possible production **Works:** full-length plays, one-acts,

children's plays **Special interest:** plays for young audiences **Regulations**: plays must be written in consultation with the theatre and based on historical and/or biographical topics proposed by the theatre **Procedure:** send 2 full-length scripts as work samples **Deadline:** ongoing program

FESTIVAL X
Rhode Island Playwrights Theatre,
58 Glenwood Ave., Pawtucket, RI 02860
Frequency: annual **Awards:** rehearsed reading/audience discussion, 2-week residency; possible grant from Rhode Island Playwrights Consortium: $2000 toward production by a Rhode Island theatre **Works:** full-length plays **Regulations:** entries must be unproduced **Procedure:** send SASE for guidelines **Deadline:** inquire (Dec. 30 in past years) **Comment:** Selected playwrights participate with director and dramaturg in casting and development process.

FIU PLAYWRIGHTS' FESTIVAL
Dept. of Theatre, Florida International University,
Miami, FL 33199   (305) 554-2895
Contact: Therald Todd, Chairperson **Frequency:** annual **Awards:** awards to be announced, production **Works:** full-length plays, one-acts **Regulations:** authors must be Florida playwrights; entries must be unproduced ; winning author must be available for production meetings and rehearsals for summer festival **Stage:** flexible, 140 seats **Audience:** "Mixed—community and university." **Procedure:** send SASE for guidelines **Deadline:** inquire **Your chances:** 80+ entries/6 judges/at least 2 readings per entry

FLETCHER CROSS AWARD
See La Pensee Discovery! Theatre Awards listing in this section.

FLORIDA STUDIO THEATRE MINI FESTIVAL/
NEW PLAY FESTIVAL
1241 N. Palm Ave., Sarasota, FL 34236 (813) 366-9017
Contact: Jack Fournier, New Play Director **Frequency:** annual **Awards:** $200, workshop production (spring-summer) for each of 3 plays selected for New Play Festival from Mini Festival; 10 staged readings in Mini Festival (fall, spring); travel, housing **Specifications:** maximum cast: 8; simple set **Stage:** proscenium, 163 seats **Audience:** "Older community. The theatre tries to educate, enlighten and expand its audience's taste." **Procedure:** send SASE for guidelines **Deadline:** inquire

FMCT PLAYWRIGHTS COMPETITION
Fargo-Moorhead Community Theatre, Box 644, Fargo, ND 58107 (701) 235-1901
Frequency: biennial odd years **Award:** $1000 or $500, production, travel and housing **Works:** full-length plays **Special interests:** "Midwestern theme, mythos or locale; experimental or unconventional works." **Regulations:** authors must be former or present residents of the Midwest; entries must be unpublished and unproduced except in workshops **Specifications:** maximum cast: 8, limited number of men; single set; no fly space; playing time: 90-120 minutes **Stage:** thrust, 300 seats; "excellent lighting equipment, many non-conventional avenues for actors' entrances" **Casting:** "Volunteers from community; many highly trained avocational actors." **Audience:** "Upper Midwestern, protestant, age range 35-45, 60% female, professional." **Procedure:** send SASE for guidelines **Deadline:** Dec. 1, 1991; no submissions before Jun. 1, 1991 **Notification:** Mar. 1, 1992 **Your chances:** 30-40 entries/3 judges/2 readings per entry **Future commitment:** no **Advice:** "FMCT is a high-quality, professional-level theatre dedicated to nurturing new works. Highly stylized work favored." **Comment:** The judges reserve the right to extend the competition into the following season should no winning script be selected by the 1991 deadline.

FOREST A. ROBERTS/ SHIRAS INSTITUTE PLAYWRITING AWARD
Forest A. Roberts Theatre, Northern Michigan University, Marquette, MI 49855-5364 (906) 227-2553
Contact: James A. Panowski, Director of Theatre **Frequency:** annual **Award:** $1000, production (Nov. 1991), travel, housing, residency during rehearsal **Works:** full-length plays **Regulations:** entries must be unpublished and unproduced **Stages:** proscenium; flexible **Audience:** "University theatre, wide age range." **Procedure:** send SASE for guidelines and application form **Deadline:** Nov. 17, 1990 **Notification:** Mar. 1991 **Your chances:** 400-500 entries/3 judges/2 or more readings per entry **Advice:** "Read the directions!"

FRANK McCLURE ONE-ACT PLAY AWARD
Amelia **Magazine, 329 E St., Bakersfield, CA 93304 (805) 323-4064** **Contact:** Frederick A. Raborg, Jr., Editor **Frequency:** annual **Award:** $150, publication, free copy **Works:** one-act plays, translations, adaptations and children's plays **Regulations:** entries must be unpublished; adaptors must secure permission **Playing time:** 45 minutes maximum **Audience:** "International, catholic readership that is predominantly well-educated

but representative of all walks of life." **Procedure**: send script with SASE, resume and $10 entry fee; "list acknowledgements" **Deadline**: May 15, 1990 **Notification**: approximately 3 months **Your chances**: 90-100 entries/3 judges/3-4 readings per entry **Advice**: "Be professional. All previous winners, we have noted, were members of The Dramatists Guild. We look for social or humane insights, strong plotting and conflict, intensity, fully developed characters and situations, daring and inventiveness."

GALLERY PLAYERS OF THE LEO YASSENOFF JEWISH CENTER PLAYWRITING CONTEST

1125 College Ave., Columbus, OH 43209 (614) 231-2731 **Contact**: Teri Devlin, Drama Director **Frequency**: biennial odd years **Award**: $1000, production **Works**: full-length plays, children's plays **Procedure**: send SASE for guidelines **Deadline**: inquire (Jan. 1 in 1989)

GEORGE R. KERNODLE PLAYWRITING COMPETITION

Dept. of Drama, University of Arkansas, Kimpel Hall 406, Fayetteville, AR 72701 (501) 575-2953 **Contact**: Thomas R. Jones, Director **Frequency**: annual **Awards**: 1st prize $300, 2nd prize $200; full production or workshop production **Works**: one-acts **Regulations**: authors must be residents of U.S. or Canada; entries must be unpublished and unproduced except in workshops; no more than 2 entries per author; no adaptations, musicals or children's plays **Specifications**: maximum cast: 6-8; playing time: 1 hour maximum **Procedure**: send SASE for guidelines; $3 fee upon entry **Deadline**: Jun. 30, 1990 **Notification**: Aug. 1, 1990

GERALDINE R. DODGE FOUNDATION NEW AMERICAN PLAY AWARD

Madison, NJ The Playwrights Theatre of New Jersey has requested that we discontinue this listing in 1990.

GOLDEN GATE ACTORS ENSEMBLE PLAYWRIGHTS COMPETITION

580 Constanzo St., Stanford, CA 94305 (415) 326-0336 **Contact**: Contest Administrator **Frequency**: annual **Award**: $1000, staged reading, possible production; all entries receive a written critique **Works**: full-length plays, related one-acts **Regulations**: authors must be U.S. residents; entries must be unproduced **Playing time**: 60 minutes minimum **Procedure**: send SASE for guidelines and application form; $20 fee upon entry **Deadline**: Jun. 15, 1990

GOSHEN COLLEGE PEACE PLAYWRITING CONTEST
See Peace Play Contest listing in this section.

GREAT PLATTE RIVER PLAYWRIGHTS FESTIVAL
Kearney State College, Department of Speech and Theatre, 905 W. 25th St., Kearney, NE 68849 (308) 234-8409
Contact: Jack Garrison, Festival Coordinator **Frequency:** annual **Award:** $500, production, staged reading **Works:** plays in development: full-length plays, one-acts, adaptations, musicals **Special interest:** "Subject matter dealing with the Great Plains, Midwest region. But we will accept work from any cultural background." **Regulations:** entries must be unpublished and unproduced; winners must be available for 2-week residency **Specifications:** maximum cast: 15; single set **Stages:** amphitheatre-arena flexible, 200 seats; black box, 200 seats **Casting:** open auditions for students and community members **Audience:** "General population of students and community members." **Procedure:** send script with SASE and resume **Your chances:** 50 entries/6 judges/6 readings per script **Deadline:** Mar. 15, 1990 **Notification:** Apr. 15, 1990 **Future commitment:** "The Festival shall have the rights to produce selected scirpts without payment of royalties." **Advice:** "In the historical category, judges will look most favorably on plays that are based on historical events in or around the Fort Kearney area of Nebraska. No melodramas."

HAROLD MORTON LANDON TRANSLATION AWARD
The Academy of American Poets, 177 E. 87th St., New York, NY 10128 (212) 427-5665
Contact: Nancy Schoenberger, Executive Director **Frequency:** annual **Award:** $1000 **Regulations:** authors must be U.S. citizens; entries must be verse drama translated from any language into English verse and published after Dec. 31, 1989; no anthologies or collaborations **Procedure:** send SASE for guidelines **Deadline:** Dec. 31, 1990

HEIGHTS SHOWCASE PLAYWRITING CONTEST
c/o Arts Inter Action, 711 W. 168th St., New York, NY 10032 (212) 222-8778
Contact: Eleanor Burke, President **Frequency:** periodic **Award:** up to $100, production **Works:** full-length plays, one-acts, plays for young audiences **Special interest:** works for inter-racial casting **Regulations:** entries must be unpublished and unproduced **Specifications:** plays for young audiences should be written for adult performers **Stage:** auditorium proscenium, 99 seats **Casting:** "Open auditions with special consideration for Heights

Showcase members." **Audience:** "Well mixed: seniors, young people, neighborhood, regular theatregoers." **Procedure:** send SASE for guidelines **Deadline:** Jan. 31, 1990 **Notification:** Apr. 1990 **Advice:** "Please send a clean, readable copy."

HELEN EISNER AWARD FOR YOUNG PLAYWRIGHTS
**Streisand Center at UCLA Hillel, 900 Hilgard Ave.,
Los Angeles, CA 90024 (213) 208-3081**
Contact: Gail Schwartz, Program Director **Frequency:** annual **Award:** $1000, possible production **Works:** full-length plays, one-acts, translations, adaptations, musicals, children's plays **Regulations:** authors must be under 30 years of age; entries must deal with "the struggle to express Jewish values in the contemporary world" **Procedure:** send SASE for guidelines and application form **Deadline:** winter or fall 1990 (inquire)

HENRICO THEATRE COMPANY
ONE-ACT PLAYWRITING COMPETITION
**The County of Henrico, Division of Recreation
and Parks, Box 27032, Richmond, VA 23273**
(804) 672-5100 Contact: J. Larkin Brown, Cultural Arts Specialist **Frequency:** annual **Awards:** 1st prize $250, production; runner-up $150, possible production **Regulations:** entries must be unpublished and unproduced **Specifications:** small cast, simple set preferred; no controversial material **Stage:** flexible, 100 seats **Audience:** "Younger public, students." **Procedure:** request guidelines; 2 copies of script required upon entry **Deadline:** Sept. 15, 1990 **Your chances:** 24 entries/5 judges/5 readings per entry

THE HENRY FONDA YOUNG PLAYWRIGHTS PROGRAM
Washington, DC See Very Special Arts Young Playwrights Program listing in this section.

HIGH SCHOOL PLAYWRITING CONTEST
Baker's Plays, 100 Chauncy St., Boston, MA 02111
(617) 482-1280 Contact: Contest Editor **Frequency:** annual **Awards:** $500, publication in "Best Plays from the High School" series; cash awards for 2nd and 3rd prize winners **Special interest:** issues of interest to teens **Procedure:** write for guidelines **Deadline:** inquire

HISPANIC PLAYWRIGHTS PROJECT
**South Coast Repertory, Box 2197,
Costa Mesa, CA 92628 (714) 957-2602**
Contact: José Cruze Gonzalez, Project Director **Frequency:** annual **Awards:** participation in summer workshop (early Aug. 1990) conducted by a prominent playwright/teacher, receptions, seminars with leading American theatre artists; travel, expenses, honorarium; possible commission and publication; as many as 6 plays selected: 3 plays undergo 3-week workshop culminating in a public reading and discussion; 3 plays receive dramaturgical development and private reading by a professional cast **Works:** full-length plays, one-acts **Regulations:** authors must be Hispanic American playwrights; entries may be written partially in Spanish; unproduced works preferred; no musicals **Policy:** send script with SASE, synopsis and bio **Deadline:** Apr. 13, 1990 **Notification:** May 1990 **Your chances:** 100 entries/3 judges/2 readings per entry **Comment:** Writers selected are eligible to participate in the year-round lab which continues the development process and for future commissions.

HUMBOLDT STATE UNIVERSTY
SEASON OF NEW AMERICAN PLAYS
**Theatre Arts Dept., Humboldt State University,
Arcata, CA 95521 (707) 826-3566, -4606**
Contact: Louise Williams, Coordinator **Frequency:** biennial even years **Awards:** $1000, production and residency for each of 4-5 winners **Works:** full-length plays, related one-acts, short choreographic pieces **Regulations:** authors must be professional playwrights; entries must be unproduced except in readings or workshops; no more than 1 entry per author; winning authors must be available for 2-3 week residency **Procedure:** send SASE for guidelines; 2 copies of script required upon entry **Deadline:** Oct. 1, 1990

ILLINOIS STATE FINE ARTS PLAYWRITING CONTEST
Normal, IL This contest has been discontinued.

INDIANA UNIVERSITY-PURDUE UNIVERSITY
AT INDIANAPOLIS PLAYWRITING FOR YOUTH
COMPETITION AND SYMPOSIUM
**Dept. of Theatre, IUPUI, 525 N. Blackford St.,
Indianapolis, IN 46202 (317) 274-0554, -2095**
Contact: Dorothy Webb, Director of Youth Theatre **Frequency:** biennial even years **Awards:** 1st prize $1500 (1/2 for production or reading, 1/2 for residency during symposium), showcase production or staged reading at sympsoium (mid-Mar. 1991); 3 semi-finalists

receive $500 each (for residency) **Works**: children's plays, one-acts and adaptations **Special interest**: "Well-crafted plays with strong story lines, compelling characters and careful attention to language. May include music." **Regulations**: entries must be unpublished and must not have had an Equity production; adaptors must secure permission; winner and runners-up must attend symposium **Playing time**: 45-90 minutes **Procedure**: send SASE for guidelines and application form **Deadline**: Jun. 1, 1990 **Notification**: Dec. 1990 **Your chances**: 125 entries/16 judges/2 or more readings per entry **Advice**: "Follow all rules and guidelines. Quality plays--write up, not down, to children. Write to the child within yourself."

INNER CITY CULTURAL CENTER
SHORT PLAY COMPETITION
1308 S. New Hampshire Ave., Los Angeles, CA 90006
(213) 387-1161 **Contact**: C. Bernard Jackson, Executive Director **Frequency**: annual **Awards**: cash award (1st prize $2000, 2nd prize $1500, 3rd prize $1000) or paid professional internship with film studio; publication **Works**: one-acts, translations, adaptations, children's plays **Specifications**: small cast; minimal set; playing time: 20-45 minutes; translations and adaptations must be of unpublished works **Procedure**: send SASE for guidelines; sponsoring organization (theatre, church, school, etc.) presents fully-mounted production to panel of judges; $25 fee upon entry **Deadlines**: Aug. 10, 1990 for letter of intent; Sept. 7, 1990 for completed application and fee; elimination rounds mid-Sept.--mid-Nov. 1990; finalists' presentation Dec. 1990

THE INSIDE FROM THE OUTSIDE
INTERNATIONAL PROSE/POETRY CONTEST
Bloomington, IN This contest is currently inactive.

INTERNATIONAL NEW MUSIC COMPOSERS
COMPETITION
7114 Southwest 114 Pl. Suite E, Miami, FL 33173
(305) 271-9138 **Contact**: Lorraine Silver, Coordinator **Frequency**: biennial odd years **Awards**: $2500, concert performance at Carnegie Recital Hall; possible performance for runners-up **Works**: "Musicals, operas, mixed-media pieces." **Regulations**: entries must have been completed within the last 5 years and must not have won major competitions **Procedure**: send SASE for guidelines in early 1991

THE INTERNATIONAL SOCIETY OF DRAMATISTS AWARDS
Box 1310, Miami, FL 33153   (305) 674-0538
Contact: Andrew Delaplaine, President   **Frequency**: annual
Stage: flexible, 100 seats   **Procedure**: send SASE for guidelines

ADRIATIC AWARD
Awards: 1st prize $250; certificates for 5 runners-up   **Works**: full-length plays, musicals **Regulations**: entries must not have been professionally produced (with Equity actors) more than once   **Deadline**: Nov. 1, 1990 postmark **Notification**: Mar. 1991

LINCOLN MEMORIAL CONTEST
Awards: 1st prize $100; 5 honorable mentions **Works**: one-acts   **Regulations**: entries must be unproduced **Deadline**: Jan. 15, 1990 **Notification**: Apr. 1990

PERKINS PLAYWRITING CONTEST
Award: $500   **Works**: full-length plays, translations, musicals   **Regulations**: entries must be unproduced **Deadline**: Dec. 6, 1990 **Notification**: Feb. 1991

JACKSONVILLE UNIVERSITY ANNUAL PLAYWRITING CONTEST
Division of Art, Theatre Arts and Dance,
Jacksonville University, Jacksonville, FL 32211
(904) 744-3950 Contact: Betty H. Swenson, Chair
Comments: "Because of the retirement of Dr. Davis Sikes who was the founder and Director of this program, the contest has been put 'on hold' until a successor is found and the contest re-established"; playwrights are advised to inquire before submitting materials.

JAMES D. PHELAN LITERARY AWARD
The San Francisco Foundation Awards Office,
685 Market St. Suite 94105, San Francisco, CA 94105
(415) 543-0223   Contact: Katherine L. Brody, Awards Program Coordinator   **Frequency**: annual   **Award**: $2000   **Works**: full-length plays, single and related one-acts, children's plays **Regulations**: authors must be California natives aged 20-35 as of Jan. 15, 1990; entries must be unpublished plays-in-progress **Length**: 100 pages maximum   **Procedure**: send SASE for guidelines and application form **Deadline**: Jan. 15, 1990; no submission before

Nov. 15, 1990 for 1991 competition **Notification**: Jun. 15, 1990 **Your chances**: 200+ entries/3 judges

JCC THEATRE OF CLEVELAND
DOROTHY SILVER PLAYWRITING COMPETITION
**The Jewish Community Center, 3505 Mayfield Rd.,
Cleveland Heights, OH 44118 (216) 382-4000 ext. 275**
Contact: Elaine Rembrandt, Director, Visual and Performing Arts **Frequency**: annual **Award**: $1000, staged reading, possible production **Works**: full-length plays **Exclusive interest**: "The Jewish experience." **Regulations**: entries must be unproduced **Procedure**: send SASE for guidelines **Deadline**: Dec. 15, 1990 **Notification**: Jul. 10, 1991

JEWEL BOX THEATRE PLAYWRITING AWARD
3700 N. Walker, Oklahoma City, OK 73118
(405) 521-1786 Contact: Charles Tweed, Production Director **Frequency**: annual **Award**: $500, reading, possible production **Works**: full-length plays **Special interest**: "Character rather than spectacle." **Regulations**: request guidelines and application form; 2 copies of script and "playwright's agreement" required upon entry **Deadline**: Jan. 17, 1990 **Notification**: Apr. 1990

JOHN GASSNER MEMORIAL PLAYWRITING AWARD
**New England Theatre Conference, 50 Exchange St.,
Waltham, MA 02154 (617) 893-3120**
Contact: Marie L. Philips, Executive Secretary **Frequency**: annual **Awards**: 1st prize $500, 2nd prize $250; staged reading and critique-discussion at NETC convention, referral to publishers **Works**: full-length plays, one-acts, children's plays **Regulations**: authors must be citizens of U.S. or Canada; entries must not be published, professionally produced, optioned or under consideration elsewhere; no more than 2 entries per author **Procedure**: send SASE for guidelines; $5 fee upon entry (waived for NETC members) **Deadline**: Apr. 15, 1990 postmark **Notification**: Sept. 1, 1990 **Your chances**: 150-200 entries/3-7 judges/3 readings per entry **Advice**: See "Suggestions for Playwrights" on reverse side of contest announcement, available upon request. **Comment:** The judges reserve the right to withhold the award if in their opinion no entry merits it.

KUMU KAHUA PLAYWRITING CONTEST
1770 East-West Rd., Honolulu, HI 96822
(808) 948-7677 Contact: Dennis Carroll, Juli Thompson **Frequency**: annual **Awards**: Division I: $500 for long play (50 pages or more), $300 for short play (15-50 pages); Division II: $250

for long play, $100 for short play; reading and/or production **Works**: full-length plays, single and related one-acts **Regulations**: Division I open to all authors, plays on Hawaiian subject matter only; Division II for Hawaiian residents only, non-Hawaiian subject matter, playing time: 30-150 minutes; entries must be unproduced; previous entries ineligible **Specifications**: entries must be suitable for a small theatre **Stage**: 150-200 seats **Audience**: "Varies." **Procedure**: send SASE for guidelines **Deadline**: Jan. 1, 1990 **Notification**: Apr. 1, 1990 **Your chances**: 30-40 entries/3 judges/3-12 readings per entry **Advice**: "No purely commercial material of the frothy sort."

LA PENSEE DISCOVERY! THEATRE AWARDS
511 N. 179th Pl., Seattle, WA 98133 (206) 542-8648
Contact: Willy Clark, Artistic Director **Frequency**: annual **Awards**: cash award ($300 in 1989) **Works**: full-length plays, single and related one-acts (related preferred), children's plays **Specifications**: maximum cast: 8-10; sets must be suitable for intimate stage **Stage**: flexible, 50-75 seats **Procedure**: send SASE for guidelines **Deadline**: Jan. 15, 1990 **Notification**: Apr. 15, 1990 **Your chances**: 200-300 entries/3-5 judges/3-5 readings per entry **Comment**: Formerly Allen Clark Memorial Award and Fletcher Cross Award.

LAWRENCE S. EPSTEIN PLAYWRITING AWARD
280 Park Ave. S #22E, New York, NY 10010
(212) 979-0865 **Contact**: Lawrence S. Epstein, Director **Frequency**: annual **Award**: $250, plaque **Works**: full-length plays, one-acts **Special interest**: theme varies (inquire) **Procedure**: send SASE for guidelines **Deadline**: Nov. 30, 1990

LEAH PRODUCTIONS PLAYWRIGHT CONTEST
New York, NY This contest has been discontinued.

THE LEE KORF PLAYWRITING AWARDS
The Original Theatre Works, Burnight Center,
Cerritos College, 11110 E. Alondra Blvd.,
Norwalk, CA 90650 (213) 924-2100
Contact: Georgia Well, Managing Director **Frequency**: annual **Award**: up to $500, production, reading **Works**: full-length plays or "theatre pieces" **Special interest**: "Preference will be given to authors who can arrange to join us for pre-production festivities and rehearsals." **Stages**: Burnight Center Theatre, 362 seats; Burnight Studio Theatre, 100 seats **Procedure**: send 2 copies of script with SASE **Deadline**: Jan. 1, 1990 **Notification**: May 1990 **Your chances**: 70+ entries/5 judges/3 readings per entry

LETRAS DE ORO (SPANISH LITERARY CONTEST)
**University of Miami, 1531 Brescia Ave.,
Coral Gables, FL 33124 (305) 284-3266**
Contact: Joaquin Roy, Graduate School of International Studies
Frequency: annual **Awards**: general prize $2500, publication
Works: full-length plays, one-acts, adaptations, children's plays
Regulations: authors must be U.S. residents; entries must be
unpublished and written in Spanish and must not have won a previous
award; no more than 1 entry per author **Procedure**: send SASE for
guidelines **Deadline**: Oct. 12, 1990 **Notification**: Mar. 1991
Your chances: 20 entries/25 judges/5 readings per entry

LEWIS GALANTIERE LITERARY TRANSLATION PRIZE
**American Translators Association, 109 Croton Ave.,
Ossining, NY 10562 (914) 941-1500**
Contact: Betty Becker-Theye, Chair, Honors & Awards Committee,
Kearny State College, Kearny, NE 68849 (308) 234-8521
Frequency: biennial even years **Award**: $500 **Works**: full-
length and one-act translations **Exclusive interest**: distinguished
literary translations from any language (except German) into English
Regulations: entries must have been published by an American
publisher within the past 2 years; single volumes and works in
collections are eligible **Procedure**: "Translator or publisher may
submit entry plus 10 consecutive pages of original, jacket and
available ad copy." **Deadline**: Mar. 15, 1990 **Notification**: Aug.
31, 1990

LITTLE THEATRE OF ALEXANDRIA
ONE-ACT PLAYWRITING COMPETITION
See National One-Act Playwriting Competition listing in this section.

LOIS AND RICHARD ROSENTHAL NEW PLAY PRIZE
**Cincinnati Playhouse in the Park, Box 6537,
Cincinnati, OH 45206 (513) 421-5440**
Contact: Worth Gardner, Artistic Director; Ara Watson, Playwright
in Residence **Frequency**: annual **Award**: $2000 advance on
royalties, production, $1500 stipend for residency with expenses
Works: full-length plays, related one-acts **Regulations**: entries
must be unpublished and not produced professionally; no more than 1
entry per author **Specifications**: related one-acts must constitute
a full evening's entertainment **Stages**: thrust; arena **Procedure**:
send script with SASE **Deadline**: Jan. 15, 1990; no submission
before Oct. 15, 1990 for 1991 competition **Notification**: Mar.
1990

LOVE CREEK SHORT PLAY FESTIVAL
c/o Cynthia Granville, 42 Sunset Dr.,
Croton-On-Hudson, NY 10520
Frequency: annual **Awards:** $250 first prize; mini-showcase production in New York City for finalists **Works:** short plays **Regulations:** entries must be unpublished and not produced in New York City area within past 12 months; no more than 2 entries per author **Specifications:** minimum cast: 3; simple sets and costumes; playing time: 45 minutes maximum **Stage:** flexible **Casting:** "All plays are cast within company (currently over 100 members)." **Procedure:** send script with SASE **Deadline:** Oct. 1, 1990 postmark; no submissions before Jun. 1 **Your chances:** 200+ entries **Future commitment:** credit for production if play is later produced off Broadway or published **Advice:** "Inquiries may not be acknowledged without considerable delay because of volume of entires; synopses/excerpts will not be read. Do not send inquiry without SASE. Please, no phone calls!"

MANHATTAN PUNCH LINE
FESTIVAL OF ONE-ACT COMEDIES
410 W 42nd St., New York, NY 10036   (212) 239-0827
Contact: Steve Kaplan, Artistic Director **Award:** presentation in Dec. or Jan. program **Works:** one-acts **Regulations:** entries must be unproduced **Playing time:** 45 minutes maximum **Procedure:** send script with SASE **Deadline:** Oct. 1, 1990 **Notification:** 12-16 weeks

MARC A. KLEIN PLAYWRITING AWARD
Department of Theatre,
Case Western Reserve University, 2070 Adelbert Rd.,
Cleveland, OH 44106 (216) 368-2858
Contact: Kelly Morgan, Executive Officer **Frequency:** annual **Awards:** $500, production, staged reading, travel ($500); all entries considered for workshop production **Works:** full-length plays, related one-acts, musicals **Regulations:** authors must be enrolled in U.S. colleges or universities; entries must be unpublished, unproduced and endorsed by a teacher of drama or a theatre professional **Procedure:** send SASE for guidelines **Deadline:** Apr. 1, 1990 **Notification:** mid-May 1990 **Your chances:** 35 entries/3 judges/3 readings per entry

MARGARET BARTLE ANNUAL PLAYWRITING AWARD
Community Children's Theatre of Kansas City,
8021 E. 129th Terrace, Grandview, MO 64030
(816) 761-5775 Contact: E. Blanche Sellens, Chairman, Playwriting Award **Award:** $500, possible production **Works:**

children's plays, adaptations and musicals **Regulations:** entries must be unpublished and unproduced **Specifications:** maximum cast: 8; all roles must be suitable for adult women; sets must be suitable for touring to elementary schools; playing time: 55-60 minutes; no seasonal plays; "no gratuitous violence, mature love stories, slang, cursing" **Stages:** various spaces **Audience:** grades K-6 **Procedure:** send SASE for guidelines **Deadline:** Jan. 26, 1990 **Notification:** Apr. 1990 **Your chances:** 40-60 entries/5 judges/5 readings per entry **Future commitment:** right to produce the winning play royalty-free for 1 year or 2 consecutive years; winning play may or may not be produced in 1990 **Advice:** "Suggested topics: legends, folklore, historical incidents, biographies, adaptations of children's classics." **Comment:** The judges reserve the right to withhold the award if in their opinion no entry merits it.

MARGO JONES PLAYWRITING COMPETITION
Department of Music and Drama,
Texas Woman's University, Box 23865, Denton, TX 76204
(817) 383-3586 Contact: Mary Lou Hoyle, Chairman, Selection Committee **Frequency:** biennial odd years **Award:** $1000, production **Works:** full-length plays, one-acts **Special interest:** "Plays which are about women or feature women in leading roles." **Regulations:** entries must be unpublished and unproduced **Specifications:** small cast, simple set **Stage:** proscenium **Casting:** "Students are given preference." **Audience:** "Small but enthusiastic." **Procedure:** send SASE for guidelines **Deadline:** Feb. 1, 1991 **Notification:** Apr. 1991 **Your chances:** 250 entries/3 judges/1 reading per entry **Advice:** "We are usually asked if male playwrights may submit. They may. Entries are read without that information attached."

MARKET HOUSE THEATRE
ONE-ACT PLAYWRIGHTING COMPETITION
141 Kentucky Ave., Paducah, KY 42001 (502) 444-6828
Contact: April Cochran, Executive Director **Frequency:** annual **Awards:** $50, public staged readings (spring) for 2 winners **Special interests:** "Small social issues; regional (Mid-South) interests." **Regulations:** entries must be unpublished and unproduced **Specifications:** maximum cast: 10; minimal set changes preferred; playing time: 20-60 minutes **Stage:** proscenium **Audience:** "Conservative." **Procedure:** send SASE for guidelines **Deadline:** inquire (Oct. 31 in 1989) **Future commitment:** no **Comment:** The judges may reserve the right to withhold the award if in their opinion no entry merits it.

MARK GILBERT AWARD
Saturday Night Leftovers, 282 S. Union St., Concord, NC 28025 (704) 786-4364
Contact: David Lathrop, Lori Lathrop, Producers **Frequency:** annual **Award:** $150, production **Works:** full-length plays, one-acts **Special interest:** "A good story, well told by interesting characters." **Regulations:** entries must be unpublished; no more than 3 entries per author **Specifications:** maximum cast: 10; no more than 2 sets **Stage:** flexible, 200 seats **Casting:** "Open auditions; director's discretion." **Audience:** "Intelligent, open-minded, sophisticated." **Procedure:** send script with SASE, synopsis, resume, script history and tape of any music **Your chances:** 300-400 entries/4 judges/4 readings per entry **Deadline:** Dec. 31, 1990; no submission before Sept. 1 **Future commitment:** "Option for future production." **Comment:** The judges reserve the right to withhold the award if in their opinion no entry merits it.

MARVIN TAYLOR PLAYWRITING AWARD
Sierra Repertory Theatre, Box 3030, Sonora, CA 95370 (209) 532-3120   Contact: Dennis Jones, Producing Director **Frequency:** annual **Award:** $400, production **Works:** full-length plays, adaptations, musicals **Regulations:** entries must be unpublished and have had no more than 2 productions or staged readings; adaptors must secure permission; no more than 1 entry per author **Specifications:** maximum cast: 15; no more than 2 sets **Stages:** proscenium, 99 seats; thrust, 99 seats **Audience:** "Rural, caucasian, 30's-60's, large percentage seniors." **Procedure:** send script with SASE **Deadline:** May 15, 1990 postmark **Notification:** Sept. 1, 1990 **Your chances:** 200 entries/3 judges/1-3 readings per entry

MAUDE ADAMS PLAYWRITING CONTEST
Columbia, MO   This contest has been discontinued.

McDONALD'S LITERARY ACHIEVEMENT AWARDS
Negro Ensemble Company, Box 778 Times Square Station, New York, NY 10108
Frequency: annual **Award:** $2000, travel to New York City, "literary forum and celebrity reading" **Works:** full-length plays, one-acts **Exclusive Interest:** "The Black experience in America." **Minimum length:** 20 pages **Procedure:** send script with SASE, bio and list of productions **Deadline:** Jun. 1, 1990 **Notification:** Aug. 15, 1990

MERRIMACK REPERTORY THEATRE PLAYWRITING CONTEST

Box 228, Lowell, MA 01853 (508) 454-6324
Contact: David G. Kent, Literary Manager/Dramaturg **Frequency:** annual **Awards:** cash awards ($500 in past years) for as many as 6 finalists; summer workshop productions; possible full production **Works:** full-length plays, translations, adaptations, musicals, children's plays **Special interests:** "The intellectual history of New England; women's role in the American workplace; life in the industrial city; history, cultural preservation and conflict; immigration and the clash of cultures in industrial America." **Regulations:** authors must be residents of CT, MA, ME, NH, RI, VT; entries must be unpublished and unproduced **Stage:** prosceniumthrust, 280 seats **Audience:** "Blue collar workers; Asian immigrants." **Procedure:** send script with SASE **Deadline:** Mar. 15, 1990 **Notification:** Jun. 1, 1990 **Your chances:** 300 entries/6 judges/1-2 or more readings per entry **Comment:** The judges reserve the right to withhold the award if in their opinion no entry merits it.

MIDSOUTH PLAYWRIGHTS CONTEST

Playhouse on the Square, 51 S. Cooper,
Memphis, TN 38104 (901) 725-0776, 726-4498
Contact: Jackie Nichols, Executive Director **Frequency:** annual **Award:** $500, production **Works:** full-length plays **Regulations:** entries must be unproduced and uncommitted **Specifications:** maximum cast: 10; single or unit set **Stage:** proscenium **Audience:** "20-50, college educated." **Procedure:** send script with SASE **Deadline:** Apr. 1, 1990 postmark **Notification:** Jul. 1990 **Your chances:** 500 entries/10 judges/3 readings per entry

MILLER AWARD 1990

Deep South Writers Conference,
Box 44691, University of Southwestern Louisiana,
Lafayette, LA 70504
Contact: John Fiero, Director **Frequency:** annual **Award:** $1500 **Works:** full-length plays **Exclusive interest:** "Some aspect of the life of Edward de Vere, Earl of Oxford, and/or the English Renaissance; suitability for adaptation to film or TV will be considered." **Regulations:** entries must be unpublished **Procedure:** send SASE for guidelines **Deadline:** Jul. 15, 1990 **Notification:** Sept. 1990 **Your chances:** 7 entries/2 judges plus tie-breaking 3rd reader if necessary; 2 readings per entry **Future commitment:** Conference retains 1st publication rights until Jun. 1, 1991. **Comment:** The judges reserve the right to withhold the award if in their opinion no entry merits it.

MILL MOUNTAIN THEATRE NEW PLAY COMPETITION
1 Market Square, Center in the Square,
Roanoke, VA 24011 (703) 342-5730
Contact: Jo Weinstein, Literary Manager **Frequency**: annual
Award: $500, staged reading, stipend, possible production with
travel to be determined by location of author **Works**: full-length
plays, single and related one-acts, musicals **Special interest**:
"Mixed casts, but not to the exclusion of others." **Regulations**:
authors must reside in U.S.; entries must be unpublished and
unproduced except in developmental workshops; no more than 2
entries per author **Specifications**: maximum cast: 12; unit set
preferred **Stages**: proscenium, 462 seats; flexible, 150 seats
Audience: "A conservative audience that is becoming increasingly
excited by innovative directing." **Procedure**: send SASE for
guidelines **Deadline**: Jan. 1, 1990; no submissions before Oct. 1,
1990 for 1991 deadline **Notification:** Aug. 1, 1990 **Your
chances**: 300+ entries/5 judges/2-3 readings per entry **Future
commitment**: "None, unless we have had an extensive role in the
development of the play." **Advice**: "Present your own play in a neat
professional manner." **Comment:** The judges reserve the right to
withhold the award if in their opinion no entry merits it.

MIXED BLOOD VERSUS AMERICA
Mixed Blood Theatre Company, 1501 S. 4th St.,
Minneapolis, MN 55454 (612) 338-0937
Contact: David Kunz, Script Czar **Frequency**: annual **Award**:
$2000, production **Works:** full-length plays, musicals
Regulations: authors must have had at least 1 work produced by a
professional or educational theatre (workshop production qualifies);
entries must be unproduced; no more than 2 entries per author;
previous entries ineligible **Procedure:** send script with SASE and
resume or other proof of produced work **Deadline**: Apr. 15, 1990
Notification: fall 1990

THE MOBIL PLAYWRITING COMPETITION
The Royal Exchange Theatre Company,
St. Ann's Square, Manchester M2 7DH, England
(061) 833-9333, -9938 Contact: Literary Manager
Frequency: every 2-3 years **Awards**: 1st prize £10,000, 2nd
prize £5000, 3rd prize £3000, international prize £3000, special
prizes £1000; possible production with negotiable payment, possible
publication, possible 1-year residency at Royal Exchange Theatre
Works: full-length plays **Regulations**: authors may be of any
nationality; entries must be written in English, unproduced and not on
offer elsewhere **Stage**: theatre-in-the-round, 740 seats
Procedure: send SASE for guidelines **Deadline**: inquire (Jan. 16 in

1988) **Your chances**: 1500-2000 entries/6 judges/at least 2 readings per entry, 9-10 for shortlisted scripts

THE MORTON R. SARETT MEMORIAL AWARD
Department of Theatre Arts,
University of Nevada-Las Vegas, 4505 Maryland Pkwy.,
Las Vegas, NV 89154 (702) 739-3666
Contact: Paul Harris, Professor of Theatre **Frequency**: biennial, even years **Award**: $3000, full or workshop production, residency **Works**: full-length plays, musicals **Regulations**: entries must not have been published or produced by profit-making companies **Stages:** proscenium, 570 seats; black box, 180 seats **Audience:** "Students and season subscribers." **Procedure**: send SASE for guidelines and application form; 2 copies of script required upon entry **Deadline**: Jan. 30, 1990 **Your chances**: 300 entries/25-30 judges **Comment:** "An announced winner is not mandatory for every playwriting competition."

MULTICULTURAL PLAYWRIGHTS FESTIVAL
The Group Theatre Company, 3940 Brooklyn Ave. NE,
Seattle, WA 98105 (206) 545-4969
Contact: Tim Bond, Festival Director **Frequency**: annual **Awards**: 1st prize $1000, workshop production, travel, housing for 2 winners; 4-6 rehearsed readings; participation in 2-week festival (Jun. 1991) **Works**: full-length plays, single one-acts, adaptations **Regulations**: authors must be "Asian, Black, Chicano/Hispanic or Native American and must be U.S. residents"; entries must not have been given full Equity production; no musicals or children's plays **Specifications**: maximum cast: 10 preferred; small sets **Stage**: modified thrust, 200-213 seats **Audience:** "Middle income, ethnically diverse." **Procedure:** send script with SASE, resume and cover letter, mark "Attn: Festival" **Deadline**: Sept. 15, 1990 postmark **Notification:** Feb. 1991 **Your chances:** 200 entries/9 judges/1-8 readings per entry **Advice:** "Send us your entries early to avoid the last minute rush."

NATIONAL ARCHIVES PLAYWRITING COMPETITION
National Archives and Records Administration,
Educational Branch, NEE-E, National Archives,
Washington, DC 20408 (202) 523-3347
Contact: Chairman **Frequency**: annual **Awards**: 1st prize $450, 2nd prize $250; possible production **Works**: full-length plays without act breaks, one-acts, musicals **Exclusive interest:** "Scripts based on any event(s) within the past 200 years which deal with the issues raised by the Bill of Rights or by the 14th and 15th Amendments." **Regulations:** entries must be unpublished and

unproduced and "must be based on records held by National Archives, its field branches, and/or any of the presidential libraries"; no more than 1 entry per author **Specifications:** maximum cast: 6-8; few scenes; minimal set and lighting requirements; no fly space; 1 wing 3'x6'; no more than 3 instruments for musicals; playing time: 45-90 minutes preferred **Stage:** 26' wide by 12'6" deep **Audience:** "Interested in historic plays; general public, educators." **Procedure:** send SASE for guidelines **Deadline:** Jan. 15, 1990 **Notification:** Apr. 1990

NATIONAL JEWISH THEATER PLAY WRITING COMPETITION
5050 W. Church St., Skokie, IL 60077 (312) 675-2200
Contact: Sheldon Patinkin, Artistic Director **Frequency:** undetermined **Awards:** 1st prize $2000, workshop production, possible mainstage production, 5-week residency; 2nd prize $500, reading, housing **Works:** full-length plays **Exclusive interest:** "The contemporary Jewish experience." **Specifications:** "Scripts should not be about the holocaust." **Stage:** open, 250 seats **Procedure:** send SASE for guidelines **Deadline:** inquire (Dec. 1 in 1989)

NATIONAL MUSIC THEATER CONFERENCE
Eugene O'Neill Memorial Theater Center Suite 901,
234 W. 44th St., New York, NY 10036
(212) 382-2790 **Contact:** Paulette Haupt, Artistic Director **Frequency:** annual **Award:** development, possible staged reading, $250 stipend, travel, housing and board for Conference (Aug.) in Waterford, CT **Works:** musicals, musical adaptations **Regulations:** authors must be U.S. citizens; entries must be unproduced and unoptioned; adaptors must secure permission; participants must be in residence for entire conference period **Procedure:** request guidelines and application form **Deadline:** Feb. 1, 1990 (tentative date; inquire)

NATIONAL ONE-ACT PLAY CONTEST
Actors Theatre of Louisville, 316 W. Main St.,
Louisville, KY 40202 (502) 584-1265
Contact: Michael Bigelow Dixon, Literary Manager **Frequency:** annual **Award:** $1000, possible production **Works:** single and related one-acts **Regulations:** authors must be citizens or residents or U.S.; entries must not be published or professionally produced; no more than 2 entries per author; previous entries ineligible **Maximum length:** 60 pages **Stages:** thrust, 650 seats; thrust, 150 seats **Audience:** "A cross-section of the Louisville community." **Procedure:** send script with SASE **Deadline:** Apr. 15, 1990

postmark **Notification:** fall 1990 **Your chances:** 160 entries/judging by ATL staff/2 readings per entry **Advice:** "See contest rules in brochure."

NATIONAL ONE-ACT PLAYWRITING COMPETITION
Little Theatre of Alexandria, 600 Wolfe St., Alexandria, VA 22314 (703) 683-5778
Contact: Chairman, Playreading Committee **Frequency:** annual **Awards:** 1st prize $350, 2nd prize $250, 3rd prize $150; possible production **Works:** single one-acts **Exclusive interest:** "Stage plays only!" **Regulations:** entries must be unpublished and unproduced; no more than 1 entry per author **Specifications:** single set preferred; few scene changes; playing time: 20–60 minutes **Stage:** proscenium, 210 seats **Audience:** "Sophisticated theatre audience; conservative." **Procedure:** request guidelines; entry fee may be announced **Deadline:** Mar. 31, 1990 postmark **Notification:** Dec. 1990 **Your chances:** 100 entries/6-8 judges/4-6 readings per entry **Advice:** Criteria for judging are concept, dramatic action, characterization, dialogue, stageability and technical requirements; "judges are favorably inclined toward scripts which have a running time of 20–60 minutes; in which a precis of the play precedes abstract works; and in which a description of each character appears, either at the beginning or as each character first appears on stage." **Comment:** Theatre reserves the right to withhold any or all awards.

NATIONAL PLAY AWARD
National Repertory Theatre Foundation, Box 71011, Los Angeles, CA 90071 (213) 629-3762, 626-5944
Contact: Lloyd Steele, Literary Manager **Frequency:** biennial even years **Awards:** $7500 to playwright; $5000 to qualified professional theatre to aid production **Works:** full-length plays, one-acts comprising a full evening **Exclusive interest:** "Original plays conceived for production on the living stage." **Regulations:** entries must not be published or produced with a paid Equity cast and may not have won a major award; previous entries ineligible; no musicals, translations or adaptations **Procedure:** send SASE for guidelines or send script with SASE to National Play Award, 630 N. Grand Ave. Suite 405, Los Angeles, CA 90012 **Deadline:** Jul. 1, 1990 postmark **Notification:** early 1992 **Your chances:** 1100 entries/8 preliminary readers and 5 judges/2-3 readings per entry **Future commitment:** no **Comment:** The judges reserve the right to withhold the award if in their opinion no entry merits it, "but this has never happened."

NATIONAL PLAYWRIGHTS CONFERENCE/ NEW DRAMA FOR TELEVISION PROJECT

Eugene O'Neill Memorial Theater Center Suite 901, 234 W. 44th St., New York, NY 10036 (212) 382-2790 **Contact**: Peggy Vernieu, Administrator **Frequency**: annual **Award**: development, staged reading or videotaping, stipend, travel, housing and board for Conference in Waterford, CT **Works**: original full-length plays, single and related one-acts **Regulations**: authors must be U.S. residents; entries must be unproduced and uncommitted; no adaptations; no more than 1 entry per author per category; stage and TV **Procedure**: send SASE for guidelines from New York office Sept.–Nov. 1990 **Deadline**: Dec. 1, 1990 postmark **Notification**: Apr. 1991 **Your chances**: 1200+ entries/varying number of judges and readings per entry **Comment**: See Backalenick, Irene, "In the Shadow of O'Neill," *TheaterWeek* (Aug. 21, 1989), 28–31.

NATIONAL PLAYWRIGHTS SHOWCASE

Erie, PA This contest has been discontinued.

NATIONAL TEN-MINUTE PLAY CONTEST

Actors Theatre of Louisville, 316 W. Main St., Louisville, KY 40402 (502) 584-1265 **Contact**: Michael Bigelow Dixon, Literary Manager **Frequency**: annual **Awards**: $1000 Heideman Award, production **Works**: short plays **Special interests**: "Plays with 3 or more characters aged 18–28." **Regulations**: entries must be unproduced; no more than 2 entries per author **Specifications**: no more than 1 set; maximum length: 10 minutes, 10 pages **Stage**: black box **Procedure**: send SASE for guidelines **Deadline**: inquire (Dec. 1 in 1989) **Your chances**: 2000 entries/6 judges/2 readings per entry **Future commitment**: inquire

NETWORK NEW MUSIC THEATER AWARDS PROGRAM

National Music Theater Network, 1457 Broadway Suite 1111, New York, NY 10036 (212) 382-0984 **Contact**: C. Carroll Carter Jr., Executive Director **Frequency**: annual **Awards**: $1000 to writer/composer team; $4000 to first theatre to produce work **Works**: musicals, operas **Regulations**: authors must be American writers and composers; entries must be suitable for general audiences **Procedure**: send SASE for guidelines and application form; $30 fee upon entry **Deadline**: Jun. 30, 1990 **Notification**: Sept. 30, 1990 **Comment**: Formerly Seagram's New Music Theater Awards Program.

NEW AMERICAN COMEDY FESTIVAL
**Ukiah Players Theatre, 1041 Low Gap Rd.,
Ukiah, CA 95482 (707) 462-1210**
Contact: Catherine Babcock Magruder, Artistic Director
Frequency: biennial even years **Awards**: $300, staged reading, travel (up to $300), lodging, per diem during festival for 2 winners **Works**: full-length comedies **Regulations**: entries must be unpublished and unproduced; winning playwrights must attend Festival in Aug. 1990 **Specifications**: small cast, simple set preferred **Stage**: proscenium, 133 seats **Casting**: "Company directors will cast from available local actors." **Audience**: "A mixed audience in age and background in this rural northern California community." **Procedure**: send SASE for guidelines and application form **Deadline**: Feb. 1, 1990 **Notification**: May 1990 **Your chances**: 200 entries/5 judges/3 readings per entry **Comment**: The judges reserve the right to withhold the award if in their opinion no entry merits it.

NEW WORLD THEATER NEW PLAY COMPETITION
**7600 Red Rd. Suite 212, South Miami, FL 33143-5424
(305) 663-0208, -0223** **Contact**: Kenneth A. Cotthoff, Executive Director **Frequency**: annual **Awards**: $500, production for as many as 3 winners **Works**: full-length plays **Special interests**: Florida locations or themes; interracial and/or inter-ethnic casts; strong female roles **Regulations**: entries must not be published or professionally produced **Specifications**: maximum cast: 4; single full set, "may have minor secondary or several minimal sets"; modest production requirements **Procedure**: send SASE for guidelines **Deadline**: May 1, 1990 **Notification**: Oct. 1990 **Comments**: "In addition to the usual elements of plot, characterization, dialogue, etc., plays will be judged in the following areas: entertainment value, relevance in today's world, broadness of appeal." "Authors must be willing to see play developed in workshop!" New World Theater claims "customary subsidiary rights" to winning plays.

NFJC HEBREW TRANSLATION COMMISSION
**National Foundation for Jewish Culture,
330 Seventh Ave. 21st Floor, New York, NY 10001
(212) 629-0500** **Contact**: Andrea Aronson Morgan, Program Officer **Award**: up to $1000 to be matched by producing theatre **Works**: translations **Regulations**: entries must be first translations or first stageworthy translations into English of Hebrew plays **Procedure**: nomination by theatre interested in producing translation; send SASE for guidelines **Deadline**: ongoing program

1990 ANNUAL ONE-ACT FESTIVAL COMPETITION
Virginia Beach Parks and Recreation,
Virginia Beach Recreation Center, Kempsville,
800 Monmouth Ln., Virginia Beach, VA 23464-2998
(804) 495-1892 Contact: Eileen M. Gatliffe, Special Operations
Coordinator **Awards**: production (Jan.), videotape and plaque for
each of 3 winners **Works**: one-acts **Special interests**: realistic
comedies and dramas **Specifications**: maximum cast: 7; simple
technical demands; playing time: 30-45 minutes; no obscene language
or situations **Audience**: "Mature." **Procedure**: send SASE for
guidelines **Deadline**: inquire (Nov. 15 in 1989) **Your chances**:
60-80 entries/3 judges/3-5 readings per entry **Comment**: Formerly
listed as Ones at Eight Annual One-Act Festival.

NO EMPTY SPACE THEATRE PLAYWRITING CONTEST
568 Metropolitan Ave., Staten Island, NY 10301
Contact: James E. Stayoch, Producing Director **Frequency**:
biennial even years **Award**: $500, possible production **Works**:
full-length plays, one-acts, translations, adaptations, musicals,
children's plays **Regulations**: entries must be unpublished and
unproduced **Specifications**: "Technical considerations will not
affect winning but may effect production." **Procedure**: send SASE
for guidelines **Deadline**: Dec. 31, 1990; no submissions before Feb.
Your chances: 100 entries/2 judges **Advice**: "Serious work."

NORTHBAY PLAYWRIGHTING CONTEST
Department of Theatre Arts, Sonoma State University,
Rohnert Park, CA 94928 (707) 664-2474
Contact: Elizabeth Craven, Project Director **Frequency**: biennial
even years **Award**: $1000, production **Works**: full-length plays,
adaptations **Regulations**: entries must be unpublished and
unproduced; adaptations must be of material in the public domain;
winning author must be available for 2-week residency **Procedure**:
send SASE for guidelines and application form; $10 fee upon entry
Deadline: Oct. 1990 (inquire)

NORTHWEST PLAYWRIGHTS GUILD COMPETITION
Box 95259, Seattle, WA 98145 (206) 365-6026
Contact: Sharon Glantz, Project Director **Works**: full-length
plays, one-acts, musicals, children's plays **Awards**: 3 evenings of
staged readings of selected plays **Special Interest**: "International
themes." **Regulations**: playwrights must reside in AK, ID, MT, OR,
WA or WY **Procedure**: send script with SASE, synopsis and entry
fee: Northwest Playwrights Guild dues ($30 1st year, $20 yearly
renewal; see listing in Special Programs) **Deadline**: inquire (Apr. 30
in 1989)

OFF-OFF BROADWAY ORIGINAL SHORT PLAY FESTIVAL
Double Image Theatre, 445 W. 59th St., New York, NY 10019 (212) 245-2489 **Contact**: William Talbot, Festival Coordinator **Frequency**: annual **Award**: publication by Samuel French (see Publishers) **Works**: segments of full-length plays, one-act plays, translations, adaptations, musicals and children's plays **Regulations**: entries must be unpublished products of theatres, professional schools or colleges that have fostered playwriting for at least 2 years **Playing time**: 40 minutes or less **Audience**: "New York City." **Procedure**: nomination by producing organization; guidelines available in Feb. **Deadline**: Apr. 1990 (inquire) **Notification**: May 1990 **Your chances**: 140 entries/6 critics as judges

OGLEBAY INSTITUTE TOWNGATE THEATRE PLAYWRITING CONTEST
See Towngate Theatre Playwriting Contest listing in this section.

ONES AT EIGHT ANNUAL ONE-ACT FESTIVAL
See 1990 Annual One-Act Festival Competition listing under "N" in this section.

ON THEMES OF RURAL AMERICA
See Arrow Rock Lyceum Theatre National Playwrights Competition listing in this section.

PAUL T. NOLAN AWARD
Deep South Writers Conference, USL Box 44691, University of Southwestern Louisiana, Lafayette, LA 70504 **Contact**: John Fiero, Director **Frequency**: annual **Awards**: 1st prize $200, possible publication; 2nd prize $100 **Works**: one-acts **Regulations**: entries must be original plays; no adaptations or musicals; no more than 3 entries per author **Procedure**: send SASE for guidelines; $5 fee upon entry **Deadline**: Jul. 15, 1990 **Notification**: "Just prior to Deep South Writers Conference (see Special Programs) in Sept." **Your chances**: 50 entries/3 judges/up to 3 readings per entry **Future Commitment**: right to 1 production, first publication until Jun. 1, 1991 **Comments**: Entries will not be returned.

PEACE PLAY CONTEST
Goshen College, Theatre Office, Goshen, IN 46526 (219) 535-7393 **Contact**: Lauren Friesen, Director of Theatre **Frequency**: biennial odd years **Award**: $500, production **Works**: single and related one-acts **Regulations**: entries must not be

published or professionally produced and must deal with peace and conflict resolution **Maximum cast**: 8 **Stage**: semi-thrust--410 seats **Casting**: "Students; non-traditional casting; cold-reading auditions." **Audience**: "College faculty and students." **Procedure**: send SASE for guidelines **Deadline**: inquire (Dec. 31 in 1989) **Your chances**: 100 entries/3 judges/4 readings per entry

PEN TRANSLATION PRIZE
PEN American Center, 568 Broadway, New York, NY 10012 (212) 334-1660
Contact: John Morrone, Program Coordinator **Frequency**: annual **Award**: $3000 **Works**: translations **Regulations**: entries must be book-length translations from any language into English published in U.S. during current calendar year **Procedure**: send SASE for guidelines; 2 copies of book required upon entry **Deadline**: inquire (Dec. 31 in 1989)

PHILADELPHIA BAR ASSOCIATION THEATRE WING PLAYWRITING COMPETITION
One Reading Center, Philadelphia, PA 19107 (215) 238-6300 **Contact**: Theatre Wing Committee, Playwriting Contact **Frequency**: annual **Award**: $5000, possible production **Works**: full-length plays **Exclusive interest**: "Works which address some aspect of the legal profession." **Regulations**: entries must be unpublished and must not have been professionally produced or have won major awards **Procedure**: request guidelines **Deadline**: inquire (Nov. 15 in 1989)

PLAYS FOR A NEW AMERICA
Department of Theatre and Dance, University of Alabama, Box 870239, Tuscaloosa, AL 35487 (205) 348-5283
Contact: Paul Castagno, Director of Theatre **Frequency**: annual **Award**: $1000, production **Works**: full-length plays **Special interests**: "Positive forces in America; humanistic concerns; non-realistic and post-modern format." **Regulations**: entries must be unpublished and unproduced **Procedure**: send SASE for guidelines; small fee upon entry **Deadline**: Mar. 15, 1990 **Notification**: May 1, 1990

PLAYWRIGHT'S FORUM AWARDS
Theatreworks, University of Colorado, Box 7150, Colorado Springs, CO 80933 (719) 593-3232, -3275
Contact: Whit Andrews, Producing Director **Frequency**: annual **Awards**: 2 awards of $200, production, travel ($350) **Works**: single and related one-acts **Special interests**: "Experimental work and comedy." **Regulations**: entries must be unpublished and

unproduced; no more than 1 entry per author **Specifications**: maximum cast: 12; modest technical requirements; playing time: 1 hour maximum **Stage:** thrust, 185 seats **Audience:** "Diverse." **Procedure:** send SASE for guidelines **Deadline**: Dec. 15, 1990 **Notification:** Mar. 1, 1991 **Your chances:** 800 entries/10 judges/2 readings per entry **Advice:** "We like passion, theatricality, risk taking; honest dialogue as opposed to an attempt to impress. A little good, old fashioned outrageousness doesn't hurt, either."

PORTLAND STATE UNIVERSITY
NEW PLAYS IN PROGRESS SERIES
Dept. of Theatre Arts, Box 751, Portland, OR 97207
(503) 464-4612 **Contact**: Pauline E. Peotter, Director
Frequency: annual **Award**: production with royalty, residency
Works: full-length plays, one-acts **Regulations**: authors must be residents of OR or WA; entries must be unproduced; no more than 1 entry per author; authors must attend at least 1 week of rehearsals (local authors must attend 6 weeks) during Oct.-Nov. 1990 **Procedure**: send script with SASE **Deadline**: Jan. 8, 1990 **Notification:** spring 1990

PURGATORY THEATER
NATIONAL PLAYWRITING COMPETITION
Box 666, Durango, CO 81302 (303) 247-9000 ext. 231
Contact: Ron Sanford, Executive Producer **Frequency**: annual **Award**: $2000, production **Works**: full-length plays **Regulations**: entries must be unpublished and unproduced and must not have won major awards; no more than 2 entries per author **Specifications**: maximum cast: 10; playing time: approximately 2 hours; "no nudity, no obscenity, no issues or activities included for shock value only" **Stage:** platform-thrust **Audience:** "Mainly adults, resort oriented." **Procedure:** send SASE for guidelines **Deadline**: Apr. 1, 1990 **Notification:** Jun. 1990 **Advice:** "Only the first 250 entries will be considered."

QRL POETRY SERIES
Quarterly Review of Literature, **Princeton University, 26 Haslet Ave., Princeton, NJ 08540 (609) 921-6976**
Frequency: annual **Award**: $1000, publication **Works**: full-length plays, single and related one-acts, translations **Exclusive interest**: "Poetic plays." **Length**: 40-89 pages **Procedure**: send SASE for guidelines; $20 fee upon entry includes subscription **Deadlines**: May 1990, Nov. 1990 (inquire)

RADIO DRAMA AWARDS
Madison, WI This contest is inactive in 1990.

REGIONAL CHILDREN'S THEATRE COMPETITION 1990
**Columbia Entertainment Co., 309 Parkdale Ave.,
Columbia, MO 65202 (314) 874-5628**
Contact: Betsy Phillips, Chairperson **Frequency:** annual **Award**:
$250, production in Dec. 1990 **Works:** children's full-length plays,
musicals **Exclusive interest:** "Large-cast plays with characters
of all ages to be presented by our theatre school pupils, aged 8-15."
Regulations: entries must be unpublished and unproduced except in
staged readings or workshops **Specifications**: maximum cast: 40;
"children will be moving set pieces; costumes can be built; however,
we prefer to use what we have in stock" **Stage:** 180 seats;
"primarily we work on a thrust or proscenium" **Casting:** "Every
child in our theatre school gets a part with lines. We do double cast
larger roles." **Audience:** "Parents, general public and children,
median age 12 years." **Procedure:** send SASE for guidelines
Deadline: Jun. 30, 1990 postmark; no entries before Feb.
Notification: Aug. 15, 1990 **Your chances:** 33 entries (based
on 2nd year)/8 judges/3-8 readings per entry **Advice:** "Please
remember that young people (ages 8-15) enjoy portraying diverse
human or fantastical beings. They have experienced many of life's
lessons at earlier ages than adults. Our 'ideal' play is one that has a
message without moralizing, does not talk down to the audience and is
fun and challenging for our students to act in." **Comment:** The
judges reserve the right to withhold the award if in their opinion no
entry merits it.

RENATO POGGIOLI TRANSLATION AWARD
**PEN American Center, 568 Broadway,
New York, NY 10012 (212) 334-1660**
Contact: Christine Friedlander **Frequency**: annual **Award**: $3000
grant **Works**: translations **Special interest**: "The focus of the
prize is on Italian translation, not plays." **Regulations**: authors must
be "beginning and promising translators working on their first
book-length translations from Italian into English"; works-in-progress
accepted **Procedure**: send letters of application, curriculum vitae
including the candidate's Italian studies, statement of purpose, sample
of translation with original Italian text **Deadline**: Feb. 1, 1990
postmark **Notification:** May 1990 **Comment:** It is preferred
that the grant period be spent in Italy.

THE RICHARD RODGERS PRODUCTION AWARD
**American Academy and Institute of Arts and Letters,
633 W. 155th St., New York, NY 10032 (212) 368-5900**
Contact: Lydia Kaim, Assistant to the Executive Director
Frequency: annual **Awards**: up to $100,000 and/or developmental
grants of up to $15,000 for workshop productions by New York City

not-for-profit theatres **Works:** musicals **Regulations**: authors must be citizens or permanent residents of U.S. and must not be established in the field; entries must not have been commercially produced; no more than 1 entry per author; previous entries ineligible **Procedure:** send SASE for guidelines and application form **Deadline**: inquire (Nov. 6 in 1989) **Your chances:** 180 entries/9 judges **Advice:** "Innovative and experimental work."

ROBERT J. PICKERING AWARD
FOR PLAYWRITING EXCELLENCE
**Coldwater Community Theater, 89 S. Division,
Coldwater, MI 49036 (517) 278-2389, 279-7963**
Contact: J. Richard Colbeck, Chairman, Play Selection Committee **Frequency**: annual **Awards**: 1st prize $200, production, housing to attend performance, production agreement; 2nd prize $75; 3rd prize $25 **Works:** full-length plays, children's plays **Exclusive interest:** works of interest to a Midwestern audience **Regulations**: entries must be unproduced **Stage:** proscenium, 500 seats **Procedure:** send SASE for guidelines **Deadline**: inquire (Nov. 15 in 1989) **Your chances:** 200 entries/6 judges/6 readings per entry

RUBY LLOYD APSEY PLAYWRITING COMPETITION
Birmingham, AL This contest is inactive in 1990.

SAN DIEGO JUNIOR THEATRE
PLAYWRITING COMPETITION
**Casa del Prado Room #208, Balboa Park,
San Diego, CA 92101 (619) 239-1311**
Contact: James Saba **Frequency:** annual **Award:** $1000 **Works:** children's plays, adaptations and musicals **Special interests:** "Hip, new, innovative and exciting works to be enjoyed by audiences of all ages." **Regulations:** entries must be unproduced; adaptors must secure permission **Specifications:** entries must be suitable for performers in 8-18 age range **Procedure:** send SASE for guidelines **Deadline:** Aug. 1, 1990 **Advice:** "Please follow professional script format."

SCHOLASTIC WRITING AWARDS
**Scholastic, Inc., 730 Broadway, New York,
NY 10003 (212) 505-3404 Contact**: Chuck Wentzel, Director, Awards Program **Frequency**: annual **Awards**: cash prizes of $50-$125; 2 $1000-scholarships **Works:** one-act plays, screenplays, radio and TV scripts **Regulations**: authors must be students in grades 7-12; entries must be unpublished **Playing time:** 30 minutes **Procedure:** send SASE for guidelines and application form **Deadline**: Jan. 17, 1990 postmark **Notification:** May 1990

Your chances: 1500 entries/15 judges/3 readings per entry **Advice:** "For young playwrights: edit, edit, edit. Be medium specific when writing."

SEAGRAM'S NEW MUSIC THEATER AWARDS
See Network New Music Theater Awards Program listing in this section.

S. ELIZABETH POPE PLAYWRITING COMPETITION
Bridgewater State College Alumni Association,
Box 13, Bridgewater, MA 02324 (508) 697-1288
Contact: Philip Conroy, Director, Alumni Association **Frequency:** annual **Award:** $3000, production **Works:** full-length plays **Regulations:** entries must be unpublished and unproduced **Procedure:** send SASE for guidelines **Deadline:** inquire (Nov. in 1989)

SETC NEW PLAY PROJECT
Department of Performing Arts, Clemson University,
Clemson, SC 29634-1505 (803) 656-3043
Contact: Clifton S. M. Egan, Chairman, New Play Project **Frequency:** annual **Award:** $250, staged reading, travel, publicity and recommendation to the O'Neill Theater Center (see National Playwrights Conference listing in this section) **Works:** full-length plays, related one-acts **Regulations:** entries must be unpublished and unproduced **Procedure:** send SASE for guidelines **Deadline:** Jul. 31, 1990; no submission before Mar. 15 **Notification:** Oct. 1990 **Your chances:** 180 entries/15 judges/1 initial reading per entry, 5 in final round

SIENA COLLEGE PLAYWRIGHT'S COMPETITION
Theatre Program, Dept. of Fine Arts, Siena College,
Loudonville, NY 12211 (518) 783-2381
Contact: Mark A. Heckler, Director of Theatre **Frequency:** biennial even years **Award:** $2000, production, up to $1000 for travel and housing **Works:** full-length plays **Regulations:** entries must be unpublished and unproduced; no musicals; winning author must participate in 4-week residency program (Jan.-Feb. 1991) **Specifications:** maximum cast: 10, 3-6 preferred; single or unit set; entries must be suitable for college-age performers **Stages:** proscenium; thrust **Audience:** college and local community **Procedure:** before entering send notification of entry including play title, author's name, address, phone number, resume and SASE (inquire for more details) **Deadline:** Jun. 30, 1990 postmark; no submission before Feb. 1 **Your chances:** 300+ entries/3 judges/1-3 readings per entry **Advice:** "Submit scripts

suitable for undergraduate theatre students in a liberal arts college rather than a pre-professional training program."

THE SOCIETY OF MIDLAND AUTHORS DRAMA AWARD
c/o Chicago Tribune, 435 N. Michigan Ave., Chicago, IL 60611 (312) 222-1154
Contact: Rick Kogan, General Awards Chairman **Frequency**: annual **Award**: $400, staged reading, workshop or full production **Works**: full-length plays, one-acts **Regulations**: authors must be current residents of IA, IL, IN, KS, MI, MN, MO, ND, NE, OH, SD or WI; entries must have been given their 1st reading or production in 1989 **Procedure**: send SASE for guidelines and application form **Deadline**: Feb. 15, 1990 **Notification**: spring 1990 **Your chances**: varying number of entries/3 judges/3 readings per entry

SOURCE THEATRE
NATIONAL PLAYWRITING COMPETITION
1809 14th St. NW, Washington, DC 20009
(202) 462-1073 Contact: Pat Murphy Sheehy, Artistic Director **Frequency**: annual **Awards**: 1st prize $250, production; finalists $50, workshop production **Works**: full-length plays, one-acts, musicals **Regulations**: entries must not have been professionally produced **Procedure**: send script with SASE, synopsis and resume **Deadline**: Mar. 15, 1990 **Notification**: Jun. 1, 1990 **Comment**: "All entries will also be considered for SourceWorks reading series and The Washington Theatre Festival" (see Special Programs).

SOUTH CAROLINA NEW PLAY FESTIVAL
Trustus Theatre, Box 11721, Columbia, SC 29211
(803) 254-9732 Contact: Jim Thigpen, Artistic Director **Frequency**: annual **Awards**: 1st prize cash award, production; 2 runners-up receive cash awards, staged readings **Works**: full-length plays, one-acts, translations, adaptations, children's plays **Regulations**: authors must have some connection with South Carolina; entries must be unproduced, but plays with previous readings or workshops are preferred; no musicals **Specifications**: maximum cast: 8 with doubling; single set preferred **Stage**: flexible, 99 seats **Casting**: "Open; color-blind." **Audience**: "A marvelous cross-section of theatregoers and non-theatregoers." **Procedure**: send script with SASE **Deadline**: Apr. 1, 1990 **Notification**: Jun. 1, 1990 **Your chances**: 35 entries in 1989/3 judges/4 readings per entry **Comments**: "We are unique in that our seats are over-stuffed swivel rocking chairs, and we have a bar that serves wine and beer." The judges reserve the right to withhold the award if in their opinion no entry merits it.

SOUTHEAST REGION YOUNG PLAYWRIGHT AND CHILDREN'S THEATRE FESTIVAL

Theatre Winter Haven, Box 1615, Winter Haven, FL 33882
(813) 299-2672 Contact: Ruthann Benson, Director of Theatre School; Thomas Altman, Playwright in Residence **Frequency:** annual **Awards:** 1st prize $300, 2nd prize $200, 3rd prize $100; production in summer festival, up to $750 travel, housing **Regulations:** authors must be aged 23 or younger; entries must be unpublished; no adaptations **Procedure:** send 2 copies of script with SASE, playwright's date of birth and contact information on title page and $5 entry fee **Deadline:** Jan. 15, 1990 **Notification:** Mar. 15, 1990

SOUTHERN PLAYWRIGHTS COMPETITION

Center for Southern Studies, 114 Martin Hall,
Jacksonville State University, Jacksonville, AL 36265
(205) 231-5226 Contact: Steven J. Whitton
Award: $1000, production (May 1990) **Works:** full-length plays **Exclusive interest:** "The Southern experience." **Regulations:** authors must be natives or residents of the South; entries must be unproduced **Procedure:** write or phone for guidelines and application forms **Deadline:** Feb. 15, 1990

STANLEY DRAMA AWARD

Department of Languages and Literature,
Wagner College, 631 Howard Ave.,
Staten Island, NY 10301 (718) 390-3256, -3100
Contact: Director **Frequency:** annual **Award:** $1000, possible production **Works:** full-length plays, related one-acts, musicals **Regulations:** entries must not be published or professionally produced; entries must be recommended by a theatre professional or teacher of creative writing or drama; former Stanley winners ineligible **Procedure:** send SASE for guidelines and application form **Deadline:** Sept. 1, 1990 postmark **Notification:** Mar. 1991 **Your chances:** 100 entries/10 judges/1-4 readings per entry

THE STEINBECK PLAYWRITING COMPETITION

The Western Stage of Hartnell College,
156 Homestead Ave., Salinas, CA 93901 (408) 755-6990
Contact: Joyce Lower, Dramaturg **Frequency:** annual **Awards:** 1st prize cash award, production with royalty, residency, possible publication; staged reading for all finalists; winner selected from readings **Works:** full-length plays **Exclusive interest:** "Works in the spirit of John Steinbeck." **Maximum cast:** 60 **Regulations:** entries must be unproduced except in readings, workshops; no more than 1 entry per author **Stages:** proscenium, 540 seats; modified

thrust, 200 seats; arena, 120 seats; "environmental staging on our large stage" **Casting:** "Most actors are in or have recently graduated from MFA or equivalent programs; limited Equity contract." **Audience:** "Diverse." **Procedure:** send SASE for guidelines **Deadline:** Dec. 31, 1990 postmark; no submissions before Oct. 1 **Your chances:** 500-1000 entries/15 judges/5-6 readings per entry **Advice:** "Remember that the spirit of Steinbeck encompasses an enormous range of human experience."

SUMMERFIELD G. ROBERTS AWARD
The Sons of the Republic of Texas,
5942 Abrams Rd. Suite 222, Dallas, TX 75231
(214) 343-2145 Contact: Maydee J. Scurlock **Frequency:** annual **Award:** $2500 **Works:** full-length plays **Exclusive interest:** "Life in the Republic of Texas." **Regulations:** entries must have been completed during the calendar year preceding deadline **Procedure:** send 5 copies of script **Deadline:** Jan. 31, 1990 **Notification:** early Apr. 1990 **Comment:** Scripts will not be returned.

THE SUSAN SMITH BLACKBURN PRIZE
3239 Avalon Pl., Houston, TX 77019 (713) 522-8529
Contact: Emilie S. Kilgore, Board of Directors **Frequency:** annual **Awards:** 1st prize $5000; runner-up $1000 **Regulations:** authors must be women of any nationality, writing in English; entries must be unproduced or produced within 1 year of deadline **Procedure:** nomination by professional artistic director, literary manager or dramaturg; 2 copies of script required upon nomination **Deadline:** inquire (Sept. 22 in 1989)

TCG TRANSLATION/ADAPTATION COMMISSIONS
Theatre Communications Group, 355 Lexington Ave.,
New York, NY 10017 (212) 697-5230
Contact: Tony Kushner, Director of Literary Services **Award:** up to $1000 to be matched by producing TCG-member theatre **Works:** translations, adaptations **Regulations:** entries must be first or first stageworthy translations or adaptations of classic or contemporary plays or nondramatic works in any foreign language **Procedure:** application from TCG-member theatre interested in producing work **Deadline:** ongoing program

THE TEN-MINUTE MUSICALS PROJECT
Box 461194, West Hollywood, CA 90046
(213) 656-8751 Contact: Michael Koppy, Producer **Frequency:** annual **Award:** $250, development toward production in a collection **Works:** musical one-acts and excerpts **Special**

Interest: "Short musical scenes." **Specifications:** maximum cast: 12; playing time: 5-15 minutes with sung material comprising at least 2/3 of length; excerpts from longer works must be "completely self-contained" **Procedure:** write or phone for guidelines **Deadline:** Mar. 1, 1990 **Your chances:** 150 entries/9 selections in 1988-89 **Advice:** The Ten-Minute Musicals Project was initiated to encourage composers, librettists and lyricists to create complete short stage musicals. Works can be based on original stories, or, as has often been the case, on extant short stories."

TENNESSEE WILLIAMS/NEW ORLEANS LITERARY FESTIVAL ONE-ACT PLAY CONTEST
Dept. of English, University of New Orleans, New Orleans, LA 70148 (504) 949-9805
Contact: W. Kenneth Holditch, Board of Directors **Frequency:** annual **Award:** $500, staged reading at Tennessee Williams Festival (Mar.) **Works:** one-acts **Exclusive interest:** American subject matter **Regulations:** entries must be unpublished; no musicals **Stage:** proscenium **Procedure:** send script with SASE and $5 fee (check payable to Tennessee Williams Literary Festival) **Deadline:** Feb. 1, 1990 postmark **Your chances:** 200 entries/6 judges/2-4 readings per entry

THEATRE EXPRESS NATIONAL ONE-ACT COMEDY PLAYWRITING CONTEST
90 Wyman St., Lowell, MA 01852 (508) 459-2342
Contact: D.K. Oklahoma **Awards:** production with royalties for 5 winners **Works:** one-acts **Exclusive interest:** comedies **Specifications:** small cast, simple set; playing time: 45-75 minutes **Regulations:** entries must be unpublished; previously developed works preferred **Stage:** Nashoba Valley Dinner Theatre, Westford, MA **Audience:** general **Procedure:** send script with SASE, script history and brief resume **Deadline:** Jan. 15, 1990

THEATRE MEMPHIS NEW PLAY COMPETITION
630 Perkins St. Extended, Memphis, TN 38117-4799
(901) 682-8323 Contact: Martha Graber, Iris Dichtel, Co-Chairmen, New Play Competition **Frequency:** triennial **Awards:** $2500, production, travel, lodging; possible production of runners-up **Works:** full-length plays, related one-acts **Regulations:** entries must not have been professionally produced except in workshops or staged readings; previous entries must be substantially revised and so noted on title page; no musicals **Stages:** proscenium, 435 seats; black box, 100 seats **Casting:** "Open auditions for anyone in the community." **Audience:** "Over 40, middle to upper class." **Procedure:** send SASE for guidelines **Deadline:** Oct. 1, 1990

Notification: early 1991 **Your chances:** 500 entries/10 final round readers/2 readings per entry **Comments:** The judges reserve the right to withhold the award if in their opinion no entry merits it.

THEATREWORKS/USA COMMISSIONING PROGRAM
890 Broadway, New York, NY 10003 (212) 688-0745
Contact: Barbara Pasternack, Literary Manager **Award:** step commissioning process, production **Works:** children's musicals **Special interests:** historical and biographical topics; adaptations of classics and contemporary literature **Specifications:** maximum cast: 5-6 with doubling; set suitable for touring; playing time: 1 hour **Procedure:** send script with SASE or treatment with sample scenes and SASE **Deadline:** ongoing program **Advice:** "Contact us for a schedule of New York City performances; see the kind of work we do."

THEODORE WARD PRIZE FOR PLAYWRITING
Columbia College Chicago, Theatre/Music Center,
72 E. 11th St., Chicago, IL 60605 (312) 663-9462
Contact: Chuck Smith, Facilitator **Frequency:** annual **Awards:** 1st prize $2000, production, travel, housing; 2nd prize $500, staged reading, audio tape **Works:** full-length plays **Regulations:** authors must be of African-American descent; entries must not be published or professionally produced and must be copyrighted; no more than 1 entry per author **Casting:** students **Stage:** black box, 70 seats **Procedure:** send script with SASE, synopsis, resume, script history **Deadline:** Jul. 2, 1990 postmark **Notification:** Oct. 1990 **Your chances:** 80 entries/5 judges/varying number of readings per entry **Comment:** The judges reserve the right to withhold the award if in their opinion no entry merits it.

THIRD STEP THEATRE COMPANY
SPRING FESTIVAL OF STAGED READINGS
1179 Broadway 3rd Floor, New York, NY 10001
(212) 545-1372 Contact: Margit Ahlin, Literary Manager **Frequency:** annual **Awards:** cash award to best play; staged readings followed by discussions **Works:** full-length plays, one-acts, translations, adaptations **Special interests:** "Women and minority playwrights." **Regulations:** no more than 2 entries per author; "no 1-person 'plays' or kitchen drama" **Casting:** "Interracial, often non-traditional." **Procedure:** send 15-page dialogue sample with synopsis for each submission **Deadline:** Jan. 15, 1990 **Notification:** 3 months **Your chances:** 100 entries **Advice:** "Plays should be highly dramatic, socially relevant, lean toward the avant garde, the daring."

TOWNGATE THEATRE PLAYWRITING CONTEST
Oglebay Institute, Oglebay, Wheeling, WV 26003
(304) 242-4200 **Contact**: Debbie ' Hynes, Performing Arts Specialist **Frequency**: annual **Award**: $300, production, some travel **Works**: full-length plays **Regulations**: entries must not be published or professionally produced **Specifications**: no grid or fly space **Stage**: proscenium, 171 seats **Procedure**: send SASE for guidelines **Deadline**: Jan. 1, 1990 postmark **Notification**: May 1, 1990 **Your chances**: 70-100 entries/8-10 judges/1 or more readings per entry **Comment**: The judges reserve the right to withhold the award if in their opinion no entry merits it.

TOWSON STATE UNIVERSITY PRIZE FOR LITERATURE
College of Liberal Arts, Towson, MD 21204
(301) 321-2128 **Contact**: Annette Chappell, Dean, College of Liberal Arts **Frequency**: annual **Award**: $1000 **Works**: single plays, collections **Regulations**: authors must have been Maryland residents for 3 years at time of award and not over 40 years of age; entries must have been published within 3 years prior to nomination or be scheduled for publication within the year **Procedure**: send SASE for guidelines and application form; 4 copies of book required upon entry **Deadline**: May 1, 1990 postmark **Notification**: Sept. 1, 1990 **Your chances**: 10-15 entries/9 judges **Comment**: Entry materials are not returned.

24TH STREET EXPERIMENT
ANNUAL PLAYWRIGHT COMPETITION
Our Lady of the Lake University, 411 Southwest 24th St., San Antonio, TX 78285 (512) 435-2103
Contact: Virginia Hardy **Awards**: $200; staged reading for winner and 3 runners-up **Works**: full-length plays, one-acts, translations, adaptations **Exclusive interest**: "Contemporary themes in new and interesting formats." **Regulations**: entries must be unpublished and unproduced **Specifications**: small cast preferred; playing time: 2 hours **Stage**: proscenium **Audience**: "Socially conscious, mixed ethnic." **Procedure**: send SASE for guidelines **Deadline**: Mar. 1, 1990 **Your chances**: 20 entries normally received

UNICORN THEATRE
NATIONAL PLAYWRIGHT'S COMPETITION
3820 Main St., Kansas City, MO 64111 (816) 531-7529
Contact: Jan Kohl, Literary Manager **Frequency**: annual **Award**: $1000, production with possible residency **Works**: full-length plays **Regulations**: entries must not be published or professionally produced; no musicals or historical plays; no more than 2 entries per author **Specifications**: maximum cast: 10; contemporary settings

Procedure: send script with SASE, 1-page synopsis, cover letter and brief biography **Deadline:** Mar. 1, 1990 **Notification:** Jun. 1990 **Future commitment:** 5% subsidiary rights

UNIVERSITY OF CINCINNATI PLAYWRITING CONTEST/ FESTIVAL OF NEW WORKS
Dept. of Theater, Mail Location 003, Cincinnati, OH 45221 (513) 475-5471 Contact: Michael Hankins, Artistic Director of Drama **Frequency:** biennial odd years **Awards:** $750 for full-length play, $250 for one-act; possible production with development, royalty, travel, housing **Works:** full-length plays, one-acts, musicals **Regulations:** entries may not have been produced professionally; no children's plays; no more than 2 entries per author **Stage:** black box, 100 seats **Procedure:** send SASE for guidelines **Deadline:** inquire (Sept. 30 in 1989) **Your chances:** 400 entries/4 judges/2 readings per entry **Advice:** "Write honestly."

UNIVERSITY OF LOUISVILLE
GRAWEMEYER AWARD FOR MUSIC COMPOSITION
School of Music, University of Louisville, Louisville, KY 40292 (502) 588-6907
Contact: David R. Harman, Executive Secretary **Frequency:** annual **Award:** $150,000 in 5 annual installments of $30,000 each **Works:** musicals, operas **Regulations:** entries must have premiered during the past 5 years and must be sponsored by professional musical organizations or individuals **Procedure:** send SASE for guidelines and application form; $30 fee upon entry **Deadline:** Jan. 26, 1990 **Notification:** late spring 1990 **Comment:** "Large musical genre: choral, orchestral, chamber, electronic, song-cycle, dance, opera, musical theatre, extended solo work."

VERMONT PLAYWRIGHTS AWARD
The Valley Players, Box 441, Waitsfield, VT 05673
Contact: Howard Chapman, Chairperson **Frequency:** annual **Award:** $1000, possible production **Works:** full-length plays **Regulations:** authors must be Vermont residents; entries must be unpublished and unproduced, "but previous workshops and readings are encouraged"; no musicals **Specifications:** entries must be suitable for the community and the facility **Procedure:** send SASE for guidelines and application form **Deadline:** Aug. 1, 1990 **Notification:** Dec. 1990

VERMONT REPERTORY THEATRE
NATIONAL PLAYWRITING CONTEST
Box 366, Ft. Ethan Allen, Winooski, VT 05404
(802) 655-9620 Contact: Robert R. Ringer, Producing Director
Frequency: annual **Award**: $1000, production **Works**: full-length
plays, translations, adaptations **Regulations**: entries must be
unproduced; no sit-coms or "cutesy" material **Specifications**:
maximum cast: 10; simple production requirements **Stage**: 3/4
thrust-flexible--140 seats **Audience**: "Professionals and college
students." **Procedure**: send SASE for guidelines; 3 copies of script
required upon entry **Deadline**: Jun. 30, 1990 **Your chances**: 400
entries/2-3 judges **Advice**: "Professional, well-written scripts
that investigate man's existence, social issues."

VERY SPECIAL ARTS YOUNG PLAYWRIGHTS PROGRAM
Education Office, John F. Kennedy Center,
Washington, DC 20566 (202) 662-8899
Contact: Coordinator **Frequency**: annual **Award**: production at
John F. Kennedy Center; travel, housing for playwright, teacher and
chaperone **Works**: full-length plays, single and related one-acts,
musicals, children's plays **Exclusive interest**: disability
Regulations: authors must be students (with or without disabilities),
12-18 years of age; entries must be unproduced **Specifications**:
small cast, simple set preferred **Audience**: "Children and adults,
many disabled individuals." **Procedure**: send SASE for guidelines and
application form **Deadline**: Feb. 19, 1990 **Notification**: Apr.
1990 **Your chances**: 100+ entries/7 judges/2 readings per entry
Comments: Scripts are not returned. Formerly The Henry Fonda
Young Playwrights Program.

THE VIRGINIA PRIZE FOR PLAYWRITING
Virginia Commission for the Arts, James Monroe Bldg.,
101 N. 14th St. 17th Floor, Richmond, VA 23219-3683
(804) 225-3132 Voice/TDD Contact: Commission Office
Frequency: annual **Award**: $10,000 **Works**: full-length plays,
one-acts, plays-in-progress with 1 act completed **Regulations**:
authors must reside in Virginia; entries must be unpublished and must
not have been professionally produced; no more than 1 entry per
author; undergraduates ineligible; no musicals **Procedure**: send
SASE for guidelines; 3 copies of script required upon entry
Deadline: Jan. 15, 1990 **Notification**: Jun. 1, 1990 **Your
chances**: 100-150 entries/3 judges **Comment**: The judges
reserve the right to withhold the award if in their opinion no entry
merits it.

WAREHOUSE THEATRE COMPANY ONE-ACT COMPETITION
Box 2077, Stephens College, Columbia, MO 65215
(314) 443-0784 **Contact**: Jenny Friend, Artistic Director
Frequency: annual **Award**: $200; production or staged reading
Works: one-acts **Special interest**: works by, for or about women
Regulations: authors must be high shcool or college students; entries
must be unpublished and unproduced **Procedure**: send SASE for
guidelines; $7.50 fee upon entry **Deadline**: inquire (Nov. 4 in 1989)

WEST COAST ENSEMBLE
COMPETITION FOR FULL-LENGTH PLAYS
Box 38728, Los Angeles, CA 90038 (213) 871-8673
Contact: Les Hanson, Artistic Director **Award:** $500, production
Regulations: entries must not have been produced in Southern
California **Maximum cast:** 12 **Procedure:** send script with SASE
Deadline: Nov. 1, 1990

WESTERN PUBLIC RADIO PLAYWRITING CONTEST
Ft. Mason Center, San Francisco, CA 94123
(415) 771-1160 **Contact**: Leo C. Lee, Project Director
Frequency: annual **Awards**: $300, production for WPR's *California
Radio Theatre* series for 3 winners **Works**: one-act radio plays
Regulations: entries must be original works **Playing time:** 30
minutes **Procedure**: send script with SASE **Deadline**: Jun. 15,
1990

WICHITA STATE UNIVERSITY PLAYWRITING CONTEST
University Theatre, Box 31, Wichita State University,
Wichita, KS 67208 (316) 689-3185
Contact: Bela Kiralyfalvi, Professor of Theatre **Frequency**: annual
Award: production, travel, housing **Works**: full-length plays,
related one-acts **Regulations**: authors must be students in U.S.
colleges; entries must be unpublished and unproduced; no children's
plays **Specifications**: small theatre; playing time: 90 minutes
minimum **Stage**: flexible, 100 seats **Audience**: "Typical university
audience." **Procedure**: send script with SASE **Deadline**: Feb. 15,
1990 **Notification**: Apr. 15, 1990 **Your chances**: 40-50
entries/3 judges/3 readings per entry **Advice**: "Don't send the first
draft!"

WINGS THEATRE COMPANY 1990 NEW PLAYS CONTEST
521 City Island Ave., City Island, NY 10464
(212) 885-1938 Contact: Jeffery Corrick, Artistic Director
Frequency: annual **Awards**: production with royalty for as many
as 3 plays; staged readings for 10 finalists **Works**: full-length plays,
musicals **Special interests**: "Plays that are strong in theme and

explore social, moral or philosophical issues." **Regulations**: authors must be U.S. playwrights; entries must not be published or commercially produced **Stage**: flexible, 75 seats **Procedure**: send script with SASE **Deadline**: inquire (probably Dec. 31, 1990) **Your chances**: 500 entries/10 judges/1-5 readings per entry

WRITER'S DIGEST WRITING COMPETITION
1507 Dana Ave., Cincinnati, OH 45207 (513) 531-2222
Contact: Competition Director **Frequency**: annual **Awards**: overall winner: a trip to New York and lunch with 4 editors or agents; script winner: electronic typewriter; publication in booklet **Works**: first 15 pages of full-length plays, one-acts, children's plays **Regulations**: entries must be unpublished and unproduced; no more than 1 entry per author; previous entries ineligible **Specifications**: standard format **Procedure**: send SASE for guidelines; 1-page synopsis required upon entry **Deadline**: May 31, 1990 **Notification**: Oct. 30, 1990 **Your chances**: 500 entries/2 judges

YEAR-END SERIES (Y.E.S.) NEW PLAY FESTIVAL
Department of Theatre, Northern Kentucky University, Highland Heights, KY 41076 (606) 572-5560
Contact: Jack Wann, Project Director **Frequency**: biennial even years **Awards**: $400, production, expenses, for each of 3 winners **Works**: full-length plays, single and related one-acts, musicals **Regulations**: entries must be unproduced; no more than 1 entry per author; author must visit in Apr. 1991 **Specifications**: entries must be suitable for actors aged 17-25; small orchestra for musicals **Stages**: proscenium; black box **Procedure**: send SASE for guidelines and application form **Deadline**: Dec. 15, 1990 **Your chances**: 300-400 entries/3-9 judges/3-9 readings per entry

YOUNG PLAYWRIGHTS FESTIVAL
The Foundation of the Dramatists Guild, 234 W. 44th St., New York, NY 10036 (212) 575-7796
Contact: Nancy Quinn, Producing Director **Frequency**: annual **Award**: staged reading or production with royalty, travel, residency; 1-year membership in the Dramatists Guild **Works**: full-length plays, one-acts **Regulations**: authors must be under 19 years of age as of Jul. 1, 1990 **Procedure**: send script with SASE and brief cover letter **Deadline**: Oct. 1, 1990 **Comment**: See Gregg, Steve, "New Writers on Stage," *Dramatics* (Jan. 1989), 7-10.

YOUNG PLAYWRIGHTS FESTIVAL
Pegasus Players, 1145 W. Wilson Ave., Chicago, IL 60640
(312) 878-9761 Contact: Arlene Crewdson, Artistic Director
Frequency: annual **Award:** $500, production (Jun. 1990)
Works: full-length plays, one-acts, translations, adaptations, musicals **Special interests:** "Social value; works stressing a moral center." **Regulations:** entries must be unpublished and unproduced; authors must be Chicago residents, 8th grade-high school **Procedure:** send SASE for guidelines and application form **Deadline:** Feb. 1, 1990 **Notification:** Mar. 1990

The following contests either did not respond to our 1990 questionnaire or came to our attention too late to be included in our survey. We advise that playwrights inquire before submitting materials.

ELMIRA COLLEGE ORIGINAL PLAY AWARD
Elmira College Department of Theatre, Elmira, NY 14901
Award: $1000, funding for production **Works:** full-length plays, adaptations **Regulations:** adaptors must secure permission; no musicals **Procedure:** send SASE for guidelines **Deadline:** inquire

THE LIVE OAK THEATER NEW PLAY AWARD
311 Nueces St., Austin, TX 79701
Contact: Mari Marchbanks **Awards:** $1000, possible production for 2 winners: best play and best play by a Texas resident; possible directed readings of runners-up **Works:** full-length plays **Regulations:** authors must be U.S. citizens; entries must not be produced professionally **Procedure:** send SASE for information on future awards **Deadline:** inquire (Nov. 1 in 1989)

THE QUEENS THEATRE NETWORK, INC. PLAY AWARDS
The Cultural Environ, 46-12 Queens Blvd.,
Sunnyside, Long Island, NY 11104 (718) 361-1008
Awards: staged reading for each of 3 winners: best full-length play, best one-act, best theatre piece for young audiences **Regulations:** authors must be residents of Queens County; entries must be unpublished and unproduced; no adaptations **Procedure:** phone for information on future awards; $5 fee in 1989 **Deadline:** inquire (Dec. 15 in 1989)

- Notes -

Special Programs

Guidelines for applying for participation in special programs listed in this section:

Read each listing thoroughly and carefully.

Unless an individual listing specifies other procedures, playwrights should send a stamped, self-addressed envelope for guidelines and application forms.

Apply for programs well in advance of deadlines, and be certain that all required materials accompany each application. Do not expect return of any materials not accompanied by self-addressed mailers or envelopes, adequately stamped and large enough to accommodate the materials to be mailed.

ACT I CREATIVITY CENTER
4550 Warwick Blvd. #1201, Kansas City, MO 64111
Contact: Charlotte Plotsky **Program:** 1 week-2 month residencies for adults at lake-front home **Accommodations:** private rooms; meals provided Mon-Sat. a.m. **Fee:** based on ability to pay **Procedure:** write to D.G. Plotsky for information packet; $10 fee upon application **Deadline:** 1 month prior to desired residency **Your chances:** 4-8 spaces available **Comment:** Center is located at 457 Lucy Rd., Lake Ozark, MO 65049.

ACTORS' ALLIANCE, INC.
AAI, JAF Box 7370, New York, NY 10116
(718) 768-6110 Contact: Melanie Sutherland, Juanita Walsh, Co-Artistic Directors **Program:** a resident ensemble theatre company; activities include weekly workshop meetings, productions and reading series, fundraising parties **Remuneration:** travel and small fee for performance **Fee:** $25 annual membership **Comments:** "Although we prefer those writers who are available for Monday night workshops, we will consider out-of-town submissions for Associate Membership." See Actors' Alliance, Inc. listing in Theatres.

THE ALLIANCE OF RESIDENT THEATRES/
NEW YORK, INC.
131 Varick St. Room 904, New York, NY 10013
(212) 989-5257 Contact: Kate C. Busch, Executive Director **Program:** a membership support organization for the off Broadway and off off Broadway theatre; programs and services include resources, consultations, seminars, telephone support, job board computerized bulletin board, internship placements; various publications include *Theater Times* bi-monthly newspaper available to

New York donors of $50 or more; membership categories: Theatre Members, Associate Theatre Members, Professional Affiliates **Dues:** $125 per year for Professional Affiliate **Procedure:** phone for eligibility requirements

THE AMERICAN ALLIANCE FOR THEATRE AND EDUCATION
c/o Department of Theatre Arts, Virginia Tech, Blacksburg, VA 24061 (703) 231-7624
Contact: Roger L. Bedard, Executive Secretary **Program:** a membership organization formed with the merger of the American Association for Theatre in Secondary Education and the American Association of Theatre for Youth; services include AATE Unpublished Play Reading Project (open to non-members) and selection and promotion of promising new plays for elementary and secondary schools; publications include directory, quarterly newsletter, quarterly *Youth Theatre Journal* and triannual *Drama/Theatre Teacher* (some subscriptions available to non-members) **Fees:** $48 individual, $30 student or retiree, $75 organization, $65 foreign member

AMERICAN COLLEGE THEATRE FESTIVAL
NEW PLAY PREVIEW PROGRAM
Dept. of Theater Arts, Film and Television, UCLA, 405 Hilgard Ave., Los Angeles, CA 90024
Contact: John Cauble, *PAC/ACTF News* Editor **Program:** playwrights willing to have their works premiered as entries in ACTF are sought by the Development Committee of the Playwriting Awards Committee; donors and schools willing to sponsor and produce selected works are also sought **Comment:** See American College Theatre Festival Awards listing in Contests.

AMERICAN INDIAN COMMUNITY HOUSE
842 Broadway, New York, NY 10003 (212) 598-0100
Contact: Theater Program Director **Program:** an organization for New York's American Indian population; programs include Theater Department, library, newsletter, weekly radio program on WBAI-FM; resident theatre company; Native Americans in the Arts (see Theatres) develops and produces works by and about American Indians

AMERICAN MUSIC CENTER
250 W. 54th St. Suite 300, New York, NY 10019
Contact: Nancy S. Clarke, Executive Director **Program:** national service organization fostering and encouraging the creation, performance, publication and recognition of contemporary American music; services include circulating library of American music, advocacy for creative artists and their music, resource information,

semi-annual newsletter, grants and awards program; network for composers, lyricists and librettists **Dues:** $30 per year

AMERICAN PLAYWRIGHT PROGRAM
Westbeth Theatre Center, 151 Bank St.,
New York, NY 10014 (212) 691-2272
Contact: Ted Snowdon, Literary Manager **Program:** a developmental program in which selected scripts receive staged readings, those continuing in program are further developed until 3 or 4 are selected for full showcase production **Works:** full-length plays, adaptations **Specifications:** small cast, simple set for intimate 60-seat theatre **Procedure:** send SASE for guidelines **Deadline:** ongoing program **Notification:** 6 months

AMERICAN-SCANDINAVIAN FOUNDATION
127 E. 73rd St., New York, NY 10021
Contact: Exchange Division **Program:** grants and fellowships for graduate study in Denmark, Finland, Norway, Iceland and Sweden for U.S. citizens and permanent residents who have completed undergraduate study; $2000 grants for short visits; $8000 fellowships for a full academic year **Deadline:** Nov. 1, 1990

ARIZONA STATE UNIVERSITY GUEST LECTURESHIP
Dept. of Theatre, Arizona State University,
Tempe, AZ 85287 (602) 965-5359
Contact: Lin Wright, Chair **Program:** a 2-year maximum visiting professorship in beginning playwriting; maximum salary $34,000; for a published and professionally produced dramatist with an established reputation **Procedure:** request guidelines **Comment:** "The playwright has traditionally premiered a show with ASU faculty and staff and has assisted students with staged readings of their works."

ARTISTS FOUNDATION
8 Park Plaza, Boston, MA 02116 (617) 227-2787
Contact: Netta Davis, Acting Fellowship Director **Program:** fellowships of $9500 or $500 to finalists in 19 categories including Playwriting & Music Composition; for artists at least 18 years of age who have resided for at least 6 months prior to deadline in Massachusetts; undergraduate or graduate students in field of application ineligible **Works:** full-length plays, one-acts **Procedure:** request guidelines and application form from Fellowship Dept. after Sept. 1, 1990 **Deadline:** inquire (usually early Oct.)

ARTIST TRUST
1331 3rd Ave., 517 Jones Bldg., Seattle, WA 98101
Contact: David Mendoza, Director **Program:** 20 annual fellowships
of $5000 available to professional artists in all disciplines who are
residents of Washington **Procedure:** request guidelines

ARTS INTERNATIONAL
Institute of International Education,
809 United Nations Plaza, New York, NY 10017
(212) 984-5370 Contact: Barbara C. McLean, Program Director
Program: a membership organization providing services and
information on international exchange of professional artists; services
include publications, technical assistance, facilitation and advocacy,
data bank on sources of funding and production, work spaces and
facilities for artists; newsletter; consultations ($25 per hour)

ASCAP MUSICAL THEATRE WORKSHOP
1 Lincoln Plaza, New York, NY 10023 (212) 870-7545
Contact: Bernice Cohen, Director of Musical Theatre Activities
Program: 10 Monday night sessions under the direction of Charles
Strouse; participating composers and lyricists present selections from
works-in-progress to panels of professionals in all aspects of theatre;
sessions begin Oct. 29, 1990 **Fee:** none **Procedure:** send cassette
including 4 songs (preferably theatre songs), resume of theatre and
musical background and SASE **Deadline:** Aug. 3, 1990; inquire for
opening date **Notification:** Sept. 1990

ASOLO TOURING THEATER COMMISSIONS
Drawer E, Sarasota, FL 34230 (813) 355-7115
Contact: Robert G. Miller, Artistic Director **Program:** a step-
commissioning process of script development; workshop production
Works: 1-hour plays, adaptations **Specifications:** maximum cast:
5; works must be suitable for touring to upper elementary, junior high
and high schools **Remuneration:** negotiable commission
Procedure: request Information Sheet for Playwrights; "unsolicited
script will be read if it falls within the guidelines" **Deadline:**
ongoing program; "seasons are selected in Dec. of the preceding year"
Notification: 6 months

ASSITEJ/USA
Theatre & Film Department, Brigham Young University,
Provo, UT 84602 (801) 378-4574
Contact: Harold R. Oaks, President **Program:** an international
membership organization for professional theatre for young audiences;
services include international networks, New Plays program,
information resources, exchanges, forums, festivals; publications

include *TYA Today* **Fees:** $40 individual; $25 student or retiree; $30 library; $65-$85 organization; $65 individual or organization outside U.S.A.

THE ASSOCIATED WRITING PROGRAMS
Old Dominion University, Norfolk, VA 23529
(804) 440-3839 Contact: Gale Arnoux, Director of Services
Program: a national membership organization serving as advocate for authors and students and encouraging growth in university and college creative writing programs; *Job List* includes opportunities for playwrights

ASSOCIATION FOR THEATRE IN HIGHER EDUCATION
c/o Theatre Service, Box 15282,
Evansville, IN 47716 (812) 474-0549
Program: a membership organization serving university and college theatres, teachers and students; programs include playwriting (see Christina Crawford Awards listing in Contests); annual conference features playwriting sessions and staged readings **Fees:** $50 individual; $30 student or retiree

ASSOCIATION OF HISPANIC ARTS
173 E. 116th St., New York, NY 10029
Contact: Jane Delgado, Executive Director **Program:** a service organization for Hispanic artists and arts organizations; services include monthly newsletter; future plans include a directory of Hispanic playwrights

ATLANTIC CENTER FOR THE ARTS
1414 Art Center Ave., New Smyrna Beach, FL 32168
(904) 427-6975 Contact: Donna Blagdan, Special Projects Director **Program:** opportunities for associate artists to work with internationally-known Master Artists in Residence in 3-week interdisciplinary residencies **Fee:** $200 tuition plus expenses **Procedure:** phone to request brochures; Master Artist selects associate **Your chances:** 50 applications received annually **Comments:** Past Master Artists in Residence include Edward Albee, Romulus Linney, Joshua Sobol and Ted Tally.

AT THE FOOT OF THE MOUNTAIN PROGRAMS
2000 S. 5th St., Minneapolis, MN 55454 (612) 375-9487
Contact: Rebecca Rice, Co-Artistic Director **Programs:** collaboration by women of color on works to be performed by people of color; plays by and about women; Coming of Age Project: productions by and about elders and adolescents **Procedure:** send SASE for guidelines

AUSTRALIAN WRITERS' GUILD
60 Kellett St., Kings Cross,
New South Wales 2011, Australia
Contact: Angela Wales, Executive Secretary **Program:** trade union providing marketing information and minimum basic agreement; programs include meetings, seminars, publications, 6-month membership for visiting writers **Procedure:** request guidelines

THE AUTHORS LEAGUE FUND
AND THE DRAMATISTS GUILD FUND
234 W. 44th St., New York, NY 10036 (212) 391-3966
Contact: Susan Drury, Administrator **Program:** interest-free loans to meet the immediate and demonstrated needs of published or produced working professional writers **Procedure:** request guidelines and application form; documentation of publication or production required upon application **Response:** 4-6 weeks

BAILIWICK REPERTORY ANNUAL DIRECTORS' FESTIVAL
3212 N. Broadway, Chicago, IL 60657 (312) 883-1090
Contact: David Zak, Executive Director **Program:** production of 50 new one-act plays: musicals, comedies, dramas, adaptations **Playing time:** 50 minutes maximum **Procedure:** request guidelines **Deadline:** apply Dec.-Jan.

BANFF CENTER SCHOOL OF FINE ARTS
MUSIC THEATRE PROGRAM
Box 1020, Banff, Alberta, Canada TOL 0C0
Contact: John Metcalf, Artistic Head **Program:** residence and workshop for composers and librettists; participants attend rehearsals and workshop productions **Accommodations:** room, meals **Remuneration:** limited scholarships available **Procedure:** send score with SASE, resume and cassette tape **Deadline:** ongoing program **Notification:** 6 weeks

BANFF CENTER SCHOOL OF FINE ARTS
PLAYWRIGHTS' COLONY
Box 1020, Banff, Alberta, Canada TOL 0C0
Contact: John Murrell, Program Head **Program:** 6-week residency (May-Jun.) for senior Canadian playwrights to work on final revision in preparation for rehearsal and/or production **Procedure:** writers, producers, directors or dramaturgs may send script with SASE **Deadline:** Feb. 1, 1990

BEST PLAY COMPANY
Box 444 Times Square Station, New York, NY 10108
(212) 695-5641 Contact: David Kerry Heefner
Program: a not-for-profit organization which develops one play at a time through readings, staged readings, workshops; various theatre professionals (actors, directors, playwrights, designers, technicians, attorneys and press representatives) participate in the development process **Procedure:** send script with SASE **Deadline:** ongoing program **Comment:** "BEST will work with the author over whatever period of time it takes to get the play in really producible shape."

BLUE MOUNTAIN CENTER
Blue Mountain Lake, New York 12812 (518) 352-7391
Contact: Harriet Barlow, Director **Program:** 4-week residencies (Jun.-Nov.) **Special interest:** social, economic or environmental problems **Fee:** none **Procedure:** request guidelines; 10-page work sample, 3 recommendations required upon application **Deadline:** inquire **Your chances:** 15 spaces available

BMI/LEHMAN ENGEL MUSICAL THEATRE WORKSHOP
Broadcast Music, Inc., 320 W. 57th St.,
New York, NY 10019 (212) 586-2000 ext. 258
Contact: Jean Banks, Senior Director; Norma Grossman, Director, Musical Theatre **2 Programs: COMPOSER-LYRICIST WORK-SHOP** (Sept.-May) 2-hour weekly sessions for composers and lyricists **Procedure:** send letter of inquiry; lyricist include 3 contrasting lyrics (comedy, ballad, other); composer include 3 contrasting compositions on cassette; composer/lyricist include 3 contrasting songs (comedy, ballad, up-tempo) on cassette; provide short set-up for each song or lyric; send SASE with materials **Deadline:** Aug. 1, 1990; interviews held before Labor Day **LIBRETTISTS WORKSHOP** program for writers of all genres which analyzes and discusses current and past musicals; students are encouraged to join with composers/lyricists workshops for collaborations; specific assignments to solve problems **Procedure:** send excerpts from works published, produced or in-progress from any medium; include one sample of humorous writing; send SASE with materials **Deadline:** May 1, 1990

BRITISH AMERICAN ARTS ASSOCIATION
49 Wellington St., London WC2E 7BN, England
Contact: Jennifer Williams, Executive Director **Program:** information service and clearing house for exchange between British and American cultural activities; services include information, advice, advocacy and technical assistance to professionals in all disciplines throughout Great Britain and U.S. **Procedure:** request guidelines

BRITISH THEATRE ASSOCIATION
Cranbourn Mansions, Cranbourn St., London, WC2H 7A9, England   Phone: (01) 734-1664
Contact: Ron Haddon, Administrator   **Program:** a membership organization acting as a clearinghouse for information on theatre; services and activities include comprehensive theatre reference library of over 250,000 holdings, training courses in theatre skills, playwrights' workshops, script assessment, discounts on theatre tickets and theatre supplies, lectures and events and publication of the theatre magazine *Drama*   **Procedure:** request application form and details of annual membership

BRODY ARTS FUND
California Community Foundation, 3580 Wilshire Blvd.
Suite 1660, Los Angeles, CA 90010   (213) 413-4042
Contact: Program Administrator   **Program:** a $2500 fellowship awarded to a resident of Los Angeles County, awarded triennially to emerging artists in literary and media arts (including playwrights)   **Special interest:** artists in "expansion arts" field (inner-city, rural, minority or tribal arts)   **Procedure:** request application, available summer 1990   **Your chances:** 400 applications/15 fellowships awarded   **Deadline:** fall 1990 (inquire)

BUSH ARTIST FELLOWSHIP
First National Bank Bldg. E-900, St. Paul, MN 55101
Contact: Sally Dixon, Program Director   **Program:** as many as 15 annual grants of $24,000 plus $6240 for production and travel for playwrights, fiction and non-fiction writers, composers, visual artists and choreographers; recipients must be at least 25 years of age and residents of MN, SD or ND for 12 of the past 36 months   **Deadline:** late Oct. (inquire)   **Notification:** 5 months

CAC PLAYWRIGHT'S FORUM
Contemporary Arts Center, Box 30498,
New Orleans, LA 70190 (504) 523-1216
Contact: Julie Hebert, Artistic Director   **Program:** workshop providing opportunities for staged readings, workshop and full productions for local and visiting professional playwrights, translators, composers, librettists and lyricists   **Fee:** none   **Procedure:** phone for meeting times; bring script to meeting   **Deadline:** ongoing year-round program   **Your chances:** 8-10 spaces available

CALIFORNIA THEATRE COUNCIL

1824 N. Curson Ave., Los Angeles, CA 90046;
Box 46320, Los Angeles, CA 90048
(213) 874-3163 (answering service) **Program:** a
membership organization for individuals and theatres; programs and
services include annual California Theatre Conference, publications
include *West Coast Plays* (anthology, see Publishers), *West Coast
Theatre Directory* **Comment:** When *The Playwright's Companion
1990* went to press, this program's office was under construction;
playwrights are advised to write for information.

CENTER FOR ARTS INFORMATION

1285 Avenue of the Americas 3rd Floor,
New York, NY 10019 (212) 977-2544
Contact: Laura Green, Executive Director **Program:** a resource
center for the not-for-profit arts; 6500-volume library has books,
pamphlets, directories and information on funding agencies and service
organizations; publication program offers information on grants, jobs
and arts management and administration; publications include
newsletters *FYI* and *Spaces*

CENTER THEATER YOUTHEATRE PROGRAM

1346 W. Devon, Chicago, IL 60660 (312) 508-0200
Contact: Hilary Hammond, Literary Manager **Program:** workshop
productions of plays performed by young people, including mentally
and physically handicapped young people; most works are created by
improvisation; works which may be adapted to performers' needs will
be considered **Procedure:** send script with SASE

CENTRAL OPERA SERVICE

Metropolitan Opera, Lincoln Center, New York, NY 10023
Contact: Maria F. Rich, Executive Director **Program:** membership
organization serving as catalyst for new ideas and programs and as
respondent to needs of the operatic and musical theatre community;
programs and services include national conferences, information
service, various directories and quarterly *COS Bulletin* which
features a column detailing opportunities **Dues:** $20 per year
individual membership; $50 per year institutional membership

CHATEAU DE LESVAULT

Onlay, 58370 Villapourçon, France
Contact: Bibbi Lee, Director **Program:** residency (May-Oct.) at
classical-style French country house; for artists and writers working
on specific projects **Accommodations:** room, meals, utilities
Fee: 3600 francs per month **Deadline:** 2 months prior to desired
date of residency

CHICAGO DRAMATISTS WORKSHOP
1105 W. Chicago Ave., Chicago, IL 60622
(312) 633-0630   Contact: Russ Tutterow, Artistic Director
Program: a developmental and service organization for Chicago-area playwrights; programs include readings, classes, workshops, symposia, discussions, panels, productions, festivals, talent coordination, marketing services and referrals to producing theatres; selective admission of Chicago-area playwrights   **Fee:** $75 per year
Procedure: prospective members invited to attend public sessions prior to script submission and interview; phone for information

CINTAS FOUNDATION FELLOWSHIP PROGRAM
Institute of International Education,
809 United Nations Plaza, New York, NY 10017-3580
(212) 984-5564   Contact: Rebecca A. Sayles, Program Officer
Program: fellowships designed "to foster and encourage the professional development and recognition of talented creative artists" of direct Cuban lineage   **Your chances:** 130 applicants/10 fellowships awarded/1 playwright selected   **Deadline:** Mar. 1, 1990

CITY OF ATLANTA BUREAU OF CULTURAL AFFAIRS
236 Forsyth St. Suite 402, Atlanta, GA 30303
Program: semi-annual individual grants of $500-$2500 and annual fellowships of $8000 for Atlanta residents of "demonstrated artistic ability"   **Deadlines:** Oct., Nov. 1990; May 1991 (inquire)
Notification: 3 months

COLUMBIA COLLEGE CHICAGO NEW MUSICALS PROJECT
Music/Theater Center, 72 E. 11th St., Chicago, IL 60605
(312) 663-9462   Contact: Sheldon Patinkin, Artistic Director
Program: a 4-month workshop with directors and dramaturg for composer-writer teams with full-length works in first stages of development; possible staged reading or production   **Remuneration:** weekly stipends   **Regulations:** material must be unproduced and original or in the public domain   **Procedure:** submit a rough draft of libretto and songs or full treatment with SASE, samples of previous work, history of project, tape of music, biographies   **Notification:** 2-3 months after receipt of material   **Deadline:** ongoing program
Notification: 2-3 months

COMPOSERS/LIBRETTISTS STUDIO
New Dramatists, 424 W. 44th St., New York, NY 10036
(212) 757-6960   Contact: Ben Krywosz, Special Projects Director   **Program:** a 2-week exercise workshop (Dec. 1990) dealing with the composer-librettist relationship; participants work with members of New Dramatists on series of collaborative exercises;

resulting pieces rehearsed with singers and presented in open recital **Acommodations**: housing **Remuneration**: $200 weekly stipend, travel **Procedure**: send tape of work, including material written for voice, with SASE, cover letter and resume **Deadline**: Jul. 1, 1990 **Notification**: late Aug. 1990 **Your chances**: 5 spaces available **Comment**: See New Dramatists listing in this section.

COORDINATING COUNCIL
OF LITERARY MAGAZINES LIBRARY
666 Broadway 11th Floor, New York, NY 10012
(212) 614-6551 Program: a library of magazines, useful to playwrights interested in publication; *Directory of Literary Magazines* ($9.95) **Procedure**: phone for appointment

CORNELL CENTER FOR THE PERFORMING ARTS
NEW WORKS PROGRAM
430 College Ave., Cornell University, Ithaca, NY 14850
(607) 254-2700 Contact: Janet Salmons-Rue, Outreach Director **Program**: residencies of 7-10 days for rehearsals and staged readings of new plays **Accommodations**: housing **Remuneration**: honorarium, travel **Procedure**: send query/synopsis; no unsolicited script **Deadline**: Apr. 30, 1990

CUMMINGTON COMMUNITY FOR ARTS
R.R. 1, Box 145, Cummington, MA 01026
(413) 634-2172 Contact: Helen Lang, Gloria Gowdy **Program**: 1-3 month residencies on 100 acres in Berkshires for artists in all disciplines **Accommodations**: living/studio space in private cottages or 2 main houses; Children's Program of supervised activities for 5-12 year olds (Jul.-Aug.) **Fee**: $10-$17 per day; work exchanges available **Procedure**: request guidelines; resume, work samples in triplicate, $10 fee required upon application **Deadlines**: Jan. 1, 1990 for Apr.-May; Mar. 1, 1990 for Jun.-Aug.; Jun. 1, 1990 for Sept.-Nov. **Your chances**: up to 20 spaces available

DEEP SOUTH WRITERS CONFERENCE
Box 44691, University of Southwestern Louisiana,
Lafayette, LA 70504
Program: annual writers' conference held in Sept., "to discover, develop, celebrate and promote excellence in prose and verse"; faculty-led workshops, individual counseling, discussions, lectures, readings **Deadline**: Jul. 15, 1990 **Comment**: See Miller Award and Paul T. Nolan Award in Contests.

D.H. LAWRENCE FELLOWSHIP
Department of English, Humanities 217,
University of New Mexico, Albuquerque, NM 87131
Contact: Scott P. Sanders, Chair, D.H. Lawrence Fellowship Committee **Program:** award of $2100 and 4-week residency (Jun.-Aug. 1990) for a writer of fiction, poetry, drama or creative non-fiction; writer must be working in English language; resident may be asked to present a reading, lecture or 1-time consultation service under auspices of the university **Accommodations:** private 4-room residence at D.H. Lawrence Ranch outside Taos **Procedure:** send letter explaining reasons for desiring the fellowship, outline of planned work during residency, work sample, resume and $10 fee **Deadline:** Jan. 31, 1990 **Advice:** "The fellowship will be awarded to the applicant whose recent work shows the greatest promise of benefitting contemporary letters."

DISCOVERY '90
Choate Rosemary Hall, Box 788, Wallingford, CT 06492
(203) 269-1113 Contact: Terrence Ortwein
Program: a 3-week residency (Jul. 1990) for development of previously unproduced one-act scripts for production by secondary schools **Accommodations:** housing, meals **Remuneration:** $700 stipend **Procedure:** submit script with SASE or request guidelines **Deadline:** Mar. 1, 1990 **Notification:** May 1, 1990

DOBIE-PAISANO PROJECT
University of Texas, Main Bldg. 101, Austin, TX 78712
(512) 471-7213 Contact: Audrey N. Slate, Coordinator
Program: 1 or 2 annual fellowships of $1200 stipend and 6-month residency at Paisano Ranch; recipients must be native Texans or Texas residents, or work must focus on Texas and the Southwest **Accommodations:** maintenance, utilties **Procedure:** request guidelines; 4-page application form, work samples in triplicate required upon application **Deadline:** Jan. 15, 1990

DORLAND MOUNTAIN COLONY
Box 6, Temecula, CA 92390 (714) 676-5039
Contact: Helén Vigil **Program:** residencies of 1-3 months on 300-acre Dorland Preserve in Palomar Mountains near San Diego; accommodations for writers and artists with clear direction and substantial accomplishment in field **Accommodations:** individual studios, weekly potluck, no electricity **Fee:** $150 per month **Procedure:** request guidelines; letter of intent, resume, work samples, all in triplicate, required upon application **Deadlines:** Mar. 1, 1990; Sept. 1, 1990 **Notification:** 2 months **Your chances:** 6 spaces available

DORSET COLONY HOUSE FOR WRITERS
Box 519, Dorset, VT 05251 (802) 867-2223
Contact: John Nassivera, Director **Program:** 1 week-2 month residencies (Sept.-May) for writers of serious purpose and "record of professional achievement" **Accommodations:** private room with desk; library/sitting room, dining room, kitchen available **Fee:** voluntary $50 per week **Procedure:** submit query with resume and description of proposed project; indicate desired dates of residency

DOUBLE IMAGE THEATRE/
NEW VOICES AT GREENE STREET CAFE
445 W. 59th St., New York, NY 10019 (212) 245-2489
Contact: Judith Clinton; Brian Chavanne, Coordinator **Program:** a series of public readings followed by moderated discussions designed to nurture and expose new writers and develop new projects; open to unpublished, unproduced works **Works:** full-length plays, one-acts **Procedure:** send query/synopsis **Deadline:** ongoing program **Notification:** 2 months **Your chances:** 12 scripts developed each year **Comment:** 80% of works read in New Voices series go on to production by the theatre and other theatres.

DRAMA LEAGUE OF NEW YORK
PLAYWRIGHT ASSISTANCE AWARDS
165 W. 46th St. Suite 601, New York, NY 10036
(212) 302-2100 Contact: Playwrights Awards Committee
Program: $1000 awards to playwrights **Procedure:** nomination by artistic director of a New York not-for-profit theatre or selection from unsolicited submissions

DRAMA PROJECT
Box M 151 First Ave., New York, NY 10003
(212) 674-1166 Contact: Doug Moston, Artistic Director
Program: a workshop of actors, directors and playwrights who collaborate in the development of new plays; during 10-week sessions the playwright's works are read by actors and regularly critiqued as the development progresses; roles are cast from actors within the group, and staged readings are created for public audiences including the industry (also literary agents); works from staged readings selected for workshop productions held at Riverside Shakespeare **Fee:** $110 **Procedure:** send SASE for guidelines

DRAMATIC RISKS
60 E. 4th St. #19, New York, NY 10003 (212) 353-1965
Contact: Mark Grant Waren, Executive Director **Program:** new play development **Procedure:** send SASE for guidelines

THE DRAMATISTS GUILD, INC.
234 W. 44th St., New York, NY 10036 (212) 398-9366
Contact: David E. LeVine, Executive Director **Program:** the professional association of playwrights, composers and lyricists (produced and unproduced) in the U.S.; services include use of standard contracts, contract counseling, advice on relationships with producers and agents, emergency toll-free number, script-retrieval and royalty collection, symposia in major U.S. cities, reference library, Committee for Women, Kleban Foundation grants (see listing in this section), The Dramatists Guild Fund (See The Authors League Fund and the Dramatists Guild Fund listing in this section), access to health insurance, complimentary ticket program; publications include quarterly journal and monthly newsletter **Fee:** $50 per year **Procedure:** send script or other proof or authorship of a play with SASE and annual fee **Comment:** See the Foundation of the Dramatists Guild listing in this section.

THE EDWARD F. ALBEE FOUNDATION, INC.
14 Harrison St., New York, NY 10013 (212) 226-2020
Contact: David Briggs, Foundation Secretary **Program:** 1-month residencies (Jun. 1–Oct. 1) at the William Flanagan Memorial Creative Persons Center ("The Barn") in Montauk, Long Island, for writers and artists demonstrating talent and need **Accommodations:** private room **Fee:** none **Procedure:** request guidelines; letter of intent, resume, work samples, 2 recommendations required upon application **Deadline:** Apr. 1, 1990 for Jun.-Sept. 1990 season **Notification:** May 1990 **Your chances:** 6 spaces available

ENSEMBLE STUDIO THEATRE INSTITUTE
549 W. 52nd St., New York, NY 10019 (212) 581-9603
Contact: Curt Dempster, Artistic Director **Program:** 1-week residencies at summer conference in Tannersville, NY; playwrights-in-residence work under guidance of the dramaturg serving as residency director as well as theatre's literary department; daily conferences, periodic readings **Accommodations:** room, meals **Fee:** $350 per week **Procedure:** send script with SASE and letter of intent **Best time:** Apr.-Aug. **Notification:** 1 month

FAIRCHESTER PLAYWRIGHTS PROJECT
20 Dogwood Dr., Danbury, CT 06811 (914) 965-4212
Contact: Dan Rustin, Director **Program:** membership organization for playwrights residing in Fairfield County, CT, or Westchester County, NY; biweekly readings of members' works by professional actors **Fee:** $6 per month **Procedure:** submit script of 1 full-length or 2 one-act plays-in-process, with SASE and SAS postcard **Deadline:** ongoing program

FEEDBACK SERVICES/FEEDBACK THEATREBOOKS
305 Madison Ave. Suite 411, New York, NY 10165
(212) 687-4185 Contact: Walter J. Meserve, Editor-in-Chief
Program: a resource information service providing script critiques, query letter and synopsis preparation, script preparation, topical research, correspondence courses in playwriting; publications include 2 annual reference books: *The Playwright's Companion: A Submission Guide to Theatres and Contests in the U.S.A.* and *Who's Where in the American Theatre* **Procedure:** send SASE for specific information

FINE ARTS WORK CENTER
Box 565, Provincetown, MA 02657 (508) 487-9960
Contact: Mary MacArthur, Executive Director **Program:** 10-16 week residency (May 22-Sept. 11, 1990); composers considered when space is available; participants must be recipients of recognized individual fellowships and awards or winners of other selected juried competitions from 1988-1990; programs include readings, films, exhibitions, performances, informal discussions with visiting writers **Accommodations:** newly renovated living quarters and separate studio space **Fee:** $4000 **Procedure:** application by sponsoring organization (recognized arts organization, foundation or state or regional arts agency); include resume, writer's letter of intent, work samples, letter from sponsor stating the nature of the award, amount and time frame and a statement of potential benefit to artist of residency **Deadline:** Apr. 15, 1990 **Notification:** 6 weeks

FIRSTSTAGE
6817 Franklin Ave., Los Angeles, CA 90028
(213) 850-6271 Contact: Literary Manager **Program:** a membership organization "dedicated to bringing together writers, actors and directors in the development of new material for stage and film"; weekly readings and discussions; possible workshop productions **Fee:** $100 yearly; $30 per quarter **Procedure:** send script with SASE and resume **Deadline:** ongoing program **Your chances:** 100 applications/all are accepted

FLORIDA STUDIO THEATRE ARTISTS COLONY
1241 N. Palm Ave., Sarasota, FL 34236 (813) 366-9017
Contact: Dorean Pucciatti **Program:** residencies (Apr.-Nov.) of varying length for writers, directors and designers in FST living-center; program includes private work time and opportunity for interaction with staff and administrative and technical involvement in FST activities and productions **Accommodations:** bedroom, common living area, shared kitchen and bath **Fee:** $7.50 per day **Deadline:** applications due 1 month prior to expected residency **Your chances:** up to 6 spaces available

THE FOUNDATION CENTER
79 Fifth Ave. at 16th St., New York, NY 10003
(212) 620-4230   Program: an independent national service organization providing information on private philanthropic giving; national network of library reference collections available; publications include *Grants for Arts and Cultural Programs* and *Grants to Individuals*

THE FOUNDATION OF THE DRAMATISTS GUILD
234 W. 44th St., New York, NY 10036 (212) 575-7795
Contact: Mary Rodgers, President   **Program:** Sponsoring organization for projects which encourage and assist dramatists and students of dramatic writing and which foster an appreciation of dramatic works; programs include the George and Elisabeth Marton Prize (by nomination only) for the encouragement of new American playwrights and the annual Young Playwrights Festival (see Contests) which identifies and encourages playwrights under the age of 19 and conducts school workshops and a school tour   **Comment:** See The Dramatists Guild listing in this section.

FRANK SILVERA WRITERS' WORKSHOP
317 W. 125th St. 3rd Floor, New York, NY 10027
(212) 662-8493   Contact: Byron C. Saunders, Executive Director   **Program:** an annual Writers' Laboratory for Afro-American authors, other minorities and women; programs include Monday Readings/Critique Series (Sept.-Jun., 7:30 p.m.), staged readings, Writers'/Directors' Showcase productions   **Special interest:** "Plays that depict minority lifestyles."   **Procedure:** send script with SASE   **Your chances:** hundreds of submissions/35 participants accepted   **Advice:** "Attend the Monday Readings and the writing workshops."

FREDERICK DOUGLASS CREATIVE ARTS CENTER WRITING WORKSHOPS
168 W. 46th St., New York, NY 10036 (212) 944-9870
Contact: Fred Hudson, Artistic Director   **Program:** 2 sessions each year of 12-week writing workshops: beginning and advanced playwriting; weekly meetings; advanced session includes readings, possible production; sessions in other genres including television and film also offered   **Remuneration:** produced playwright receives $300   **Fees:** $70 for each session   **Procedure:** inquire for guidelines   **Deadlines:** early Jan. 1990 for Mar.-Jun. 1990; early Sept. 1990 for Oct. 1990-Jan. 1991 (inquire)

FULBRIGHT SCHOLAR PROGRAM
Council of International Exchange of Scholars,
3400 International Dr. NW #M-500,
Washington, DC 20008
Contact: M. Carlota Baca, Director **Program:** grants in research and university lecturing for periods ranging from 3 months to a full academic year in more than 100 countries; for scholars in virtually all disciplines and academic ranks; professionals, retired faculty and independent scholars are encouraged; recipient must be U.S. citizen with Ph.D. or comparable professional qualifications, teaching experience and, for some countries, foreign language proficiency **Remuneration:** benefits vary by country but generally include travel, stipend, book and baggage allowances; some travel for dependents and tuition allowance for children **Procedure:** request guidelines **Deadlines:** vary by program; inquire

FUND FOR NEW AMERICAN PLAYS
John F. Kennedy Center, Washington, DC 20566
(202) 416-8024 Contact: Deborah Dixon, Project Director
Program: fund to assist not-for-profit regional theatres in the production of American plays; financial assistance for the creation of excellence in production (4-week rehearsal periods, residencies for playwrights, possible guest actors and theatre artists) **Remuneration:** $10,000 stipend to playwright; no funds for technical requirements **Procedure:** producing company may submit as many as 3 original plays with detailed budgets outlining ordinary production expenses and additional funds needed **Deadline:** inquire **Comment:** Program is supported by the Kennedy Center, American Express and the President's Committee on Arts and Humanities.

THE GATHERING
The Whole Theater, 544 Bloomfield Ave.,
Montclair, NJ 07042 (201) 744-2996
Contact: Pat Andrews **Program:** a women's project meeting for readings on the last Monday of each month; open to all women; purpose is "to share and promote women's activities in the theatre" **Procedure:** call for information

GS PLAYWRIGHTS' PROJECT
George Street Playhouse, 9 Livingston Ave.,
New Brunswick, NJ 08901 (201) 846-2895
Contact: Wendy Liscow, Project Director **Program:** 6-8 playwrights are invited to weekly meetings for 6-8 weeks during which their plays will be read **Procedure:** participation by invitation **Comment:** This is the first year of the program; playwrights for the first session have been chosen.

HAMBIDGE CENTER FOR CREATIVE ARTS & SCIENCES
Box 339, Rabun Gap GA 30568
(404) 874-6672 (Nov.-Apr.), 746-5718 (May-Oct.)
Contact: Ray Pierotti, Executive Director **Program:** 2 week—2 month resident fellowships (May-Oct.) to individuals seeking solitude for the pursuit of professional excellence in all areas of arts, humanities and sciences **Accommodations:** private cottage with kitchen, bath and work studio, evening meal **Fees:** $8-$15 per day depending upon ability to pay; some aid available **Procedure:** send SASE with 45¢ postage for guidelines **Notification:** 5-8 weeks

HAWTHORNDEN CASTLE
INTERNATIONAL RETREAT FOR WRITERS
Lasswade Midlothian, Scotland EH18 1EG
Program: residencies of 4-6 weeks (Feb.-Jul., Sept.-Dec.) in remote castle outside Edinburgh; for dramatists, novelists, poets or other creative writers who have published at least 1 book or have had a play professionally produced **Accommodations:** study-bedrooms, communal breakfast and evening meal; daytime silence rule in effect **Deadline:** late Sept. (inquire) **Notification:** 3 months **Your chances:** spaces available for 5 fellows

HELENE WURLITZER FOUNDATION
Box 545, Taos, NM 87571 (505) 758-2413
Contact: Henry A. Sauerwein Jr., Director **Program:** 3-6 month residencies (Apr.-Sept.) for creative artists in all media **Accommodations:** residents maintain their own accommodations and provide their own food **Fee:** none **Procedure:** request guidelines; letter of intent and work samples required upon application

THE HENRY FONDA YOUNG PLAYWRIGHTS PROJECT
Washington, DC See Very Special Arts Young Playwrights Program listing in Contests.

INSTITUTE OF OUTDOOR DRAMA
CB #3240, NCNB Plaza, University of North Carolina,
Chapel Hill, NC 27599 (919) 962-1328
Contact: Mark R. Sumner, Director **Program:** a research/ resource and advisory agency providing communications services for producers and information for those interested in outdoor drama, encouraging established playwrights and composers to create new outdoor dramas and advising new playwrights interested in writing outdoor dramas; services and activities include a roster of artists and production personnel, professional consultation and feasibility study appraisal, annual auditions for summer employment in outdoor drama, conferences, lectures, symposia, occasional reading of

scripts by produced playwrights (query/synopsis required prior to submission); publications include   books, bulletins, visual aids and monthly newsletter

INTAR HISPANIC AMERICAN MUSIC THEATRE LABORATORY
New York, NY This program has been discontinued.

INTAR HISPANIC PLAYWRIGHTS-IN-RESIDENCE LABORATORY
Box 788 Times Square Station, New York, NY 10108
(212) 695-6134, -6135   Contact: Maria Irene Fornes, Program Director   **Program:** a 20-week residency program (fall 1990-spring 1991) for professional Hispanic playwrights writing mainly in English; intensive work sessions culminating in staged reading **Remuneration:** $2500 stipend **Procedure:** submit script with SASE and biography **Deadline:** Jun. 30, 1990 **Notification:** early fall 1990

INTERNATIONAL THEATRE INSTITUTE OF THE UNITED STATES (ITI/US)
220 W. 42nd St., New York, NY 10036 (212) 944-1490
Contact: Louis A. Rachow, Library Director   **Program:** an organization with centers in 77 countries, founded by UNESCO "to promote international exchange of knowledge and practice in the theatre arts"; programs and services include assistance for theatre artists traveling internationally, reference library documenting theatre activities in 150 countries and housing 11,500 plays from 92 countries, information and consultation service on international theatre activities and on international copyright, Music Theatre Committee, Theatre of Nations biennial international festival, quarterly newsletter

THE INTERNATIONAL WOMEN'S WRITING GUILD
Drama Consortium, Box 810 Gracie Station,
New York, NY 10028 (212) 737-7536
Contact: Hannelore Hahn, Executive Director **Program:** an alliance of women writers in U.S., Canada and abroad; programs include workshops, networking between women writers, lists of literary agents and workshops which have agreed to read members' works, job placement, insurance programs; *Membership Services: Network* newsletter; script-reading program with cooperating theatres **Fees:** $30; $45 foreign member

THE JAMES THURBER PLAYWRIGHT-IN-RESIDENCE
The Thurber House, 77 Jefferson Ave.,
Columbus, OH 43215 (614) 464-1032
Contact: Michael J. Rosen, Literary Director **Program:** a 1-quarter teaching residency for a playwright who has "had at least 1 play published and/or produced by a significant company" and who shows aptitude for teaching; resident teaches 1 course in The Ohio State University's Dept. of Theatre; "the majority ot the writer's time will be reserved for current writing projects"; possible public reading or production of resident's work **Accommodations:** housing in Thurber's boyhood home; book center, local writers' center, museum available **Remuneration:** $5000 stipend **Deadline:** inquire; applications available Sept. 1990 for 1991-92 residency **Comment:** In 1990 the position has been awarded to Don Nigro, the 1988 resident; his play will be mounted during the spring of 1991, making that season unavailable for other residencies.

JEROME PLAYWRIGHT-IN-RESIDENCE FELLOWSHIPS
The Playwrights' Center, 2301 Franklin Ave. E,
Minneapolis, MN 55406 (612) 332-7481
Program: annual fellowships of $5000; access to The Playwrights' Center services, for playwrights who have not had more than 2 professionally produced plays; Fellows must be U.S. citizens or permanent residents and must spend fellowship period (Jul.-Jun.) in residence **Procedure:** phone or write for application forms, available after Dec. 1, 1990 **Deadline:** Feb. 1, 1990 **Notification:** Apr. 1990 **Your chances:** 300 applications/6 fellowships awarded **Comment:** See The Playwrights' Center listing in this section.

JOHN SIMON GUGGENHEIM
MEMORIAL FOUNDATION FELLOWSHIPS
90 Park Ave., New York, NY 10016 (212) 687-4470
Program: 6 month-1 year fellowships to further the development of scholars and artists by assisting them to engage in research in any field and creation in any of the arts; fellowships awarded in 2 annual competitions: one open to citizens and permanent residents of U.S. and Canada, other open to citizens and permanent residents of Latin America and the Caribbean; fellows must "have already demonstrated exceptional capacity for productive scholarship or exceptional creative ability in the arts"; amount of grants adjusted to the needs of the fellows; the Foundation may subsidize publication of important contributions produced by holders of fellowsihps **Your chances:** 3,144 U.S. and Canadian applicants in 1989/198 fellowships awarded/no playwrights selected **Deadline:** inquire; final selection of fellows for 1990 will be made in March 1990

KEY WEST LITERARY SEMINAR
Box 391-D, Sugarloaf Shores, FL 33044
Program: an annual 4-day seminar (Jan.), events include panel discussions, readings, cocktail receptions, video and performance art; 1990 participants include Christopher Durang, Maria Irene Fornes, Emily Mann, Wendy Wasserstein, Lanford Wilson; writers' workshop precedes seminar **Fee:** $200; additional fee for workshop **Procedure:** send SASE for guidelines

KLEBAN FOUNDATION
The Dramatists Guild, 243 W. 44th St.,
New York, NY 10036 (212) 398-9366
Program: grants of $150,000 each, paid in 3 annual installments, for lyricists (and possibly for librettists) working on American musicals; for individuals who have not had Broadway productions for the past 2 years **Procedure:** request guidelines; work samples and letter detailing activities and intentions required upon application **Deadline:** inquire **Comment:** Submitted materials will not be returned.

LEAGUE OF CHICAGO THEATRES/
CHICAGO THEATRE FOUNDATION
67 E. Madison Suite 2116, Chicago, IL 60603
(312) 977-1730 Contact: Diane O. Economos, Executive Director **Program:** a trade and service organization for Chicago artists, theatres and theatre personnel, providing programs and services in marketing, promotion, advocacy and general resources; publications include bimonthly *Theatre Chicago* magazine, monthly *Theatre Chicago Guide, Marketing Promotions Guide* and *Theatre Chicago Reference Book* **Membership dues:** $250-$1500, based on theatre's budget **Affiliate Fees:** $35 individual; $100 organization

THE LEE STRASBERG THEATRE INSTITUTE
115 E. 15th St., New York, NY 10003 (212) 533-5500;
7936 Santa Monica Blvd., Los Angeles, CA 90046
(213) 650-7777 Program: Playwrights & Company: a forum in which acting students write scenes and/or one-act plays; works in progress are presented for discussion and critique, possible staged readings, productions **Procedure:** Institute registration required; request guidelines

THE LEHMAN ENGEL MUSICAL THEATRE WORKSHOP
1605 N. Cahuenga Blvd. #216, Hollywood, CA 90028
(213) 465-8818 Contact: John Sparks, Co-Director **Program:** workshop for composers, lyricists and librettists meeting every 5th week (Mon.-Thurs. evenings Sept.-Jun.); based on curriculum

developed by Lehman Engel; 1st year: music, lyric and book writing assignments; 2nd year: selected writers work independently and bring projects to workshop sessions **Fee:** $100 (including nonrefundable $25 application fee); possible work-study program **Procedure:** request guidelines and application form; work samples required upon application **Deadline:** Aug. 1, 1990 **Notification:** Sept. 1990

LITERARY MANAGERS AND DRAMATURGS OF AMERICA
c/o CASTA, CUNY Graduate Center, 33 W. 42nd St., New York, NY 10036 (212) 642-2657
Contact: Anne Cattaneo, President **Program:** a national membership organization offering job referral, information resources, *LMDA Review* quarterly newsletter; activities include workshops and symposia, public panels, membership meetings, annual national conference; assistance in dealing with theatres to obtain professional and courteous treatment of playwrights who submit scripts **Fees:** $35 per year active (voting) member; $25 per year associate (associate membership open to playwrights, artistic directors, agents, other theatre professionals and members of the public concerned with dramaturgy); $15 per year student; $75 per year institution

LOS ANGELES THEATRE ALLIANCE/ LEAGUE OF PRODUCERS
644 S. Figueroa, Los Angeles, CA 90017 (213) 614-0556
Contact: Karen Rushfield, Executive Director **Program:** a membership service organization of theatres and producers in Los Angeles; services include networking opportunities, roundtable discussions, resource center, audience development and marketing services, newsletter, professional job bank; membership restricted to organizations, but services available to individuals

LOS ANGELES THEATRE CENTER PROGRAMS
514 S. Spring St., Los Angeles, CA 90013
(213) 627-6500 Contact: Bill Bushnell, Artistic Producing Director **The Women's Project:** a workshop for Los Angeles women playwrights **Young Playwrights Lab:** a developmental workshop for Los Angeles residents aged 15-22 **Latino Theatre Lab:** a workshop for Latino actors, playwrights and directors; collaborative projects; works may be included in LATC season **Playwrights' Unit:** regular sessions for established Los Angeles playwrights **Asian American Theatre Project:** an access point for emerging Asian artists to "mainstream" theatre **Black Theatre Artists Workshop:** a forum for research and presentation of new plays by black writers; a contact point for writers, directors and actors **Music Theatre Lab:** playwrights, composers and lyricists

explore a musical expression of "the kind of cutting-edge theatre for which LATC is known" **Procedure:** send SASE for specific information

LUDWIG VOGELSTEIN FOUNDATION
Box 4924, Brooklyn, NY 11240
Contact: Frances Pishny, Executive Director **Program:** small foundation offering fewer than 50 annual grants (average grant: $2500) to individuals in arts and humanities; no scholarships **Procedure:** send SASE for guidelines

MACDOWELL COLONY
100 High St., Peterborough, NH 03458 (603) 924-3886
Contact: Christopher Barnes, Resident Director **Program:** residencies of approximately 6 weeks in wooded semi-rural setting for writers, visual artists, composers and film/video artists **Fee:** determined by resident **Procedure:** request forms 8 months prior to date of desired residency; work samples, recommendations, fee required upon application

MANHATTAN PLAYWRIGHTS UNIT
338 W. 19th St., New York, NY 10011 (212) 989-0948
Contact: Saul Zachary, Co-Founder/Director **Program:** organization of experienced, active playwrights; works-in-progress shared at weekly meetings **Procedure:** send cover letter with SASE and resume

MARY INGRAHAM BUNTING INSTITUTE
34 Concord Ave., Cambridge, MA 02138
Contact: Fellowship Coordinator **Program:** various annual fellowships for women scholars, writers, artists and musicians in residence; recipient must have Ph.D. or equivalent professional experience **Accommodations:** private office, course auditing privileges, access to Harvard and Ratcliffe facilities **Deadline:** Oct. 1, 1990 **Notification:** Apr. 1991

MARY ROBERTS RINEHART FUND
Dept. of English, George Mason University,
4400 University Dr., Fairfax, VA 22030
(703) 323-2220 Contact: Roger Lathbury
Program: 2 grants ("currently around $950") presented biennially in odd years to non-produced and non-published dramatists who need assistance to complete works **Exclusive interest:** "Strong narrative quality." **Procedure:** nomination by established writer, agent or editor; submit 30-page sample of nominee's work; written recomendation not needed **Deadline:** inquire for upcoming deadline

McKNIGHT FELLOWSHIPS
The Playwrights' Center, 2301 Franklin Ave. E,
Minneapolis, MN 55406 (612) 332-7481
Program: fellowships of $10,000 with provisions for professional workshops, "to recognize playwrights whose work has made a significant impact on the contemporary theatre"; subsidy, supplementary assistance and professional encouragement; 2-month residency at The Playwrights' Center; selection based on resume and plan for Fellowship year; recipients must be U.S. citizens and must have a minimum of 2 professional productions **Procedure:** request guidelines after Oct. 2, 1990 **Deadline:** Dec. 1, 1990 **Your chances:** 150 applications/6 fellowships awarded **Comment:** See The Playwrights' Center listing in this section.

MEET THE COMPOSER
2112 Broadway Suite 505, New York, NY 10023
Program: a national composers' service organization which fosters the creation, performance and recording of music by American composers and develops new audiences for contemporary music; programs and services include grants for composer fees to not-for-profit organizations that present their works; the composers Performance Fund and Affiliate Newtork, Orchestra Residencies Program, the Composer/Choreographer Project, Meet the Composer/Reader's Digest Commissioning Program and Jazz Program; publications include *Composers in the Marketplace: How to Earn a Living Writing Music* and *Commissioning Music* **Procedure:** application to specific program submitted by not-for-profit sponsoring organization; additional information available on request

MERCANTILE LIBRARY ASSOCIATION WRITERS STUDIO
17 E. 47th St., New York, NY 10017
Contact: Dorothy Gardner, President; Charlotte Myska, Director of Programs **Program:** not-for-profit private lending library of 220,000 volumes; programs and services include residencies for playwrights and librettists engaged in current projects, privileges of Mercantile Library membership: access to all library resources (200,000 volumes); activities include lectures, forums, readings, book discussions, meetings with other literary organizations **Accommodations:** carrel space, storage for computers and typewriters; access to special reference collection of 19th century American and British literature **Fee:** $300 for 3 months, renewable up to 1 year **Procedure:** request application form; work samples and resume required upon application; unpublished writers eligible if they can provide evidence of serious intent **Deadline:** ongoing program **Notification:** 2 weeks **Your chances:** 17 carrel spaces available

MERELY PLAYERS
Box 606, New York, NY 10108 (212) 799-2253
Contact: Monica Hays, President **Program:** a membership organization of actors, directors and writers; activities include script development through 18 regularly scheduled Monday night readings and 2 Second Step staged readings (Sept.-May) **Special interest:** plays dealing with minority issues **Fee:** $72 annual membership **Procedure:** submit script with SASE; playwright who has had 2 scripts accepted may become member **Deadline:** ongoing program

MIDWEST PLAYLABS
The Playwrights' Center, 2301 Franklin Ave. E,
Minneapolis, MN 55406 (612) 332-7481
Program: a 2-week retreat (Jul. 30-Aug 12, 1990) during which new, unpublished, unproduced full-length plays are developed with assistance from professional acting company and nationally recognized directors and dramaturgs; revised plays receive public readings; Pre-Conference (May 18-21, 1990) **Accommodations:** room, meals **Remuneration:** stipend, travel **Procedure:** request guidelines and application forms, available after Jan. 2, 1990 **Deadline:** Mar. 1, 1990 **Notification:** Apr. 30, 1990 **Your chances:** 300 applications/6 plays selected **Comment:** See The Playwrights' Center listing in this section.

MILDRED I. REID WRITERS COLONY
Penacook Rd., Contoocook, NH 03229 (603) 746-3625
Contact: Mildred I. Reid, Director **Program:** 1-6 week residencies (Jul.-Aug.) for beginning writers who wish to work under guidance and for professionals and semi-professionals; programs include private consultation, evening readings, classes **Accommodations:** single or double rooms, kitchen facility, breakfast **Fee:** at least $115 per week **Procedure:** send query **Your chances:** 100+ applications/ 30+ writers selected

MILLAY COLONY FOR THE ARTS
Steepletop, Box 3, Austerlitz, NY 12017
(518) 392-3103 Contact: Ann-Ellen Lesser, Executive Director **Program:** 1-month residency for artists **Accommodations:** room, studio, meals **Fee:** none **Procedure:** request guidelines, application form; work samples, 1 recommendation required upon application **Deadlines:** Feb. 1, 1990 for Jun.-Sept. 1990; May 1, 1990 for Oct. 1990-Jan. 1991; Sept. 1, 1990 for Feb.-May 1991 **Your chances:** 5 spaces available

MONEY FOR WOMEN/
BARBARA DEMING MEMORIAL FUND, INC.
Box 40-1043, Brooklyn, NY 11240
Contact: Pam McAllister, Administrator **Program:** semi-annual grants averaging $500-$1000 for U.S. residents who are feminists "active in the arts whose work speaks for peace and social justice and in some way sheds light upon the condition of women or enhances self-realization"; grants awarded for specific projects other than study **Procedure:** send SASE for application form **Deadlines:** Feb. 1, 1990; Jul. 1, 1990 **Your chances:** 150 applications/10 grants

MONTALVO CENTER FOR THE ARTS
Box 158, Saratoga, CA 95071 (408) 741-3421
Contact: Elisabeth Challener, Executive Director **Program:** 3-month residencies on 175-acre arts center near San Francisco for playwrights and/or composers with evidence of professional activity and recognition **Accommodations:** apartment **Fees:** $100 per month individual; $115 per month per couple; limited assistance available **Procedure:** request application form; letter of intent, resume, work sample and 3 references required upon application **Deadline:** ongoing program **Notification:** 1 month **Your chances:** 5 spaces available

MOUNT SEQUOYAH NEW PLAY RETREAT
Department of Drama, 406 Kimpel Hall,
University of Arkansas, Fayetteville, AR 72701
(501) 575-2953 Contact: Thomas R. Jones
Program: summer residency/workshop: play development with directors and actors, staged reading with critique by theatre professional **Accommodations:** housing, meals **Works:** one-acts, scenes from longer plays **Fee:** to be announced ($500 in 1989); fellowships available **Procedure:** request guidelines; $5 upon application **Deadline:** inquire (May 15 in 1989)

MUSICAL THEATRE LAB
Box 188, Pound Ridge, NY 10576 (914) 764-4412
Contact: Stuart Ostrow, Producer **Program:** a developmental workshop for new, production-ready works; 12 public workshop performances **Remuneration:** weekly stipend for 6 weeks **Procedure:** send script with SASE and cassette tape of music **Deadline:** ongoing program **Comment:** Jun.-Aug. address: Agassiz House, Radcliffe College, 10 Garden St., Cambridge, MA 02138 (617) 495-8676.

NATIONAL ENDOWMENT FOR THE ARTS
OPERA MUSICAL THEATER PROGRAM
NEA, Nancy Hanks Center, 1100 Pennsylvania Ave. NW, Washington, DC 20506 (202) 682-5447
Contact: Gertrude J. Saleh **Program:** annual grants or commissions awarded to professional producing organizations, independent producers, artist-producers, artistic associates and national and regional service organizations **Procedure:** request guidelines and "Intent to Apply Card" **Deadline:** card must be returned to NEA by Feb. 1, 1990

NATIONAL ENDOWMENT FOR THE ARTS
THEATER PROGRAM
**NEA, Nancy Hanks Center Room 608,
1100 Pennsylvania Ave. NW, Washington, DC 20506
(202) 682-5425 Contact:** Ben Cameron
Program: 1-year fellowships of $10,000-$17,500 plus additional $2500 for residency at a professional theatre; awarded to playwrights whose work has been professionally produced within the past 5 years **Deadline:** May 31, 1990 **Your chances:** 228 applications in 1989/19 grants awarded

THE NATIONAL FOUNDATION FOR JEWISH CULTURE
**330 Seventh Ave. 21st Floor, New York, NY 10001
(212) 629-0500 Contact:** Andrea Aronson Morgan, Program Officer **Program:** an umbrella organization for programs and services in contemporary Jewish theatre in North America; services include information resources and consultation for theatres interested in producing plays on Jewish topics, advocacy, newsletter and catalogue, NFJC Playwrights' Travel Grant Program (see listing in this section), NFJC Hebrew Translation Commission (see Contests)

NATIONAL INSTITUTE FOR OPERA AND MUSIC THEATER
**John F. Kennedy Center, Washington, DC 20566
(202) 965-2800 Contact:** Maria L. Thompson, Program Manager
Program: a not-for-profit arts organization that supports American creators and performers during the early stages of their careers; grants to individuals and collaborative teams **Procedure:** request guidelines and application form in late summer; $20 fee upon application **Deadline:** late fall (inquire)

THE NATIONAL MUSIC THEATER NETWORK
**1457 Broadway Suite 1111, New York, NY 10036
(212) 382-0984 Contact:** C. Carroll Carter Jr., Executive Director **Program:** a service organization "committed to the discovery, evaluation and promotion of new music theatre"; services

include professional evaluations, listing of selected works in national catalogue, Sampler Series of excerpt concert performances; works must not have received a major production **Fee:** $30 for evaluation **Procedure:** send SASE for guidelines **Deadline:** ongoing program **Comment:** See Network New Music Theater Awards listing in Contests.

NEW AMERICAN PLAYS SERIES
New York Theatre Group, Box 1557,
New York, NY 10011 (718) 624-4680
Program: "A long-term developmental process of readings, workshops and full productions designed to explore different facets of contemporary American writing for the theatre by established and unknown writers." **Works:** full-length plays, one-acts **Special interests:** "Plays that challenge and provoke current social, political or cultural preconceptions; non-naturalistic styles." **Procedure:** "Send first 15-20 pages of script with SASE or SAS postcard." **Notification:** 3-6 months **Your chances:** 200-300 applications/ 10-20 new participants selected **Comment:** Formerly New American Theatre Project.

NEW CITY THEATER DIRECTOR'S FESTIVAL
1634 11th Ave., Seattle, WA 98122 (206) 323-6801
Contact: John Kazanjian, Artistic Director **Program:** an annual spring showcase for Seattle directors, playwrights and actors; plays receive one performance; 5 best plays run in repertory for 2 weeks **Works:** one-acts **Fee:** $30 **Procedure:** director should submit project (director is responsible for finances including playwright's royalty); all projects are accepted **Deadline:** Jan. 1, 1990

NEW COLLEGE PLAYWRIGHTS
The Playwrights' Center, 2301 Franklin Ave. E.,
Minneapolis, MN 55406 (612) 332-7481
Program: a 3-week conference of intensive classes and workshops (Jun.), for college-age writers, actors and directors interested in playwriting; participants receive college credit and a 1-year membership at The Playwrights' Center **Fee:** $500; scholarships available **Procedure:** phone or write for guidelines, available Mar. 1990 **Deadline:** Apr. 30, 1990 **Comment:** See The Playwrights' Center listing in this section.

NEW DRAMATISTS
424 W. 44th St., New York, NY 10036 (212) 757-6960
Contact: Joel K. Ruark, Managing Director **Program:** a membership organization open to all playwrights residing in New York City area and those residing elsewhere who can advantageously use

membership; services include developmental laboratory, library, loan fund, free ticket service for Broadway and off Broadway shows, international exchanges, ScriptShare national distribution service, Arnold Weissberger Award (see Contests), Composer/ Librettists Studio (see listing in this section); publications include bimonthly newsletter and monthly bulletin providing information on funding, competitions and other opportunities **Deadline:** Sept. 15, 1990 **Notification:** Spring 1991

THE NEW HARMONY PROJECT
Box 276, Ladoga, IN 47954
Program: annual 2-week conference (May-Jun.) for writers with unproduced, unoptioned works; Pre-Conference Weekend **Works:** plays, musicals, screenplays, teleplays **Accommodations:** housing, meals **Remuneration:** stipend, transportation **Procedure:** request guidelines **Deadline:** inquire (Dec. 1 in 1989)

NEW INDEPENDENTS PROJECT
The Play Works Company, Box 25152,
Philadelphia, PA 19147 (212) 236-8488
Contact: Christopher J. Rushton, Director **Program:** a 1-year (Sept. to Sept.), 7-step script development program, from consultation through play lab to public staged reading, which "fosters independent full-scale productions of new plays"; emphasis is on area playwrights, but program is open to all **Works:** full-length plays, one-acts, translations, adaptations, musicals **Fee:** $45 per year **Procedure:** send 2 scripts with SASE **Deadline:** spring (inquire) **Your chances:** 50 spaces available

THE NEW JERSEY PLAYWRIGHTS WORKSHOP
385 Ocean Blvd., Sea Verge 7S, Long Branch, NJ 07740
(201) 229-5491 Contact: Mary Ann Greco, Executive Director **Program:** a membership organization for New Jersey-based playwrights; programs include weekly classes in beginning and advanced playwriting, workshop readings with critiques, seminars, playwrights' speaker series, minority group program, high school and regional theatre outreach programs **Fee:** $150 for 10 class sessions **Procedure:** send SASE for information **Deadlines:** inquire (Sept. 15 and Dec. 15, 1989 for classes)

NEW WORKS THEATRE PLAYWRIGHTS' WORKSHOP
3926 Iowa St., San Diego, CA 92104 (612) 284-1105
Contact: Jack G. Barefield, Executive Director **Program:** a limited-membership, developmental workshop for experienced, published/produced writers in San Diego area (a writer whose work is promising may be accepted); programs include cold and rehearsed

readings of works-in-progress, possible public readings and full productions with local actors **Special interest:** educational entertainments for schools for which member playwrights write and actors perform for royalties and fees **Procedure:** send script with SASE and attend a meeting **Deadline:** ongoing program

NEW YORK FOUNDATION FOR THE ARTS
5 Beekman St. Suite 600, New York, NY 10038
(212) 233-3900 Contact: Lynda A. Hansen, Director; David Green, Assistant Director **Program:** a service organization offering Artists-Residencies in New York schools and communities, consultation services for arts in education, fiscal and advisory services for artists working on individual projects, fellowships, loans, conferences, workshops, seminars, publications; Artist Fellowship Program offers $7000 to playwrights and composers with 2 years residency in New York, professional accomplishment and commitment to professional careers; Artists' New Works Program: assistance for New York residents in development of arts projects (film, video, theatre, music and literature), sponsorship for not-for-profit status, fiscal management assistance, proposal reviews, fund-raising counsel (request guidelines) **Deadline:** Sept. 1990 (inquire); no application before Jun. 1, notification: 8 months

NFJC PLAYWRIGHTS' TRAVEL GRANT PROGRAM
National Foundation for Jewish Culture,
330 Seventh Ave. 21st Floor, New York, NY 10001
(212) 629-0500 Contact: Andrea Aronson Morgan, Program Officer **Program:** a travel grant of up to $250 for a playwright to work with a not-for-profit theatre in the U.S. or Canada during rehearsal of a previously unproduced play with a Jewish theme **Procedure:** producing theatre must request guidelines and application form **Deadline:** application due at least 1 month prior to 1st rehearsal

NORTH CAROLINA ARTS COUNCIL
VISITING ARTIST PROGRAM
Community Development Section,
North Carolina Arts Council, Dept. of Cultural Resources,
Raleigh, NC 27611 (919) 733-7897
Contact: Sheila Wright, Artists-In-Residence Coordinator
Program: residencies of 9 months-1 year (maximum term of participation: 4 years) for professional, committed artists at 58 community and technical colleges; artists-in-residence work for the communities in which the institutions are located, presenting workshops, lecture/demonstrations, in-school activities, readings and productions; "self-development time is set aside for artists to devote

to their own work"; masters degree or equivalent experience and training required, possible interview   **Remuneration:** negotiable salary ($17,000- $25,000) plus benefit package   **Procedure:** "Call or write prior to Feb. 1, 1990 for application; samples of work, resume and 3 reference letters are required."   **Best time:** "Nov. and Dec. are excellent months to contact us."   **Deadline:** Feb. 1, 1990   **Notification:** Mar. 31, 1990   **Your chances:** 248-280 applicants in all disciplines/70-140 residents selected; "no quotas; from theatre discipline we normally receive 30-50 applications, of which 3-8 are playwrights"   **Financial support:** grants and fellowships available to North Carolina artists   **Comment:** "Applicants may also be eligible for the Artists-In-Schools Program (grades K-12) and may participate in one or both types of residencies (community colleges or schools)."

NORTHWEST PLAYWRIGHTS GUILD
Box 95259, Seattle, WA 98145   (206) 365-6026
Contact: Sharon Glantz, President   **Program:** a service organization and information resource for playwrights; support services include in-house staged readings, public readings, bank of members' scripts, newsletter; discounts on Guild workshops (with such writers as Maria Irene Fornes and Jean-Claude van Itallie), script preparation services   **Fees:** $30 first year, $20 per year thereafter   **Procedure:** send fee for first year; all applicants accepted   **Comment:** See Northwest Playwrights Guild Competition in Contests.

NORTHWOOD INSTITUTE
ALDEN B. DOW CREATIVITY CENTER
Midland, MI 48640-2398   (517) 832-4478
Contact: Carol Coppage, Executive Director   **Program:** 10-week residency (mid-Jun.--mid-Aug. 1991) for artists in all disciplines whose project is "new and innovative" and has potential for impact in its field;   no families or pets   **Accommodations:** furnished apartment, study area,   meals   **Remuneration:** modest stipend, travel, project costs   **Procedure:** request guidelines, application form; resume, work samples, project budget required upon application   **Deadline:** Dec. 31, 1990   **Notification:** Apr. 1, 1991   **Your chances:** 4 spaces available

OLLANTAY CENTER FOR THE ARTS
Box 636, Jackson Heights, NY 11372   (718) 565-6499
Contact: Pedro R. Monge, Director   **Program:** a multi-art center (visual arts, literature, folk arts) serving mainly the Hispanic population the New York area; programs include writing workshops, staged readings, encounters with Hispanic writers resulting in publications; Traveling Theatre Playwriting Workshop: full bilingual

traveling productions of unproduced plays **Special interest:** the Latin American experience **Procedure:** send script with SASE for traveling workshop **Comment:** "An anthology of one-act plays—the first one-act plays to appear by Hispanics—will be published during the season."

O'NEILL OPERA/MUSIC THEATER CONFERENCE
New York, NY See National Music Theater Conference listing in Contests.

OREGON WRITERS COLONY
Box 15200, Portland, OR 97215 (503) 771-0428
Contact: Marlene Howard **Program:** 1-4 week residencies **Accommodations:** housing in a log house owned by Oregon Writers Colony **Fee:** $100 per week; some financial assistance available **Procedure:** request guidelines for "Colonyhouse" **Deadline:** inquire

PADUA HILLS PLAYWRIGHTS' WORKSHOP/FESTIVAL
Box 461450, Los Angeles, CA 90046 (213) 281-6799
Contact: Cheryl Bianchi, Executive Director **Program:** 6-week summer workshop in playwriting "with emphasis on developing the voice of the playwright"; program includes student readings with professional actors and participation in Padua Playwrights Festival; instructors include Maria Irene Fornes, Murray Mednick, David Henry Hwang, John Steppling, Alan Bolt, Lin Hixon, Jon Robin Baitz **Fee:** $1000 **Procedure:** request brochure; letter of intent and writing samples required upon application **Deadline:** May 15, 1990 **Notification:** early June 1990 **Your chances:** 100 applications/ 25 participants selected **Comment:** "Playwrights are invited to participate in the Festival. We do not accept scripts. Application is for students of the Workshop only."

PALENVILLE INTERARTS COLONY
2 Bond St., New York, NY 10012 (212) 254-4614
Contact: Patrick Sciarratta, Colony Director; Joanna M. Sherman, Artistic Director, Bond Street Theatre **Program:** 1-8 week residencies (Jun. 1-Sept. 30) for artists with at least 3 years' professional experience in their fields who "demonstrate a high level of artistic ability"; "active theatre space"; programs and services include readings, development with ensemble, full productions **Works:** full-length plays, one-acts, translations, adaptations, musicals, children's plays **Special interests:** "Artists who possess an appreciation of the global implication of their efforts; physical, skills-oriented theatre; socially-relevant satire."
Accommodations: private or semi-private room or cabin, studio

space, meals **Fee:** $250 per week suggested; grants related to specific projects available **Procedure:** send script with SASE and cover letter **Deadline:** Apr. 1, 1990; "applications are accepted after the deadline on a first come, first served basis; no grants/discounts available after deadline" **Notification:** within 4 weeks **Your chances:** 100+ applications/50 residencies available/ 1-2 playwrights accepted **Advice:** "Artists in all disciplines, and arts groups, are encouraged to apply."

PEN AMERICAN CENTER
568 Broadway, New York, NY 10012 (212) 334-1660
Contact: Karen Kennerly, Executive Director **Program:** a member of International PEN association of writers; activities include Freedom to Write and Freedom to Read; readings, symposia and other public events; translator-publisher resources; publisher-writer programs; publications include *Grants and Awards Available to American Writers;* annual awards include Renato Poggioli Award (see Contests); the PEN Writers' Fund (see listing in this section) **Fee:** $60 annually **Procedure:** "Apply to Membership Committee. Playwrights must have had at least 2 full-length plays produced by reputable theatres."

PEN TO STAGE PRODUCTIONS
Box 1253 Old Chelsea Station, New York, NY 10011
Contact: W. Squier **Program:** a developmental collective of New York City-area actors, directors, designers and writers dedicated to the development and promotion of the stage works of new American artists; weekly reading series; possible public presentation; programs include The Readings Workshop: cold readings of plays in progress, The Developmental Workshop: open rehearsals of plays in progress, The Open Workshop: staged readings, The Festival of New Works: minimally produced new plays presented in repertory **Works:** full-length plays, one-acts, adaptations, musicals **Specifications:** works must be 'theatrical' in nature **Fees:** "'Members' contribute whatever they can whenever they attend; 'Active Members' contribute a set amount on a monthly basis in exchange for a vote in major artistic decisions." **Procedure:** send dialogue sample (10 page maximum) typical of playwright's work, brief resume and SAS postcard **Notification:** 1-2 months **Your chances:** "Membership is open; we increase the size of the workshop to suit the number of members." **Advice:** "Playwrights who have been most successfully served by our organization are those who have been willing to extend themselves for the benefit of the other artists involved."

PEN WRITERS' FUND
**PEN American Center, 568 Broadway,
New York, NY 10012 (212) 334-1660**
Contact: Christine Friedlander, Program Coordinator **Program:** interest-free loans and grants of up to $1000 in emergency assistance for published or produced writers in financial difficulties **Procedure:** request guidelines **Your chances:** 150 applications/ 9-12 playwrights awarded funds; membership is limited to 15 **Comment:** "The PEN Writers' Fund also administers the PEN Fund for Writers and Editors with AIDS; grants range from $500 to $1000."

PERFORMING ARTS RESEARCH CENTER
**The New York Public Library at Lincoln Center,
111 Amsterdam Ave., New York, NY 10023
(212) 870-1639 (Billy Rose Theatre Collection),
(212) 870-1663 (Rodgers & Hammerstein Archives)**
Contact: Richard M. Buck, Assistant to the Chief **Program:** extensive collection of non-circulating research materials on theatre, music, dance, film, radio and TV; for in-depth research by advanced students, professionals, authors and specialists

PHILADELPHIA DRAMA GUILD PLAYWRIGHTS' PROJECT
Philadelphia, PA Philadelphia Drama Guild has requested that we discontinue this listing.

THE PHILADELPHIA THEATRE COMPANY'S MENTOR PROJECT
**Bourse Bldg, Suite 735, 21 S. 5th St.,
Philadelphia, PA 19106 (215) 592-8333**
Contact: Lynn M. Thomson, Artistic Associate/Literary Manager **Program:** 6-month residency program in which a master playwright-in-residence (Michael Weller in 1990; Arthur Kopit in 1989) conducts seminars and works closely with 2 apprentice playwrights **Procedure:** apprentices chosen through nationwide search; write for guidelines in Apr. 1990

PLAYFORMERS
20 Waterside Plaza #5A, New York, NY 10010
(212) 685-5394 Contact: Romola Allrud, Artistic Director **Program:** not-for-profit playwrights' support group meeting biweekly; professional readings of works-in-progress; calendar set at start of season **Fee:** voluntary contribution of $105 per year, $35 per quarter to support "a wine and cheese buffet at each meeting and clerical expenses" **Procedure:** send script with SASE, resume and bio; phone for details **Deadline:** ongoing program **Your chances:** 10 applications; new members accepted only when vacancies occur

Comments: "Membership is limited to 15; visitors are welcome. We are contemplating an Annex with a separate program of its own because many wish to join who can't because of our limitation or who aren't on a suitable professional level."

PLAYMARKET
Box 9767, Wellington, New Zealand
Phone: Wellington (04) 758-405 Contact: Ann Paetz, Administrator **Program:** New Zealand's principal agency for playwrights; services include script advisory and critiquing, arrangements for workshop productions of promising scripts, script preparation and distribution, contract negotiation and royalty collection; publications include *The Playmarket Directory of New Zealand Plays and Playwrights* and *New Zealand Theatrescripts* **Procedure:** request guidelines

THE PLAYWRIGHT/DIRECTOR WORKSHOP
c/o Charles Maryan, Director,
777 West End Ave. Apt. 6C, New York, NY 10025
(212) 864-0542 Program: a course designed for developing directors and playwrights, dealing with the process of a play from manuscript to production; 2 terms of 16 weeks each are held from Oct.-May **Fee:** $320 per 16-week term **Procedure:** send script with SASE; interview required **Your chances:** 20-30 applicants/ 1-2 new participants accepted **Comment:** "By design this is a very small group: no more than 12 including both directors and playwrights. More than 30 plays have been produced in U.S.A. We also accept screenwriters."

PLAYWRIGHT EXCHANGE
The Play Works Company, Box 25152,
Philadelphia, PA 19147 (212) 236-8488
Contact: Christopher J. Rushton, Director **Program:** an exchange of playwrights among The Play Works Company (see Theatres) and theatres in Boston, Chicago and New York City which produce the works of exchanged writers **Procedure:** send SASE for information; participants selected by program officers

THE PLAYWRIGHT IN RESIDENCE NEW WORKS PROGRAM
River Arts Repertory, Box 1166, Woodstock, NY 12498
(914) 679-2100 Contact: Marguerite Feitlowitz, Literary Manager **Program:** residency (Jul.-Aug.) in Woodstock for purpose of developing a script for a staged reading or full production; for plays not produced in New York City **Remuneration:** stipend **Procedure:** request guidelines before Mar. 1990; no requests for 1991 program before Oct. 1990 **Notification:** Jun. 1, 1990

THE PLAYWRIGHTS' CENTER
2301 Franklin Ave. E, Minneapolis, MN 55406
(612) 332-7481 **Program**: a service organization for playwrights; programs include developmental services (readings, staged readings, workshops, classes); conferences; exchanges with theatres and other programs; Jones Commissioning Program for one-acts; Playwrights-in-the Schools Residency Program; Storytalers professional touring company; Young Playwrights program for writers under 19 (see listing in this section); New College Playwrights (see listing in this section); fellowships: 6 annual Jerome Playwrights-in-Residence Fellowships of $5000 (see listing in this section), 6 annual McKnight Fellowships of $10,000 (see listing in this section); Midwest PlayLabs (see listing in this section); *Subtext* newsletter

PLAYWRIGHTS' CENTER OF CHICAGO
3716 N. Clark St., Chicago, IL 60613 **(312) 271-3468**
Contact: James W. MacDowell, Artistic Director **Program**: a membership organization for Chicago-area playwrights; activities include cold readings, workshops, staged readings, showcase productions of original scripts, classes in dramaturgy and other areas of theatre **Fees**: $100 per year; varying fees for classes **Procedure**: send SASE for guidelines and application form; membership fee required upon application **Deadline**: ongoing program

THE PLAYWRIGHTS' CENTER OF SAN FRANCISCO
1001 Pine St. #803, San Francisco, CA 94109
(415) 928-4451 **Contact**: Mona Scheyer, Reading Director **Program**: a membership organization for Bay Area playwrights; programs include weekly reading-critiques and DramaRama national competition (see Contests) **Procedure**: send SASE for guidelines

THE PLAYWRIGHTS FOUNDATION
Box 1191, Mill Valley, CA 94942 (415) 381-3311
Contact: Nonah Holmgren, President **Program**: a developmental support organization for northern California playwrights; programs include annual Bay Area Playwrights Festival: 4-6 workshop productions of new plays; Staged Reading Series: readings of 8-12 scripts per year (unsolicited scripts accepted), panel discussions and workshops led by established artists, publication of *Re:Write* newsletter, playwright- in-residence fellowships

PLAYWRIGHTS' PLATFORM
164 Brayton Rd., Boston, MA 02135
(617) 254-4482, 427-7450 **Contact**: Beverly Creasey, President **Program**: a membership organization for authors with unpublished, unproduced plays; participants are encouraged to become

members; services and activities include a developmental program of
weekly workshops, staged readings, referral and dramaturgical
services, newsletter; Annual One-Act Festival (summer); Festival of
Full-Length Plays (Jul.) for members' unproduced plays, deadline:
Mar. 20 1990 **Remuneration:** percentage of box office for Festival
production **Fee:** $15 per year **Procedure:** send script with SASE
Deadline: ongoing program

PLAYWRIGHT'S PREVIEW PRODUCTIONS, LTD.
Hartley House Theatre, 413 W. 46th St.
New York, NY 10036 (212) 289-2168
Contact: Frances W. Hill, James Keeler, Co-Artistic Directors
Program: developmental program (Sept.–May) for plays not
previously produced in the New York City area; activities include
staged readings, workshops, possible productions **Works:** small-
cast full-length plays and one-acts, small-scale musicals **Special
interest:** contemporary issues **Procedure:** send script with SASE
Deadline: ongoing program **Comment:** See Emerging Playwright
Award listing in Contests.

PLAYWRIGHTS THEATRE OF NEW JERSEY
33 Green Village Rd., Madison, NJ 07940
(201) 514-1787 Contact: Kate Clark, Literary Manager
Program: a service organization for playwrights and a theatre
producing new plays; services and activities include New Play
Development Program (see listing immediately following), The
Teachers and Playwrights Conference, Playwrights Information Center
offering advice to writers and sponsoring playwriting symposiums,
state-wide playwriting-in-the-schools program and playwriting-for-
teachers project, Madison Young Playwrights Festival (productions of
works by 4th-12th grade participants in city-wide playwriting-in-
the-schools program), special needs projects for playwrights (work
with senior citizens, the physically handicapped, teenage substance
abusers, juvenile offenders; playwriting-in-prisons initiative), "gifted
and talented playwriting symposiums" for students from various
school districts, adult playwriting classes

PLAYWRIGHTS THEATRE OF NEW JERSEY
NEW PLAY DEVELOPMENT PROGRAM
33 Green Village Rd., Madison, NJ 07940
(201) 514-1787 Contact: Kate Clark, Literary Manager
Program: development of unproduced plays by American playwrights; activities include readings, staged readings and workshop
productions, liason with other theatres **Works:** full-length plays,
one-acts, musicals **Special interest:** American works
Accommodations: housing **Remuneration:** living expenses

Procedure: send script with SASE, 1-page synopsis, script development history and resume **Deadline:** ongoing program **Notification:** 3 months **Your chances:** 500-800 applications/ 15-20 playwrights accepted **Comment:** "Our mission statement: 'A professional not-for-profit theatre dedicated to the development of new plays and writers for the stage.'"

THE PLAYWRIGHTS' UNIT
1733 Kilbourne Pl. NW, Washington, DC 20010
(202) 667-3623 Contact: Ernest Joselovitz, Administrator **Program:** 3-tier program for DC, MD and VA playwrights: **The Unit**, the permanent professional playwrights workshop; **The Forum**, apprenticeship program of continual 2-month sessions of 8-10 member groups; both offering biweekly meetings with roundtable discussions, in-house and public readings, intensive workshop readings, playlab; and **Associate Membership**, sharing free theatre ticket privileges, Playwrights-Read-Playwrights discussions, newsletter; additional programs include special classes in Re-Writes, Acting for Playwrights, From Script to Screen; Annual Playwrights Conference in Sept.: workshops, panels, guest speakers, food **Fees:** The Unit $60 for 6 months; The Forum $80 per 3-month session; Associate $20 per year **Procedure:** The Unit: send script with SASE, interview required; The Forum: registration in Jan., May, Sept. (priority to Associate Members); Associate: letter or application anytime **Your chances:** The Unit: 10 applications/3-4 playwrights accepted; The Forum: 40-50 applications per session/36 playwrights accepted; Associate: 75 applications/all accepted **Comments:** "1990 will be our 6th Conference; in 1989 over 140 playwrights attended."

THE PRESTON JONES NEW PLAY SYMPOSIUM
Houston, TX 77277 This program has been discontinued.

PRIMAFACIE/WESTFEST
Denver Center Theatre Company, 1050 13th St., Denver, CO 80204 (303) 893-4200
Contact: Barbara E. Sellers, Producing Director **Program:** an annual new play festival; 2-week residency (Apr. 30-May 12) includes rehearsal and staged reading by members of DCTC Acting Company; 3-4 scripts from series are chosen for full production **Works:** full-length plays **Maximum cast:** 12 **Procedure:** send script with SASE **Deadline:** Dec. 30, 1990 **Your chances:** 600 submissions/8-10 scripts selected **Comments:** PrimaFacie readings are held concurrently with the production run of new plays selected from the previous year's festival. Previous winners of PrimaFacie are produced in WestFest.

PRIMARY STAGES COMPANY
584 Ninth Ave., New York, NY 10036 (212) 333-7471
Contact: Seth Gordon, Literary Manager **Program:** a developmental program of readings, workshop productions, full productions; for American playwrights with unproduced plays or plays not produced in New York or in need of development **Remuneration:** stipend for full production **Procedure:** send script with SASE, cover letter and resume **Deadline:** ongoing program **Notification:** 1-6 months **Comment:** See 45th Street Theatre listing in Theatres.

PRINCESS GRACE FOUNDATION-U.S.A.
174 E. 80th St., New York, NY 10021 (212) 744-3221
Contact: Inge Heckel, Pamela Signorella **Program:** scholarships, apprenticeships and fellowships for young artists working in theatre, dance and film **Procedure:** nomination by artistic director of theatre where artist is working; request guidelines

PROFESSIONAL ASSOCIATION OF CANADIAN THEATRE/PACT COMMUNICATIONS CENTER
64 Charles St. E, Toronto, Ontario, Canada M4Y 1T1
(416) 968-3033 **Contact:** Catherine Smalley, Executive Director **Program:** the national service and trade association for professional English-language theatres in Canada; services include government advocacy, negotiation of collective agreements, public awareness programs, PACT Communications Center serving as charitable wing to improve and expand communications and information services; publications include *Behind the Scenes: A guide to Canadian non-profit professional theatres and theatre-related resources*, monthly *Artsboard* bulletin of job opportunities, *Canada on Stage* yearbook of theatrical activity

PUERTO RICAN TRAVELING THEATRE PLAYWRIGHTS' WORKSHOP
141 W. 94th St., New York, NY 10025 (212) 354-1293
Contact: Allen Davis III, Director **Program:** workshop (Oct.-Jul.) with beginning and professional units for New York City-area residents; Hispanic writers preferred, but open to non-Hispanics; activities include weekly meetings, discussions, readings, development, staged readings for 1-2 workshop productions **Procedure:** professionals send full-length play with SASE and resume; beginners phone above number and leave name and number **Deadline:** Sept. 30, 1990 **Notification:** 1 month **Comment:** "We are a bilingual organization; all works are produced in English and in Spanish."

PUERTO RICAN TRAVELING THEATRE
TRAINING UNIT FOR YOUNGSTERS
141 W. 94th St., New York, NY 10025
(212) 354-1293 Contact: Allen Davis III, Director
Program: a bilingual (English and Spanish) training program (Jan.-Jul.) in all aspects of theatre for youngsters aged 14 and over; class includes about 250 participants **Procedure:** phone in fall for information

RAGDALE FOUNDATION
1260 N. Green Bay Rd., Lake Forest, IL 60045
(312) 234-1063 Contact: Jill Harris, Acting Director
Program: 1 week-2 month residencies **Accommodations:** private room, meals **Fee:** $70 per week; financial assistance may be available upon statement of need **Procedure:** request guidelines; letter of intent, resume, work samples, 3 recommendations required upon application **Deadline:** 3-6 months prior to date of desired residency **Your chances:** 12 spaces available

RED MOON ENSEMBLE
WRITERS AND ACTORS WORKSHOP
Box 2122 Times Square Station, New York, NY 10108
Contact: Jamie Richards **Program:** ongoing weekly workshop directed by Todd Peters and using acting ensemble; readings of plays-in-progress followed by moderated discussions; selected works receive staged readings in Red Moon's Playreading Series **Fee:** $50 per month **Procedure:** send SASE for information

RED OCTOPUS THEATRE COMPANY
ORIGINAL SCRIPTS WORKSHOP
Box 1403, Newport, OR 97365 (503) 265-9231
Contact: Bernadette Robinson, Managing Director **Program:** 2-3 week developmental workshop for as many as 10 unproduced works-in-progress (one-acts or excerpts from full-length plays); program includes collaboration with director and actors, staged readings at Newport Performing Arts Center, possible production **Works:** full-length plays, one-acts, adaptations, musicals **Accommodations:** housing **Remuneration:** small honorarium, partial travel **Procedure:** send script with SASE **Deadline:** Oct. 15, 1990 **Notification:** Dec. 1990 **Your chances:** 50-75 applications/6-10 playwrights accepted

THE ROCKEFELLER FOUNDATION GRANTS
1133 Avenue of the Americas, New York, Ny 10036
(212) 869-8500 Contact: Karen Kaplan This program is undergoing changes; playwrights are advised to inquire.

THE ROCKEFELLER FOUNDATION'S BELLAGIO STUDY AND CONFERENCE CENTER

Bellagio Center Office, 1133 Avenue of the Americas, New York, NY 10036 (212) 869-8500
Program: 4-or 5-week residencies at Villa Serbelloni on Lake Como, Italy, for scholars and artists "of achievement with significant publications, compositions or shows to their credit" in any discipline; spouses welcome; no children or pets; women and minority scholars encouraged **Accommodations:** private room with bath, study, meals **Fee:** none **Procedure:** request guidelines **Deadline:** applications due 12 months prior to expected residency **Your chances:** 500 applications/135 residents selected **Comment:** Center is closed mid-Dec.--mid-Jan. each year.

ROUNDABOUT THEATRE'S CREATIVE CONNECTION

Roundabout Theatre Conservatory, 100 E. 17th St., New York, NY 10003 (212) 420-1360
Contact: Janet McCall, Conservatory Director **Program:** playwriting classes offered each fall and spring **Fee:** inquire **Procedure:** send SASE for guidelines

SASKATCHEWAN WRITERS/ARTISTS COLONIES

Box 3986, Regina, Saskatchewan S0A 4T0 Canada (306) 757-6310 Contact: Paul Wilson
Programs: 3 colonies: St. Peter's College in Muenster; Fort San, Echo Valley; Emma Lake **Fee:** $40 per week **Procedure:** phone or write for guidelines for each colony; resume, work samples, work plan and 2 references required upon application

THE SCRIPT REVIEW

Box 925, Arlington Heights, IL 60006
Contact: Timothy Mooney **Program:** a newsletter providing reports on new manuscripts to literary managers, dramaturgs, artistic directors, producers, theatre programs and agents; program included occasional readings **Fees:** $10 for listing; $20 for subscription **Procedure:** send script with SASE and listing fee

SHENANDOAH PLAYWRIGHTS RETREAT

ShenanArts, Route 5, Box 167-F, Staunton, VA 24401 (703) 248-1868
Contact: Robert Graham Small, Director **Program:** a fellowship for a 3-week residency (Jul-Aug.) at Pennyroyal Farm, for the purpose of providing "a stimulating, challenging environment for playwrights and screenwriters to test and develop new work"; activities include personal writing time; readings by writers of their own works, discussions with directors and dramaturgs, workshops

providing "on-the-feet/on-the page" explorations of each play with acting company, public staged readings, discussions; individual residencies of 3-6 weeks during spring-summer also available (submit proposal) **Works:** full-length plays, one-acts, translations, adaptations **Remuneration:** fellowships available, based on competition for admission: The Jack Morrison Playwriting Fellowship and The Retreat Alumni Fellowship (inquire), American College Theatre Festival Fellowships (see American College Theatre Festival listing in Contests) **Procedure:** send 2 bound copies of script typed in standard format, SASE, personal statement of writing background, SAS postcard **Deadline:** Apr. 1, 1990 **Notification:** after Jun. 1, 1990 **Your chances:** 300+ applications/12 participants accepted **Comment:** See Virginia Playwriting Fellowships and Virginia TheatreWorks II listings in this section.

THE SONGWRITERS GUILD OF AMERICA
276 Fifth Ave. Suite 306, New York, NY 10001
Contact: Lewis M. Bachman, Executive Director **Program:** a voluntary national association operated by and for songwriters in all areas of music; programs and services include advice and protection for songwriters in dealings with publishers, a series of educational programs, contract review, collection service for non-performance royalties, health and life insurance, ASK-A-PRO and Song Critique programs, lyric- and song-writing classes **Procedure:** request application form for Full membership (for published composers and lyricists) or Associate membership (for those who wish to learn about songwriting); $45 deposit required upon application **Dues:** $55-$350 per year full member; $45 per year associate member

SOURCEWORKS
Source Theatre Company, 1809 14th St. NW,
Washington, DC 20009 (202) 462-1073
Contact: Pat Murphy Sheehy, Artistic Director **Program:** at least 20 evenings (Oct.-May) of script-in-hand productions of original new works or "theatre rarities"; host organization for emerging projects from Washington area playwright support groups and new production companies **Procedure:** send SASE for guidelines

SOUTHEAST PLAYWRIGHTS PROJECT
Box 14252, Atlanta, GA 30324 (404) 985-8023
Contact: Shery Sheppard Kearney, Executive Director **Program:** a service organization for playwrights and dramaturgs who reside, or who have resided, in the Southeast; programs include script development (cold readings, rehearsed and staged readings, non-performance workshops, bi-monthly Writers' Lab and Writers' Gym) and career development (dramaturgical advice, retreats,

networking, mentor program, free theatre tickets); internships in literary management available; programs planned for the future include script circulation service, fellowships, emergency loan fund, classes, publications of directories of dramaturgs and directors **Works:** full-length plays, one-acts, translations, adaptations, musicals, children's plays **Fees:** $25 Subscribing Member (receives mailings, newsletter and workshop discounts); $50 General, Full or Associate Member **Procedure:** "Associate and Full Members (eligible for script development beyond Writers' Lab level) are elected by committee in Feb. based on script submissions and/or productions." **Your chances:** Full Members: 10-20 applications/1-4 participants accepted; Associates: 75 applications/7-8 participants accepted

SOUTHERN ILLINOIS UNIVERSITY PLAYWRIGHT'S WORKSHOP
Carbondale, IL   This program is currently inactive.

SOUTHWEST THEATRE ASSOCIATION/ MARIE LAYTON BLISS NEW PLAYS PROGRAM
Norman, OK   This program is currently inactive.

S.T.A.G.E.
Box 214820, 4633 Insurance, Dallas, TX 75221
(214) 559-3917   Contact: Julie Holman, Executive Director
Program: a membership organization for playwrights, actors, designers and directors in southwestern U.S.; services include resource and script library, audition callboards, career counseling, advice on resume preparation and contracts, publication of *Center Stage*, Exposure/Stages: production of original one-acts for 4 nights in July (inquire) **Fee:** $35

STAGES
The Philadelphia Theatre Company, Bourse Bldg. Suite 735, 21 S. 5th St., Philadelphia, PA 19106
(215) 592-8333   Contact: Lynn M. Thomson, Literary Manager
Program: a 2-week developmental program (spring) of workshop productions; activities include classes, guest artists and speakers, readings, workshops; pre-program Weekend Writers Retreat (Mar. 1991) **Works:** full-length plays, one-acts **Regulations:** works must be unproduced or substantially revised **Accommodations:** housing **Remuneration:** stipend, travel **Procedure:** send script with SASE, synopsis and resume **Deadline:** Dec. 15, 1990 **Notification:** Apr. 1991 **Your chances:** 600 submissions/3 scripts selected

STAGE II WORKSHOPS
**Long Wharf Theatre, 222 Sargent Dr.,
New Haven, CT 06511 (203) 787-4284**
Contact: James Luse, Literary Analyst **Program:** a developmental residency (Dec.-Mar.) providing 3 weeks of rehearsals, 3 weeks of performances before an audience, with playwright in residence for the entire time; opportunity to rewrite; possible full production **Accommodations:** housing **Remuneration:** stipend **Procedure:** submit through agent (preferred method), or send query/synopsis with dialogue sample, resume, professional recommendation and production experience **Deadline:** ongoing program, decisions made in Oct. **Your chances:** 200 submissions/4 playwrights selected

THE SUNDANCE INSTITUTE PLAYWRIGHTS LABORATORY
RR 3, Box 624-B, Sundance, UT 84604 (801) 225-8844
Contact: David Kirk Chambers **Program:** a 3-week developmental program (Jul.) providing intensive workshops and readings of unproduced full-length plays and one-acts **Accommodations:** room, meals **Remuneration:** travel **Procedure:** nomination of playwright and specific script by a committed not-for-profit theatre **Your chances:** 200 nominations/10 playwrights selected **Deadline:** Dec. 15, 1990 **Comments:** Other programs: Film Composers Laboratory for professional composers, Independent Feature Film Program for screenwriters and filmmaking teams (inquire). See Bannon, Barbara M., "Letter From Sundance," *TheaterWeek,* Sept. 18, 1989, 15-16.

TCG OBSERVERSHIP PROGRAM
**Theatre Communications Group, 355 Lexington Ave.,
New York, NY 10017 (212) 697-5230**
Contact: Arthur Bartow, Associate Director **Program:** semi-annual grants in 3 categories: Category I/Affiliated Artists (artists holding salaried positions with TCG affiliated theatres) and Category II/Unaffiliated Artists offer grants of up to $2000 for inter-city travel in U.S. and Canada, $75 per diem to enable "theatre artists to extend their artistic boundaries by exploring the work of colleagues in other locations," trips of at least 1 week including visits to no fewer than 3 theatres; Category III/Rehearsal Observerships offers grants for inter-city travel to enable writers whose work is receiving full production at a TCG Constituent theatre to be in residence for a minimum of 2 weeks during rehearsal period **Procedure:** application or nomination by TCG Constituent theatres **Deadlines:** Feb. 15, 1990; Sept. 15, 1990

THEATER IN THE WORKS
112 Fine Arts Center, University of Massachusetts, Amherst, MA 01003 (413) 545-3490, -0681
Contact: Virginia Scott, Resident Dramaturg **Program:** a 2-week residency (Jul.) for development of substantially unproduced plays-in-process with limited practical requirements and/or small-scale musicals; playwright spends first week working with director and dramaturg, second week with professional company; two book-in-hand performances before audience invited to discuss the play with the playwright **Works:** full-length plays, related one-acts **Accommodations:** housing **Remuneration:** $325 weekly stipend, travel **Procedure:** send script with SASE **Deadline:** Mar. 15, 1990 **Notification:** May 15, 1990 **Your chances:** 4 spaces available

THEATRE ARTISTS WORKSHOP OF WESTPORT, INC.
17 Morningside Dr. S, Westport, CT 06880
(203) 227-5836 Contact: Doug Scott, President **Program:** a not-for-profit membership organization for professional-caliber playwrights, composers, librettists and lyricists; activities include development in collaboration with member actors, directors and other theatre artists; readings, staged readings, workshop productions, peer evaluations **Fee:** $50 initial fee; $200 per year **Procedure:** send SASE for guidelines and application form **Deadline:** ongoing program

THEATRE BAY AREA
2940 16th St. Suite 102, San Francisco, CA 94103
(415) 621-0427 Contact: Jean Schiffman, Communications Director **Program:** a membership and resource organization for theatre artists in the San Francisco area; support services available; publications include *Callboard* monthly magazine and *Theatre Directory of the San Francisco Bay Area* ($15 for non-members, $12 for members) which includes resources for playwrights **Fees:** $27 per year individual, $32 per year organization **Procedure:** send dues

THEATRE COMMUNICATIONS GROUP (TCG)
355 Lexington Ave., New York, NY 10017
(212) 697-5230 Contact: Peter Zeisler, Director; Tony Kushner, Director of Literary Services **Program:** the national organization for America's professional not-for-profit theatres; programs and services include conferences, seminars, TCG Translation/Adaptation Commissions (see Contests), TCG Observership Program (see listing in this section), a theatre resource library and computerized data bank; publications include *Dramatists*

Sourcebook (see The Playwright's Library), *American Theatre* magazine (see Publishers and The Playwright's Library) and *Plays in Process/New Plays USA* (see Publishers), *ArtSEARCH* bulletin of job opportunities, *Theatre Profiles* guide to TCG'S 200+ constituent theatres

THEATRE DEVELOPMENT FUND
1501 Broadway, New York, NY 10036
Contact: Henry Guettel, Executive Director   **Program:** a not-for-profit service organization dedicated to the development of professional theatre and encouraging the production of new plays and musicals, increasing audiences for all performing arts and working to resolve problems within the theatre community; programs include TKTS half-price booth in Times Square, the Costume Collection, the Theatre Access Project making theatre available to handicapped theatregoers, NYC/On Stage 24-hour telephone service providing information on performances in New York (212) 587-1111 or out of state 1 (800) STAGENY

THIRD STEP THEATRE COMPANY
SPRING FESTIVAL OF STAGED READINGS
New York, NY   See listing in Contests.

TYRONE GUTHRIE CENTER
Annaghmakerrig, Newbliss, County Monaghan, Ireland
Contact: Bernard Loughlin, Resident Director   **Program:** 1–3 week residencies for all artists who have had work published or produced **Accommodations:** private apartment in a country house; music and rehearsal room available   **Fee:** 1000 Irish pounds per month for artists from abroad   **Procedure:** request application form; work sample, resume and letter of intent required upon application **Deadline:** ongoing program   **Notification:** 1 month   **Advice:** "Particular consideration will be given to clear outline of project to be undertaken at the Center."

UCROSS FOUNDATION
2836 US Hwy. 14–16 E, Clearmont, WY 82835
Contact: Heather Burgess, Director   **Program:** 2 week–4 month residencies in rural ranching community   **Accommodations:** living and studio space, meals   **Deadlines:** Mar. 1, 1990 for Aug.–Dec. 1990; Oct. 1, 1990 for Jan.–May 1991   **Notification:** 6–8 weeks

UNIVERSITY OF ALABAMA
NEW PLAYWRIGHTS' PROGRAM
Dept. of Theatre & Dance, Box 870239, University of Alabama, Tuscaloosa, AL 35487-0239 (205) 348-9032
Contact: Director **Program:** a developmental residency (Sept.-May) for emerging playwright with previous experience; activities include staged reading, workshop or full production; resident may offer limited workshops and oversee staging of student work **Special interest:** unproduced scripts **Accommodations:** housing **Remuneration:** stipend, travel **Procedure:** send script with SASE and cover letter describing ways script might benefit from staged reading and dramaturgy **Deadline:** ongoing program **Notification:** 6-8 weeks

UNIVERSITY OF WISCONSIN
MADISON SCHOOL OF THE ARTS AT RHINELANDER
610 Langdon Room 727, Madison, WI 53703
Program: summer courses in theatre: playwriting, improvisational drama, story-telling and dramatization and play analysis lab; professional playwright leads workshop for 10 advanced playwrights; classes available in other areas **Fee:** $120 for 1 week

VIRGINIA CENTER FOR THE ARTS
Mt. San Angelo, Sweet Briar, VA 24595 (804) 946-7236
Contact: William Smart, Director **Program:** 3 week-3 month residential fellowships on 445-acre estate; for professional playwrights, composers and lyricists **Accommodations:** room, private studio, meals **Fee:** $20 per day **Procedure:** request guidelines; letter of intent, resume, work samples, 2 recommendations and $15 filing fee required upon application **Deadlines:** Jan. 25, 1990 for May-Sept. 1990; Apr. 25, 1990 for Sept. 1990-Jan. 1991; Sept. 25, 1990 for Jan.-May 1991 **Notification:** 8 weeks **Your chances:** 24 spaces available

VIRGINIA PLAYWRIGHTS FELLOWSHIPS
ShenanArts, Route 5, Box 167F, Staunton, VA 24401 (703) 248-1868 Contact: Robert Graham Small, Director **Program:** 1 or 2 annual fellowships of $2000 and acceptance to 1990 Shenandoah Valley Playwrights Retreat (see listing in this section) for playwrights and screenwriters who have resided in Virginia for major portion of past year; students ineligible **Works:** full-length plays, one-acts, translations, adaptations **Procedure:** send 2 copies of a draft of the scipt with SASE, a personal statement of writer's background and SAS postcard **Deadline:** Apr. 1, 1990 **Notification:** Jun. 1, 1990 **Your chances:** 300+ applications/ 12 participants selected

VIRGINIA THEATREWORKS III
ShenanArts, Bo 167-F, Route 5, Staunton, VA 24401
(703) 248-1868   Contact: Robert Graham Small, Director
Program: annual 3-day weekend workshop/conference (Jul.) in Richmond, VA, for playwrights to meet and interact with Virginia theatre artists, directors and actors; participants observe rehearsals and take part in workshops and discussions on playwriting **Fee:** $100
Procedure: send SASE for guidelines

VOLUNTEER LAWYERS FOR THE ARTS (VLA)
1285 Avenue of the Americas 3rd Floor,
New York, NY 10019 (212) 977-9270
Program: a national organization arranging free legal representation and counseling for artists and not-for-profit organizations unable to afford private counsel and with arts-related legal problems; services include educational program of seminars on not-for-profit incorporation, legal workshops, national conferences; publications include *Law & the Arts* quarterly journal ($35 annual subscription) and guides covering issues in copyright, contracts, privacy and libel, as well as several publications on legal and business essentials for artists

THE WASHINGTON THEATRE FESTIVAL
Source Theatre Company, 1809 14th St. NW,
Washington, DC 20009 (202) 462-1073
Contact: Pat Murphy Sheehy, Artistic Director   **Program:** annual program (Jul.-Aug.) involving small professional theatres "on and around 14th Street"; The New Play Showcase: 10 evenings of full productions of full-length plays or evenings of one-acts, Theatre Row Events: 10 workshop productions receive 1-3 performances each, The Ten-Minute Play Competition: 3-night event with at least 25 entries **Remuneration:** $75 grand prize; awards presented at Festival Awards Ceremony   **Procedure:** send SASE for guidelines

WEST COAST PLAYWRIGHTS WORKSHOP
Box 2370, Mill Valley, CA 94242 (415) 388-5200
Contact: Michelle Swanson, Robert Hedley, Artistic Directors
Program: a developmental workshop which collaborates with Marin Theatre Company (see Theatres), The Ensemble Theatre of Marin, the College of Marin Drama Dept. and Iowa Playwrights Workshop; programs and services include a variety of workshops and long-term developmental work with selected writers   **Fee:** tuition for workshops (inquire) **Procedure:** send SASE for guidelines

WESTFEST
Denver, CO   See PrimaFacie/WestFest listing in this section.

WHETSTONE THEATRE COMPANY
PLAYWRIGHTS PROGRAM
Box 800, Putney, VT 05346 (802) 387-4355
Contact: Tamara Tormohlen, Managing Director   **Program:** a developmental program for plays not professionally produced; activities include public workshops, staged readings, discussions, possible production **Accommodations:** housing **Remuneration:** stipend, possible travel **Works:** full-length plays, one-acts, translations, adaptations, musicals, children's plays **Procedure:** send script with SASE **Your chances:** 30 submissions/1 production plus 5–6 staged readings

WOMEN IN THEATRE FESTIVAL
64 Wyman St., Jamaica Plain, MA 02130
(617) 524-0971 Contact: Sophie Parker, Festival Director
Program: organization providing exposure for women in theatre arts and nurturing women's theatre network; services include publication of *Women in Theatre Resource Guide* and annual multi-cultural/multi-racial festival (Mar.) of previously mounted productions of new works in association with Massachusetts performing arts centers and universities **Procedure:** send SASE for guidelines **Deadline:** fall 1990; inquire (Sept. 30 in 1989) **Notification:** Nov. 1990

THE WOMEN'S PROJECT AND PRODUCTIONS
See listing in Theatres.

WOW (WOMEN ONE WORLD) CAFE
59 E. 4th St., New York, NY 10003 (212) 460-8067
Contact: Claire Moed, WOWette-at-large   **Program:** a cooperative membership organization for women playwrights, producers, directors and performers (men are welcome if event is coordinated by a woman); program provides an opportunity for playwrights to see and work in plays that may be presented in readings, staged readings or workshops; members are expected to cooperate in all aspects of the program; meetings generally take place on Tuesday evenings **Remuneration:** members may share in box office receipts **Procedure:** send SASE for guidelines

THE WRITERS ROOM
153 Waverly Place 5th Floor, New York, NY 10014
Contact: Renata Rizzo-Harvi, Executive Director **Program:** an urban writers colony in Greenwich Village open 24 hours, 7 days a week, and offering highly subsidized work space to more than 125 writers annually; writers of all genres welcome; programs and services include monthly readings **Accommodations:** work space, library/lounge, kitchen facilities **Fee:** rent of $150 per quarter **Procedure:** request application form; three references and $50 application fee required upon application

YADDO
Box 395, Saratoga Springs, NY 12866 (518) 584-0746
Contact: Myra Sklarew, President **Program:** 1-2 month residencies for professional artists **Accommodations:** room, studio space, meals **Fee:** "Voluntary contribution of $20 per day is encouraged to help defray the cost of the residency; no qualified artist will be denied admission on the basis of inability to contribute to cost." **Procedure:** send work samples, two sponsors' letters and $20 application fee **Deadlines:** Jan. 15, 1990 for 1990-91; Aug. 1, 1990 for remaining winter 1990-91 space **Notification:** 6 weeks after deadline

THE YARD
325 Spring St., New York, NY 10013 (212) 206-7885
Contact: Walt Sado, Administrative Director **Program:** 6-8 week residencies (May 15-Jun. 30) in Chilmark, Martha's Vineyard, for collaborations of choreographer and artist from any other discipline on new work; 2 selected teams work with performing artists; works premiere in 100-seat Barn Theater; possible Boston and/or New York performance in Sept. **Remuneration:** stipend **Procedure:** submit joint proposal **Deadline:** Dec. 15, 1990 **Notification:** Feb. 1991

YELLOW SPRINGS INSTITUTE
Art School Rd., Chester Springs, PA 19425
(215) 827-9111 Contact: Vesna Todorovic Miksic, Associate Director **Program:** annual Artists' Residency Fellowships (Apr.-Nov.) in dance, performance art, sound research, experimental theatre and interdisciplinary forms for the development of new, unproduced works; residents must have at least 3 years professional experience in field **Special interest:** "Projects that merge or transcend traditional disciplines and reveal new perspective on contemporary life." **Accommodations:** room, meals, supplies, facilities, technical support **Procedure:** send SASE for guidelines and application form by mid-fall 1990; project description and

supporting materials required upon application **Deadline:** Dec. 14, 1990 **Notification:** spring 1991

YOUNG PLAYWRIGHTS
The Playwrights' Center, 2301 Franklin Ave. E, Minneapolis, MN 55406 (612) 332-7581
Program: year-round activities for playwrights under 19 years of age: Young Playwrights Summer Playwriting Conference (scholarships and college credit available); mentorships with professional playwrights; readings and workshops with theatre professionals; Playwrights Center classes; Play Readings and Shoptalks; Young Playwrights Newsletter; teacher training **Fee:** $500 tuition; financial aid/scholarship available **Procedure:** phone or write for application forms, available Mar. 1990 **Your chances:** 75 applications/15-30 playwrights selected **Comment:** See The Playwrights' Center listing in this section.

ZEN MOUNTAIN MONASTERY
Box 197D, S. Plank Rd., Mt. Tremper, NY 12457
Contact: Geoffrey Arnold, Information Officer **Program:** artist-in-residencies (1-month minimum) available for professional, working artists seriously interested in completing a body of work while engaging in authentic Zen practice in traditional monastic setting; daily meditation and monastic activities integrated with 5-6 hours for art work **Procedure:** send letter of application and portfolio

Publishers

Guidelines for submitting work to the publishers listed in this section:

Read each listing thoroughly and carefully and follow any advice offered. Do not expect a publisher to alter its exclusive interests or specifications in order to publish your play.

Comply exactly with each publisher's stated submission policy. Be certain that appropriate materials accompany each submission (see The Playwright's Checklist and individual listings).

Do not expect a publisher to return any materials, or respond to any correspondence, not accompanied by self-addressed mailers or envelopes, adequately stamped and large enough to accommodate the materials to be mailed.

AMELIA MAGAZINE
See Frank McClure One-Act Play Award listing in Contests.

AMERICAN THEATRE MAGAZINE
Theatre Communications Group, 355 Lexington Ave., New York, NY 10017 (212) 697-5230
Contact: Jim O'Quinn, Editor **Publication**: monthly magazine **Works**: full-length plays, one-acts, translations, adaptations, children's plays **Special interests**: contemporary works; translations; works produced by TCG theatres **Readership**: general **Submission policy**: solicited script **Your chances:** 5 plays published **Remuneration**: negotiable fee; complimentary copies

THE AMERICAS REVIEW AND ARTE PUBLICO PRESS
University of Houston, 4800 Calhoun, Houston, TX 77004 (713) 749-4768 Contact: Nicolás Kanellos, Publisher **Works**: full-length plays, one-acts, adaptations, musicals, children's plays **Guidelines**: authors must be Hispanic; works must be written in either Spanish or English; unpublished works only for *The Americas Review;* writers published by Arte Publico Press are usually those previously published in *The Americas Review* **Submission policy:** unsolicited script with SASE **Response**: 3 months **Remuneration**: *The Americas Review* : fee, 2 copies; Arte Publico Press: negotiable royalty, complimentary copies

ANCHORAGE PRESS, INC.
Box 8067, New Orleans, LA 70182 (504) 283-8868
Contact: Orlin Corey, Editor **Press:** specialty house **Works:** children's plays: full-length plays, one-acts, translations, adaptations, musicals **Guidelines:** works must be previously produced plays (at least 3 productions required, 5 preferred), written for trained actors **Readership:** "All working theatres, whether educationally based, community or professional." **Submission policy:** unsolicited script with SASE and proof of productions (reviews, programs); professional recommendation; agent submission **Response:** 30 days query; 120 days script **Your chances:** 1000+ submissions/10 plays published **Remuneration:** 50% of royalties, 10% of play sales; 10 copies **Advice:** "Read the literature in the field; see a current Anchorage Press catalogue; work in the theatre in general; master the development of plays through productions first."

APALACHEE QUARTERLY
Box 20106, Tallahassee, FL 32316
Contact: Barbara Hamby, Co-Editor **Publication:** literary quarterly **Works:** one-act plays, translations, adaptations, performance-art and experimental pieces **Submission policy:** unsolicited script with SASE **Response:** 2-3 months **Remuneration:** "Fee when grant money is available; 2 copies and discount of additional copies." **Comment:** A special theme issue is published once each year.

ARAN PRESS
1320 S. Third St., Louisville, KY 40208 (502) 636-0115
Contact: Tom Eagan, Editor & Publisher **Works:** full-length plays, one-acts, translations, adaptations **Special interests:** "We concentrate on 5 markets: professional theatre, community theatre, summer stock, dinner theatre and college/university theatre." **Guidelines:** "Standard play format; typed. All subjects." **Readership:** "Hopefully our readers are producers!" **Submission policy:** query/synopsis preferred; unsolicited script with SASE **Response:** 2 weeks **Your chances:** 200-300 submissions/50 plays published **Remuneration:** 50% production royalty, 10% book royalty **Advice:** "We issue a catalogue each year of the plays we publish." **Comment:** Writers subsidize publication: $100 for full-length play, $50 for one-act.

ART CRAFT PLAY COMPANY/
HEUER PUBLISHING COMPANY
233 Dows Bldg., Cedar Rapids, IA 52406
(319) 364-6311 Contact: C. E. McMullen, Editor & Publisher
Works: 3-act plays, one-acts, musicals **Guidelines:** "Material

must be within the scope of high school students." **Submission policy**: unsolicited script with SASE; query/synopsis **Best time**: early spring **Response**: 2 months **Remuneration**: "Either outright payment or percentage; 12 copies."

ARTE PUBLICO PRESS

See The Americas Review and Arte Publico Press listing in this section.

BAKER'S PLAYS

100 Chauncy St., Boston, MA 02111 (617) 482-1280
Contact: John B. Welch, Editor **Works**: full-length plays, one-acts, adaptations, musicals, children's plays, chancel dramas **Special interests**: religious plays; "mature plays for teen actors" for Plays for Young Adults Division **Guidelines**: previously produced plays preferred; length: 24-80 pages **Readership**: "High school, community, university and children's theatre; religious theatre." **Submission policy**: unsolicited script with SASE; query/synopsis; agent submission **Response**: 1 week query; 4 months script **Your chances**: 800 submissions/20-15 plays published **Remuneration**: "From 50%-80%; 6 copies." **Program**: High School Playwriting Contest (see Contests) **Advice**: "Get it produced. Collaborate with an understanding director and actors." **Comment**: Baker's publishes as many as 25 scripts for the amateur market each year.

BALL STATE UNIVERSITY FORUM

Ball State University, Muncie, IN 47306 (317) 285-8456
Contact: Bruce W. Hozeski, Editor-in-Chief **Publication**: quarterly journal of humanities **Works**: full-length plays, one-acts, translations, adaptations **Guidelines**: works must be unpublished **Submission policy**: unsolicited script with SASE **Response**: 4 months **Remuneration**: 1 copy and offprints

THE BELLINGHAM REVIEW

The Signpost Press, Box 4065, Bellingham, WA 98227
Contact: Shelley Rozen, Editor **Publication**: semi-annual small-press periodical publishing short plays, poetry and fiction **Works**: one-acts **Guidelines**: works must be unpublished; length: under 5000 words preferred **Submission policy**: unsolicited script with SASE **Response**: 2-3 months **Remuneration**: 1 copy; 1 year subscription

BOX 749 MAGAZINE
411 W. 22nd St., New York, NY 10011 (212) 989-0519
Contact: David Ferguson, Editor-in-Chief **Works:** full-length plays, one-acts, translations **Guidelines:** works must be unpublished **Submission policy:** unsolicited script with SASE **Response:** 3 months **Remuneration:** 3-5 copies

BROADWAY PLAY PUBLISHING INC.
357 W. 20th St., New York, NY 10011 (212) 627-1055
Contact: Christopher Gould, President **Works:** full-length plays **Special interest:** contemporary American works; innovative works by new playwrights **Guidelines:** length: 80 minutes; no auto-biographical or historical material **Submission policy:** unsolicited script with SASE; query/synopsis with dialogue sample and resume; professional recommendation; agent submission **Response:** immediate query; 4 months script **Remuneration:** royalty:10% book, 80% amateur, 90% stock; 10 copies **Advice:** "Write something we've never seen before."

BROOKLYN REVIEW
Department of English, Brooklyn College,
Brooklyn, NY 11230 (718) 780-5195
Contact: Playwriting Editor **Publication:** annual journal of poetry, fiction, drama **Works:** one-acts **Maximum length:** 15 pages **Submission policy:** unsolicited script with SASE **Deadline:** inquire (Dec. 15 in 1989) **Response:** 2 months **Your chances:** approximately 3 plays published each year **Remuneration:** 2 copies

CALLALOO
Department of English, Wilson Hall,
University of Virginia, Charlottesville, VA 22903
(804) 924-6637 **Contact:** Charles H. Rowell, Editor
Publication: journal of arts and letters **Works:** one-acts, translations **Guidelines:** works must be previously unpublished; previously produced works preferred **Specifications:** script should be unbound and with pages numbered; length: 50 typed, double-spaced pages **Readership:** "American, African and European." **Submission policy:** unsolicited script with SASE and resume; agent submission **Best time:** Aug.-May **Response:** 3 months **Your chances:** 15 submissions/1 play published **Remuneration:** "$10 per printed page, 1 copy of journal and several offprints." **Future commitment:** "Publication acknowledgement if reprinted or republished."

THE CAPILANO REVIEW
2055 Purcell Way, North Vancouver, BC, Canada V7J 3H5
(604) 986-1911   Contact: Dorothy Jantzen, Editor
Publication: arts quarterly **Works:** one-acts **Guidelines:** works must be unpublished **Submission policy:**   query with proposal **Response:** 2 months **Remuneration:** $12 per page up to $48; 2 copies

CASTA-INSTITUTE FOR CONTEMPORARY EAST EUROPEAN DRAMA AND THEATRE
Graduate Center of the City University of New York, 33 W. 42nd St. Room 1222, New York, NY 10036
(212) 790-4209, -4464   Contact: Daniel C. Gerould, Alma H. Law, Co-directors **Works:** translations of Eastern European plays written since 1945 **Special interests:** published or unpublished translations for listing in bibliographies; translations-in-progress; previously published bibliographies of Polish and Soviet plays **Submission policy:** query/synopsis

CHILD LIFE MAGAZINE
Box 567, Indianapolis, IN 46206 (317) 636-8881
Contact: Steve Charles, Editor **Publication:** magazine published 8 times a year **Works:** one-act children's plays, adaptations, "playlets" **Special interests:** "Health-related themes; works for classroom or living-room staging, for children aged 8-11." **Submission policy:** unsolicited script with SASE **Deadline:** 8 months in advance for seasonal works **Response:** 10 weeks **Remuneration:** approximately 8¢ per word; up to 10 copies **Future commitment:** magazine buys all rights

CHILDREN'S PLAYMATE MAGAZINE
1100 Waterway Blvd., Box 567, Indianapolis, IN 46206
(317) 636-8881 ext. 249   Contact: Elizabeth Rinck, Editor **Works:** children's plays **Special interest:** "Health-related themes." **Guidelines:** works must be unpublished; length: 500-800 words **Submission policy:** unsolicited script with SASE **Deadline:** 8 months in advance for seasonal works **Response:** 10 weeks **Remuneration:** approximately 8¢ per word

COACH HOUSE PRESS, INC.
Box 458, Morton Grove, IL 60053 (708) 967-1777
Contact: David Jewell, Publisher **Works:** plays for senior adults **Special interests:** "Human intelligence, our caring and cooperative natures, and our innate zest for life." **Readership:** "Older adults and activity directors of senior adult recreation centers and nursing facilities." **Submission policy:** unsolicited script with SASE and

resume; query/synopsis with resume; professional recommendation; agent submission; "include notes on experience with production: observations, changes made" **Best times**: Nov.-Mar., summer **Response**: 1 month query; 3-4 months script **Remuneration**: 10% script sales, 50% performance royalty **Advice**: "Get at least one first-class production of your play and rewrite/tighten based on your observations with an audience."

CONFRONTATION
English Department,
C.W. Post College of Long Island University,
Greenvale, NY 11548 (516) 299-2391
Contact: Martin Tucker, Editor **Publication**: general magazine **Works**: one-acts **Guidelines**: works must be unpublished **Readership**: "A literate audience." **Submission policy**: unsolicited script with SASE **Response**: 8-10 weeks **Remuneration**: $15-$75; 1 copy

CONTEMPORARY DRAMA SERVICE
Meriwether Publishing, Ltd., 885 Elkton Dr.,
Colorado Springs, CO 80907 (303) 594-4422
Contact: Ted Zapel, Associate Editor **Works**: full-length plays, one-acts, adaptations, musicals, plays for young audiences, monologues **Special interests**: "One-act comedies or musicals that can be performed by young people in church or school"; produced plays preferred **Specifications**: "No serious, legitimate-theatre plays; no excessive profanity or x-rated subject matter." **Readership**: "Youngsters and non-denominational church folk." **Submission policy**: unsolicited script with SASE; query/synopsis **Response**: 2 weeks-2 months **Your chances**: 1200 submissions/50-60 plays published **Remuneration**: book and performance royalties or fee for amateur and publishing rights **Advice**: "Send for our catalogue and guidelines; enclose $1 for postage."

DEKALB LITERARY ARTS JOURNAL
555 N. Indian Creek Dr. Clarkston, GA 30021
(404) 299-4119 **Contact**: Charleise Young, Editor **Publication**: literary and arts magazine published 3 times a year **Works**: one-acts **Guidelines**: works must be unpublished **Submission policy**: unsolicited script with SASE **Response**: 4 months **Remuneration**: 1 copy

DIMENSION
Box 26673, Austin, TX 78755 (512) 345-0622
Contact: A. Leslie Willson, Editor **Works:** translations **Exclusive interest:** translations of contemporary works originally written in German; stage plays, radio plays, musicals **Submission policy:** unsolicited script with SASE **Response:** 6 months

DRAMA BOOK PUBLISHERS
260 Fifth Ave., New York, NY 10001
(212) 725-5377 Contact: Ralph Pine, Editor-in-Chief **Works:** full-length plays, translations, musicals **Special interest:** plays previously produced on Broadway **Guidelines:** works must be produced on Broadway, off Broadway or in London **Submission policy:** professional recommendation **Remuneration:** advance against royalties

DRAMATIC PUBLISHING COMPANY
311 Washington St., Box 109, Woodstock, IL 60098
(815) 338-7170 Contact: Sally Fyfe, Editor
Works: full-length plays, one-acts, adaptations, musicals, children's plays **Special interest:** produced plays **Minimum length:** 30 minutes for one-act **Readership:** "Elementary, junior high, high school, college, community and professional teachers/directors." **Submission policy:** unsolicited script with SASE; professional recommendation; agent submission **Response:** 3 months **Your chances:** 500-600 submissions/8-12 plays published each year **Remuneration:** "By contract." **Advice:** "If work has been produced, include reviews and photos."

DRAMATICS MAGAZINE
3368 Central Pkwy., Cincinnati, OH 45225-2392
(513) 559-1996 Contact: Don Corathers, Editor
Publication: monthly educational magazine **Works:** full-length plays, one-acts, translations, adaptations **Special interests:** produced plays preferred; "roles that are within the range of high school students and plays that address the concerns of young people aged 16-20" **Guidelines:** works must be unpublished; "no photocopies of dot matrix printouts, please" **Readership:** "Teens to young adults, generally brighter than average, very interested in theatre; also 3500 high school and college theatre directors." **Submission policy:** unsolicited script with SASE; query/synopsis; professional recommendation; agent submission; solicited script **Response:** 2 weeks query; 6 weeks script **Your chances:** 500 submissions/5 plays published **Remuneration:** flat payment of $100-$200; 5 copies (negotiable) **Future commitment:** "We buy first serial rights only."

DRAMATIKA
429 Hope St., Tarpon Springs, FL 34689
Contact: John Pyros, Editor **Works**: one-acts **Guidelines**: scripts must be camera ready, 8"x11" **Submission policy:** unsolicited script with SASE **Response**: 1 month **Remuneration**: copies

DRAMATISTS PLAY SERVICE
440 Park Ave. S., New York, NY 10016 (212) 683-8960
Contact: F. Andrew Leslie, President **Works**: full-length plays, one-acts, translations, adaptations, musicals, children's plays **Exclusive interest**: plays for amateur and stock markets **Guidelines**: works must be produced; production in New York City preferred **Submission policy:** unsolicited script with SASE, production history and reviews; professional recommendation; agent submission **Response**: 2 weeks **Remuneration**: advance against royalties; 10% book royalty, 80% amateur royalty, 90% stock royalty; copies

EARTH'S DAUGHTERS
Box 41 Central Park Station, Buffalo, NY 14215
Publication: feminist journal **Works**: full-length plays, one-acts, translations, adaptations, children's plays, **Special interests**: "Experience and creative expression of women." **Submission policy:** unsolicited script with SASE **Response**: 2 months **Remuneration**: 2 copies **Comment**: Usually excerpts are published; occasionally an issue is devoted to a complete playscript.

ELDRIDGE PUBLISHING COMPANY, INC.
Box 216, Franklin, OH 45005 (513) 746-6531
Contact: Nancy Vorhis, Editor **Works**: full-length plays, one-acts, adaptations, musicals, children's plays, Christmas plays **Special interests**: "Fun, light-hearted material as well as some serious works; larger-cast plays do better for schools, so more students can become involved"; produced works preferred **Specifications**: "Nothing x-rated!" **Readership**: "Elementary, middle and high schools; community theatres; churches. We have a widely varied market, but do not reach inner city." **Submission policy:** unsolicited script with SASE; query/synopsis **Response**: 3 weeks query; 3 months script **Your chances**: 350 submissions/20 plays published; "99% of our submissions are unsolicited" **Remuneration**: flat payment of $125 or more; 35% collected royalties; 12 copies **Advice**: "Have the play produced locally to work out any 'bugs' before submission. Remember, stage action is critical. Keep dialogue snappy."

ENCORE PERFORMANCE PUBLISHING
Box 692, Orem, UT 84057 (801) 225-0605
Contact: Michael C. Perry, President **Works:** full-length plays, one-acts, translations, adaptations, musicals, children's plays **Special interests:** Christian and family messages; holiday plays **Guidelines:** works must have had at least 2 amateur or professional productions **Submission policy:** unsolicited script with SASE **Response:** 8 weeks **Your chances:** 5-10 plays published each year **Remuneration:** 10% book royalty, 50% performance royalty

EVENT
Box 2503, Douglas College, New Westminster, BC, Canada V3L 5B2 (604) 520-5400
Contact: Dale Zieroth **Publication:** arts journal published 3 times a year (Mar., Jul., Nov.) **Works:** one-acts **Guidelines:** unpublished plays by both new and established writers **Submission policy:** send SASE for guidelines **Remuneration:** honorarium

FREELANCE PRESS
Box 548, 56 Center St., Dover, MA 02030
(617) 785-1260 Contact: Elizabeth Bickford, Managing Editor **Works:** musicals and musical adaptations for young audiences **Special interests:** "Works based on classics; large casts." **Guidelines:** entries must be unpublished and less than 50 pages in length; scripts may be bound or unbound; scores must be camera ready **Submission policy:** unsolicited script with SASE; simultaneous submissions accepted **Best time:** fall-spring **Response:** 2 weeks query; 1 month script **Your chances:** 10-15 submissions/6 plays published **Remuneration:** royalty $50/$35, complimentary copies

HAWAII REVIEW
University of Hawaii Manoa, English Department,
1733 Donaghho Rd, Honolulu, HI 96822 (808) 948-8548
Contact: Dellzell Chenoweth, Editor-in-Chief **Publication:** literary journal published once every 3 quarters **Works:** full-length plays, one-acts, translations, adaptations **Submission policy:** unsolicited script with SASE **Response:** 3-4 months **Remuneration:** 2 copies

HELICON NINE
Box 22412, Kansas City, MO 64113 (913) 345-0802
Contact: Gloria Vando Hickok, Editor **Publication:** literary and arts journal published 3 times a year **Works:** full-length plays, one-acts, translations and adaptations **Exclusive interest:** works by women **Submission policy:** unsolicited script with SASE **Response:** 3 months **Remuneration:** 1-year subscription; 2 copies **Comment:** One-acts and excerpts are published.

HEUER PUBLISHING COMPANY

See Art Craft Play Company/Heuer Publishing Company listing in this section.

I. E. CLARK, INC., PUBLISHERS

St. John's Rd., Box 246, Schulenburg, TX 78956
(409) 743-3232 Contact: M. A. Berckenhoff, Manager, Editorial Dept. **Works:** full-length plays, one-acts, translations, adaptations, musicals, children's plays **Guidelines:** works must have had "2 or 3 previous productions directed by someone other than the author" **Submission policy:** unsolicited script with SASE **Response:** 6 months-1 year **Your chances:** 1000 submissions/10-15 plays published, "over half of which are by our established authors" **Remuneration:** royalty **Advice:** "Get produced by a superb director and polish your play according to his advice. Ask yourself: why, with thousands of good plays available, would anybody want to do my play?"

INSTRUCTOR MAGAZINE

730 Broadway, New York, NY 10003 (212) 505-3000
Works: children's plays **Special interest:** holiday and seasonal themes; roles for young performers **Submission policy:** unsolicited script with SASE **Response:** 6-8 weeks **Remuneration:** $75-$125 **Deadline:** "Submit seasonal plays 6 months before season."

LATIN AMERICAN LITERARY REVIEW

2300 Palmer St., Pittsburgh, PA 15218 (412) 351-1477
Contact: Yvette Miller, Editor **Publication:** semi-annual journal **Works:** one-acts, translations **Exclusive interests:** one-acts by U.S. writers of Latin American origin; translations of Latin American plays, contemporary works preferred **Maximum length:** 20 pages **Submission policy:** unsolicited script with SASE **Deadlines:** Feb. 1, 1990; inquire for fall deadline **Response:** 6 months **Remuneration:** 2 copies

LILLENAS DRAMA RESOURCES/
LILLENAS PUBLISHING COMPANY

Box 419527, Kansas City, MO 64141
(816) 931-1900 ext. 319 Contact: Paul M. Miller, Editor **Works:** full-length plays, one-acts, adaptations, musicals, children's plays, sketches, skits **Special interests:** unproduced plays preferred; "scripts must reflect a philosophical/religious point of view, in keeping with Christianity" **Specifications:** works must be suitable for church and school production; length: full-length plays 90 minutes-2 hours; one-acts 30-45 minutes; sketches and skits shorter

Readership: "Somewhat conservative Christians of all ages."
Submission policy: send SASE for current guidelines sheet **Best time**: "Christmas plays in fall for following year." **Response**: 2 weeks query; 2-3 months script **Your chances**: 200 submissions/12-15 plays published **Remuneration**: flat payment: $5 per page; 10% royalty; 25 copies **Advice**: "Know our market; if Christmas is your thing, find a new angle; visit a Christian bookstore and look over Lillenas script formats."

THE MASSACHUSETTS REVIEW
Memorial Hall, University of Massachusetts, Amherst, MA 01003 (413) 545-2689
Contact: Drama Editor **Publication:** quarterly review of literature, arts, current affairs **Works:** one-acts **Length:** 25-30 pages **Submission policy:** unsolicited script with SASE **Best time:** Oct. 1-Jun. 1 only **Response:** 1-2 months **Remuneration:** $50; 2 copies

MODERN INTERNATIONAL DRAMA
Theatre Dept., SUNY, Binghamton, NY 13905
(607) 777-2704 Contact: George E. Wellwarth, Co-editor
Publication: semi-annual journal **Works:** translations of previously untranslated plays **Guidelines:** "Consult inside front cover for format." **Readership:** "Academic and professional theatre." **Submission policy:** unsolicited script with SASE and author's permission **Response:** 1 week query; 1 month script, if submitted Sept.-May **Your chances:** 20 submissions/4 plays published **Remuneration:** 3 copies

MODERN LITURGY
160 E. Virginia St. Suite 290, San Jose, CA 95112
(408) 286-8505 Contact: Ken Guentert, Editorial Director
Works/exclusive interest: "Short sketches suitable for presentation during worship services, classes and religious celebrations."
Maximum length: 10 minutes **Specifications:** "Minimum props."
Readership: "Worship planners and artists." **Submission policy:** unsolicited script with SASE **Best time:** 1 year before issue date
Response: 2 months **Remuneration:** subscription; 5 copies

NEW AMERICAN WRITING
2920 W. Pratt, Chicago, IL 60645 (312) 764-1048
Contact: Maxine Chernoff, Paul Hoover, Editors **Publication:** semi-annual poetry magazine **Works:** one-acts, translations
Special interests: "Plays that use language well and offer progressive and lively points of view." **Maximum length:** 30 pages **Submission policy:** unsolicited script with SASE

Deadlines: Jan. 1, 1990 for spring issue; Jul. 1, 1990 for fall issue
Response: 2 months   **Remuneration:** $5 per page when funds are available; 2 copies

NEW PLAYS INCORPORATED
Box 371, Bethel, CT 06801   (203) 792-4342
Contact: Patricia Whitton, Publisher   **Works:** children's plays, translations, adaptations and musicals   **Special interest:** "Out of the ordinary plays to be performed for young audiences by adults and teens."   **Guidelines:** works must be produced ("by someone other than the author")   **Specifications:** works must be 45-90 minutes in length; bound scripts preferred   **Readership:** "Looking for high-quality writing, depth of theme."   **Submission policy:** professional recommendation; simultaneous submissions accepted   **Your chances:** 300-500 submissions/2-4 plays published, "often from writers we are already working with"   **Remuneration:** 50% production royalties, 10% script sales; 6 copies   **Advice:** "Read our catalogue; it will give a better idea of our interests."

OBSIDIAN II: BLACK LITERATURE IN REVIEW
Department of English, Box 8105,
North Carolina State University, Raleigh, NC 27695
(919) 737-3870   Contact: Gerald Barrax, Editor
Publication: literary journal published 3 times a year   **Works:** full-length plays, one-acts   **Exclusive interest:** black writers   **Guidelines:** works must be unpublished; length: 25-30 pages; no simultaneous submissions   **Submission policy:** 2 copies of unsolicited script with SASE   **Response:** 2 months   **Your chances:** approximately 3 plays published each year   **Remuneration:** 2 copies

ORACLE PRESS
Baton Rouge, LA   This press has requested that we discontinue its listing.

PAJ PUBLICATIONS
See Performing Arts Journal listing in this section.

PENNSYLVANIA REVIEW
525 CL, University of Pittsburgh, Pittsburgh, PA 15260
(412) 624-0026   Contact: Deborah Pursifull, Managing Editor
Publication: semi-annual literary magazine   **Works:** one-acts   **Guidelines:** works must be unpublished   **Submission policy:** unsolicited script with SASE   **Deadlines:** Apr. 1, 1990; inquire for fall deadline   **Notification:** 8-10 weeks   **Remuneration:** $5 per page, 1 copy

PERFORMING ARTS JOURNAL
**PAJ Publications, 131 Varick St. Suite 902,
New York, NY 10013 (212) 243-3885, -3974**
Contact: Bonnie Marranca, Gautam Dasgupta, Co-Publishers/ Editors
Works: full-length plays, translations, adaptations **Special
interests**: "20th century performance and drama in any language;
specializing in critical essays, plays in translation, American
avant-garde work." **Submission policy:** query/synopsis
Response time: 1-2 months **Remuneration**: advance; option and/
or royalty **Comments:** Playwrights should contact directory
assistance if phone number has been changed. See PAJ Publications
listing in this section.

PIONEER DRAMA SERVICE, INC.
Box 22555, Denver, CO 80222 (303) 759-4297
Contact: Shubert Fendrich **Works**: children's plays **Special
interest**: "We deal primarily in the educational theatre market."
Guidelines: "All material should be produced prior to submission;
unpublished; 30-75 minutes playing time; large casts."
Specifications: "Single set preferred; no obscene language or
overly mature situations." **Submission policy:** unsolicited script
with SASE; query/synopsis **Best time**: Nov.-Mar. **Response**:1
week-1 month **Your chances**: 150 submissions/15 plays published
Remuneration: varies **Advice**: "Check our catalogue to make sure
your play is the type of thing we use; query."

PLAYERS PRESS, INC.
Box 1132, Studio City, CA 91604 (818) 789-4980
Contact: Robert W. Gordon, Senior Editor **Works**: full-length plays,
one-acts, translations, adaptations, musicals, children's plays;
performing arts books **Guidelines**: works must be produced
Specifications: "No pornography or objectionable material."
Readership: "Professional, semi-professional and amateur theatres
and the reading public." **Submission policy:** query/synopsis
Response: 30 days query; 12 months script **Your chances**: 300
submissions/5-25 plays published **Remuneration**: negotiable royalty

PLAYS
Baton Rouge, LA Publication of this magazine has been discontinued.

PLAYS IN PROCESS
**Theatre Communications Group, 355 Lexington Ave.,
New York, NY 10017 (212) 697-5230**
Contact: Tony Kushner, Director of Literary Services **Works**:
full-length plays, one-acts, translations, adaptations, musicals,
children's plays **Guidelines**: works must have been produced during

the current season by a TCG constituent theatre **Readership**: "Subscribership: mainly non-profit theatres in U.S., Canada and abroad, college and university theatres and libraries." **Submission policy**: nomination by artistic director or literary manager of producing theatre; request nomination form from Literary Services Dept.; 5 copies of script required upon nomination **Best time**: "As early in season as possible." **Deadline**: Jun. 30, 1990 **Response**: 3 months **Your chances**: 100–150 submissions/12 plays published **Remuneration**: 10 copies **Comments**: Related program: *New Plays USA* biennial anthology series of plays selected from Plays in Process circulation and *American Theatre* magazine (see listing in this section); playwright receives royalty and 6 copies. See Theatre Communications Group listing in Special Programs.

PLAYS, THE DRAMA MAGAZINE FOR YOUNG PEOPLE
120 Boylston St., Boston, MA 02116   (617) 423-3157
Contact: Elizabeth Preston, Managing Editor   **Works**: one-act children's plays and adaptations **Guidelines**: adaptations must be of works in public domain; 20–30 minutes playing time preferred for junior-senior high, 15–20 minutes for middle grades, 8–15 minutes for lower grades **Specifications**: "Sets should be simple enough for young people to erect without too much trouble; low-cost materials, nothing elaborate." **Readership**: "Public schools and libraries—teachers and drama directors." **Submission policy**: unsolicited script with SASE; query/synopsis for adaptation; no simultaneous submission **Response**: 2 weeks **Your chances**: 250–300 submissions/25–30 plays published **Remuneration**: "Varying rates on acceptance; 1 copy." **Future commitment**: "We buy all rights." **Advice**: Send SASE for style sheet.

PORTLAND REVIEW
Box 751, Portland, OR 97207 (503) 464-4468
Contact: James Carr, Editor **Publication**: arts journal published once every 3 quarters **Works**: one-acts **Special interest**: experimental works **Submission policy**: unsolicited script with SASE **Response**: 6 weeks **Remuneration**: 1 copy

RESOURCE PUBLICATIONS
160 E. Virginia St. #290, San Jose CA 95112
(408) 286-8505   Contact: Ken Guentert, Editorial Director **Works**: short plays, collections **Exclusive interest**: works for religious education classes, youth ministry or celebrations **Guidelines**: works must be unpublished; length: 7–15 minutes **Submission policy**: unsolicited script with SASE   **Response**: 2 months **Remuneration**: royalty

SALOME
5548 N. Sawyer Ave., Chicago, IL 60625
(312) 539-5745 **Contact:** Effie Mihopoulos, Editor
Publication: journal of performing arts **Works:** one-acts
Exclusive interest: "Works dealing with the arts or with artistic
characters." **Submission policy:** unsolicited script with SASE
Response: time varies **Remuneration:** 1 copy

SAMUEL FRENCH, INC.
45 W. 25th St., New York, NY 10010 (212) 206-8990
Contact: Lawrence Harbison, Editor **Works:** full-length plays,
one-acts, translations, adaptations, musicals, children's plays
Special interests: "Light comedies, mysteries, Broadway and off
Broadway hits." **Guidelines:** "We prefer professional stageplay
format, an example of which is our publication *Guidelines* ($3
including postage)." **Submission policy:** unsolicited script with
SASE; query/synopsis; professional recommendation; agent
submission **Response:** 1 week query; 2-12 months script **Your
chances:** 1500 submissions/"few" plays published **Remuneration:**
10% book royalty, 80% amateur royalty, 90% stock royalty; 10
copies with discount on additional copies **Advice:** "Have it succeed on
the Island of Manhattan."

SCHOLASTIC SCOPE
730 Broadway, New York, NY 10003 (212) 505-3000
Contact: Deborah Sussman, Senior Editor **Works:** plays for
teenagers **Special interests:** problems of contemporary
teenagers: family, job, school; comedy, mystery, science fiction;
plays about minorities **Readership:** 7th-12th graders **Guidelines:**
works must be suitable for teenagers with 4th-5th grade reading
ability; characters in 14-18 age range; length: 1000-6000 words
Submission policy: unsolicited script with SASE **Response:**
time varies **Remuneration:** $200 or more

SCHOLASTIC VOICE
730 Broadway, New York, NY 10003 (212) 505-3122
Contact: Forrest Stone, Editor **Publication:** magazine distributed
through schools **Works:** plays for teenagers **Guidelines:** works
must be 1000-6000 words in length and suitable for teenagers with
at least 8th grade reading ability **Submission policy:** unsolicited
script with SASE **Response:** time varies **Remuneration:** "Varies;
we pay fairly well." **Advice:** "Send us anything rated 'PG-13.'"

SCRIPTS AND SCRIBBLES
141 Wooster St., New York, NY 10012 (212) 473-6695
Contact: Daryl Chin, Consulting Editor **Works**: full-length plays, one-acts, performance-art texts and scenarios **Submission policy**: query/synopsis **Exclusive interests**: non-traditional works; works produced outside New York City **Response**: 3-4 months **Remuneration**: 25 copies

SINISTER WISDOM
Box 3252, Berkeley, CA 94703
Contact: Elana Dykewomon, Editor **Publication**: literary and arts quarterly **Works**: one-acts, excerpts from full-length plays **Exclusive interests**: "Works by women reflecting the diversity of women; lesbian/feminist themes." **Guidelines**: maximum length: 3000 words; no heterosexual material **Submission policy**: unsolicited script with SASE **Response**: 2-6 months **Remuneration**: 2 copies

STORY LINE PRESS
325 Ocean View Ave., Santa Cruz, CA 95062
(408) 426-5539 Contact: Robert McDowell, Editor **Works**: full-length plays, one-acts, translations **Special interest**: poetic plays **Submission policy**: query with brief project description/proposal **Response**: 2 weeks query; 2 months script **Remuneration**: royalty **Comment**: Press publishes 9 books each year: poetry, criticism, fiction.

SWIFT KICK
1711 Amherst St., Buffalo, NY 14214 (716) 837-7778
Contact: Robin Kay Willoughby, Editor **Publication**: quarterly magazine **Works**: full-length plays, one-acts, translations, adaptations, children's plays, musicals, performance-art pieces **Exclusive interest**: experimental, unconventional works; works generally considered "unproducible" **Guidelines**: works must be unpublished **Readership**: "Very small, crosses all category lines." **Submission policy**: unsolicited script with SASE; query/synopsis; include information on simultaneous submissions **Best time**: summer **Response**: 3-6 months **Your chances**: 1 submission/"1 play published in 1 of 7 issues" **Remuneration**: 3 copies **Advice**: "Order sample copy; have the outlook of Tzara or Beckett."

TEJAS ART PRESS
207 Terrell Rd., San Antonio, TX 78209 (512) 826-7803
Contact: Robert Willson, Editor **Works**: full-length plays, one-acts **Guidelines**: authors must be American Indians; works must be unpublished and scheduled for first production **Submission policy**:

unsolicited script with SASE **Response**: 1 month **Remuneration**: negotiable royalty; copies

TEMBLOR: CONTEMPORARY POETS
4624 Cahuenga Blvd. #307, North Hollywood, CA 91602
(818) 449-1276 Contact: Leland Hickman
Publication: semi-annual prose and poetry journal **Works**: full-length plays, one-acts, translations **Exclusive interest**: contemporary experimental poetic works **Guidelines**: works must be unpublished **Submission policy**: unsolicited script with SASE **Response**: 2 months

THEATER
222 York St., New Haven, CT 06520 (203) 436-1568
Contact: Joel Schechter, Editor **Publication**: triennial journal **Works**: full-length plays, one-acts, translations, adaptations **Guidelines**: works must have received one major production only **Submission policy**: query/synopsis **Response**: 2 months **Your chances**: 1 play published in each issue **Remuneration**: approximately $150 and/or copies

THIRD WOMAN PRESS
c/o Chicano Studies, Dwinelle Hall,
University of California, Berkeley, CA 94720
(415) 642-0240 Contact: Norma Alarcón, Editor
Works: full-length plays, one-acts, translations, adaptations **Exclusive interests**: plays in English or Spanish written by or on behalf of U.S. Hispanic women and Third World women **Submission policy**: unsolicited script with SASE **Response**: 6 weeks **Remuneration**: copies **Comment**: Press publishes short one-acts and excerpts from longer works.

TSL PRESS
Mussman Bruce Publishers, 139 W. 22nd St.,
New York, NY 10011 (212) 741-1032
Press: small press **Works**: translations **Submission policy**: solicited script **Remuneration**: fee; copies **Comment**: A small press which publishes books by and about visual artists and new translations of plays.

UBU REPERTORY THEATER PUBLICATIONS
See Ubu Repertory Theater listing in Theatres.

UNITED ARTS
141 Wooster St., New York, NY 10012 (212) 473-6695
Contact: Daryl Chin, Editor **Publication:** journal published 3-4
times a year **Works:** one-acts, translations **Exclusive interest:**
unconventional, avant garde works **Submission policy:** query/
synopsis **Response:** 6-8 weeks **Remuneration:** copies

UNIVERSITY OF MISSOURI PRESS
BREAKTHROUGH SERIES
See Breakthrough Series listing in Contests.

WATERFRONT PRESS
52 Maple Ave., Maplewood, NJ 07040 (201) 762-1565
Contact: Kal Wagenheim, President **Press:** small press **Special
interest:** Hispanic works **Submission policy:** solicited script
Response: 1 month **Your chances:** plays published "very
occasionally" **Remuneration:** 10% royalty; 10 copies

WEST COAST PLAYS
California Theatre Council, Box 48320,
Los Angeles, CA 90048
(213) 874-3163 (answering service)
Works: full-length plays, one-acts, translations, adaptations,
musicals, children's plays, performance-art pieces **Guidelines:**
works must have received their first U.S. production west of the
Rockies **Submission policy:** send SASE for guidelines
Remuneration: up to $100 advance against royalty; copies
Comments: When *The Playwright's Companion 1990* went to press,
the California Theatre Council's office was under construction;
playwrights are advised to write for information. See California
Theatre Council listing in Special Programs.

WILLOW SPRINGS
P.U.B., Box1063,
Eastern Washington University, Cheney,WA 99004
(509) 458-6429 Contact: Gillian Conoley, Editor
Publication: semi-annual literary journal **Works:** one-acts,
translations **Special interests:** "Craftsmanship, imagination."
Submission policy: unsolicited script with SASE **Response:** 1-2
months **Remuneration:** 4 copies

WOMEN IN PERFORMANCE:
A JOURNAL OF FEMINIST THEORY
New York University, Tisch School of the Arts, Performance Studies, 721 Broadway 6th Floor, New York, NY 10003 (212) 998-1625
Contact: Katheryn White, Editorial Board **Publication:** semi-annual journal **Works**: full-length plays, one-acts, translations **Exclusive interest**: works by, for and about women; special interest in feminist performance theory **Guidelines**: works must be unpublished **Submission policy:** query/synopsis **Response:** 3 months query; several months script **Your chances:** 50-100 submissions/2 new plays published each year **Comment:** Staged reading program has been discontinued.

Agents

Suggestions for contacting the agents listed in this section:

A playwright hoping to secure the services of an agent should send a brief query letter describing his or her work and a resume providing details of plays produced or published and awards and honors received.

Agents do not welcome unsolicited scripts or phone calls from authors whose work they do not know.

"The Literary Agent," an informational brochure on the standard practices of and services offered by agents (see The Playwright's Library) is available free with SASE from the Society of Author's Representatives, Box 650 Old Chelsea Station, New York, NY 10113.

The Dramatists Guild (see Special Programs) also provides advice on the playwright-agent relationship and will send a list of agents to Guild members on request.

AGENCY FOR THE PERFORMING ARTS
888 Seventh Ave., New York, NY 10106
(212) 582-1500
Agents: Richard Krawetz, Rick Leed

ALAN WILLIG AND ASSOCIATES
337 W. 43rd St. Suite 1B, New York, NY 10036
(212) 586-4300

ANNA-MARIE McKAY
400 W. 43rd St. #3A, New York, NY 10036
(212) 564-6990

ANN ELMO AGENCY
60 E. 42nd St., New York, NY 10165
(212) 661-2880

ARTISTS AGENCY, INC.
230 W. 55th St. Suite 29D, New York, NY 10019
(212) 245-6960
Agents: Jonathan Russo, Barry Weiner

BERTHA KLAUSNER INTERNATIONAL LITERARY AGENCY
71 Park Ave., New York, NY 10016
(212) 685-2642

BRET ADAMS
448 W. 44th St., New York, NY 10036
(212) 765-5630
Agents: Bret Adams, Mary Harden

DORESE AGENCY
1400 Ambassador St., Los Angeles, CA 90035
(213) 556-0710
New York City answering service: (212) 580-2855
Agent: Alyss Dorese

THE DRAMATIC PUBLISHING COMPANY
311 Washington St., Woodstock, IL 60098
(815) 338-7170
Agent: Susan Sergel

ELISABETH MARTON AGENCY
96 Fifth Ave., New York, NY 10011
(212) 255-1908
Agents: Elisabeth Marton, Tonda Marton

ELLEN NEUWALD
902 N. Ronda Sevilla, Laguna Hills, CA 92653
(714) 380-7987

E.M.A.
161 E. 65th St., New York, NY 10021
(212) 517-7180
Agent: Jeannine Edmunds

EVELYN J. POWERS
2311 Windingbrook Ct., Bloomington, IN 47401
(812) 336-5643

FIFI OSCARD ASSOCIATES
19 W. 44th St., New York, NY 10036
(212) 764-1100

FLORA ROBERTS, INC.
157 W. 57th St., New York, NY 10019
(212) 355-4165
Agents: Sarah Douglass, Flora Roberts

THE GERSH AGENCY
103 W. 42nd St., New York, NY 10036
(212) 997-1818
Agents: Mary Meagher, Scott Yoselow

GRAHAM AGENCY
311 W. 43rd St., New York, NY 10036
(212) 489-7730
Agent: Earl Graham

HAROLD MATSON COMPANY
276 Fifth Ave. Suite 303W, New York, NY 10001
(212) 679-4490

HELEN HARVEY ASSOCIATES
410 W. 24th St., New York, NY 10011
(212) 675-7445
Agents: Helen Harvey, Marion Matera

HELEN MERRILL
435 W. 23rd St. Suite 1A, New York, NY 10011
(212) 691-5326

HUTTO MANAGEMENT
405 W. 23rd St., New York, NY 10011
(212) 807-1234
Agent: Jack Hutto

INTERNATIONAL CREATIVE MANAGEMENT
40 W. 57th St., New York, NY 10019
(212) 556-5600
Agents: Bridget Aschenberg, Mitch Douglas, Wiley Hausam

JOYCE P. KETAY
334 W. 89th St. #4F, New York, NY 10024
(212) 799-2398

KATHE TELINGATOR
435 Bergen St., Brooklyn, NY 11217
(718) 230-4910

THE LANTZ OFFICE
New York City: 888 Seventh Ave. Suite 2500,
New York, NY 10106 (212) 586-0200
Agent: Robert Lantz

THE LANTZ OFFICE
Los Angeles: 9255 Sunset Blvd. Suite 505,
Los Angeles, CA 90069 (213) 858-1144
Agent: Jack Thal

LOIS BERMAN
240 W. 44th St., New York, NY 10036
(212) 575-5114

LUCY KROLL AGENCY
390 West End Ave. Suite 9B, New York, NY 10024
(212) 877-0627 877-0556
Agents: Barbara Hogenson, Lucy Kroll, Holly Lebed

MARGARET RAMSAY, LTD.
14a Goodwin's Ct., St. Martin's Ln., London WC2, England
Agents: Tom Ehrhardt, Margaret Ramsay

MARJE FIELDS
165 W. 46th St., New York, NY 10036
(212) 764-5740
Agent: Ray Powers

MICHAEL IMISON PLAYWRIGHTS
New York City: Box 1006 Ansonia Station,
New York, NY 10023 (212) 874-2671
Agent: Abbe Levin
London: 28 Almeida St., London N1 1TD, England
(01) 354-3174
Agents: Alan Brodie, Michael Imison

PARAMUSE ARTISTS ASSOCIATES
1414 Avenue of the Americas, New York, NY 10019
(212) 758-5055 **Agent:** Shirley Bernstein

PEREGRINE WHITTLESEY
345 E. 80th St., #31F, New York, NY 10021
(212) 737-0153

ROBERT A. FREEDMAN DRAMATIC AGENCY, INC.
1501 Broadway #2310, New York, NY 10036
(212) 840-5760
Agents: Robert A. Freedman, Selma Luttinger

ROSENSTONE/WENDER
3 E. 48th St., New York, NY 10017
(212) 832-8330
Agents: Renata Cobbs, Howard Rosenstone

SAMUEL FRENCH, INC.
45 W. 25th St., New York, NY 10010   (212) 206-8990
Agents: Lawrence Harbison, William Talbot

SCOTT HUDSON
215 E. 76th St., New York, NY 10021
(212) 570-9645

THE SHUKAT COMPANY
340 W. 55th St. #1A, New York, NY 10019
(212) 582-7614
Literary Representatives/Personal Managers: Scott Shukat,
Peter Shukat

SUHRKAMP VERLAG
175 Fifth Ave., New York, NY 10010
(212) 460-1653
Agent: Thomas Thornton

SUSAN SCHULMAN LITERARY AGENCY
454 W. 44th St., New York, NY 10036
(212) 713-1633

THE TANTLEFF OFFICE
360 W. 20th St. #4F, New York, NY 10011
(212) 627-2105
Agent: Jack Tantleff

WILLIAM MORRIS AGENCY, INC.
1350 Avenue of the Americas, New York, NY 10019
(212) 586-5100
Agents: Peter Franklin, George Lane, Biff Liff, Gilbert Parker,
Esther Sherman, Jerome Talbert

WRITERS & ARTISTS AGENCY
70 W. 36th St. Suite 501, New York, NY 10018
(212) 947-8765   **Agent:** William Craver

Appendices

Cross Reference to Special Interests

Cross Reference to Special Programs

The Playwright's Calendar

The Playwright's Library

Cross Reference to Special Interests

While the theatres, contests, programs and publishers included in this cross reference have expressed a special or exclusive interest in the topics under which they are listed, many of them have other interests as well. Many theatres, contests, programs and publishers not listed below, while not claiming a special interest, also accept works indicated by the following headings. Some special interests noted in individual listings are too specific ("the life of Edward de Vere, Earl of Oxford," for example) or too general (such as "American themes" or "social/political issues") to warrant headings. Those special interests which call for value judgments (such as "literary merit" or "theatricality") are also not included.

Avant Garde & Experimental Works, New Forms
(See also Multi-Media Works.)

Theatres: **Academy Theatre** 3, **Actors Lab Arizona** 6, **AMAS Repertory** Theatre 11, The **American Place** Theatre 14, **American Stage Festival** 16, **At the Foot of the Mountain** 21, **BoarsHead: Michigan Public** Theater 27, **Bond Street** Theatre 27, **Brigham Young Theatre** & Film Dept. 29, **Burbage Theatre** Ensemble 31, The **Changing Scene** 36, The **Chicago Theatre Co.** 37, **Clavis** Theatre 41, **Coney Island USA** 43, **Contemporary Arts Center** 43, **Creation Production** Co. 46, **Dell'Arte Players** Co. 50, **Dixon Place** 52, **Dreiske Performance** Co. 54, The **Empty Space** Theatre 56, **45th Street** Theatre 62, **Friends & Artists** Theatre Ensemble 63, **Fulton Opera House** 63, **Heartland** Theatre Co. 70, **Jacksonville University** Division of Art, Theatre Arts and Dance 80, **Just Us** Theater Co./Club Zebra 82, **L.A. Designers'** Theatre 84, **La Mama** Experimental Theatre 85, The **Mark Taper Forum** 94, **Medicine Show** Theatre Ensemble 96, **Music-Theatre Group**/Lenox Arts Center 102, **New Play** Productions 107, **New York Theatre Workshop** 111, **Northlight** Theatre 112, **Omaha Magic** Theatre 117, **Payson Playmakers** 120, **Playmakers** (FL) 128, **Playwright's Alliance** 129, **The Road Company** 140, **Round House** Theatre 141, The **Salt Lake Acting Co.** 142, **San Diego Repertory** Theatre 142, **Seven Stages** 145, **Soho Repertory** Theatre 148, **Stages Trilingual** Theatre 151, **Storefront** Theatre 153, **Syracuse Stage** 155, **Theater for The New City** 158, **Theatre X** 166, **Third Step** Theatre Co. 166, **Walnut Street** Theatre 175, The **Wilma** Theatre 180, **Woolly Mammoth** Theatre Co. 181

Contests: FMCT Playwrights Competition 210, **Playwright's Forum** Awards 232, The **Richard Rodgers Production** Award 234, **Third Step Theatre Co.** Spring Festival of Staged Readings 241, **24th Street Experiment** Annual Playwright Competition 242

Publishers: Apalachee Quarterly 303, **Broadway Play** Publishing 305, **Performing Arts Journal** 314, **Portland** Review 315, **Scripts and Scribles** 317, **Swift Kick** 317, **Temblor:** Contemporary Poets 318, **United Arts** 319

Biblical/Christian Themes

Theatres: **Acacia** Theatre 3, **A.D. Players** 9, **Company Theatre** 43, **Lamb's Players** Theatre 86, **Saltworks** Theatre Co. 142

Publishers: Baker's Plays 304, **Encore Performance** Publishing Co. 310, **Lillenas** Publishing Co. 311, **Modern Liturgy** 312, **Resource** Publications 315

Biographical & Historical Works

Theatres: AMAS Repertory Theatre 11, **American Living History** Theater 13, **Artreach** Touring Theatre 20, **Boston Shakespeare** Co. 28, **Chicago Medieval Players** 37, **City Theatre** (CA) 40, **The Coterie Inc.** 45, **Cumberland County** Playhouse 48, **Dixie College** Theatre 52, **Great North American History** Theatre 68, **Intermountain** Actors Ensemble 78, **Mary Baldwin College** Theatre 95, **Merrimack Repertory** Theatre 96, **N.C. Black Repertory** Co. 103, **New Jersey Shakespeare Festival** 106, **The Old Slocum House** Theatre 116, **R.A.P.P.** Resident Theatre Co. 137, **Shakespeare & Company** 145, **Teatro Dallas** 156, **Theatre West Virginia** 165, **Theatreworks/USA** 166, **Walnut Street** Theatre 175, **Young People's Theatre** Co. of Delaware Valley 184

Contests: **Festival Theatre of Biography & History** Commissions 208, **Great Platte River** Playwrights Festival 212, **Margaret Bartle** Annual Playwriting Award 220, **Merrimack Repertory Theatre** Playwriting Contest 223, **Miller** Award 1990 223, **National Archives** Playwriting Competition 225, **Theatreworks/USA** Commissioning Program 241

Children's Plays, Concerns of Youth

Theatres: **Academy** Theatre 3, **A.D. Players** 9, **Arkansas Arts Center Children's** Theatre 18, **Artreach** Touring Theatre 20, **Arvada Center** for the Arts & Humanities 20, **California Theatre Center** 32, The **Children's Theatre Co.** 37, **Community Children's Theatre** 42, The **Coterie** Inc. 45, **Creative Arts Team** 46, **Creative** Theatre 46, The **Delray Beach** Playhouse 50, **Emmy Gifford** Children's Theater 56, **Ensemble Theatre** of Cincinnati 57, **Fairbanks Drama Association** & Fairbanks Children's Theatre Inc. 59, **FMT** 61, The **Great–American Theatre** Co. 68, **Hangar** Theatre 69, **Heritage Artists Ltd.** 71, **Honolulu Theatre** for Youth 74, **Little Broadway** Productions 88, **Looking Glass** Theatre 89, **Main Street** Theater (TX) 92, **Market House** Theatre 94, **Marriott Lincolnshire** Theatre 94, **Merry–Go–Round** Playhouse 97, **Miami Beach** Community Theatre 97, The **New Conservatory** 105, **Northside** Theatre Co. 112, **Oak Ridge** Community Playhouse 113, **Old Creamery** Theatre Co. 115, **Pegasus Players** 121, **Pennyrile** Players Theatre 122, **Periwinkle** National Theatre for Young Audiences 123, **Portland Repertory** Theatre 131, **Prairie Players** Youth Theatre 132, **Pulse Ensemble** Theatre 135, **Pushcart** Players 135, **Seaside Music** Theater 143, **Seattle Children's** Theatre 143, **Stage One:** Louisville Children's Theatre 150, The **Street Theater** 153, The **Theater at Monmouth** 158, **Theatre IV** 160, **Theatre of Youth** Co. 162, **TheatreWorks/USA** 166, The **Thirteenth Street Children's Theatre** Ensemble 167, **Young People's Theatre** Co. of Delaware Valley 184, **Young Performers Theatre** 184

Contests: **Anna Zornio** Memorial Children's Theatre Playwriting Award 194, **DC Art/Works** Playwrights Competition 204, **Festival Theatre of Biography and History** Commissions 208, **High School Playwriting** Contest 213, **Indiana University–Purdue University at Indianapolis Playwriting for Youth** Competition and Symposium 214, **Margaret Bartle** Annual Playwriting Award 220, **Regional Children's Theatre** Competition 1990 234, **San Diego Junior Theatre** Playwriting Competition 235, **Southeast Region Young Playwright** and Children's Theatre Festival 238

Programs: The **American Alliance for Theatre & Education** 251, **Asolo Touring Theater** Commissions 253,

ASSITEJ/USA 253, **At the Foot of the Mountain** Programs 254, **Center Theater Youtheatre** 258, **New Works Theatre Playwrights' Workshop** 278, **Playwrights Theatre** of New Jersey 286

Publishers: **Anchorage** Press 303, **Child Life** Magazine 306, **Children's Playmate** Magazine 306, **Dramatics** Magazine 308, **Eldridge** Publishing Co. 309, **Freelance** Press 310, **Instructor** Magazine 311, **New Plays Incorporated** 313, **Pioneer Drama Service** Inc. 314, **Plays:** The Drama Magazine for Young People 315, **Scholastic Scope** 316, **Scholastic Voice** 316

Ethnic & Minority Authors & Themes

Theatres: **Alabama Shakespeare** Festival (Black) 9, **American Jewish** Theatre 13, The **American Line** 13, The **American Place** Theatre 14, **Asian American** Theater Co. 20, **At the Foot of the Mountain** 21, The **Bilingual Foundation** of the Arts (Hispanic) 25, **Borderlands Theater**/Teatro Fronterizo (Latino American, Native American) 28, The **Chicago Theatre** Co. (African American) 37, **Company One** Theater 42, **Contemporary Arts Center** 43, **Crossroads** Theatre Co. (Afro-American, African, W. Indian) 47, **Duo** Theatre (Hispanic American) 55, **East West Players** (Asian American) 55, **El Teatro Campesino** 56, **Experimental Theatre** of The Puertorican Atheneum (Puerto Rican, Hispanic) 59, **Folksbeine** Theater (Jewish) 62, **Havurat Yisrael** Theatre Group (Jewish) 70, **NTAR Hispanic American** Theatre 78, **JCC Center Stage** (Jewish) 81, **Jewish Repertory** Theatre 81, **Jomandi Productions** Inc. (African American) 82, **Just Us** Theater Co./Club Zebra (Black American) 82, **Los Angeles Theatre Center** 90, **Magic Theatre** 91, **Merrimack Repertory** Theatre 96, **Mills College** Theatre 98, **National Jewish** Theater 102, **Native Americans** in the Arts 103, **N.C. Black Repertory** Co. 103, **Negro Ensemble** Co. 104, **New Federal** Theatre 105, **New Mexico Repertory** Theatre (Hispanic) 106, The **New Theatre of Brooklyn** 109, **New York Theatre Workshop** 111, **Oakland Ensemble** Theatre (Black American) 113, **One Act** Theatre Co. 117, **Pan Asian Repertory** Theatre 119, The **Penumbra** Theatre Co. (African American) 122, **Puerto Rican Traveling** Theatre (Hispanic) 134, **Repertorio Español** (Hispanic) 138, **Rites & Reason** (Afro-American) 139, **San Diego Repertory** Theatre 142, The **Seattle Group** Theatre 143, **Seven Stages** (Black) 145, **South Coast Repertory** 148, **Studio Arena** Theatre 154, **Teatro Dallas** 156, **Theatre Rhinoceros** 163, **Third Step** Theatre Co. 166, **Three**

Brothers Theatre (Black) 167, **University of Arizona** Department of Drama (Hispanic, Native American) 172, **Victory Gardens** Theater 173, **Wisdom Bridge** Theatre 180

Contests: **Black Dramatists** Festival 198, **Borderlands Theater**/Teatro Fronterizo New Play Search (Latino American, Native American) 199, **Chicano** Literary Contest 201, **Cornerstone:** Penumbra Theatre Co. National Playwright Competition (Afro-American) 203, **Dayton Playhouse** Playwriting Competition 204, **Emerging Playwright** Award 206, **Helen Eisner** Award for Young Playwrights (Jewish) 213, **Hispanic Playwrights** Project 214, **JCC Theatre** of Cleveland Dorothy Silver Playwriting Competition (Jewish) 217, **Lorraine Hansberry** Playwriting Award (Black) 193, **McDonald's** Literary Achievement Awards (Black) 222, **Multicultural Playwrights** Festival 225, **National Jewish Theater** Play Writing Competition 226, **Theodore Ward** Prize for Playwriting (Afro- American) 241, **Third Step Theatre Co.** Spring Festival of Staged Readings 241

Programs: **American Indian Community House** 251, Association of **Hispanic Arts** 254, **At the Foot of the Mountain** Programs 254, **Brody Arts Fund** 257, **Cintas Foundation** Fellowship Program (Cuban) 259, **Frank Silvera** Writers' Workshop 265, **INTAR** Hispanic Playwrights-in-Residence Laboratory 268, **Los Angeles Theatre Center** Programs (Latino, Asian American, Black) 271, The **National Foundation for Jewish Culture** 276, **NFJC Playwrights Travel Grant** Program (Jewish) 279, **Ollantay Center** for the Arts (Hispanic) 280, **Puerto Rican Travelirq Theatre** Playwrights' Workshop (Hispanic) 288, The **Rockefeller Foundation's Bellagio Study and Conference Center** 290

Publishers: The **Americas Review and Arte Publico** Press (Hispanic) 302, **Latin American Literary** Review 311, **Obsidian II:** Black Literature in Review 313, **Scholastic Scope** 316, **Tejas Art** Press (American Indian) 317, **Third Woman** Press (Hispanic) 318, **Waterfront Press** (Hispanic) 319

Gay & Lesbian Themes & Characters

Theatres: **Alice B.** Theatre 10, **Celebration** Theatre 34, The **Glines** 66, **Theatre Rhinoceros** 163, **3-Dollar Bill** Theatre 168

Publisher: **Sinister Wisdom** 317

Health & Disability

Theatres: **Creative** Productions 46, **Fairmount Theatre of the Deaf** 60, **Paul Bunyan** Playhouse 120, **Saltworks Theatre Co.** 142, **Stop-Gap Co.** 152

Contests: DC **Art/Works** Playwrights Competition 204, **Very Special Arts** Young Playwrights Program 244

Programs: **Center Theater Youtheatre** Program 258, **Playwrights Theatre of New Jersey** 286

Publishers: **Child Life** Magazine 306, **Children's Playmate** Magazine 306

Multi-Media Works
(See also Avant Garde & Experimental Works, New Forms.)

Theatres: **Contemporary Arts Center** 43, **FMT** 61, **Just Us** Theater Co./Club Zebra 82, **Mettawee River** Co. 97, **Music-Theatre Group**/Lenox Arts Center 102, The **Open Eye New Stagings** 118, The **Play Works** Co. 124, **San Diego Repertory** Theatre 142, **Soho Repertory** Theatre 148, **Theater for The New City** 158, **Underground Railway** Theater 171, **Vineyard** Theatre 174, The **Wilma** Theatre 180

Contest: **International New Music Composers** Competition 215

Multi-Ethnic or Non-Traditional Casting

Theatres: **Alice B.** Theatre 10, **AMAS Repertory** Theatre 11, **American Folk** Theater 12, The **American Line** 13, **Apple Corps** Theatre 17, **Berkshire Public** Theatre 25, **Borderlands Theater**/Teatro Fronterizo 28, **Chicago Medieval** Players 37, **City Stage** Theatre Co. 39, **Company One** Theater 42, **Daughter** Productions 49, **Detroit Center** for the Performing Arts 51, **Detroit Repertory** Theatre 51, **El Teatro Campesino** 56, **Fairmount Theatre of the Deaf** 60, **Friends & Artists** Theatre Ensemble 63, **Hartford Stage** Co. 70, **Heights Showcase** 71, **Jomandi Productions** Inc. 82, **L.A. Designers'** Theatre 84, **Mill Mountain** Theatre 98, **Mills College** Theatre 98, **Milwaukee Repertory** Theatre 99, The **New Rose** Theatre 107, **New Tuners** Theatre 109,

Oakland Ensemble Theatre 113, **On Stage Productions:** On Stage Children 117, The **Seattle Group** Theatre 143, **Takoma Theatre** Inc. 155, **TheatreWorks** 165, **Third Step** Theatre Co. 166, **Victorian** Theatre 173, **West Coast Ensemble** 177

Contests: **Aggie Players** Playwriting Competition 191, **Borderlands Theater**/Teatro Fronterizo New Play Search 199, **Celebration of One-Acts** 201, **Heights Showcase** Playwriting Contest 212, **Mill Mountain Theatre** New Play Competition 224, **New World Theater** New Play Competition 229, **Peace Play** Contest 231, **South Carolina New Play** Festival 237, **Third Step Theatre Co.** Spring Festival of Staged Readings 241

Program: **At the Foot of the Mountain** Programs 254

Musicals, Operas

Theatres: **Alhambra** Dinner Theatre 10, **Allenberry** Playhouse 10, **AMAS** Repertory Theatre 11, **American Music Theatre Festival** 14, **Attic** Theatre (MI) 22, **Barn** Players 24, **Broadway Tomorrow** Musical Theatre 30, **Coconut Grove** Playhouse 41, **The Coterie Inc.** 45, **Country Dinner** Playhouse 45, **Creative** Productions 46, **Creative** Theatre 46, The **Delray Beach** Playhouse 50, **Derby** Dinner Theatre 51, **Dixie College** Theatre & Pioneer Players 52, **Fairbanks Light Opera** Theatre 59, **Firehouse** Theatre (NE) 60, **Ford's** Theatre 62, **Goodspeed** Opera House 67, **Heritage Artists** 71, **Kalamazoo** Civic Players 83, **Lake George** Dinner Theatre 85, **Lakewood** Little Theatre 85, **Lawrence Welk** Resort Theatre 87, **Light Opera** of Manhattan 87, **Little Broadway** Productions 88, **Marriott Lincolnshire** Theatre 94, **Musical Theatre Works** 101, **Music-Theatre Group**/Lenox Arts Center 102, **New Tuners** Theatre 109, **Omaha Magic** Theatre 117, **Paper Mill** Playhouse 119, **Payson Playmakers** 120, The **Play Works** Co. 129, **Provo Community** Theatre 134, **Puerto Rican Traveling** Theatre 134, **Royal Court** Repertory 141, **Seaside Music** Theater 143, The **Snowmass Repertory** Theatre 147, **Soho Repertory** Theatre 148, **Stanley Hotel** Theatre 152, **Tennessee Repertory** Theatre 156, **Theatre on The Square** 163, **TheatreWorks** 165, **TheatreWorks/ USA** 166, The **Thirteenth Street Children's Theatre** Ensemble 167, **Triangle** Theatre Co. 170, **Upstairs** Dinner Theatre 172, **Vineyard** Theatre 174, **West Bank Downstairs** Theatre Bar 176, **West End** Dinner Theatre 178, **Young People's Theatre** Co. of Delaware Valley 184, **Zephyr** Theatre Complex 185

Contests: ACTF **Musical Theater** Award 192, **American Musical Theater** Festival 194, **BMI University Musical Show** Competition 198, **International New Music Composers** Competition 215, **National Music Theater Conference** 226, **Network** New Music Theater Awards Program 228, The **Richard Rodgers** Production Award 234, The **Ten-Minute Musicals** Project 239, **University of Lousiville Grawemeyer** Award for Music Composition 243, **TheatreWorks/USA Commissioning** Program 241

Programs: **American Music Center** 251, **ASCAP Musical Theatre** Workshop 253, **Banff Center School of Fine Arts Music Theatre Program** 255, **BMI/Lehman Engel** Musical Theatre Workshop 256, **Central Opera** Service 258, **Columbia College Chicago** New Musicals Project 259, **Composers/ Librettists Studio** 259, **Kleban** Foundation 270, The **Lehman Engel** Musical Theatre Workshop 270, **Los Angeles Theatre Center** Programs 271, **Meet the Composer** 273, **Musical Theatre Lab** 275, **National Endowment for the Arts** Opera Musical Theater Program 276, **National Institute** for Opera and Music Theater 276, The **National Music Theater Network** 276, The **Songwriters Guild** of America 291

Publishers: **Contemporary Drama Service** 307, **Freelance** Press 310

Mysteries

Theatres: **Apple Corps** Theatre 17, **Coconut Grove** Playhouse 41, The **Delray Beach** Playhouse 50, **Fountain Square** Players 63, **Lakewood Little** Theatre 85, **Market House** Theatre 94, **New Phoenix** 106, **Royal Court** Repertory 104, **Source** Theatre Co. 148, **Stanley Hotel** Theatre 152

Publishers: **Samuel French Inc.** 316, **Scholastic Scope** 316

One-Acts & Short Plays

Theatres: **Academy** Theatre 3, The **Acting Group** 4, **Actors Alliance** Theatre 5, **Actors Theatre of Louisville** 7, **Actors Theatre of St. Paul** 8, **American Living History** Theater 13, **Arvada Center** for The Arts & Humanities 20,

Atlantic Community College Theatre 21, **Barn** Players 24, **Brooklyn Theatre** Ensemble 30, **Carroll College** Little Theatre 34, **Cheyenne** Little Theatre Players 37, **City Stage** Theatre Co. 39, **Clavis** Theatre 41, **Company One** Theater 42, **The Coterie Inc.** 45, **Dixon Place** 52, **Ensemble Studio** Theatre 57, **Gary Young Mime** Theatre 64, **Hangar Theatre** 69, **Little Broadway** Productions 88, **Manhattan Punch Line** Theatre 93, **Mill Mountain** Theatre 98, **One Act** Theatre Co. 117, **Pennsylvania Stage** Co. 122, **Prairie Players** Youth Theatre 132, **Puerto Rican Traveling** Theatre (musicals) 134, **Quaigh** Theatre 135, **Senior Acting Program** of the Barn Players 144, The **Thunderbird** Theater Co. 168, **West Bank Downstairs** Theatre Bar 176

Contests: **A Directors' Theatre** Annual Young Playwrights' Competition 191, **Anna Zornio Memorial Children's Theatre** Playwriting Award 194, **Celebration of One-Acts** 201, **Chicano** Literary Contest 201, **Christina Crawford** Awards 202 **DC Art/Works** Playwrights Competition 204, The **Dogwood National One-Act Play** Competition 205, **Drury College** 1-Act Playwriting Contest 206, **Dubuque Fine Arts Players** 13th Annual One-Act Playwriting Contest 206, **Exposure/Stages** 207, **Frank McClure** One-Act Play Award 210, **George R. Kernodle** Playwriting Competition 211, **Henrico Theatre Co.** One-Act Playwriting Competition 213, **Inner City Cultural Center** Short Play Competition 215, **Kumu Kahua** Playwriting Contest 217, **Lincoln Memorial** One-Act Contest 216, **Love Creek Short Play** Festival 220, **Manhattan Punch Line Festival** of One-Act Comedies 220, **Margaret Bartle** Annual Playwriting Award 220, **Market House Theatre** One-Act Playwrighting Competition 221, **National One-Act Play** Contest (KY) 226, **National One-Act Playwriting** Competition (VA) 227, **National Ten-Minute Play** Contest 228, **1990 Annual One-Act Festival** Contest 230, **Off-Off Broadway Original Short Play** Festival 231, **Paul T. Nolan** Award 231, **Peace** Play Contest 231, **Playwright's Forum** Awards 232, **Scholastic** Writing Awards 235, The **Short Play Awards Program** 193, The **Ten-Minute Musicals** Project 239, **Tennessee Williams/ New Orleans Literary Festival** One-Act Play Contest 240, **Theatre Express** National One-Act Comedy Playwriting Contest 240, The **Virginia Prize** for Playwriting 244, **Warehouse Theatre Co.** One-Act Competition 245, **Western Public Radio** Playwriting Contest 245, **Writer's Digest** Writing Competition 246

Programs Discovery '90 261, **S.T.A.G.E.** 292

Publishers: **Apalachee Quarterly** 303, The **Bellingham Review** 304, **Brooklyn Review** 305, **Callaloo** 305, **Capilano Review** 306, **Child Life Magazine** 306, **Confrontation** 307, **Contemporary Drama Service** 307, **DeKalb Literary Arts** Journal 307, **Dramatika** 309, **Event** 310, **Latin American Literary** Review 311, The **Massachusetts Review** 312, **Modern Liturgy** 312, **New American Writing** 312, **Obsidian II:** Black Literature in Review 313, **Pennsylvania** Review 313, **Portland** Review 315, **Salome** 316, **Scholastic Scope** 316, **Scholastic Voice** 316, **Sinister Wisdom** 317, **United Arts** 319, **Willow Springs** 319

Published Works

Contests: **ATA Award** for Literary Translation from the German 196, **Harold Morton Landon** Translation Award 210, **Lewis Galantiere** Literary Translation Prize 219, **PEN Translation** Prize 232, **Towson State University** Prize for Literature 242

Puppetry

Theatres: **Center for Puppetry Arts** 35, **Mettawee River** Co. 97, **Underground Railway** Theater 171

Radio Plays

Theatre: **Company One** Theater 42

Contests: **Scholastic** Writing Awards 235, **Western Public Radio** Playwriting Contest 245

Publisher: **Dimension** 308

Regional/Local Writers & Themes

NORTHEAST
Theatres: **About Face** Theatre Co. 2, **Atlantic Community College** Theatre 21, **Broadway Tomorrow Musical** Theatre 30, **Brooklyn Theatre** Ensemble 30, **Browns Head** Repertory Theatre 31, **Contemporary Theatre** of Syracuse 44, The **Gallery Players** of Park Slope 64, **Gloucester Stage** Co. 66,

Huntington Guild Theatre Co. 75, **Merrimack Repertory Theatre** 96, **Oldcastle** Theatre Co. 115, **Philadelphia Drama Guild** 124, The **Theatre of Newburyport** 162, **Vermont Theatre Co.** 173

Contests: **Clauder** Competition for Excellence 202, **Merrimack Repertory Theatre** Playwriting Contest 223, **Vermont** Playwrights Award 243, The **Queens Theatre Network Inc.** Play Awards 247

Programs: **American Indian Community House** 251, **Artists Foundation** 252, **Fairchester Playwrights** Project 263, **New Dramatists** 277, **New Independents** Project 278, The **New Jersey Playwrights** Workshop 278, **Ollantay Center** for the Arts 280, **Pen to Stage** Productions 282, **Playwright Exchange** 284, **Puerto Rican Traveling Theatre** Playwrights' Workshop 288

SOUTH/SOUTHEAST

Theatres: **Academy** Theatre 3, **Alabama Shakespeare** Festival 9, **Arkansas Repertory** Theatre 19, **Cumberland County** Playhouse 48, **Ensemble Theatre of Florida** 58, The **Firehouse Theatre** Inc. (AL) 61, **North Carolina Shakespeare Festival** 112, **The Road Company** 140, **Roadside** Theater 140, **Southern Appalachian** Repertory Theatre 149, **Southern Rep** 149, **Tennessee Repertory** Theatre 156, **Theatre-in-the-Works** Inc. (FL) 161

Contests: **CAC** New Play Competition 199, **Festival of Southern Theatre** 208, **FIU** Playwrights' Festival 209, **Market House Theatre** One-Act Playwriting Competition 221, **New World Theater** New Play Competition 229, **South Carolina New Play** Festival 237, **Southern Playwrights** Competition 238, **Towson State University** Prize for Literature 242, The **Virginia Prize** for Playwriting 244

Programs: **City of Atlanta** Bureau of Cultural Affairs 259, The **Playwrights' Unit** 287, **Southeast Playwrights** Project 291, **Virginia Playwrights Fellowships** 296

MIDWEST

Theatres: **Brown Grand** Theatre 31, The **Cricket** Theatre 47, **FMT** 61, **Free Street Theater** 63, **Heartland** Theatre Co. 70, **Horse Cave** Theatre 75, **Kearney State College** Theatre 83, **Madison Repertory** Theatre 91, **Mad River** Theatre Works 91, **Northlight** Theatre 112, **Paul Bunyan**

Playhouse 120, **Players Theatre** of Columbus 128, **Remains** Theatre 137, **Rochester Civic** Theatre 140, **Victory Gardens** Theater 173

Contests: **Arnold & Dorothy Burger** Playwriting Competition 195, **Cleveland Public Theatre** Festival of New Plays 202, **FMCT** Playwrights Competition 210, **Great Platte River** Playwrights Festival 212, **Robert J. Pickering** Award 235, The **Society of Midland Authors** Drama Award 237, **Young Playwrights** Festival (IL) 247

Programs: **Bush Artist Fellowship** 257, **CAC Playwright's Forum** 257, **Chicago Dramatists** Workshop 259, **League of Chicago Theatres** 270, **Playwrights' Center** of Chicago 285

WEST/SOUTHWEST
Theatres: **Arizona Theatre** Co. 18, **Borderlands Theater**/Teatro Fronterizo 28, **Cheyenne** Little Theatre Players 37, **Creede Repertory** Theatre 47, **Intermountain** Actors Ensemble 78, The **Julian** Theatre 82, **Montana Repertory** Theater 100, **New Mexico Repertory** Theatre 106, The **Salt Lake Acting Co.** 142, **South Coast Repertory** 148, **Stages** Repertory Theatre (TX) 150, **Tale Spinners** Theater 156, **Theatre West** 164

Contests: **Borderlands Theater**/Teatro Fronterizo New Play Search 199, **California Young Playwrights** Project 200, **James D. Phelan** Literary Award 216, **Summerfield G. Roberts** Award 239

Programs: **Brody** Arts Fund 257, **Dobie–Paisano** Project 261, **Los Angeles Theatre Center** Programs 271, **New Works Theatre Playwrights' Workshop** 278, The **Playwright's Center** of San Francisco 285, The **Playwrights Foundation** 285, **S.T.A.G.E.** 292, **Theatre Bay Area** 294

Publisher: **West Coast Plays** 319

NORTHWEST
Theatres: The **Empty Space** Theatre 56, **Idaho Shakespeare Festival** 76, **Perseverance** Theatre 124, **Portland Repertory** Theatre 131, **Triad Ensemble** 169

Contests: **Northwest Playwrights Guild** Competition 230, **Portland State University** New Plays in Progress Series 233

Programs: **Artist Trust** 253, **New City Theater** Director's
Festival 277, **Northwest Playwrights Guild** 280

Publisher: **West Coast Plays** 319

OUTSIDE CONTINENTAL U.S.A./INTERNATIONAL

Theatres: **California Repertory** Co. 32, **Chicago Medieval**
Players 37, **Experimental Theatre** of the Puertorican Atheneum
59, **Honolulu Theatre** for Youth 74, **Magic Theatre** 91, **One
Act** Theatre Co. 117, **Shakespeare & Company** 145, **Stages
Trilingual** Theatre 151, The **Wilma** Theatre 180

Contests: **Kumu Kahua** Playwriting Contest 217, **Northwest
Playwrights Guild** Competition 230

Programs: **American/Scandinavian Foundation** 252, **Arts
International** 253, **Australian Writers' Guild** 255, **Banff
Center School of Fine Arts Playwrights' Colony** 255,
British American Arts Association 256, **British Theatre**
Association 257, **PEN American Center** 282, **Playmarket** 284

Publisher: **CASTA** 306

Rural or Small-Town Settings & Themes

Theatres: **Arrow Rock Lyceum** Theatre 19, **Browns Head**
Repertory Theatre 31, **Cumberland County** Playhouse 48, **Mad
River** Theater Works 91, **The Road Company** 140

Contest: **Arrow Rock Lyceum** Theatre National Playwrights
Competition 196

Program: **Brody** Arts Fund 257

Second Productions, Previously Produced Works

Theatres: **Coney Island USA** 43, The **Second Stage** 144,
Theatre Rapport 163

Contests: **American College Theatre Festival** Awards
191-4, **FEAT** Playwriting Festival 207, **The Society of
Midland Authors** Drama Award 237, **University of Louisville
Grawemeyer** Award for Musical Composition 243

Program: **Women in Theatre** Festival 298

Publishers: **American Theatre** Magazine 302, **Anchorage Press** 303, **Baker's** Plays 304, **Callaloo** 305, **Contemporary Drama Service** 307, **Drama Book Publishers** 308, **The Dramatic Publishing** Co. 308, **Dramatics** Magazine 308, **Dramatists Play Service** 309, **Eldridge** Publishing Co. 309, **Encore Performance** Publishing Co. 310, **I. E. Clark** Publishers 311, **New Plays Incorporated** 313, **Pioneer Drama Service** 314, **Players** Press 314, **Plays in Process** 314, **Samuel French Inc.** 316, **Theater** 318, **West Coast Plays** 319

Seniors' Issues, Older Actors & Audiences

Theatres: The **Adelphian Players** 8, **Barn** Players 24, **Creative** Productions 46, **Glass Unicorn** Productions 66, **Senior Acting Program** of the Barn Players 144, **Stop-Gap** Co. 152, **Sunset** Playhouse 154

Programs: **At the Foot of the Mountain** Programs 254, **Banff Center School of Fine Arts Playwrights' Colony** 255

Publisher: **Coach House** Press 306

Spanish-Language Plays

Theatres: **Duo** Theatre 55, **Post Theatre** Co. 131, **Puerto Rican Traveling** Theatre 134, **Repertorio Español** 138, **Stages Trilingual** Theatre 151, **Thalia** Spanish Theatre 157

Contests: **Borderlands Theater**/Teatro Fronterizo New Play Search 199, **Chicano** Literary Contest 201, **Hispanic Playwrights** Project 214, **Letras de Oro** (Spanish Literary Contest) 219

Programs: **Puerto Rican Traveling Theatre** Playwrights' Workshop 288, **Puerto Rican Traveling Theatre** Training Unit for Youngsters 289

Publishers: The **Americas Review and Arte Publico Press** 302, **Third Woman** Press 318

Student Authors, Young Playwrights

Contests: **A Directors' Theatre** Annual Young Playwrights' Competition 191, **American College Theatre Festival** Awards 191-4, **BMI University Musical Show** Competition 198, **California Young Playwrights** Project 200, **Christina Crawford** Awards 202, **Helen Eisner Award** for Young Playwrights 213, **High School Playwriting** Contest 213, **Marc A. Klein** Playwriting Award 220, **Scholastic** Writing Awards 235, **Southeast Regional Young Playwright** and Children's Theatre Festival 238, **Very Special Arts** Young Playwrights Program 244, **Warehouse Theatre** Co. One-Act Competition 245, **Wichita State University** Playwriting Contest 245, **Young Playwrights** Festival (NY) 246, **Young Playwrights** Festival (IL) 247

Programs: **Artists Foundation** 252, The **Associated Writing Programs** 254, **Association for Theatre in Higher Education** 254, **At the Foot of the Mountain** Programs 254, **Los Angeles Theatre Center** Programs 271, **New College Playwrights** 277, **Playwrights Theatre of New Jersey** 286, **Puerto Rican Traveling Theatre** Training Unit for Youngsters 289, **Young Playwrights** (MN) 300

Translations (into English), Adaptations

Theatres: **Alabama Shakespeare** Festival (literary ad.) 9, The **Arkansas Arts Center** Children's Theatre (ad. classics) 18, **Bloomsburg Theatre** Ensemble (tr. classics) 26, **Borderlands Theater**/Teatro Fronterizo (ad., tr. Latino American) 28, The **Charlotte Shakespeare** Co. 36, **Chicago Medieval** Players (ad. medieval, Renaissance) 37, The **Children's Theatre Co.** (ad.) 37, The **Clarence Brown** Co. (classics, E. European, Latin American) 40, **The Coterie Inc.** (ad. classics) 45, **CSC:** Classic Stage Co. (ad. other genres, European classics) 48, **Drama Committee** Repertory Theatre (ad. prose classics) 54, **El Teatro Campesino** (ad. classics) 56, The **Great-American Theatre** Co. (ad. children's classics) 68, **Honolulu Theatre** for Youth (ad. fairy tales, classics) 74, **Indiana Repertory** Theatre (ad. classics) 78, **INTAR** Hipanic American Theatre 78, **Intiman** Theatre Co. (classics) 79, **Lamb's Players** Theatre (ad. classics) 86, **Little Broadway** Productions (children's musical ad. classics) 88, **Long Island Stage** (tr. classics) 88, **Los Angeles Theatre Works** (ad. classics) 90, **Marin** Theatre Co. (tr. classics) 93, **Mettawee River** Co. (ad. myths, legends) 97, **Missouri Repertory** Theatre

100,   **Nebraska Theatre Caravan** (classics) 104,   The **New Rose** Theatre (classics) 107,   The **New Theatre of Brooklyn** (tr.) 109,   **New York Theatre Workshop** 111,   **North Carolina Shakespeare Festival** (ad. classics) 112,   **Northlight** Theatre (tr. and ad. "lost" plays) 112,   **Odyssey** Theater Co. (NY) (ad. literary works) 114,   **Paper Mill** Playhouse (musical ad.) 119, **Portland Repertory** Theatre (ad. classics) 131,   **Post Theatre** Co. 131,   **R.A.P.P.** Resident Theatre Co. (tr. and ad. classics) 137, **Remains** Theatre (ad.) 137,   **River Arts Repertory** 139, **Round House** Theatre (tr. classics) 141,   **Shakespeare & Company** (ad. E. Wharton, H. James & contemporaries) 145,   **Stage One:** Louisville Children's Theatre (ad.) 150,   **Stages Trilingual** Theatre (tr. Spanish, French) 151,   **Stage West** (MA) (ad. other genres, neglected classics, 20th century European) 151,   The **Studio Theatre** (tr. new Asian, European) 154,   **Theater Emory** (tr. and ad. classics) 158,   The **Theatre of Newburyport** (tr. and ad.) 162,   **Theatre West Virginia** (ad. well-known works) 165, **Three Rivers** Shakespeare Festival (classics) 168,   **Ubu Repertory** Theater (tr. French) 171,   The **Will Geer Theatricum Botanicum** (tr. classics) 179,   The **Wilma** Theatre (tr. and ad. international works) 180,   **Yale Repertory** Theatre (tr.) 183

Contests: ASF Translation Prize (Scandinavian) 196,   **ATA Award** for Literary Translation from German 196,   **Borderlands Theater**/Teatro Fronterizo New Play Search (ad., tr. Latino American) 199,   **Elmira College** Original Play Award (ad.) 247, **Harold Morton Landon** Translation Award (verse) 212,   **Lewis Galantiere** Literary Translation Prize (any language except German) 219,   **Margaret Bartle** Annual Playwriting Award (ad. children's classics) 220,   **NFJC Hebrew Translation** Commission 229, **PEN Translation** Prize 232,   **Renato Poggioli** Translation Award (Italian) 234,   **TCG Translation/Adaptation** Commissions 239, **TheatreWorks/USA Commissioning Program** 241

Publishers: American Theatre Magazine (tr.) 302,   **CASTA** (tr. East European since 1945) 306,   **Dimension** (tr. German) 308, **Freelance Press** (ad. children's classics) 310,   **Latin American Literary** Review (tr. Latin American literature) 311,   **Modern International Drama** (tr.) 312,   **New American Writing** (tr.) 312,   **Peforming Arts Journal** (tr.) 314,   **Plays:** The Drama Magazine for Young People (ad. children's) 315,   **TSL Press** (tr.) 318,   **Willow Springs** (tr.) 319

Urban Settings & Themes

Theatres: The **Adelphian** Players 8, **Free Street** Theater 63, **Ironbound** Theatre 79

Contest: **DC Art/Works** Playwrights Competition 204

Program: **Brody** Arts Fund 257

Women Authors, Women's Issues and Roles

Theatres: A **Directors' Theatre** 8, **Alice B.** Theatre 10, **At the Foot of the Mountain** 21, **Capital Repertory** Co. 33, **Company One** Theater 42, **Daughter** Productions 49, **Friends & Artists** Theatre Ensemble 63, **Horizons:** Theatre from a Woman's Perspective 74, **Horizon Theatre** Co. 74, **Idaho Shakespeare Festival** 76, The **Immediate Theatre** 77, **Kalamazoo** Civic Players 83, **Lace** Productions 83, **Los Angeles Theatre** Center 90, **Mary Baldwin College** Theatre 95, **Mills College** Theatre 98, The **New Theatre** of Brooklyn 109, **One Act** Theatre Co. 117, **San Diego Repertory** Theatre 142, **Seven Stages** 145, **Springboard** Theatre 150, **Stages Repertory** Theatre 150, **Studio Arena** Theatre 154, **Syracuse Stage** 155, **Texas A & I** University Theatre 157, **Third Step** Theatre Co. 166, The **Tower Players** of Hillsdale College 169, **Wisdom Bridge** Theatre 180, **Women's Interart Center** 181, The **Women's Project** and Productions 181, **Works by Women** 182

Contests: **Dayton Playhouse** Playwriting Competition 204, **Margaret Bartle** Annual Playwriting Award 220, **Margo Jones** Playwriting Competition 221, **Merrimack Repertory** Theatre Playwriting Contest 223, **New World** Theater New Play Competition 229, The **Susan Smith Blackburn** Prize 239, **Third Step** Theatre Co. Spring Festival of Staged Readings 241, **Warehouse Theatre Co.** One-Act Competition 245

Programs: At the **Foot of the Mountain** Programs 254, **Frank Silvera** Writers' Workshop 265, **The Gathering** 266, The **International Women's Writing Guild** 268, **Los Angeles Theatre Center** Programs 271, **Mary Ingraham Bunting** Institute 272, **Money for Women**/The Barbara Deming Memorial Fund Inc. 275, The **Rockefeller Foundation's Bellagio** Study and Conference Center 290, **Women in Theatre** Festival 298, **WOW (Women One World) Cafe** 298

Publishers: **Earth's Daughters** 309, **Helicon Nine** 310,
Sinister Wisdom 317, **Third Woman Press** 318, **Women in
Performance**: A Journal of Feminist Theory 320

Cross Reference to Special Programs

Membership & Service Organizations, Resource Information Services

Actors' Alliance Inc. 250, The **Alliance of Resident
Theatres**/New York 250, The **American Alliance for Theatre
and Education** 251, **American Indian Community House** 251,
American Music Center 251, **Arts International** 253,
ASSITEJ/USA 253, The **Associated Writing Programs** 254,
Association for **Theatre in Higher Education** 254, Association
of **Hispanic Arts** 254, **Australian Writers' Guild** 255, **British
American Arts** Association 256, **British Theatre** Association
257, **California Theatre Council** 258, **Center for Arts
Information** 258, **Central Opera** Service 258, **Chicago
Dramatists** Workshop 259, **Coordinating Council of Literary
Magazines** Library 260, The **Dramatists Guild** 263,
Fairchester Playwrights Project 263, **Feedback Services/**
Feedback Theatrebooks 264, **FirstStage** 264, The **Foundation
Center** 265, The **Foundation of the Dramatists Guild** 265,
Institute of Outdoor Drama 267, **International Theatre
Institute** of the United States 268, The **International Women's
Writing Guild** 268, **League of Chicago Theatres**/Chicago
Theatre Association 270, **Literary Managers and Dramaturgs** of
America 271, **Los Angeles Theatre Alliance**/League of
Producers 271, **Manhattan Playwrights** Unit 272, **Meet the
Composer** 273, **Merely Players** 274, **National Foundation** for
Jewish Culture 276, **National Institute** for Opera and Music
Theater 276, The **National Music Theater** Network 276, **New
Dramatists** 277, **New Independents** Project 278, The **New
Jersey Playwrights** Workshop 278, **New York Foundation** for
the Arts 279, **Northwest Playwrights Guild** 280, **Ollantay**
Center for the Arts 280, **PEN** American Center 282, **Pen to Stage**
Productions 282, **Performing Arts Research Center** 283,
Playformers 283, **Playmarket** 284, The **Playwrights' Center**
285, **Playwrights' Center of Chicago** 285, The **Playwrights'
Center** of San Francisco 285, **Playwrights' Platform** 285,
Playwrights Theatre of New Jersey 286, The **Playwrights'
Unit** 287, **Professional Association of Canadian
Theatre**/PACT Communications Center 288, The **Songwriters**

Guild of America 291, **Southeast Playwrights Project** 291, **S.T.A.G.E.** 292, **Theatre Artists Workshop** of Westport 294, **Theatre Bay Area** 294, **Theatre Communications Group** 294, **Theatre Development Fund** 295, **Volunteer Lawyers** for the Arts (VLA) 297, **Women in Theatre** Festival 298, **WOW (Women One World) Cafe** 298

Play Development Programs

(For theatres and contests offering play development programs, see individual listings.)

Actors' Alliance Inc. 250, **American Playwright** Program 252, **ASCAP Musical Theatre** Workshop 253, **Asolo Touring Theatre** Commissions 253, **At the Foot of the Mountain** Programs 254, **Banff Center** School of Fine Arts Music Theatre Program (residency) 255, **Banff Center** School of Fine Arts Playwrights' Colony (residency) 255, **BEST** Play Co. 256, **BMI/Lehman Engel Musical Theatre** Workshops 256, **CAC Playwright's Forum** 257, **Center Theater Youtheatre** Program 258, **Chicago Dramatists Workshop** 259, **Columbia College Chicago** New Musicals Project 259, **Composers/Librettists Studio** 259, **Cornell Center** for the Performing Arts New Works Program (residency) 260, **Discovery '90** (residency) 261, **Double ImageTheatre** New Voices at Greene Street Cafe 262, **Drama Project** 262, **Dramatic Risks** 262, **Ensemble Studio Theatre Institute** (residency) 263, **Fairchester** Playwrights Project 263, **Firststage** 264, **Frank Silvera** Writers' Workshop 265, **Frederick Douglass Creative Arts Center** Writing Workshops 265, **The Gathering** 266, **GS Playwrights' Project** 266, **INTAR Hispanic Playwrights-in-Residence** Laboratory (residency) 268, The **Lee Strasberg Theatre Institute** 270, The **Lehman Engel Musical Theatre** Workshop 270, **Los Angeles Theatre Center** Programs 271, **Manhattan Playwrights Unit** 272, **Merely Players** 274, **Midwest PlayLabs** (residency) 274, **Mount Sequoyah** New Play Retreat (residency) 275, **Musical Theatre Lab** 275, **New American Plays** Series 277, **New College Playwrights** 277, **New Independents** Project 278, The **New Jersey Playwrights** Workshop 278, **New Works Theatre Playwrights' Workshop** 278, **New York Foundation** for the Arts 279, **New York Theatre** Playwrights' Workshop 278, **Padua Hills** Playwrights' Workshop/Festival (residency) 281, **Palenville** Interarts Colony (residency) 281, **Pen to Stage** Productions 282, The **Philadelphia Theatre Company's Mentor Project** (residency)

Production Programs, Festivals
(Also see Play Development Programs.)

Professional Appointments

Script Services: Critiques, Script Preparation, Marketing/Distribution
(For theatres and contests offering script services, see individual listings.)

American College Theatre Festival New Play Preview Program 251, **American Playwright** Program 252, **Chicago Dramatists** Workshop 259, **Feedback Services**/Feedback Theatrebooks 264, **Frank Silvera** Writers' Workshop 265, **The International Women's Writing Guild** 268, **Merely Players** 274, **Mount Sequoyah** New Play Retreat 275, **New Dramatists** 277, **Northwest Playwrights Guild** 280, **Playmarket** 284, **Playwright Exchange** 284, The **Script Review** 290, **Southeast Playwrights Project** 291

Sources of Financial Support

American-Scandinavian Foundation 252, **Artists Foundation** 252, **Artist Trust** 253, The Authors League Fund and **The Dramatists Guild Fund** 255, **Brody** Arts Fund 257, **Bush Artist Fellowship** 257, **Cintas Foundation** Fellowship Program 259, **City of Atlanta** Bureau of Cultural Affairs 259, **Drama League of New York** Playwright Assistance Awards 262, **Fulbright Scholar** Program 266, **Fund for New American Plays** 266, **Jerome Playwright-in-Residence** Fellowships 269, **John Simon Guggenheim** Memorial Foundation Fellowships 269, **Kleban** Foundation 270, **Ludwig Vogelstein** Foundation 272, **Mary Ingraham Bunting** Institute 272, **Mary Roberts Rinehart** Fund 272, **McKnight Fellowships** 273, **Money for Women**/Barbara Deming Memorial Fund Inc. 275, **National Endowment for the Arts** Opera Musical Theater Program 276, **National Endowment for the Arts** Theater Program 276, **New York Foundation** for the Arts 279, **NFJC** Playwrights' Travel Grant Program 279, **PEN** Writers' Fund 283, The **Playwrights' Center** 285, **Princess Grace Foundation-U.S.A.** 288, **Rockefeller Foundation** Grants 289, **TCG Observership** Program 293, **Virginia Playwrights Fellowships** 296

Training Programs, Classes
(Also see individual listings.)

New College Playwrights 277, **Puerto Rican Traveling Theatre** Training Unit for Youngsters 289, **Roundabout Theatre's** Creative Connection 290, **University of Wisconsin** Madison School of the Arts at Rhinelander 296, **Young Playwrights** (MN) 300

Work Spaces

Mercantile Library Association Writers Studio 273, The **Writers Room** 299

Writers' Colonies, Retreats, Conferences
(Also see residencies indicated under Play Development Programs.)

Act I Creativity Center 250, **Atlantic Center** for the Arts 254, **Blue Mountain** Center 256, **Chateau de Lesvault** 258, **Cummington Community** for the Arts 260, **Deep South Writers Conference** 260, **Dobie-Paisano** Project 261, **Dorland Mountain Colony** 261, **Dorset Colony House** for Writers 262, The **Edward F. Albee Foundation** Inc. 263, **Fine Arts Work Center** 264, **Florida Studio Theatre** Artists Colony 264, **Hambidge Center** for Creative Arts & Sciences 267, **Hawthornden Castle** International Retreat for Writers 267, **Helene Wurlitzer** Foundation 267, **Key West Literary Seminar** 270, **MacDowell Colony** 272, **Mildred I. Reid** Writers Colony 274, **Millay Colony** for the Arts 274, **Montalvo Center** for the Arts 275, **New College Playwrights** 277, The **New Harmony Project** 278, **Northwood Institute** Alden B. Dow Creativity Center 280, **Oregon Writers Colony** 281, **Palenville** Interarts Colony 281, **Ragdale Foundation** 289, The **Rockefeller Foundation's Bellagio Study and Conference Center** 290, **Sasketchewan Writers/**Artists Colonies 290, **Shenandoah** Playwrights Retreat 290, **Tyrone Guthrie Center** 295, **Ucross Foundation** 295, **Virginia Center** for the Arts 296, **Virginia Theatreworks III** 297, **Yaddo** 299, **The Yard** 299, **Yellow Springs** Institute 299, **Zen Mountain Monastery** 300

The Playwright's Calendar 1990

Contests, special programs and publishers listed in this calendar are those whose specific deadlines for this year were announced prior to publication of *The Playwright's Companion 1990*. For information on ongoing activities, deadlines yet to be announced and deadlines falling after December 31, 1990, playwrights should consult individual listings and request guidelines.

January

1 Cummington Community for Arts 260
Kumu Kahua Playwriting Contest 217
The Lee Korf Playwriting Awards 218
Mill Mountain Theatre New Play Competition 224
New American Writing 312
New City Theater Director's Festival 277
Towngate Theatre Playwriting Contest 242

8 Chicano Literary Contest 201
Portland State University New Plays in Progress Series 233

15 Dobie-Paisano Project 261
James D. Phelan Literary Award 216
La Pensee Discovery! Theatre Awards 218
Lincoln Memorial Contest 216
Lois and Richard Rosenthal New Play Prize 219
National Archives Playwriting Competition 225
Southeast Region Young Playwright and Children's Theatre
    Festival 238
Theatre Express National One-Act Comedy Contest 240
Third Step Theatre Company Spring Festival 241
The Virginia Prize for Playwriting 244
Yaddo 299

17 Jewel Box Theatre Playwriting Award 217
Scholastic Writing Awards 235

21 Actors Theatre of Houston & Masterscriptor's Literary Service
    National Playwright Competition 191

25 Virginia Center for the Arts 296

26 Margaret Bartle Annual Playwriting Award 220
University of Louisville Grawemeyer Award 243

30 The Morton R. Sarett Memorial Award 225

31 Atlantic Community College Playwrights' Weekend 197
D.H. Lawrence Fellowship 261
Dubuque Fine Arts Players 13th Annual One-Act Contest 206
Heights Showcase Playwriting Contest 212
Summerfield G. Roberts Award 239

February
1 Arnold Weissberger Award 196
Banff Center School of Fine Arts Playwrights' Colony 255
Christina Crawford Awards 202
Cleveland Public Theatre Festival of New Plays 202
Columbia Theatre Players' Annual New Play Contest 203
Jerome Playwright-in-Residence Fellowships 269
Latin American Literary Review 311
Millay Colony for the Arts 274
Money for Women/Barbara Deming Memorial Fund 275
National Endowment for the Arts Opera Musical Theater
  Program 276
National Music Theater Conference (tentative deadline) 226
New American Comedy Festival 229
North Carolina Arts Council Visiting Artist Program 279
Renato Poggioli Translation Award 234
Tennessee Williams/New Orleans Literary Festival Contest 240
Young Playwrights Festival (IL) 247
15 Aggie Players Playwriting Competition 191
Cornerstone: Penumbra Theatre Company Competition 203
The Society of Midland Authors Drama Award 237
Southern Playwrights Competition 238
TCG Observership Program 293
Wichita State University Playwriting Contest 245
19 Very Special Arts Young Playwrights Program 244

March
1 Borderlands Theater/Teatro Fronterizo New Play Search 199
Cintas Foundation Fellowship Program 259
Cummington Community for Arts 260
Discovery '90 261
Dorland Mountain Colony 261
Midwest PlayLabs 274
The Ten-Minute Musicals Project 239
24th Street Experiment Annual Playwright Competition 242
Ucross Foundation 295
Unicorn Theatre National Playwright's Competition 242
15 Great Platte River Playwrights Festival 212
Lewis Galantiere Literary Translation Prize 219
Merrimack Repertory Theatre Playwriting Contest 223
Plays for a New America 232
Source Theatre National Playwriting Competition 237
Theater in the Works (MA) 294
20 Playwrights' Platform (Festival) 285
31 Bob Clark New Playwright Contest 199
National One-Act Playwriting Competition (VA) 227

April

May

June

30 George R. Kernodle Playwriting Competition 211
INTAR Hispanic Playwrights-in-Residence Laboratory 268
Network New Music Theater Awards 228
Plays in Process 314
Regional Children's Theatre Competition 1990 234
Siena College Playwright's Competition 236
Vermont Repertory Theatre National Playwriting Contest 244

July
 1 Composers/Librettists Studio 260
National Play Award 227
New American Writing 312
 2 Theodore Ward Prize 241
 15 Deep South Writers Conference 260
The Dogwood National One-Act Play Competition 205
Miller Award 1990 223
Paul T. Nolan Award 231
 31 SETC New Play Project 236

August
 1 Arnold and Dorothy Burger Playwriting Competition 195
BMI/Lehman Engel Musical Theatre Composer-Lyricist
  Workshop 256
The Lehman Engel Musical Theatre Workshop 270
San Diego Junior Theatre Playwriting Competition 235
Vermont Playwrights Award 243
Yaddo 299
 3 ASCAP Musical Theatre Workshop 253
 10 Inner City Cultural Center Short Play Competition (letter of
  intent) 215
 30 Festival of Firsts Playwriting Competition 208

September
 1 Dorland Mountain Colony 261
Millay Colony for the Arts 274
Stanley Drama Award 238
 7 Inner City Cultural Center Short Play Competition (completed
  application; see listing in Contests) 215
 15 Henrico Theatre Company One-Act Playwriting Competition 213
Multicultural Playwrights Festival 225
New Dramatists 277
TCG Observership Program 293
 25 Virginia Center for the Arts 296
 30 Puerto Rican Traveling Theatre Playwrights' Workshop 288

October
 1 Ferndale Repertory New Works Competition 208
Humboldt State University Season of New American Plays 214
Love Creek Short Play Festival 220
Manhattan Punch Line Festival of One-Act Comedies 220

Mary Ingraham Bunting Institute 272
Theatre Memphis New Play Competition 240
Ucross Foundation 295
Young Playwrights Festival (NY) 246
12 Letras de Oro (Spanish Literary Contest) 219
15 Bloomington Playwrights Project Contest 198
Celebration of One-Acts 201
David Library Award for Playwriting on Freedom or Americana
   (deadline may be earlier; see listing) 192
Red Octopus Theatre Company Original Scripts Workshop 289

November
1 Adriatic Award 216
American-Scandinavian Foundation 252
Beverly Hills Theatre Guild-Julie Harris Award 197
CAC New Play Competition 199
West Coast Ensemble Competition for Full-Length Plays 245
15 The Ann White Theatre 7th Annual Contest 195
17 Forest A. Roberts/Shiras Institute Playwriting Award 210
30 Dayton Playhouse Playwriting Competition 204
Lawrence S. Epstein Playwriting Award 218

December
1 ACTF College Musical Theater Award 192
Columbia Pictures Television Award 192
Drury College 1-Act Playwriting Contest 206
Lorraine Hansberry Playwriting Award 193
McKnight Fellowships 273
National Playwrights Conference/New Drama for Television
   Project 228
National Student Playwriting Award 193
The Short Play Awards Program 193
6 Perkins Playwriting Contest 216
14 Yellow Springs Institute 299
15 JCC Theatre of Cleveland Dorothy Silver Playwriting
   Competition 216
Playwright's Forum Awards 232
Stages 292
The Sundance Institute Playwrights Laboratory 293
The Yard 299
Year-End Series (Y.E.S.) New Play Festival 246
30 PrimaFacie/WestFest 287
31 Biennial Promising Playwright Award 197
Harold Morton Landon Translation Award 212
Mark Gilbert Award 222
No Empty Space Theatre Playwriting Contest 230
Northwood Institute Alden B. Dow Creativity Center 280
The Steinbeck Playwriting Competition 238

The Playwright's Library

The Playwright's Library is a selective list of articles, periodicals, books and brochures which we believe to be valuable to dramatists at various stages in their careers.

Articles

Ambush, Benny Sato, "Pluralism to the Bone," *American Theatre* (Apr. 1989), 5.

Bobkoff, Ned, "No Magic Formula: Mark Medoff talks about training actors and playwrights," *Dramatics* (Jan. 1989), 31-37.

Catron, Louis E., "Using Foreshadowing to Keep Your Stories on Track," *Writer's Digest* (Feb. 1989), 35-37;

Clinton, Edward, "Forever Young," *Writer's Digest* (Jun. 1989), 72, 70-71.

Holden, Jan, "An Answer to the Question: When are you going to try writing a real play?'" *Theater* (Winter 1988-89), 72.

Lee, Robert E., "The Only Playwriting Tools You'll Ever Need," *Writer's Digest* (May 1989), 34-36.

London, Todd, "Opening a Door Up Left: Designers and Playwrights Seek a Fuller Partnership," *American Theatre* (Mar. 1989), 38-39.

Patrick, Robert, "Playwriting 101: A syllabus, in 18 verses of doggerel," *Dramatics* (May 1989), 7.

Ramsey, Dale, "Common Sense, Construction, Crisis. With an Eye on the Audience," *Dramatists Guild Quarterly* (Spring 1989), 40-49.

Riddell, Richard, "The Academy Flunks Out," *American Theatre* Jun. 1989), 44-45.

Slaton, Gram, "The Potato Head Factor: More Myths & Misconceptions About New Play Development," *Subtext: The Newsletter of the Playwrights' Center* VI (Winter 1989), 1, 4.

Straczynski, J. Michael, "The Basic Tools of Script Structure," *Writer's Digest* (Aug. 1989), 17-19.

Yankowitz, Susan, "From the Playwright's Hammer," *Theatre* (Winter 1988-89), 89-91.

Periodicals and Magazines

American Theatre, New York: Theatre Communications Group; a monthly magazine dealing with the professional not-for-profit theatre in the U.S.; including articles, reviews, play texts; special "Plays and Playwrights" section provides information on opportunities and announces results of playwriting competitions.

Dramatics, Cincinnati: The International Thespian Society; a monthly magazine for teachers and students of drama.

Theater, New Haven, CT: Yale School of Drama; a magazine, published 3 times a year, including essays, reviews, new play texts, interviews, discussions of theatre events from around the world.

Theater Week, New York: That New Magazine, Inc.; a weekly magazine including articles on American theatre, interviews, reviews, show listings for New York City and nationwide.

TDR, Cambridge, MA: The MIT Press; a quarterly journal covering experimental performance, dance, ritual, mime, theatre, performance art and popular entertainment.

The Writer, Boston: The Writer, Inc.; a monthly magazine for aspiring writers; each Sept. issue focuses on play markets.

Writer's Digest, Cincinnati: Writer's Digest; a monthly magazine for aspiring writers.

Books

Archer, William. *Play-Making: A Manual of Craftsmanship.* Boston: Small, Maynard and Co., 1912.

Busfield, Roger M. Jr. *The Playwright's Art.* Westport, CT: Greenwood Press, 1958.

Catron, Louis E. *Writing, Producing, and Selling Your Play.* Englewood Cliffs, NJ: Prentice-Hall, Inc., 1984.

Cohen, Edward M. *Working on a New Play*. New York: Prentice-Hall, Inc., 1988.

Cole, Toby, ed. *Playwrights on Playwriting*. New York: Hill and Wang, 1960.

Egri, Lagos. *The Art of Dramatic Writing*. New York: Simon and Schuster, 1960.

Else, Gerald F. (trans. and intro.). *Aristotle Poetics*. Ann Arbor, MI: The University of Michigan Press, 1967.

Grebanier, Bernard. *Playwriting: How to Write for the Theatre*. New York: Barnes & Noble, 1961.

Griffiths, Stuart. *How Plays Are Made: The Fundamental Elements of Play Construction*. Englewood Cliffs, NJ: Prentice-Hall, Inc., 1982.

Hornby, Richard. *Script into Performance: A Structuralist Approach*. New York: Paragon House Publishers, 1987 (paperback edition).

Lawson, John Howard. *Theory and Technique of Playwriting*. New York: G. P. Putnam's Sons, 1949.

MacGowan, Kenneth. *A Primer of Playwriting*. New York: Random House, 1951.

Meserve, Mollie Ann, compiler. *Who's Where in the American Theatre 1990 Edition*. New York: Feedback Theatrebooks, 1989.

Mitchell, Angela E. and Gillian Richards, eds. *Dramatists Sourcebook 1989-90 Edition*. New York: Theatre Communications Group, 1989.

Rowe, Kenneth Thorpe. *Write That Play*. New York: Funk & Wagnalls Co., 1939.

Smiley, Sam. *Playwriting: The Structure of Action*. Englewood Cliffs, NJ: Prentice-Hall, Inc., 1971.

Weales, Gerald. *A Play and Its Parts*. New York: Basic Books, 1964.

Brochures

"Copyright Basics" (R1), Register of Copyrights, Library of Congress, Washington, DC 20559 (202) 287-9100; free brochure of the U.S. Copyright Office.

"Guidelines," Samuel French, Inc., 45 W. 25th St., New York, NY 10010; sample of format preferred by Samuel French ($3).

"A Handbook for Literary Translators," PEN American Center, 568 Broadway, New York, NY 10012; free brochure containing a model contract, information on "The Responsibilities of Translation" and a "Manifesto on Translation."

"Highlights of the New Copyright Law" (R99), Register of Copyrights, Library of Congress, Washington, DC 20559 (202) 287-9100; free brochure of the U.S. Copyright Office.

"The Literary Agent," Society of Authors' Representatives, Inc., Box 650 Old Chelsea Station, New York, NY 10113; free brochure explaining services provided by agents, standard practices of agents, a list of tasks which agents cannot perform, advice on "How to Find an Agent" and a list of SAR members with addresses.

Index to Listings

Index to Listings

ADVERTISEMENTS

APPLE II-E W/ L.Q. PRINTER.
$1.00/double spaced page. Minor spelling/punctuation correction. Fast turn around. **S. WAGNER, 907 Bonner, Alturas, CA 96101 (916) 233-4480**

MURI H. JORGENSON
P.O. Box 3548, Clearlake, CA 95422
(707) 995-0128
Professional word processing specializing in playscripts. Letter quality print. Free spell check, punctuation, and free disc storage. Legible handwritten material accepted. Prompt/confidential. Send SASE for rate sheet and sample play format. 30 years experience.

S & T TYPING/WORD PROCESSING SERVICE
P.O. Box 8033, Manchester, CT 06040
(203) 646-4720
Accurate/confidential/prompt. IBM compatible PC with letter quality print. Spell check/1 year free disk storage. From $1.25/double spaced page plus postage. Legible handwritten OK.

TEXTSCRIBE, INC.
3100 McKinnon #1000, Dallas, TX 75201
Phone: (214) 720-4565
$2.00 double spaced page + postage or delivery. Free spell check. Fast turn around. ASCII disk available.

TYPING/WORD PROCESSING SERVICE. Reliable, prompt, professional. Editing available. Accepting rough-typed, cassette, legible hand-written. Free: paper copy, disk storage. Rates decrease as pages increase. **SALLY RICH DESIGNS . . . words; P.O. Box 126; Darby, PA 19023 (near Philadelphia) Phone (215) 583-3157; Fax (215) 583-3479.**

WORDS UNLIMITED-Professional, Accurate and Confidential Word Processing Service. Manuscripts, scripts, screenplays, WORDPERFECT, Laserjet printer. Reasonable rates including disk storage and spell check. 20 years experience. **Call (212) 542-5003. NASS Member.**

TheaterWeek

28 W. 25th Street, 4th Floor, New York, NY 10010 (212) 627-2120

*We know it's
hard to keep up
with the latest
in the theater.*

●

*Unless you
subscribe to
TheaterWeek.*

Only $49 for a full year
—that's 94¢ a week!

28 West 25th Street, Fourth Floor, NY, NY 10010   212-627-2120

☐ $49 for 52 issues of THEATERWEEK ($74 outside USA)
☐ $29 for 26 issues of THEATERWEEK ($42 outside USA)
☐ Payment enclosed.   ☐ VISA   ☐ Mastercard
☐ This is a renewal subscription.
Account # _____
Exp. Date: _____ Signature _____

Name _____ _____
Address _____
City/State/Zip _____

Please allow 6 to 8 weeks for processing.   PC

What magazine tells you how to draw a groundplan, what a dramaturg does, where to find a theatre scholarship, why we work so hard, and who put the bop in the bop-bop-she-bop?
Send us the coupon and we'll show you.

A new play by Barrie Stavis
On the road with The Acting Company
Set design: a how-to series

DRAMATICS

DRAMATICS

Mail to:
Dramatics
3368 Central Parkway
Cincinnati, Ohio 45225

Send $2 with this coupon and we'll rush you a copy of our next issue. Or take a flyer and subscribe, for only $15 a year.

☐ I enclose $2 for the next issue of Dramatics.
☐ Please enter my subscription. I enclose $15 for one year.

NAME

ADDRESS

CITY   STATE   ZIP

C

SAMUEL FRENCH
THEATRE & FILM BOOKSHOPS

PLAYS, and BOOKS on FILM, THEATRE and the MOTION PICTURE INDUSTRY

Everything for the <u>playwright, actor</u>...

Plays (largest selection in the world) • Acting Technique
Playwrighting • Theatre Theory and History • Dialect Tapes
Agent Labels • and more

...and <u>filmmaker</u>

Business of Film • Screenplays • Screenwriting • TV and Video
Industry Directories • Reference • • Animation • Special Effects
Biographies • Theory and History • and more

WORLDWIDE MAIL ORDER
mail: 7623 Sunset Blvd., Hollywood, CA 90046
phone: (800) 8-ACT NOW (US)
(800) 7-ACT NOW (CA)

send for a copy of our
1990 FILM BOOK CATALOGUE ($3.00 postpaid)
Basic Play Catalogue & 1990 Supplement ($3.25 postpaid)

Samuel French, Inc. *Play Publishers and Authors Representatives*

New from Feedback Theatrebooks

WHO'S WHERE IN THE AMERICAN THEATRE 1990 Edition **Your new annual guide to theatre artists across the United States:** producers, directors, managers, performers, designers, writers, teachers, publishers, editors, agents and others working in the American theatre today. Cross references. **Publisher's price: $10.95** (shipping included).

Mail orders only. Prepayment must accompany order. New York residents add sales tax.

**Feedback Theatrebooks, Dept. PC
305 Madison Avenue, Suite 1146
New York, NY 10165**

- Notes -

✳✳✳✳✳✳✳✳✳✳✳✳✳✳✳✳✳✳✳✳✳✳✳✳✳✳✳✳✳✳✳✳✳✳✳✳

The Playwright's Companion 1991

- To be published in December 1990.

- More than 1,100 up-to-date listings of theatres, playwriting contests, programs, publishers and agents.

- The marketing tips, script format guidelines and cross references that have helped to make *The Playwright's Companion* "a goldmine" (*Dramatics*) and "an indispensable resource for playwrights" (*Library Journal*).

- Special Publisher's Price: $19.95* (shipping and handling included).

- To order your copy of *The Playwright's Companion 1991,* complete the form below and mail it, along with your check or money order, to Feedback Theatrebooks, 305 Madison Ave., Suite 1146, New York, NY 10165. Please allow 3-4 weeks for delivery.

The Playwright's Companion 1991

Order Form

Name: _____

Address: _____

City, State, Zip: _____

Phone: (_____)_____

No. copies: ____@$19.95 each. Payment enclosed: $____
Prepayment must accompany order.
*NY residents add sales tax.

Feedback Theatrebooks, 305 Madison Ave.,
Suite 1146, New York, NY 10165. Thank you!

✳✳✳✳✳✳✳✳✳✳✳✳✳✳✳✳✳✳✳✳✳✳✳✳✳✳✳✳✳✳✳✳✳✳✳✳